Beyond
THE TRAILS

WITH HERB & LOIS CRISLER
In Olympic National Park

By
Francis E. Caldwell

Francis E Caldwell

First Edition, 1998

Printed by Olympic Graphics Arts, 640 South Forks Ave., P.O. Box 1698, Forks, WA 98331

Library of Congress Cataloging-in-Publication Data
Caldwell, Francis E. - Beyond the Trails
        Pacific Northwest History
        Includes biography references
        Wildlife photography

        ISBN 0-9662667-0-6 (paperback)

        Published by ANCHOR PUBLISHING
        1335 West Eleventh Street, Port Angeles, WA 98363-5507
        To order, call 360-457-3009 FAX: 360-452-1342
        email: dlc@olypen.com

CREDITS:
Designed by: Olympic Graphic Arts, Inc.
Cover design: Katie Page
Map, Copyright ©1994 by Richard A. Pargeter.

Black & White photos:
Chapman, Hazle M. (compliments Ruby El Hult) Pgs., 10, 37, 59, 89, 99, 100, 101, 102, 103, 109, 115, 128, 129, 130, 131, 140, 144, 157, 194, 196.
Crisler Collection (compliments Ruby El Hult) Pgs., 17, 22, 23, 32, 36, 40, 46, 49, 80, 83, 89, (Thompson Studio, 57), 127, 152, 171, 186.
Kellogg, Bert, Collection, (compliments Port Angeles Library) Pg. 2, 12, 26, 33.

Color photos:
Bauer, Erwin & Peggy; cougar.
Larsen, Calvin; (2 aerials) 1. Mt. Carrie & Mt. Olympus, 2. Queets Basin & Mount Olympus.
Whiting, David; Castle-in-the-Cat
All photos not listed by the author.

Dedication

Dedicated to Ruby El Hult, without whose help this manuscript would never have been completed, and to Hazle M. Chapman, whose black and white photos, taken while with the Crislers during the 1940s, grace many pages.

Contents

Lois reminisces about pioneer mountaineers who first trod the Olympic Mountains. Horse tracks and manure in Queets Basin. Texan spends winter in Elwha Basin. Lois recalls early ascents of peaks by Seattle Mountaineers. Female climbers on Mount Olympus. Winona Bailey tries to walk on a cloud at Humes Glacier. Jack McGlone's first ascent of East Peak not recorded. Lois describes a mountain meadow. Roosevelt elk lifestyles. Photographing large herd of elk in the Bailey Range. Photographing black bear at Dodwell-Rixon Pass. Photographing a bull elk fight.

First electricity at Hume's Ranch. The process of editing film at Hume's Ranch. Herb's preoccupation while making movie. Herb ignores letter telling him he must wear a dinner jacket for big showings at Chicago Geographic Society. Lois claims perils of trekking in Olympics nothing like shopping for new evening dress. Ruby El Hult drives the green truck. The Crislers thrill to see their names on the marquee at the Metropolitan Theater in Seattle. Ruby El Hult describes attending the premier showing of BEYOND THE TRAILS. The Crislers preview their film for Walt Disney. Lois writes a derogatory column about Walt Disney Associates. Disney offers to buy Crisler's film and puts the Crislers under contract. The "Olympic Squirrel" (Herb) confronts the red-haired "Chicago Jaguar" over dress code for showing at Orchestra Hall. The long drive back to California. Showing for the Sierra Club in Berkeley and the Wilderness Society in Port Angeles.

Springtime at Hume's Ranch. Joys of being back in the Olympic Rain Forest after surviving the perils of a nation-wide tour. Looking for elk calves on the Hoh River. Lois writes about the joys of backpacking. Ruby El Hult's mid-summer visit to Hume's Ranch. Caught smooching in the swing. Photographing elk in the Bailey Range. The last lecture circuit. Crislers watch preview of the Disney release, THE OLYMPIC ELK. Listening to Starker Leopold expound on wilderness future. The Crislers receive orders from Disney to move to the Tarryall Mountains of Colorado. Leaving Hume's Ranch.

Introduction

Although this book is about Herbert and Lois Crisler's experiences in the Olympic Mountains and at Hume's Ranch on the Elwha River, other important characters are the area's wildlife, especially "Olympic" or Roosevelt elk, **Cervus elaphus roosevelti,** the true "kings" of the Olympic Mountains.

Without elk, Olympic National Park might never have been established, because, before it was a Park, it was an elk reserve. Although many other animals call the Park home, without elk Herb Crisler wouldn't have had magnificent animal subjects for his movie, BEYOND THE TRAILS. The Disney movie, THE OLYMPIC ELK, filmed entirely by Crisler, wouldn't have thrilled millions. Without the majestic elk, this book wouldn't have been written, because for half a century I've been hunting, photographing and admiring elk. Although I've photographed big game in Africa, Asia, Alaska, Canada and the American West, I have a special, profound admiration for elk.

Throughout this book Herb Crisler mentions the "spirit of the Olympics" many times. The "spirit" came to him one stormy night in 1930, while on a 30-day survival trip, without food or gun, across the Olympic Mountains. Caught in a blizzard, starving, he holed up in a shallow cave at the terminal of Hoh Glacier and spent the night wondering if he was going to survive the storm.

A few people have died, and others have simply disappeared, in the Olympic Mountains over the years. It's no place to take chances or be foolish.

I'd never thought much about Crislers' "spirit", until one night in 1990 while backpacking the Skyline Trail. I decided if I was going to write a book about Crisler, I should at least step in his boot tracks along as much of his old route across the Olympic Mountains, between his far-flung camps, as possible.

I left most of my camp at Three Prune, then set out at daylight, carrying only a sleeping bag, camera gear and a little food. I stashed the sleeping bag and food where tiny Kimta Creek crossed the trail, then continued to Lake Beauty. By the time I returned to my bag, that would be 12 miles of rugged going. The high elevation sections of the Skyline Trail are simply a poorly-maintained way path. I knew it was going to be tight getting back before dark, and misjudged how bad the "trail" was in this high, desolate area, where snow hangs on until August.

Coming back, darkness caught me a quarter of a mile from my sleeping bag. On a switchback, I walked off the trail on an elk path and had a difficult time finding the trail again in the darkness. After that I groped along, searching out the trail foot by foot with my feet, and by feeling the huckleberry bushes lining the trail with my hands. Finally I reached my bag, ate some jerky and a candy bar, then crawled in.

The night was clear. A full moon sailed up over the snow-covered peaks to the east and bathed the mountains with eerie, golden light. I laid in my bag, watched the stars, glancing occasionally towards where a black bear munched huckleberries nearby. I could hear his teeth raking in the leaves and berries. Finally I dropped off to sleep.

During the night I woke up. My upper body crawled with goose bumps, the skin on my head tingled, and my hair felt stiff; warning signals that something or someone was watching me! I definitely felt a **presence**! Has this ever happened to you? It was scary. I wished I had a gun.

I let out a shout, sat up, and probed the nearby shadows, expecting to see a black bear or cougar nearby. The moonlight was bright enough to have read by. Nothing moved. I crawled out of my bag, picked up a club, then walked barefooted into the nearby shadows. Nothing. I yelled and beat my club against the bushes. Still nothing.

I went back to bed, laid awake, listened and watched the stars, my club near my right hand. I though about Herb Crislers' request that his ashes be buried at Hume's Ranch, far across the mountains. How fitting, I thought, as he had loved the Olympics more than anywhere he'd been.

My creepy feeling finally went away. Wearily, I fell into a deep sleep.

Had the "spirit" of the Olympics passed by, perhaps staring down at me in the moonlight, happy to have company in this remote wilderness?

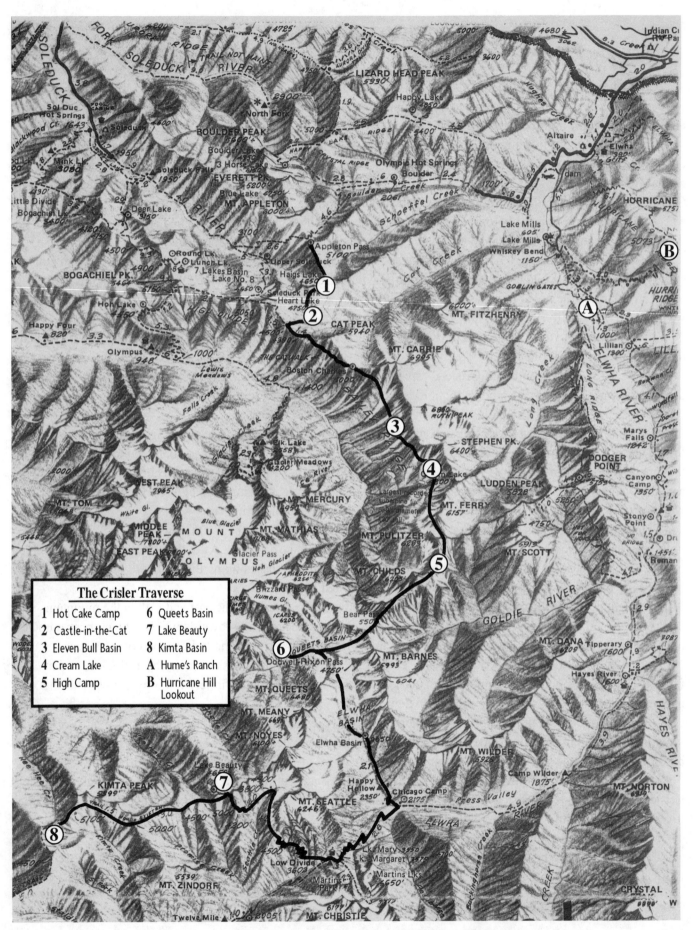

The Crisler Traverse

1 Hot Cake Camp   6 Queets Basin
2 Castle-in-the-Cat   7 Lake Beauty
3 Eleven Bull Basin   8 Kimta Basin
4 Cream Lake   A Hume's Ranch
5 High Camp   B Hurricane Hill Lookout

Map compliments of Pargeter's Map of the Olympic Mountains, Kent, WA. Copyrighted June, 1994 by R.A. Pargeter.

Georgia Photographer Comes to Peninsula

Herbert Bruce Crisler was so excited he couldn't sleep, although sleep on a troop train was nearly impossible. To suddenly be transplanted from Florida to the Pacific Northwest at the whim of the army was quite a sudden change in his young life. So much had happened in such a short time Herb's mind was whirling.

He'd married Muriel Taylor in St. Augustine, Florida, been inducted into the Army, went through a very brief basic training in Texas, then, because of his experiences as a photographer, was being shipped to the Olympic Peninsula of Washington State to work at a logging camp at Pysht, where the War Production Board was frantically trying to produce plywood from the big Sitka Spruce, called "Airplane" spruce, for the war effort.

Herb knew nothing about the Olympic Peninsula, had never heard of it actually, but it was exciting to be going there. Adventure was in his blood.

He was thankful for not being sent to Europe. Photographers were much in demand with the army. Several young men with photography skills who he'd worked with during his tenure at Eastman Kodak in Tampa, Florida, had been killed while photographing enemy positions from a small plane.

The train clanked across the deserts of the Southwest, then turned north. At dawn one morning, in northern California, Herb looked out the car window and saw an astounding sight; snow-covered Mount Shasta. Although Herb was 22 years old, Shasta was the very first mountain he'd seen. He wanted to climb it.

Strange sounding names began appearing on signs along the track. Indian names, the conductor said. Names that would twist a white man's tongue into a figure eight knot. Stands of old-growth coniferous forests lined the track through parts of northern California and Oregon.

They arrived at Vancouver Barracks on a balmy night in September, 1918. The odor of wood smoke, pine pitch and sun-dried grass reminded Herb of his native Georgia. Even in the dark, amidst the confusion of being hustled off to barracks, Herb decided he liked the Pacific Northwest.

Confusion reigned at Vancouver Barracks. The war in Europe raged unabated. Thousands of soldiers milled about, homesick, frightened, bewildered. The Barracks was a holding facility for the Northwest, where military personnel were processed, then shipped off to destinations where needed.

The detachment that was headed for the Olympic Peninsula were mustered in preparation for catching the train to Seattle. That's when Herb met the flamboyant Tom Newton, who was in charge. There was a man, Herb decided, that he'd like to get to know. Handsome, six-foot-four, energetic, lithe and muscular, he had the fluid motions of a born athlete. Tom convoluted the English language with a Norwegian accent in an amusing manner.

Tom told the detachment that they were headed for God's Country, the Olympic Peninsula. When someone asked why it was called God's Country, Tom's blue eyes sparkled. "Because after the Lord created the world, He tossed the leftover scraps into a heap known as the Olympic Mountains. Then, startled by what He had done, He created 16 feet of rain a year to wash away the leftover mess."

Tom had worked on the Peninsula on a bridge construction project and then as a logger for Merrill & Ring at their camp at Pysht. Because of his experience, the Army had ordered Tom to lead the detachment of soldiers that were headed for Pysht. To even reach such a remote place required someone with local experience.

On the train to Seattle the men gathered around Tom and pumped him about their destination. Tom gleefully complied, telling huge tales about the country and what was expected of the raw recruits. The soldiers were to be mixed in with the regular lumberjacks because of the war effort to quickly produce Sitka spruce for aircraft construction. The supply of Bauxite, imported from South America, from which aluminum was produced, had been cut off by German submarines. They would be climbing trees 250 feet high, sawing the tops off, building railroads, dragging heavy cables through thick brush where cougars and bears lived and sawing trees eight feet in diameter into logs headed for a new plywood mill at Port Angeles, and on and on. Some of the men wished they'd been assigned to the front lines instead.

After Herb told Tom he'd been sent to photograph spruce forests from the air, so the government could determine where the best stands were located, Newton went into convulsions of laughter.

"Photograph the forest," Tom choked, "Why there's so many trees on the Peninsula a blind photographer could point his camera, pull the trigger and capture all the trees anyone would ever want."

Herb saw through Tom's good-natured banter right from the start and the two hit it off and eventually became buddies.

The detachment had six hours to spend in Seattle before boarding a ship to Port Angeles. The men left their gear under the watchful eyes of Military Police guarding the station, then followed Tom to nearby First Avenue, where Tom explained one could buy an illegal shot of rot gut, and, if one had the money, some female attention as well. Being a good Southern Baptist, Herb never drank nor smoked. He left the group and wandered the waterfront, where many ships were moored.

Herb discovered outfitting stores displaying camping equipment, woolen clothing and supplies he'd never dreamed existed, supplies for miners, loggers and fishermen. The only camping equipment he'd ever owned was a sleeping bag his mother had sewn for him.

At midnight they boarded a little, soot-smeared westbound steamer. Stops were scheduled at Port Townsend; Port Williams; Port Angeles; Victoria, British Columbia and

U.S. Army Spruce Division campsite near Lake Pleasant, western Clallam County, during World War I.

Pysht. The vessel was crammed to the guards. On board were drummers selling every imaginable item needed by men working in the outdoors, construction workers, drunken loggers headed for jobs and whores headed for the construction boom on the Peninsula. After the lines were cast off Herb stood on the fantail watching the lights of Seattle disappear. Acrid coal smoke poured from the funnel as the ship steamed north through Puget Sound's quiet waters. Herb's thoughts reflected on circumstances which had placed him so far from family and home.

Herbert Bruce Crisler was born July 23, 1893 at Elberton, Elbert County, Georgia. His mother's maiden name was

Adora Bruce. Her father, Henry Bruce, owned a 500 acre plantation.

Her mother was Kesiah Vaughn. The Vaughns had lost almost everything, except their land, during the Civil War. Their livestock, except for one old horse, had either been shot for meat or rode off by soldiers. While the plantation had several slaves, all were gone, except for one old man named Joy that had hid out in a secluded gulch during the war. Crops had been taken without permission. Worst of all, the Vaughn menfolk had all been killed in the war. Three girls and the mother were left.

Henry Bruce wished desperately to serve in the Confederate Army but was so short they refused his services. After he and Kesiah married, Henry began rebuilding the 500 acre plantation, which had reverted back to nature, the fields shoulder high with brush.

Herbert's father, Jim Crisler, was a wandering man from the Blue Ridge who worked for Henry Bruce for a year. He and Adora, the oldest daughter, 15 years of age, eloped, much to Henry's disappointment. They married and lived in a nearby town. Ten months later Adora gave birth to a son. Not until Henry Bruce saw the son, his first grandchild, did he forgive Adora for eloping. The Crislers were given the opportunity to sharecrop on the Bruce plantation.

Herbert quickly became his grandfather Bruce's darling grandson. Herb loved the farm, liked to plant garden crops, hunt small game and fish. The plantation, on the Piedmont Plateau, near Peolin, about 15 miles from Danielville, in Madison County, consisted of low, red clay hills covered with short leaf pine, hemlock, white and red oak, yellow poplar, wild cherry and ash, mulberry, yellow jasmine, redbud and tulip. What tillable soil there was produced mostly cotton, and barely a living, but it was a wonderful life, especially for a small boy who loved the outdoors. Although native turkey and most deer had been killed off by soldiers during the war, the area abounded with small game, which Herb hunted with a muzzle-loading rifle his grandfather had bought for him.

By the time Herb was 10 he was picking 150 pounds of cotton a day. Pay was thirty cents a hundred. He earned about thirty-eight cents a day. Most of the money he gave to his mother.

The entire Bruce clan were expected to attend Vineyard Creek church on Sundays. Herb loved attending church, especially the week-long revival meetings after the crops had been laid by. The afternoon service was followed by a feast, as everyone brought platters of food, heaps of fried chicken, potato salad, mashed potatoes, pies, cakes and cookies. The food was laid out on tables beneath shade trees. The feast was followed by an evening service. The entire community came for these services, and it was, Herb remembered, a grand time.

Jim Crisler was a reluctant farmer and indifferent father. He frequently disappeared for weeks at a time, claiming he was looking for something better for his family than being sharecroppers . He returned home one day in 1903 and told Adora to pack, he had learned to be a photographer, and they were moving to Athens to open a photography studio.

Family group pictures were considered de rigueur, and even people who couldn't afford it frequently skimped on something in order to have their portraits taken.[1]

Once the family settled down to life in Athens, Herb began working with his father at the studio. Photography awakened some latent curiosity in Herb, and he quickly mastered mixing chemicals, loading plates and film holders for his father's view camera and even learned to print in the darkroom.

Herb had quit school in grade four. He didn't get along with his father. After a fight with Jim at age 12 he ran away and hid out in the woods near his Uncle John Draper's farm, stealing eggs and vegetables and sleeping in the barn, unknown to the Drapers. It wasn't long until he was discovered. He pleaded not to be forced to return home. Instead he went to work for his Uncle John on his farm.

During the summer of 1909, when he was 16, Herb's mother begged him to return home. Jim had left, apparently for good, and she was desperate for someone to operate the studio. Herb soon became a proficient photographer. Times were hard and business bad. He helped the family's income by trapping, and the larder by hunting squirrels and birds.

By 1911 the family of five younger brothers and sisters were desperate. Herb and his brother Henry were offered a job clearing timber for their Uncle Willie on a piece of land he owned near Paso, 200 miles south of Athens. The boys drove down in a buggy pulled by two mules. People along the way helped by feeding them and their mules. The following spring Adora and the other children arrived. Herb had planted a big garden and that was all that stood between them and starvation.

During the winter Herb, as breadwinner, decided to take Henry and spend the winter trapping along the Aucilla River in Florida. The boys had many wild experiences during three months living off the land along the river, including a scary confrontation with a man who stole their traps.

Upon returning home the boys were disappointed to see their father had returned. Herb didn't approve of the way Jim refused to support his family. Herb was 20, but sons were considered chattel of their fathers until they were 21. Herb decided to leave. Secretly packing a few belongings, he headed south for Tampa, where he heard Eastman Kodak were hiring at their finishing plant. Because he didn't doubt that Jim would send the sheriff after him, he changed his name to Loyd Smith. He didn't stop traveling until after he'd crossed the state line.

Herb liked working for Eastman Kodak, but it was seasonal, during the winter when hoards of tourists arrived to take pictures. During the summer he took a job painting the Tampa Bay hotel, a huge, Moorish structure. From the lead paint he contacted lead poisoning, which plagued him all the following winter while back at Eastman Kodak. All the money he could spare he sent to his mother, but never gave her his address.

By the following spring Herb was told by a doctor that he should spend lots of time in the fresh air to rid himself of the poison. He mentioned to his roommates at the rooming house that he thought he'd wander down and walk across the Everglades. The roommates were incredulous. No one, not even an Indian, could cross the Everglades. This only caused Herb to become more interested.

At the time, 1915, the whole southern tip of Florida, from Lake Okeechobee south, and southwest, two and a half million acres, called the Everglades simply because the "glades" seemingly stretched on forever, was unknown. Airplanes were not in use, so no one really knew what lay in the glades. Herb's research disclosed little. Common belief was that only Indians had the knowledge to live in the swamps, and they only lived in the fringes. Mosquitos, snakes, panthers and alligators would make quick work of any man caught in those swamps, was people's impressions. There had been talk about setting the glades aside as a national park, but nothing came of it.[2] Herb decided to investigate the possibilities by going to Lake Okeechobee and making the attempt. He could always turn back.

Herb's preparations for this venture were as frugal as his knowledge of the Everglades. He spent $8 on a little single shot 22 caliber rifle and a hatchet. He gave up his room and left, without saying a word to anyone of his plans.

Walking the pine scented roads across Florida did wonders for his body. He shot small game and ate whatever vegetables he could forage. After two weeks he arrived at the only store at Lake Okeechobee. He tried to buy one of the storekeeper's boats, but the man refused, saying he needed the boats to rent to fishermen. Instead, the storekeeper pointed out a tall Seminole Indian by the name of Turner, and suggested Herb ask Turner if he could ride along in his canoe, as he was headed for the south end of the lake. Herb bought a tin pail and some salt to complete his camping equipment. He would have liked a compass, but none was available. He would use the sun to guide his way southwest.

Before leaving Tampa, Herb had learned that deep-sea fishermen frequently put in at the isolated little port of Everglades, on Florida's west coast. His plan was simple. He'd walk across to Everglades, then catch a ride on a boat back to Tampa.

Turner and Herb soon became good friends. Turner admired a white man who dared walk across the Everglades. When Herb asked if anyone else had, an Indian, perhaps, Turner shook his head no, saying there was no reason to do so. During several nights they camped along the lake, Turner taught Herb how he might survive living in the Everglades. Tricks which Herb later claimed were indispensable for such an endeavor. Herb learned how to build a shield from palm fonds, laced with hemp and bolstered with big frond ribs, to protect himself from the deadly Jamaica saw grass (Cladium jamaicense) which would cut a person to ribbons if forcing one's way through unprotected. He also learned how to burn a ring of dead palm fronds around his bed before turning in, to keep snakes away, and how to avoid snake bite while walking through dense grass and brush by shuffling his feet. Herb also learned how to chop and cook palmetto cabbages.

The Everglades were a wildlife paradise, with lots of wild turkeys, deer, racoons and many beautiful birds. Ahead lay 5000 square miles of unmapped, unknown territory. Herb traveled through forests of pine, mangrove and palmetto for several days. Without a compass he steered a mighty crooked course, detouring around ponds and tangles of lianas and cypress. Occasionally he had to wade up to his shoulders, feeling every step for quicksand, holding his little sleeping pad and matches over his head. Lightning and thunder storms, accompanied by cloudbursts, frequently drenched him. His only protection from mosquitos and other biting insects was campfire smoke. Snakes slithered off roots into the water ahead of him while wading. Sometimes he encountered swamps covered with acres of beautiful, fragrant water lilies.

A month went by. The trek was becoming monotonous. Finally he noticed a break in the jungle ahead and stumbled out onto the blue waters of the Gulf of Mexico. After a swim he started walking south along the beach, uncertain whether this was the way to Everglades or not. A day later he came upon a squatter's hut. The squatter was astonished when Herb said he'd walked across the Everglades, but Herb's clothing and appearance were ample proof.

Everglades turned out to be only a little store and tavern. Herb bought new clothes and shoes. The storekeeper told him he was out of luck catching a ride to Tampa, as the boats only stopped on their way south. Northbound, on the way to market, they kept out to sea. He was told his best bet was catch a ride on a fishing boat headed south, and pay the skipper a few dollars to put him into Key West, where he could catch a ride on the new Flagler Railroad back up through Miami and make his way overland to Tampa. To see more of Florida suited Herb, and that's what he did, reaching Tampa a month later. His friends refused to believe he had walked across the Everglades, until he exposed his legs and arms. They were still covered with insect bites. [3]

During the winter of 1916 Herb worked for Eastman Kodak again. After being laid off in the spring he headed home. He learned he had a new two-year-old brother, Albert. Jim had taken one look at his new son Albert, threw his camera gear into a buggy and left. Jim never returned to his family again.

Adora, as usual, was destitute.[4] His sister Vara had married and moved to Jacksonville. Henry was working in a bakery in Atlanta. After writing to Vara, she assured Herb that he could find work there so the family moved to Jacksonville.

Again Herb assumed support for his mother and three siblings. Money went fast, and he took whatever work he could find.

In April, 1917, the United States declared war on Germany. Herb was 24, but wasn't classified 1-A because he was sole breadwinner for his family.

Herb began dating Muriel Taylor while working at a marine store in Hastings. She was the first steady girl he'd had. By mid-summer, 1918, with the war in Europe at fever pitch, Herb was reclassified and ordered to report for active duty. Photographers were badly needed to photograph enemy positions from aircraft over Germany. Herb had read in the papers that several of the photographers he knew in Tampa had already been killed while flying in light aircraft.

Muriel decided she'd go along to Saint Augustine where Herb was to be inducted.

During the trip, they decided to get married. Herb assumed he would soon be killed, and he wanted to have a son, if possible, to carry on his name.

Herb was soon on his way to Texas for a short training course. Muriel remained behind. The Army looked over his credentials, noticed he was an experienced photographer and, instead of sending him to Europe, shipped him to the Olympic Peninsula, where a photographer was needed.

Staring into the dark water off the stern, Herb wondered what lay in store for him in this strange new land. The steamer stopped at Port Townsend to unload freight and passengers, then headed around Point Wilson and into the Straits of Juan De Fuca.

At Port Angeles, the men were allowed several hours ashore while the freight was unloaded. The little town inside Ediz Hook, a natural breakwater and deep water harbor, was booming. Three mills were visible. Near the steamer dock the Ennis Creek Mill, designed to produce spruce plywood for the war effort, was under construction. Parafine's new boxwood mill and Michael Earles Puget Sound Mills and Timber Company mill, locally known as the "Big Mill" were operating.

Mud streaked Ford cars and horse-drawn wagons rumbled along planked streets over the tide flats. Talk was of the huge buildup of men and equipment of the Spruce Division, an offshoot of the United States Spruce Production Corporation, responsible for the entire project of obtaining spruce for aircraft construction, building railroads, logging and mill construction. Colonel Bryce P. Disque, U.S. Army, had been ordered to triple spruce production and had been handed an open-ended checkbook to finance the operation. What intrigued Herb were the high mountains behind the town. He longed to hike those mountains and see what they had to offer.

Walking with Tom Newton around Port Angeles, Herb was surprised to learn he was well known on the Peninsula, and that he had a handle, "Haywire Tom."

The steamer blew the "all aboard" signal. The little ship headed for Victoria, British Columbia. A heavy westerly swell caused the ship to roll and most of the passengers became seasick. At Victoria's Inner Harbor, mail and passengers were off loaded. Several Indians stood on the pier. They were dressed in white man's clothing, except they wore colorful blankets over their shoulders.

The vessel then headed for Race Rocks and set a course across the Straits for Pysht. Herb picked up a paper someone had left on the seat. The following article caught his eye:

> The little settlement [Port Angeles] has been transformed into one of the busiest on the Pacific Coast, and this boom is attributable absolutely to the demand for spruce in the construction of airplanes.
>
> The United States government has thousands of soldiers employed building miles of railway in the heart of the Olympics, to tap the finest spruce belt in the United States. The Seims, Carey-H.S. Kerbough Corporation has received a contract for 300 million board feet of spruce, amounting to $30 million, and is now erecting one of the largest mills on the coast capable of handling 1,000,000 board feet a day. Five hundred men are expected to be employed by the mill.[5]

In 1918, the Olympic Peninsula was a wild, largely unexplored country. It had been only three decades previously that the first party had crossed the Peninsula, from Port Angeles to the Pacific Ocean at the mouth of the Quinault River. Note in the above article, the writer's reference to building "miles of railway in the heart of the Olympics." The heart of the Olympics is the rugged Olympic Mountains, and little has ever been constructed there, except a few trails. Much effort was made to build railroads from the mainline to the Peninsula's forests, but a necklace of treacherous, snow-fed rivers run off the Olympic Mountains in all directions, creating obstacles for rail construction. The only railroad that was built on the Peninsula was from a rail barge terminal at Port Townsend, then along the lowlands to Port Angeles, around Lake Crescent and ended at Forks.

Pysht had no deep water harbor, so the steamer was met by small tugs towing barges. After men and freight were loaded on the barges they were towed upriver to the camp. The main Merrill & Ring camp was neatly laid out along the river. In order to have deep enough water to raft logs and tow barges, retaining pilings had been driven along both banks, then the river had been dredged. The camp had been built in 1914, and was considered the first modern camp in Clallam County. Pysht was one of three camps in western Clallam County, known as the "West End". Besides Merrill & Ring at Pysht, Goodyear Logging Company had a camp at Sekiu and Puget Sound Mills, a camp at Twin Rivers. The three were roughly 15 miles apart.

The Merrill & Ring camp didn't have the convenience of moving logs to the mills by rail. Instead the logs were moved out of the woods by rail and dumped into the Pysht River, then made into Davis rafts and towed down the Straits to market. Three steam-powered tugs, the **Wanderer, Humaconna and Wallowa** were used.

The soldiers were not to live with the civilian loggers but in army tents. Without knowing, the soldiers were entering into a hot bed of early-day union organizing that had been disrupting logging operations all over the Northwest for some time, and hadn't abated much even because of the war effort. Dismal working conditions had forced loggers to form their first union, the Industrial Workers of the World (IWW) known as the "Wobblies".

The union's goal was to force the timber companies to reduce the number of hours to the 40-hour work week, provide clean bedding and facilities and improve food.

There was a strong communistic influence in the IWW, and the timber companies flatly refused to do business with them. In order to put their demands across, a series of crippling strikes, including sabotage, had become rampant by 1917.

Soldiers were to receive civilian pay, which infuriated the loggers, since the soldiers didn't know a choker from a steam donkey. To counter the IWW, Colonel Disque formed the army's own union, the Loyal Legion of Loggers & Lumbermen, immediately dubbed the "4-L's" (Lazy Loggers and Loafing Lumbermen) by the civilian loggers. If it hadn't been for the war going on, a battle royal might have erupted between soldiers and civilians. But the regular loggers generally supported the war effort, so tolerated the army's invasion into their work place.

Herb claimed the Pysht area was a "spooky" place, not unlike the Everglades. He couldn't see the ground because of dozens of mosses, lichen and ferns. He rarely saw the sky because of the dense upper story of the old-growth rain forest or the constant overcast and fogs that plagued the country.

Being a dry summer, the soldiers were soon engaged in fighting fires, a scary job for inexperienced men. Herb made two aerial photography flights. Whether the photographs were used isn't known.

Tom Newton caused Herb no end of difficulty by claiming Herb was an experienced logger from Georgia, and getting him into jobs Herb had difficulty mastering. He was told to buck firewood for the steam yarding donkey, only to see the chunks of split fir tossed into the firebox faster than he could cut them. Then he was told to join the choker setters and was nearly killed by flying debris after falling down while trying to escape the rigging.

After about one month at Pysht, the influenza epidemic became the main topic of conversation amongst the men, but little news trickled out to the remote logging camp. Rumors were that the morgues were stacked high with bodies, and doctors were in short supply because so many were in the army.[6]

Herb obtained a three-day pass and went to Port Angeles. The Baptist preacher arranged for him to stay with a family. The following day Herb developed a raging fever. A doctor was called and Herb was told to remain in bed. Since there was no way to reach his superior officer at Pysht, he became absent without leave. After the army finally learned that he had the flu, he was moved into the hospital.

During his flu attack, Herb was asked for his next of kin's address, in case he died. After ten days he returned to Pysht. The war news was encouraging. In early November Herb was told to don his uniform and go to Port Angeles and to a certain address. In town he walked up Lincoln Street to the corner of Eighth and knocked on the door. To his surprise, Muriel opened the door. She had caught the train as soon as she received word he was in the hospital, but by the time she reached Port Angeles, Herb was back at Pysht.

Herb returned to Pysht. On November 11, the Armistice was signed. Work at Pysht came to a standstill. No one knew how the end of the war would effect the Spruce Production Division. The regular civilian crews kept working, but the army was thrown into total confusion.

Finally orders came that all soldiers were to be returned to their place of induction. Those who had been at Pysht longest were at the top of the list to be shipped home. Herb's turn didn't come until after the first of the year. Muriel was working. While on a week-end pass, they had decided to stay in Port Angeles for a year to see how they liked it. The forests, mountains, wild animals and wilderness impressed them and they wanted to see more.

At Vancouver Barracks, Herb was told that the only way he could avoid being shipped back to Florida was to prove to his commanding officer that he had a job in Port Angeles. Muriel was working for Mr. Ulmer, caring for his children. Mr. Ulmer found Herb a job at the Michael Earles Mill, so Herb was discharged and returned to Port Angeles on January 22, 1919.

What happened to the massive effort to produce spruce? With the war over, bauxite again became available and spruce wasn't needed. The Ennis Creek mill, completed about the time the war ended, never opened. It sat idle until 1929, when it was bought by Olympic Forest Products, much of it dismantled and converted into producing pulp. The mill, owned by ITT Rayonier, closed in 1997.

Howard Hughes' infamous Spruce Goose, built almost entirely of Sitka spruce, flew only once. The huge plane became the epitaph of wooden aircraft construction. It now rests in a museum in Portland, Oregon.

Millions of dollars of taxpayer's money didn't **entirely** go to waste. Peninsula railroads built by the government were eventually operated by private industry. Millions of logs were hauled to market. Eventually rails were replaced by highways and logging trucks, and, at the time of this writing, the railroads have all been abandoned.

In 1897, President Grover Cleveland set aside 2,168,320 acres of the Peninsula into the Olympic Reserve, with an estimated 61 billion board feet of old-growth timber. Of the 2,883 square miles in the Reserve, only 16 had been logged!

Today, only a tiny fraction of the Peninsula, outside of Olympic National Park, contains old-growth forest. A large portion of that forest was exported. We tried to cut it all, and would have, if it hadn't been protected by the Park.

Notes & Sources, Beyond The Trails, Chapter One.

1. Herb was born during an important era in photography. In 1889, G. Eastman began manufacturing the first photographic film on a nitrocellulose base, a material designed to meet the rugged mechanical problems associated with the new "roller photography" where, for the first time, film was inserted into an Eastman Kodak box camera, instead of being used as sheet film.

In 1897, when Herb was four, R.G. Hollaman of the Eden Musee in New York City, attempted the first story on film, a Passion Play with a cast of actors. Crisler, who would devote most of his long life and energy to producing motion-pictures, was growing up during the period when photography was actually being developed.

2. Everglades National Park, 1,400,523 acres, wasn't established until June 20, 1947, 32 years after Herb's trek. In 1915 the population of the state of Florida was only about 600,000.

3. Herb Crisler, "Crossing the Everglades," as told to Ruby El Hult.

4. Albert, during an interview with the author, before he died suddenly in 1992, remembered how destitute the family sometimes was. Adora was an avid fisherwoman, and her catch was frequently all they had to eat. Food, clothing and fuel for a cooking fire was always in short supply. Adora sometimes placed the Dutch oven into the fireplace to keep from lighting a fire in the cook stove because of a shortage of coal or wood. He remembered one period where all they had for days was biscuits, with bacon fat poured over them. Albert still had the Dutch oven. It has three legs and a recessed lid which held hot coals for baking.

5. The paper, The SPRUCE, was published by the Seims, Carey-H.S. Kerbough Corporation.

Between 25-30,000 soldiers would ultimately be working on the Peninsula. At one time, 10,000 soldiers were building railroad. About 45 miles of mainline and 20 miles of spurs were laid, at an average cost of $30,000, per mile.

Sitka spruce Picea sitchenis was commonly called "Airplane spruce" during this period. A large spruce might measure twelve foot six inches in diameter, stand two hundred fifty feet high and produce 40,000 board feet of lumber. Prior to 1948, over 106 million board feet of spruce was harvested in Washington. It was not the preferred wood, Douglas fir was. Spruce was used for boxes, barrels, crates, construction, musical instruments and, after aluminum production was cut off during World War I, for aircraft construction. Only the choice wood, free from defect, was made into plywood and framing for aircraft construction.

6. The world-wide influenza epidemic of 1918 has been called the most destructive in history. It ranks as one of the severest holocausts of disease ever recorded. More than 20 million died in only a few months. More than 50 times that many were sick. No one was allowed to enter Seattle unless they wore a face mask. Port Angeles schools, churches, theaters and other indoor public meeting places were ordered closed. The flu ban in Port Angeles wasn't lifted until November 12, one day after the Armistice.

Learning the Country. A Greenhorn Gets Initiated

From their second floor housekeeping rooms at Eighth and Lincoln, Herb and Muriel had a good view of what they thought was the top of Mount Angeles, elevation 6,454 feet.

Actually what they saw was only the lower shoulder of a very complex and rugged mountain with two false summits. The actual top is over 10 very steep, timbered and rocky airline miles from Port Angeles. In total ignorance about the local mountains, they thought climbing the mountain required only a Sunday stroll.

It was the mountains, forests and wildlife that had decided the Crislers to remain on the Olympic Peninsula. This snow-covered mountain looming south of the town thrilled Herb. The country around Pysht had been very flat. He wondered what was on top? What was on the other side?

Michael Earles "big mill" provided Herb with the promised job. Herb was 26. The mill work didn't stimulate him:

My job was stacking green lumber out in the yard to air-dry. All day, eight hours a day, five days a week I stacked boards, with strips one inch thick between to let the air through.

I began to see there was a game about this work, the reverse of when I worked for Uncle John. Everybody barely made it in time to punch the time clock by eight o'clock in the morning. Then would see how slowly they could walk to their jobs and barely keep moving all day. You got paid from the time you punched the clock in the morning until you punched out at night, and not for the work you did.[1]

After several weeks of thinking about climbing Mount Angeles, Herb decided to make the attempt. He explains what happened:

From our kitchen window we had this panoramic view of the foothills and Mount Angeles. I would spend all my leisure time looking at this big mountain that came down almost to our back yard. I thought it was like living in the Alps. All we had to do was to walk to the end of Lincoln Street. I estimated that I could get to the top in three hours.

One Thursday morning the snow was very low on the mountain. I didn't work Saturday or Sunday. I told Muriel we were going to climb to the top Saturday, stay all night and come home Sunday. I thought we could be home on Sunday in time for church at eleven o'clock. I had good equipment for mountain climbing: army shoes, wool army pants, wrap-around wool leggings, wool-lined canvas coat, a home-knit survival wool pull-on cap, slit across the face so you could see where you were going if it wasn't snowing too hard. Muriel wore a woolen union suit, a woolen dress, wool socks, hiking boots and a wool Mackinaw jacket. We had one canvas-lined wool blanket for the two of us, matches, hatchet and a poncho for shelter. We started up Lincoln Street with our army pack sacks on our backs.

(Some good soul stopped us and suggested we walk east for several blocks and find a road which went south which would take us towards Mount Angeles.) We hiked, hiked and hiked, without getting any closer to Mount Angeles. It was noon before we discovered we weren't climbing Mount Angeles after all; we had been climbing around the end of a foothill. It was disappointing. I still thought I could reach the top before dark. After a short rest we started on.

9

When we first left the road the second growth was very thick. The snow-covered branches would switch, where touched, causing a miniature snowstorm. It was a different world for me, things I'd never seen before. It was beautiful, wonderful and exciting. But the snow got deeper, the weather grew colder and the light grew dim. The top of the mountain was still far away.

I thought I would build a fire and keep it going all night, but with what? In the South it wouldn't have been any trouble. All you have to do is find a dead, yellow-pine stump, split off some pitch splinters and have a big fire going in no time. What do you do when you have no dry bark, no pitch and no dry sticks or limbs? After trying to start a fire with half a box of matches and evergreen needles I had no dry eyes! I decided the next thing to do was wrap up in the one blanket. After we got wrapped up, we soon realized that if we didn't want to stay here until the thaw next summer, we'd better get off this mountain now! That is what we did. And that is the reason no one saw buzzards flying around Mount Angeles the following spring.

It was coming down through the second growth evergreens in the snow storm where we met Webster. [2]

Ed Webster, editor and publisher of the <u>Port Angeles</u> <u>Evening News</u>, took the couple to a nearby lodge, in an area adjacent to what is now Olympic National Park, known as Heart O' The Hills. Webster built a roaring blaze in the fireplace and thawed them out. The lodge belonged to the Klahhane Club,[3] a local mountaineering group.

The Crislers were so impressed by Webster's descriptions of the club and its activities they became members that night.

After Webster discovered Herb was a photographer, interested in photographing local natural history, he encouraged him to do so. After Herb mentioned that he had worked for Eastman Kodak as a photo finisher, Webster mentioned that all photo-finishing work from Port Angeles was shipped by boat to Seattle. He suggested Herb consider starting a finishing business in Port Angeles.

Webster wished to enlarge his personal collection of natural history photos of Peninsula subjects and mentioned that he would be willing to exchange advertising, should Herb ever need any, for photos of local subjects.

A shelter along the Elwha Trail constructed by the Forest Service.

So, the aborted attempt to climb Mount Angeles resulted in meeting with an influential local newspaperman. The relationship was to become a long, mutually beneficial one. Meanwhile, Herb worked at his job:

Back to the sawmill and stacking lumber. After four weeks I decided that after a tree had been butchered and cut in strips like bacon it didn't hold the appeal for me that it did standing in the forest.

Doing Kodak finishing, especially getting a collection of negatives of interesting scenes of the country and printing scenic and wildlife post cards, looked to be a likely business and one that would give me an opportunity to get out into the mountains.[4]

What Herb needed was some subjects, preferably wildlife, for his camera. But game animals were hunted around Port Angeles, and rather wild. To accomplish this, he decided to make a backpack trip into a nearby wilderness section of the Olympic National Forest. Remembering his experiences on Mount Angeles, he went better prepared this time. However, he was still very much the greenhorn:

One of my first adventures after pictures took me up the Elwha River into the interior of the Olympics. The Olympic mountains area is one of the last wilderness regions and some of the most rugged country in the United States. With my sixty-five pound pack, consisting of sleeping bag, cooking utensils and grub, as well as film and camera, I started up the trail into this little known and, to me, unknown country.

All day I labored, puffed, and sweat under my heavy pack. Up and up to clear a deep canyon [Rica Canyon on the Elwha River], then down to the river again. I felt as if I were the first white man to come into this country and the trail was just a freak of nature. Going through a valley with such high, abrupt sides was a new experience. I felt as if those sides were closing in on me. At times this feeling was so strong it was frightening.

I had begun to watch for a likely looking level place along the trail where I could lay my sleeping bag and spend the night. All at once I broke into a small clearing in the forest with a most unusual shaped house in the middle of it. It was two stories high, with a one-story enclosed shed encircling half of it. At one end of the main part was its oddest feature, a triangular offset with two smaller one-story triangles projecting from it. The windows were composed of many rectangles the size of photographic plates. Later I found that they were such plates. Arched under the gable was a sign spelled in rusty pieces of hammered out tin cans--GEYSER HOUSE.

I stood taking it all in when a man appeared around the corner, as unusual-looking as his house. Long, iron-gray hair draped his shoulders. He wore a full beard and was dressed in a grayish-white buckskin suit.

'Hello, are you a stranger around here?' he called cordially. 'You had better come in. Be dark pretty soon.'

I approached, half delighted at a shelter for the night and half afraid of this strange man. I told him I was a photographer on a trip for pictures.

'Come on in,' he said. 'I have taken quite a few pictures myself. Made a living at it in my younger days. We are going to get along all right. Have you had supper?'

I assured him that although I hadn't, I carried plenty of grub in my pack.

'It doesn't make any difference,' he said, 'do as you like, eat your grub or eat mine or we can eat together. Everyone up here is free to do as he likes.'

That was a free and generous attitude to assume towards a stranger, I felt more magnanimous in reality than urging me to eat with him.

I found my host interesting as well as generous. 'Doc' Ludden[5] was a full-fledged hermit. For twenty years he had lived here twelve miles from a road, and twenty-five miles from town. He made his clothes and shoes from home-tanned deer and elk skins. He raised a good garden, had lots of bees and sold honey. Dr. Ludden's was a dark honey unlike any other I have ever tasted.

Dr. Ludden was a woman-hater, no fooling. 'Oh, women are all right in their place,' he said, 'but it's too hot to live there.'

When I left he invited me to stay with him on the way back and warned me that I wouldn't see any other human being until I came back. If anyone went up the Elwha into the interior he knew it. There were lots of wild cats and cougar in the country, he said, but I would be all right, he thought. They hadn't killed anyone around here for "quite a spell!"

That "quite a spell" kept popping into my head as I plodded deeper into the silent, moss-covered forests. I wondered how long quite a spell was? Maybe the time limit was running out. That night, as I slept alone in the wilderness for the first time, every little sound would wake me and then I couldn't get back to sleep for a long while.

The third day I began to feel lonely. I felt too far from civilization for my soul to communicate with it, and I had a feeling that something might jump out from behind a tree at me any moment.

That night I camped at Crackerville.[6] I lay under a bark lean-to near the river bank. I was very tense and glad that I was starting back tomorrow. For a long time I couldn't go to sleep. I thought I heard something walking in the woods. I lay motionless, earnestly wishing the river would stop making so much noise so I could hear better. It was hours before I drifted off to sleep. I awoke with a thrill of fear. The whole valley was filled with howls, growls, and wows. My nervous tension amplified the roar tenfold. It sounded like a dozen cougar and two dozen wildcats were fighting all over the valley at the same time. How long is "quite a spell" I wondered? This must be it. I could feel my heart pounding. I tried to lie perfectly still but I had a crawling sensation as if I was slipping out of the sleeping bag like a piece of spaghetti off a fork. I could feel my hair raising and the strings with which I had tied on my sleeping cap began to strangle me.

Next morning I looked over the bank expecting to see at least two dead cougars but all that remained was a conglomeration of wildcat tracks in the sand. I had all the pictures I wanted for that trip.[7]

Crisler had been a hunter since childhood, so it was natural that he began hunting around his adopted home of Port Angeles. Since wildcat and cougar were so plentiful, he decided to buy a good cat dog. Selecting a good dog, Herb wrote, was "as complicated as selecting a good wife." Eventually he decided upon Tim. Tim was partially trained, "with most of the good points and some of the bad."

The first thing Herb had to do was break Tim of running deer. Finally, after much rock throwing, Tim decided his master didn't want him to take after every deer he saw. But the desire was still there:

> I've seen Tim, when a deer jumped up, just stand and tremble. He'd been broken from running, but he still had the thrill and excitement. Like an old married man chained down--- he'd like to chase her but knew if he did he'd get in trouble.

'Doc' Ludden's Geyser House, located along the Elwha River Trail near Humes Ranch.

But when Tim hit a cat track I could tell. [Herb's referral to cat means wildcat, not cougar]. His every movement was aggressive. His nose just went, 'Let me get at that!' He'd puff for a minute, then open up and was gone. I knew to start right after him.

Sometimes I'd meet him coming back and he'd pass me going the opposite direction. The old fellow doesn't know what he's doing, I thought. He doesn't know which way the cat is headed. He'll have me hunting all over the mountains. I'd watch for a bit of mud, or better yet snow, to see the cat's print and see if we were headed in the right direction. I soon learned that when Tim started in one direction, then reversed, he was going the right way. But it mystified me. How did the dog know he was going in the right direction?

Elmer Shay's barber shop was kind of a clearing house for all local opinion, especially about fishing and hunting. There had been a hot debate about the damage a wild cat would do and it had been going on for weeks. Some said wild cats caught only squirrels, rabbits, mountain beaver, mice and other small animals and birds. I didn't know, but I found out.

Tim took a cat track on the west side of Goblins Canyon. [Two miles above present-day Lake Mills.] It led off up the side of Mt. Fitzhenry, then cut down, crossed Cat Creek and started towards the Elwha River. Suddenly Tim jumped the cat. He only gave hot chase a couple of minutes, then barked treed. This was the quickest I ever knew a cat to tree and after I shot it down the cat looked as if it were heavy with kittens. But it was a tom. After I had skinned it, I cut him open to see what he had eaten. He was stuffed full of fresh deer meat.

There was fresh snow, so I back-tracked the cat and came upon a spike buck laying amongst logs at the bottom of a slide. The cat had eaten great chunks off of the shoulders and the carcass was still warm.

By reading the tracks in the snow I could deduct what happened. The cat had walked to the upper edge of the slide and lay flat on his belly, evidently watching the deer which, by his tracks, was about eight or 10 feet away. Cat tracks, toes well spaced, snow pushed back, indicated the cat had sprung for the deer. Tracks showed the buck making long leaps at a rectangle from the way he'd been feeding. No cat tracks to be found anywhere indicated the cat was riding the deer.

Halfway down the slide something was dragging in the snow alongside the deer--maybe the cat holding onto the deer and trying to down him. A little farther the deer went to his front knees, and a much wider drag mark. Next, full grown buck with fang marks in the back of his neck. Cat tracks led away. After this, there was no question in my mind whether or not a wild cat could kill a deer.[8]

Herb had many exciting experiences chasing wildcats with Tim. The dog taught Herb a lot of tricks. Many of his experiences seem worth repeating, but only two are included for brevity sake. Crisler's extraordinary stamina and determination are evident in the following story:

Hunting cats with a dog is lots of fun, but you have to be a good woodsman and it's a young man's game and a husky one's at that. I'll give you an example. Of course this is the longest and hardest hunt I ever had. It shows what can happen to a hunter.

I left my house in Port Angeles at three o'clock one morning, drove nine miles to the end of the Morse Creek Road, hiked five miles up Cox's Valley on the trail. Tim led off on a wild cat track about six o'clock.

This cat knew all the tricks. At noon, he still hadn't treed but had kept me running all morning to stay in hearing of Tim. After noon he tried a new trick. He started climbing Hurricane Ridge. This was January and the snow got deeper and deeper. He was so light he only sank in a couple of inches. Tim would go in six or eight inches. I wallowed up to my waist. Sometimes I would go down so deep that I would use my rifle as a bar to pull myself out.

The cat went over the top [of Hurricane Ridge]--five thousand feet elevation and I had started near sea level that morning.

Going down the other side to the Lillian River we all made better time. It was hard work for me to keep in hearing distance. When I got to the river I could hear Tim half a mile up the mountain barking treed. I moved up as fast as I could. It was getting late and we had not seen a trail or road since we struck the track. I was in such a hurry I shot the cat without tying Tim and grabbed it almost as soon as he did. I never jerked the skin off a cat so fast in my life and started on a run for the Upper Elwha trail.

It was dark by the time I found it and I was still fourteen miles from the road. I started down trail at a fast trot in order to get as far as I could before it turned pitch dark. It was eleven-thirty when I got to the road and I was still 12 miles from home and 19 miles from my car.

In three months after I bought Tim I killed and collected bounty on 37 wild cats. Any fisherman has at least one story about the big one that got away. I have a story about the big cat [cougar] that got away.

With Tim and enough grub to last us two days, I started out on a cat hunting trip. The second day we came upon a cougar kill about three days old. The cougar had gnawed through the deer's ribs and eaten out his liver and heart. The tracks were cold but there was a soft snow that made them easy to follow. Tim could still get enough scent to keep him interested, so I decided to track the cat down.

Before night we came upon a small buck whose liver and heart were also gone. This kill looked much later than the first, and Tim became more excited. Since we had already tracked about seven or eight miles through snow, I was tired, so I caught and tied Tim and camped for the night.

On hunting trips, I didn't carry a sleeping bag as I had to go light in order to keep within hearing of Tim after he struck a track. It was a bitter cold night and although I kept a fire going, I couldn't keep warm. As soon as it was light enough the next morning we took up the chase.

The tracks were very large, although that was no proof that he was a large cougar. During the long night Tim and I had eaten all our grub. Now it was the middle of the afternoon and still no cougar, but two hungry hounds. The next deer I saw, I caught Tim and tied him to a tree. At the sound of the rifle shot Tim thought I had double crossed him and killed the cougar without letting him in on the fun. Tim began howling and jerking on his leash with all his weight. A half hour later, when I offered him some venison, he was still so mad he refused to touch it. I explained that I had only shot a deer and rubbed some on his nose. He couldn't hold out any longer, and got down on his belly and started gnawing on ribs. I sat on a log and gnawed a chunk of leaf fat which had chilled as soon as I removed it from the deer's insides. It was about the consistency of unsweetened chocolate and gave me quick energy.

After dinner and with enough venison for several more meals in my knapsack, we started trailing the cougar. Night came. Still no cat. That night was as miserable as the last and I was ready to go at first peep of day. Tim, full of deer meat, had found a dry place on the lower side of a leaning tree to curl up in and was so comfortable he didn't care to start trailing cougar so early. When he saw me pick up the knapsack containing the deer meat and start off he decided to go along.

We kept up this cat trailing and eating deer meat for six days, finding four cougar kills altogether. On the fifth night, in order to sleep more comfortable, I built a lean-to by placing some bark against a downed log that was high enough for me to lie under. By building a fire in front and making Tim sleep against my back, I managed to sleep quite a bit that night.

It was well after daylight when I got up and started to broil some venison. When Tim smelled this he yawned and crawled out from under the log. The minute he was outside his nose shot up and he began to sniff the air. Then he made a short semicircle and opened up with a bawl. He took out through the woods as if he'd seen what he was after. I grabbed the knapsack with my take-down rifle in it and started on the run, leaving all the venison spread out on the ground.

It wasn't long until I heard Tim bark treed and I stepped on the gas. In a short time I could see Tim down by the river with his head up in the air letting out that "sweet sound to a cat hunter's ears" roll out.

I began to look up and try to locate the cougar in one of the trees that lined the river when suddenly I caught a glimpse of something moving on a big log which hung out over the river. I jumped to where I could get a better view and there was a cougar which looked at least nine feet long moving towards the river end of the log.

I ripped off my knapsack and started assembling my rifle. My hands shook so with excitement that I couldn't get the durn thing together as easy as usual. Tim saw the cat and thought it was getting away, so he bounded up onto the log and started after him. This was too much. The cougar jumped into the water and swam to the other side before I could get my gun in shooting order. Tim jumped in after him but I didn't want to swim that icy river in freezing weather. By calling, scolding and shooting, I managed to get Tim to turn around in midstream and swim back. I put him on the leash in case he changed his mind and both of us, cold, disgusted and discouraged, went back to the fire to get something to eat.

I picked up the cougar's tracks near camp and back-trailed him to see how near he had come to me while I was sleeping. I found that he had not only walked the log we were sleeping under, but had actually stopped and stood in such a position that he was able to look down and see us![9]

Deer hunting was not always good around Port Angeles in those days. Perhaps there were too many cougar and wildcats. A lot of people relied upon wild meat, and poaching was probably rampant. One of the favorite local places to hunt was along the top of Hurricane Ridge. An old road wound around the back side, coming up from near the Elwha Ranger Station, which gave hunters access to timberline.

After getting shot at on the ridge, Herb decided to find new hunting grounds. The area he finally chose was upper Boulder Creek, above Olympic Hot Springs.

The following story is about the first big buck Herb killed. He was lucky enough to kill it close to the road. He decided to take the animal home whole. He tied the deer's front and back feet together and put him on like a back pack:

When I got to my car I laid him between the front fender and the engine hood with his

Black-tail Deer

15

head sticking out in front. This made quite an impressive sight, so I drove down town to show off to some of my friends.

There is probably only one person out of a hundred that goes hunting and gets a deer and as this was early in the hunting season I was persuaded to let the deer be displayed in front of the sporting goods store as an example of what could be done if you bought your gun and ammunition there. This brought lots of publicity and I began to get a taste of fame.

Next season I wanted to get a bigger buck and more fame. It wasn't so easy this time. I had to work longer, harder, go farther, pack harder and sweat more to get him out.[10]

Once Herb decided to become a famous hunter, nothing could stop him. He studied the habits of deer, scouted likely areas, and became one of the local expert deer hunters.

After obtaining the reputation, would-be hunters were willing to hire his services as a guide. At first Herb refused. He was ashamed for them to discover how difficult it was to bring that big trophy buck into town each season. Finally he agreed to take a few friends.

One was Dr. Roy West, the Seattle dentist who had repaired Herb's teeth after the logging accident at Pysht. Their friendship was to become a life-long one.

Herb's fame as a hunter spread. His knowledge of how to survive in the Olympic Mountains improved. Photography and scrambling around beyond the trails became his passions, then his profession, and what he became best known for on the Peninsula.

Notes & Sources, Beyond the Trails, Chapter Two

1. Herb Crisler, "Western Wildlife Photographer," courtesy Ruby El Hult.

2. Herb Crisler, "The First Climb of Mt. Angeles," as told to Ruby El Hult (Feb. 25, 1974)

3. Klahhane is an Indian word meaning "good times out-of-doors." The club had been formed by a dozen charter members in 1915. Ben Phillips was its first elected president. Their first clubhouse was the abandoned Williams' cabin at the foot of Mt. Angeles. This is undoubtedly where Webster took the Crislers that night in 1919.

4. Herb Crisler, "Western Wildlife Photographer," courtesy Ruby El Hult

5. Mr. Ludden made no pretense of being a doctor. The name was given him because he espoused the use of organic foods. He signed his name "Dok", further distancing him from the doctor title. However, on some of his stationary on file at the National Park Visitor's Center, his name was precluded by the word "Doctor." Ludden Peak (5,828 ft. el.) at the head of Long Creek, is named after him. He died Nov. 8, 1927.

6. Present-day Camp Wilder.

7. Herb Crisler. "Western Wildlife Photographer." Courtesy Ruby El Hult.

8. Ibid.

9. Ibid.

10. Ibid.

3

Photo Finishing, Building and Exploring

Herb started a photo-finishing and post card business during his spare time, while still working at the mill. At first, the drug stores, which were sending film to Seattle, refused to consider Herb's developing and finishing.

Finally Brown's Music Store gave him the break he needed. Mrs. Brown and her daughters had exposed several rolls personally, and allowed him to develop and print the film. They were delighted with his work, and agreed to begin handling film for customers. Getting pictures back the next day was something of a novelty in Port Angeles. People were accustomed to waiting a week or more.

Herb hated his job stacking lumber. As soon as the photo-finishing business picked up, he asked for his time. They needed some place to live besides the house-keeping rooms at Eighth and Lincoln. Herb rented a little house two blocks west on Eighth. He immediately converted the kitchen into a photo-finishing room, added heavy curtains to the windows and used the kitchen sink for processing. He bought several shallow pans, developer, fixer, hypo and a few safety pins for hanging film to dry. He had never required much sleep. In daytime he went looking for subjects or took care of other business. His film work was done at night, so he could get it back to the stores the next day before noon.

Behind the house he spaded enough ground to plant a garden.

Herb's first picture post cards were financed by himself. The drug stores took them only on consignment. The cards didn't sell well until the fleet came in. Sometimes a dozen naval ships anchored behind Ediz Hook. During the summer a few tourists visited the Peninsula and the cards sold well then also. Shop owners clamored for more at such times but Herb was often too busy with his photo finishing business to print post cards on short notice.

Port Angeles was a small town. Word of the fast photo-finishing service available at Brown's quickly got around and the store was swamped with orders.

Faced with such competition, the drug stores then asked Herb to do their photo finishing. Business was so good he became more independent. He no longer allowed drug stores to take his cards on consignment. They paid cash.

Herb now found himself in the same dilemma many one-man businesses have faced. With his photo-finishing

Herb Crisler postcard of Hoh Glacier from Bailey Range. Circa 1920's.

business keeping him busy he had to improvise to find time to go out and take new pictures for new post cards.

Mr. and Mrs. Taylor, Muriel's parents, decided to move to Port Angeles. Mr. Taylor suffered from chronic asthma, and had to hover over breathing vapor most of the time.

They moved in with Herb and Muriel. It fell to Herb and Muriel to support them. Mr. Taylor had been an excellent carpenter and cabinet maker, so Herb had his father-in-law's expertise to draw upon during his building jobs.

Herb and Muriel bought a large (double) lot at 231 West Third Street. The lot was level and contained several fir and madrone trees. Herb built a house on the back of the lot. Next to it he put in a vegetable garden.

Phanoy, Herb's sister, his mother and aunt came to Port Angeles to visit. Herb suggested his mother move to the area. She considered the move, declined, then left Phanoy with Herb and returned south.

Herb built a small house on the front of his lot for Phanoy to live in. Phanoy and Muriel didn't get along, so Phanoy moved in with friends. The small house in front was rented to little Will Smith. He and Herb became hunting partners.

In 1925 Herb built another house on the lot next door. Thinking his mother would come if he had a place for her to live, Herb built another two-story house at the end of Lincoln Street in 1925-26. Adora decided to remain in Georgia.

Herb and Muriel were living in their kitchen. They ate, slept, lived and used the kitchen as a darkroom.

Verne A. Samuelson, the Ford dealer located at First and Lincoln Streets, and Herb, became good friends. Samuelson was to later have considerable influence upon Herb's activities.

Herb had a beaver-like urge to forever be building something. Herb and Verne, with mostly Herb's labor, built a splendid log cabin beside a little brook in the forest near where Olympic National Park's Elwha campground is now located. They neglected to obtain a permit from the U. S. Forest Service.

The Forest Service didn't get wise to the building, as it was out of sight from the road. Verne provided Herb use of a car to reach the building site.

After the cabin was finished, Samuelson decided they had better get a permit. Verne was a well-known and prominent local businessman. He decided he'd better soften up the district ranger before he dared tell him the cabin was already built. He made several social calls, presenting a box of expensive cigars each time.

After discovering the plot, the district ranger was angry, resenting the way he'd been tricked, then shooed Samuelson out the door. Eventually his anger subsided and the permit was granted.

The Klahhane Club announced a mid-March outing. Herb jumped at the chance to go. Fifteen members decided to make the trip to Olympic Hot Springs. Herb recalled that trip many years later:

> We crossed [the Elwha River] on the covered bridge near Sisson's. The only other place to cross was not convenient. It was a cable crossing with a basket, near the ranger station, and it carried but one person at a time and took forever. [A trail existed up both sides of the Elwha River at the time.]
>
> We ran into elk on the trail. They had no fear. [1] I had my new post card camera and wanted to photograph them but had no idea how to approach the animals.
>
> All that was at the Olympic Hot Springs was a mud hole in the hillside, built up on the lower side with some logs and a few cabins with bath tubs made out of hewn cedar logs. To soak, you had to carry water in a bucket and dump it into the tubs. There was also a water mill running a generator. [2]

This may have been the first time Herb had seen elk. And his first of many, many visits to Olympic Hot Springs. The local paper carried a report of the outing:

The entire Elwha river valley seemed to be fairly alive with elk Sunday, when the 15 members of the Klahhane club returned from their week-end outing at the Hot Springs, and the best part of it was the animals seemed to have no fear of those who invaded their domain. O'Brien at one time actually had to wave his hat and yell "Shoo" to get a cow to move out of the way, while Crisler, on the pony trail just above, was snapping pictures as the herd passed single file within thirty-six feet from him. The largest herd, something over fifty, was first seen by Miss Handson, the beautiful animals being then on their way down through the grassy clearings above Wolf's ranch. Considerable amusement was afforded by Professor Flett and Mr. Blanchard getting mixed up in the midst of a small herd, which started up the mountain and then doubled back, the elk jumping to either side as they met the men coming up. There was elk sign on the slope above the trail for over two hours, and one large animal maintained his position at the foot of a rock when the club members finally left for home. Beside the elk, two black-tailed deer were seen, first being spied by Miss Chambers as they were coming up the slope; they passed within fifty yards in open timber, walking slowly along, stopping to rest and look back every thirty feet or so.

Though there was fully four feet of snow at the springs, the walking was good, being, in fact, easier than on the muddy river bottom trail. Two hours were spent in the swimming pool Saturday evening; it snowed steadily meanwhile; five feet of snow fell Saturday night. The party was entertained by Mrs. Wm. Everett and Mr. Schoeffel of the Hot Springs Co., and the menus would indeed be a surprise to larger and more pretentious hotels.

A pleasing feature was the picking of dainty white wild flowers, found growing on the mossy rocks; also the first flowering currants of the year, the bush growing out of the solid rock beneath the hanging bridge a short distance above the Elwha.[3]

If there seems to be several inconsistencies in the above story, such as "five feet of snow in one night" and picking "wildflowers", remember that Olympic Hot Springs is 2,000 feet elevation, and close to the mass of high mountains, which makes considerable difference in the weather. Down along the Elwha mid-March can be like spring.

E.B. Webster described the early-day facilities at the hot springs:

Hung on a narrow shelf on the mountainside, over a canyon threaded by the roaring Boulder in its express train speed to the Elwha and the sea, the hotel presently comes into view. A hundred-foot-high bridge is to be crossed before one reaches the hotel, the bath houses, the open air pools and the rows of tents and tent-houses where comfortable beds and abundant fresh air insure a night of deep, unbroken slumber.[4]

It was probably at Olympic Hot Springs that Herb first made the acquaintance of William "Billy" Everett, also locally known as the "Mowich Man"[5], a legendary mountain man, explorer and hunter. Billy's tales of scrambling around the Olympics and the wild, magical places he had discovered in the Bailey Range may have fanned the spark of interest, that Herb already had for wild areas in the Olympic Mountains, to a fever pitch.

The springs, on the hillside above Boulder Creek, a tributary of the Elwha River, are about 25 miles southwest of Port Angeles.

The hot springs had first been discovered in 1892 by Andrew Jacobson while on a hunting trip. Jacobson noticed steam rising and thought the mountain was about to blow up. He didn't linger. No one in Port Angeles believed him when he reported his find.

Fifteen years later Billy Everett, Thomas Farrell and Charles Anderson were in the area hunting cougar. On June 25, 1907, Everett re-discovered the hot springs. The three hunters reportedly hewed out a cedar log, flumed in hot water, then soaked. Farrell staked a mineral claim.

Later, Everett became owner. He slashed a trail from the Elwha River, a tremendous feat, as the country is steep and many windfalls cover the ground. Billy and his wife built a hand-split cedar-shake cabin and bath house. With a partner, Carl Schoeffel, they operated, and improved, the resort for many years. About the time of Herb's visit, Harry Schoeffel bought out Carl's interest.

Harry and Billy Everett's daughter Jeannette were married in 1921. After 1924 the Everetts retired to their farm on the lower Elwha. The Schoeffel's operated Olympic Hot Springs until the time it closed December 31, 1966.

About late summer of 1919, a lodge, containing a dining room, kitchen, store and meat-cooling room was operational. Resort cabins had replaced tent frames. A new 25 by 75-foot pool had been completed.

In 1920 another new lodge, containing sleeping rooms was started. [6]

Herb couldn't maintain the grueling schedule at his flourishing new business without an occasional break. The breaks were usually photo trips for more pictures. In the following story he recalls how he spent one "relaxing" vigorous weekend:

> Friday night I would clear up the remaining finishing work, then walk to Olympic Hot Springs.[7] Then on Saturday I'd climb up to the lakes [Boulder, Three Horse and Blue] and take two or three dozen post card negatives. Then I'd drop back down to the springs, have a good soak in the hot pool, rent a house-keeping cabin for $2.50, cook the food I'd brought with me and have a good sleep. Then in the morning I'd cook a quick breakfast and hike back home, have supper, do the film developing which came in on Saturday, print the Monday morning work, then deliver it to Brown's Music Store by one o'clock. [8]

Herb was fascinated by the high, snow-covered peaks which often present themselves to the viewer from various locations in the mountains behind Port Angeles. The highest peak, Mount Olympus, 7,965 feet elevation, and most surrounding peaks, are not visible from lower elevations near Port Angeles or the north Olympic Peninsula.

After Herb's first climbing experience, the unsuccessful attempt to climb Mount Angeles during the winter of 1919, he'd gained more knowledge about the challenges of travel in the rugged Olympic Mountains.

His old mentor, "Haywire" Tom Newton, was a frequent visitor. Tom loved high places and was fond of mountain climbing. Amongst his mountain climbing buddies, Newton was called the "Flying Squirrel" instead of "Haywire" or "Daredevil" Newton, names which he'd been given by fellow loggers.

The Klahhane Club was considering an attempt to climb Mount Olympus. They wanted to do so from a base camp at Queets Basin. Samuelson was appointed as climbing committee chairman. He asked Herbert Wood and Crisler if they thought it feasible to climb Olympus from Queets Basin. They didn't know, but said they'd find out.

Tom Newton was invited to lead the party. This expedition occurred during the summer of 1920. They went in from the Upper Hoh, a level trail along the river as far as Olympus ranger station. Evidently they expected to exit via Queets Basin.

At Olympus Ranger Station they met Tom Mansfield, who was working for the forest service. He was bored and decided to join the fun.

The going got steep as the way path, only an elk trail at the time, climbed ever upward to Glacier Meadows. From that point on, there was no maintained trail. They simply followed an elk trail through the woods and bushwhacked, until they reached the snout of Blue Glacier. From there the route continues on glacier ice, up to the Snow Dome, an ice field.

Herb reported that Tom was a devil to keep up with:

20

To Tom Newton everything on God's earth was expendable. It wasn't so much that he was reckless as that he knew his own prodigious strength. He could jump twenty feet downward and light on a rock like a cat, a leap that would break your jaw to follow. Lithe, with flawless balance and rhythm, when he topped a hundred-and-fifty foot fir spar tree and the severed top dropped off, leaving the tree lashing in rebound, Tom would leap to the cut end and ride it, standing free, swaying against the sky. On Sunday afternoon, when other loggers played blackjack for pastime, Tom, for recreation, would spring-board fifty feet up a fir tree.

When he climbed Olympus, he had something worth his skill at last. He climbed it like a high-rigger. The men back-packed in from the Hoh River side and made camp at Glacier Meadows. In the morning Tom led up the Snow Dome. Under a cornice he hooked his fingers over and raised his body. 'Sure, this is a good place,' he called; and reaching over, gave each young fellow a heave up, to a steep snow slope with no trace of purchase; then an upward boost.

They climbed West Peak, and Tom stood on his head on the cairn. It made the other men dizzy. He romped across the snow field to Middle Peak and on to East Peak, his party panting after. What was down he took at a leap; what was up, at a stride. From East Peak, without an instant's pause, Tom plunged over the side, so steep you couldn't see below the bulge, down towards Hoh Glacier. His shout drifted back, 'Come on!' So he was still alive. One by one the men sat down and whizzed out of sight. The one left alone on the peak was Herb Crisler, the boy from Georgia, who had never been in the mountains before. 'You can stay here and freeze to death,' he thought. 'This is it,' and over he went. Tom's shout roared through the glittering rush, 'Hey you, stand up there and jump that crevasse!' Herb made the six or eight foot leap and landed trembling, vowing in his heart if he ever got off this mountain alive, he was through with white peaks. It was not mountaineering of course, but only Tom Newton's style, a high-rigger's bold delight in risk that skill could balance towards life.

Tom took the men down Hoh Glacier on a run, jumping crevasses and shouting as he went. It was a nightmare to follow him. They siwashed it on the rocks beside the glacier that night, by a little fire of gray sticks, continually trading places by the fire during the night to keep warm. The next day the men toiled around to Glacier Meadows and their cache, except for Tom. Tom separated from his spent comrades and headed for a rendezvous with club members in Queets Basin. By squirreling away an extra day, climbing all three peaks, he had missed his purpose, to find Blizzard Pass, then go down to the Queets Basin and lead the Klahhanes back onto the mountain. He was one day late.[9]

In the fall of 1921 Herb, Al Knight and Al's brothers decided to explore the upper Sol Duc River country for new hunting possibilities. They hiked in from Sol Duc Hot Springs, backpacking a minimum of supplies because they expected to come back loaded with venison. They broke out of the timber and entered an area of beautiful meadows, with scattered patches of alpine fir, grotesquely twisted by high, relentless winds. Deer and elk sign was everywhere.

That night they camped down off the ridge in a little hollow. About midnight a rip roaring blizzard struck camp, catching the men unprepared. Gusts of wind screamed over the nearby high peaks, tore through the stumpy sub-alpine fir and threatened to put out the fire. They worked like beavers through the night, dragging in wet, snow-covered wood, hugging the fire to keep from freezing.

They named the place Windy Hollow. Whether or not anyone got a deer after the storm remains unknown, but the hunting looked so favorable, Herb decided to build a hunting shelter in the area. The lean-to shelter,

Big Blowdown of 1921.

constructed of logs and split-shake roof, built in 1922, became Herb's favorite hunting headquarters. During the 1930s, the shelter caught fire and burned. It was replaced by another not far away. Herb often came to this remote spot to hunt with his dentist friend, Dr. Roy West, Attorney Bill Long (later judge) and others. They had the area to themselves, never seeing another hunter.

The Windy Hollow shelter became the first in a chain of caches and camps which Herb would eventually build along the Bailey Range and through the Olympic Mountains, a route Herb would use for more than a decade while filming wildlife. This route now is known as the Crisler Traverse. The route is so dangerous and rugged few people, even today, attempt backpacking the Traverse.

On January 29, 1921, the Olympic Peninsula was struck by a terrible hurricane, known as the "big blow-down of twenty-one." After the 130-miles-per-hour wind died down, an estimated nine or ten billion board feet of timber lay scattered over western Clallam and

Jefferson Counties. That's enough timber to build homes for most of the families living in the state of Washington today. The storm and blow-down was a major news item.

Ed Halberg, owner of the Lincoln Theater, told Herb it was too bad he didn't have a newsreel camera to film the blow-down, that the news services would probably pay handsomely for the film.

Herb was interested, but had neither a motion-picture camera, or the money to buy one. Halberg offered to help. They located a used Pathe newsreel camera and Halberg bought it for $25. This was the first motion-

Herb Crisler flips a hotcake at camp in the Bailey Range. Hotcake appears to land on Hoh Glacier. Note famous home-made packboard that transported many tons of supplies into the back country.

picture newsreel camera to remain permanently in Clallam County. With tripod, it weighed almost 100 pounds. The camera was cranked by hand and used 35 millimeter film.

Herb photographed the big blow-down with both the newsreel and a still camera. Halberg showed the film at the Lincoln Theater. Herb then sold the film to the news services for $500. One still picture, which survives, is of an old touring car, parked beneath a jackstraw pile of windfalls which lay across the road above the car along what is, apparently, now Highway 101. Encouraged by the sale of the film, Herb became convinced that his future lay in motion-pictures. He began filming scenery and wildlife every chance he got, lugging the newsreel camera into the back country. Black and white was the only film available. Color film was unheard of.

Herb always listened attentively while visiting Billy Everett. Especially when Everett talked about the beautiful, rugged, unexplored (except by himself and Boston Charlie) wilderness which lay only a few miles south of Port

Herb Crisler in the Bailey Range in 1923.

Angeles. The area Billy described was hidden from view, even from Hurricane Ridge, because it lay behind the Bailey Range.

The Bailey Range is a series of rugged, snow-covered peaks starting at Cat Peak, including Mounts Carrie, Fairchild, Stephen Peak, Mount Ferry, and ending at Mount Childs, overlooking the headwaters of the Hoh River. These peaks, all about 6,000 feet elevation, effectively block easy access into Cream Lake Basin and the headwaters of the Hoh.

The heart of the area included Cream Lake, which Billy had discovered, and named, before the turn of the century.

Even today the upper Hoh Valley, especially Cream Lake Basin, remains one of the most inaccessible areas in the Olympic Mountain wilderness. Only three practical routes exist into the Cream Lake area. None have trails. All are difficult.

One, from the west, along the High Divide then across the infamous "Catwalk", a quarter-mile section of razor-back ridge east of Cat Peak, then east along the flanks of the Bailey Range.

Second, from Dodger Point and Ludden Peak, a shorter but very strenuous route, ending in the Bailey Range after the ascent of Mount Ferry.

Third, a long 28-mile route up the Elwha River to Elwha Basin, where the trail ends. Then up the Elwha Snowfinger to Dodwell-Rixon Pass on the extreme southeast end of the Bailey Range.

During the summer of 1924, Herb, Ed Halberg, Verne Samuelson, Al Knight and Reverend Goude, minister at the Port Angeles Baptist church, made a trip to the Bailey Range and Cream Lake. Few details exist of the trip, or route used, but they probably went in one way and out another.

Herb carried the heavy Pathe motion-picture camera into this rugged country!

That fall Herb spliced together some of the film taken on this trip and, together with film taken earlier around Port Angeles and Forks, made his very first motion-picture film, From the Mountains to the Sea.

The film was shown at the Lincoln Theater. The end of the film was a spectacular scene of the Quillayute Indian village at La Push, with surf crashing upon the magnificent, curved ocean beach, James Island loomed behind and sea gulls wheeled overhead. The end caption: "Westward the course of empire makes its way." This may sound corny today, but wasn't so presumptuous in the 1920's. Only a few decades earlier, no white men had penetrated, and resided in, the western part of the Peninsula.

Local patrons flocked to see the first motion-pictures of their beloved Peninsula. Herb was thrilled as viewers "OOO'd and AAAAHHH'd" at scenes throughout the film. Their enthusiasm, plus half the box office receipts, encouraged him to film and show more pictures of the Olympic Peninsula, and actually started Herb in his long career as a professional nature and scenic motion-picture photographer.

Herb was also an ardent fisherman. Editor Webster wrote the following:

> Two or three times each month during the summer Herbert brings in something like twenty-five trout for exhibition, but he drives out to the lake [Sutherland] at the close of each day's work.
>
> The first fall Herbert built a home; the second year, another house; yet another house the next year; a summer cottage up the Elwha; a car; yet another car; moving picture machine, enlarging machine, all the latest photographic equipment. And, "I see be th' paper," this winter Mr. and Mrs. Crisler are sojourning in Florida.
>
> As I said before, Herbert knows how to catch fish.[10]

The trip to Florida started September 29, 1923. Herb bought a new 1924 model Ford coupe late in the fall from his buddy, Verne Samuelson. Herb and Muriel drove the northern route, through Missoula, Montana and South Dakota, then on to Muriel's old home in Cleveland in 11 days. Total cost for gas, oil and meals, $56.00. We assume they camped, probably without even a tent, at night. From Cleveland they turned south and visited relatives in Georgia, then went to Florida. In the South they encountered terrible floods, washouts and torrential rains, with water on the roads so deep they had to shield their motor's ignition with a poncho.

Coming west across the southwest they encountered both sand storms and blizzards. Miles of desert roads were obliterated by sand or snow. Breaking trail in a touring car was almost like crossing the country by covered wagon before highways were constructed. Hundreds of autos were marooned in blizzards, and at least three persons perished.

The last leg of the trip, from Yuma, Arizona to Port Angeles, was made in four days, an average of over 450 miles per day. Total running time for the 12,000 mile trip was 38 days, an average of 315 miles per day. Total expenses, including a new set of tires, gas, oil, meals, hotels, etc. for the three months was $300.00 or about 2 1/2 cents a mile!

After the Crislers returned home people were astounded to read in the Port Angeles paper about the trip. The sad state of the nation's highway system was well known. Few people dared make such a long trip in 1924!

"How did you get to all those places?" they asked.

"We just followed the detour signs," Herb replied. Samuelson was ecstatic. He used Herb's story and brought out a broadside, with a picture of the "Lizzie".[11]

Herb was hooked on the Pacific Northwest by then, glad to return to the Olympic Peninsula and anxious to resume photographing.

Notes & Sources, Beyond the Trails, Chapter Three

1. Peninsula elk had been protected since the season was closed to elk hunting by the state legislature in 1905.

2. Herb Crisler Reminiscences, interview by Ruby El Hult, (Veterans Administration Hospital, Denver, Colorado, 1974).

3. Port Angeles Evening News, 18 Mar., 1919

4. E.B. Webster, Fishing in the Olympics. Port Angeles, WA, 1923

5. "Mowich" is the Indian name for deer. William (Billy) Everett, was the son of Peninsula pioneer John Everett. John Everett, a trapper and hunter for the Hudson's Bay Company, arrived at Port Crescent from Victoria, British Columbia in the early 1860's. He married a Clallam Indian. About 1863, at a time when Port Angeles consisted of only a few frame buildings along a little rutty street, John operated a "wild" meat market at the foot of Valley Street. Grouse, deer, pheasant and bear were supplied by John's partner, John Sutherland. William Everett's house and meat market, as well as other houses and the United States Customs House, operated by Collector of Customs Victor Smith, were destroyed by a flash flood, December 16, 1863.

Billy was born in 1866. His mother died at childbirth, and John was away from home hunting much of the time, so the boy was raised by a maternal aunt and uncle, a Clallam by the name of Boston Charlie, until he was old enough to accompany his father.

He became an extraordinary hunter, explorer and mountain man. He was small in stature but lithe, muscular and tough. By age 18, accompanied by his dogs, and with only a rifle, flour and coffee, he already explored much of the lower portions of the Elwha River, Boulder Creek and had even penetrated to the High Divide area between the Sol Duck, Bogachiel, Elwha and Hoh Rivers. Before Lieutenant Joseph P. O'Neal's party began exploring the interior of the Olympic Mountains in 1885 Billy had penetrated as far as Cream Lake in the Bailey Range. No man-made trails existed anywhere in the Olympic Mountains at this time. His feats were not even known to most people.

Billy and his wife developed Olympic Hot Springs. They owned land on the west side of the Elwha River, below the Lower Elwha River Bridge, where Harold Sisson now lives.

Everett is honored by two landmarks: Mount Everett at the headwaters of Boulder Creek and beautiful Lake Billy Everett in Mount Ferry Basin, near the headwaters of the Hoh River.

6. Jimmy Come Lately. 1st Edition, (1971) "Olympic Hot Springs," by Jeannette Everett Schoeffel, Clallam County Historical Society. (Port Angeles, Washington) 1971 pgs.412-415.

7. At the time, only a 12-mile, very rough horse trail led from what is now Highway 101 to the hot springs. About 2,000 feet of elevation had to be climbed to reach the springs. The trail was upgraded into a road by the forest service in the late 1920's.

8. Herb Crisler, letter to Ruby El Hult, 23 May 1974.

9. Island of Rivers. An anthology celebrating 50 years of Olympic National Park. "Pioneers of the Olympics," by Lois Crisler. Pacific Northwest National Parks & Forests Association. (Seattle, WA) 1988

This was not the first ascent of Mount Olympus. Prior to this the mountain had been climbed numerous times. Jack McGlone, a short little Irishman working under surveyor Rixon, made a solitary first ascent of East Peak in 1899, left a scrap of newsprint in a tin can, and departed. His claim went unrecorded. The scrap of paper was found by a party of The Mountaineers Club of Seattle in 1907. The party climbed all three peaks, including a first ascent of the highest, West Peak, elevation 7,965 feet.

Tom Newton died in an accident while working on the construction of Grand Coulee Dam in 1934. He had been suspended from a 100-foot-high crane over the Columbia River when the crane tipped over. His body was recovered 13 days later. He was buried at Forks.

10. E.B. Webster, Fishing in the Olympics. (Port Angeles, WA) 1923

11. Automobiles were affectionately known as "Lizzies" or "Tin Lizzies," in those days. Broadside, a term then used for a large sheet of paper, printed on one side, an advertisement, or handout brochure. This particular handbill, supposedly in Herb's words, was titled: "If I Had $100,000, and was to make another Transcontinental trip, I Would Choose a Ford Coupe." (Courtesy of Ruby El Hult)

4

Crashes

Herb was a worker, a man of action, a compulsive builder, with courage, faith in his ability to accomplish whatever he set out to do and with unlimited energy. After building three houses in Port Angeles, it's obvious that Herb could have become a building contractor. He had a successful photo finishing business, owned property and was doing okay.

However, his first love was photography, nature, wildlife and the mountains. While he did many other things to earn a living, the above pursuits were never far from his thoughts.

The Crislers wanted a child. The doctor concluded Muriel was incapable of having children. They adopted a boy only a few months old and named him Robert Bruce, the Bruce of course after Herb's maternal grandparents.

Then a series of events occurred which eventually led to a such a traumatic period in the Crislers' lives Herb later had trouble recalling particular dates and events.

He wished only to forget.

The first airplane in Port Angeles landed on Front Street between Oak and Valley, July 11, 1919.

It started after Charles A. Lindbergh's historic transatlantic flight May 20, 1927. Lindbergh had climbed into his Ryan monoplane, the Spirit of St. Louis and took off for Europe, landing in Paris thirty-three and a half hours later.

Lindbergh's sensational solo flight became the news story of the times. Talk of airplanes and the ramification of commercial trans-oceanic crossing were topics on most people's lips during this period.

Herb's interest in aviation had been fanned by the flight of the Spirit of St. Louis. The airplane, which not long before had been considered a novelty, was rapidly becoming another important machine which, like the automobile, was changing the way people thought, lived and traveled.

Back in Georgia, Herb's mechanically inclined youngest brother, Albert, joined the ranks of those interested in airplanes. He began hanging around the airport, badgering pilots to allow him to help work on the planes.

The following year, 1928, Al Gorst, a 52-year-old entrepreneur, who had started Pacific Air Transport out of Pearson Field in Vancouver, Washington, sold out for almost $100,000. He moved to the Kitsap Peninsula and started a flying school and Gorst Air Transport in Bremerton. His air taxi business did a booming business, especially while the naval fleet was in, since reaching the east side of Puget Sound from Bremerton was still an ordeal.

Round-trip tickets from Bremerton to Seattle eventually sold for as low as $1.50. While air taxi service had become available in most areas in the Pacific Northwest, those in the know about air transportation had their eyes upon roadless Alaska, which was ripe and begging for rapid transportation.

In 1929, Alaska Washington Airways sent the Alaska, a Lockheed Vega, (which, incidentally was constructed from Sitka spruce) to Alaska. Gorst followed two days later with a Keystone Loening Air Yacht and set up business in Cordova.

These happenings didn't escape observers of the air transportation business. Newspapers carried vivid stories about the historic flights. Many young men developed a passion for aviation. An aviation club was formed in Port Angeles.

Herb joined. The club rented a Piper Cub and a number of members learned to fly. Herb was more interested in the business of aviation, believing it had a great future. Herb thought any money to be made would be in commercial aviation. He considered starting a flying service.

According to Herb's brother, Captain Albert Crisler, who had a distinguished career as a flight instructor and commercial airlines pilot, Herb hoped, after acquiring an airplane, to land the mail contract between Port Angeles and Seattle.

Mail contracts were lucrative plums waiting to be picked by any aircraft owner who could demonstrate to the U.S. Postal Service they could fly from A to B with sacks of mail on a regular basis. Passenger revenue would be extra frosting on the cake.

Since the trip from Port Angeles to Seattle, although only eighty miles, took half a day, because it required either steamships or car ferries, Herb thought plenty of paying customers would use the airline services.

Herb sold his film-finishing business, part of his property in Port Angeles, mortgaged the rest, moved to Seattle, bought an airplane and started an air taxi business. As I wrote earlier, Herb was a plunger, a man of action.

The plane was a Stinson-Detroiter[1] He hired Joe Livermore as pilot. Airplanes had names in those days. They named the plane the Cirrus, after the billowing white clouds so common over Western Washington, clouds Joe hoped to avoid.

Herb bought a house at 8121 Ninth Avenue Southwest, above Boeing Field, rented an office on the top floor of the Northern Life Tower, then a new, swanky address, and hired Hazel Goodwin as secretary.

Herb also bought new clothes and became a dashing figure about town, wearing a homburg and chesterfield. Muriel, from the very first, was a reluctant partner in this venture.

The bread and butter of Crisler's air-taxi business were sight-seeing flights around Mount Rainier. Customers swarmed around the field on weekends, and they kept busy. Weekdays were slow. The mail contract to the Peninsula failed to materialize.

Back in Georgia, Albert, seventeen, wild about airplanes and motorcycles, after discovering his big brother owned an airline, thought this was the most exciting thing he'd ever heard. He almost drove his mother crazy wanting to go to Seattle and help Herbert. Finally, in desperation, he wrote and asked Herb to send him enough money so he could come to Seattle, learn to fly and become a pilot for Crisler Airlines.

Herb didn't think much of that idea, didn't have the money, and ignored the letter.

Undaunted, Albert decided he had to get to Seattle somehow.

After an uneventful summer, Joe called Herb at the office one winter day and said he had a passenger who needed to get to Portland, Oregon fast.

The weather was foggy. After talking it over, they decided not to take a chance. Navigation in those days was dead reckoning, a term which simply means visual navigation, or with only a compass. Some people assumed the term meant if you reckoned wrong--you're dead. In many instances, especially during the early days of aviation, this is exactly what happened.

Later Joe called again saying the man wanted to go so bad he offered one hundred dollars. Joe said that if Herb would come along to help, he would attempt the flight. Reluctantly, Herb agreed. One hundred dollars was quite an inducement.

Once the aircraft was airborne they entered blinding white clouds and fog. Joe flew low so they could follow highway 99, using telephone poles as a visual guide.

Near Tacoma visibility dropped right to the ground. There was no place to land. Joe was afraid he'd hit the top of a tree, so he pulled back on the stick and headed aloft in an attempt to get above the fog. Up and up they climbed. Finally they broke through into bright sunlight.

The only thing visible were the icy, white summits of Mounts Rainier and St. Helens. A fleecy white carpet of fog covered western Washington! Herb's stomach muscles tightened. He would gladly have paid the hundred dollars to be safely on the ground.

Joe decided it was too risky to either continue or return. He put the plane into a glide down through the swirling mists, looking for a hole. Finally, at about 1,000 feet elevation, a hole opened. They saw green fields, circled around, then landed in a farmer's hay pasture. Herb breathed a sigh of relief.

They had no idea where they were. A farmer came stalking towards the aircraft, looked disgustedly at the tire marks across his meadow, shook his head angrily, and said they'd come down near Centralia. The farmer led them to his house where there was a telephone.

Herb was so unnerved he drank a cup of coffee, one of only two cups of the brew he ever consumed during his entire life. Instead of helping, the coffee caused his stomach to be more upset than before.

Undaunted, the passenger tried to hire someone to drive him to Portland without success. Next, he suggested they call Portland and find out how the weather was. Swan Island Airfield reported that there was a skiff of snow on the ground, but the visibility was fair. They should be able to land without any trouble.

They took off again. Above Castle Rock they ran into a blinding snowstorm. Visibility was zero. Joe steered by compass and everyone said their own private prayers.

They broke out of the snow, looked down and saw the Columbia River. By then it was dark. The lights of Vancouver and Portland were a welcome, but confusing sight.

Airports were only strips of level ground without any navigational lights or aids in those days. They found Swan Island Airport without any trouble because the manager had thoughtfully parked several cars around the landing strip with their headlights pointed across the field.

The snow storm had proceeded them. More than a little snow covered the ground. The field was unbroken white, with alternating and confusing areas of headlights and shadows. Estimating altitude above unbroken snow was a nightmare. Joe circled several times, decided they were about 500 feet high, pushed the stick foreword and started an approach. He misjudged his altitude. The plane's landing gear slammed into the ground unexpectedly, throwing up a cloud of snow and dirt. The craft bounced, Joe gunned the engines, hauled back madly on the stick and they were airborne again.

Nonchalantly, Joe said, "Well, now we'll have that bare spot as a marker the next time around and I can judge the elevation." Herb looked down and saw the aircraft's landing gear laying upside down where they'd hit. "I didn't say a word, just hollered 'Joe', and pointed!" Herb said. Joe looked down, put his hands to his head and said, "Oh, God, we really are in trouble!"

Joe circled the field, then said, "I'll fly around until we use up all our gas--and when the motor dies I'll go in on a dead stick belly landing. Avoid chances of a fire."

Round and round the field they went. Joe instructed Herb to take all the seat cushions and place them on the floor in the passenger compartment, get the passenger to lie face down, then cover him with pads, blankets or coats, anything soft which might protect him if they crashed.

28

Herb recalled, "The passenger was very scared by this time--and so was I, but I didn't dare show it. I told him the danger was from splinters from the [wooden] plane, and the padding would protect him. He obediently laid face down and I covered him up."

Down below they could see red flashing lights of fire engines arriving at the field. The field manager had alerted ambulances and the fire department that an airplane was about to crash.

The motor coughed, sputtered, then died. Suddenly they were coasting down, the only sound was the whine of wind around the struts. Joe was afraid if he attempted a true belly landing the airplane would toboggan along on the snow and crash into the trees at the end of the field. As the plane touched down Joe tilted the wings so the craft landed on one wing tip and the fuselage to serve as a brake. The nose and wing tip plowed into the field and the plane went into a dizzy spin across the snow.

The radiator of the water-cooled engine burst open, enveloping everything in billows of steam, which probably looked like smoke to rescue crews. Suddenly the plane stopped spinning and sliding.

Before Joe and Herb could gather their wits and extract themselves they heard excited yelling and banging. Firemen, in their zeal to save the passengers from a possible explosion and fire, were chopping holes through the side of the plane, without even trying to open the doors.

Once all three were outside, ambulance personnel insisted they lie down on stretchers, although no one was hurt. The plane's port prop was shattered, the engine cylinders split apart, steam still pouring from the radiator, the fuselage appeared as if it had been attacked by an angry mob with axes.

The passenger was shaking and shivering, having lost control. He kept reaching for his billfold as if to pay Herb. Herb said, "You already paid us $100 before we left Seattle." He kept fumbling in his billfold, his hands trembling, and drew out another $100 bill. Herb repeated that he'd already paid, but the passenger threw the money at him, saying in a quavering voice, "It's worth another hundred--just to be alive!"

Herb knew insurance would not cover rebuilding the plane. They were out of business. He and Joe held a conference. Joe knew people in Portland. He thought he'd stay and try to find a job as pilot. Before the trip they'd agreed to split the $100 fare. But what about the bonus? "Let's have a celebration party," Joe suggested. "We're all still alive."

Joe called a hotel proprietor he knew and ordered arrangements for dinner for a dozen people and a band so they could dance all night. "We want to blow $100," Joe told the proprietor.

Whether or not the poor passenger attended this victory party goes unrecorded, but we assume everyone who helped at the crash scene was included. They had such a good dinner and party Herb thought the hotel must have spent $500 instead of $100.

Back in Seattle Herb was faced with settling up with the owners of the plane, closing the office and laying off his secretary. Insurance didn't begin to cover his losses.

Herb eventually lost everything he owned in the crash and Depression. Years later, his old friend Verne Samuelson, who became a millionaire in the automobile agency and banking business in Port Angeles, would say, "If you'd have taken the money you put into that plane and bought Boeing stock, think what you'd be worth now." [2]

Unexpectedly, who should walk in one day but his brother Albert. Astonished, Herb blurted, "How did you get here, kid?" He had only seen Al a few times when he was little. Al said he'd hitchhiked, rode the rails and walked.

When he learned that Herb's plane had been wrecked and there was no longer an airline, he was totally crushed. Herb found Al work around Boeing Field for a while, but it wasn't long before he hitched rides across the country again to Georgia.

Meanwhile, Herb and Muriel had to make some difficult decisions. As he had several times previously, Herb turned to photography:

> I had a Chrysler car. I thought I could get some work at one of the newspapers as a photographer.
> That was the first I knew that the Depression was coming on. Instead of hiring, they were laying off
> men and dividing up the time between the few left.

The payment was coming on the house above Boeing Field. We had no money so I took the Chrysler down to a used car salesman. I thought I'd get quite a bit for it but they were paying almost nothing. I sold it for $200. That was all I could get and I needed the money.

This was when I thought of taking penny pictures at dime stores. I tried Kress and some of the others but they weren't interested. Finally Newberry's gave me space on a percentage basis. Then I bought a penny picture camera, a 5X7. It was made especially to take five poses to one strip of negative. You took five exposures, cut up the strips and you had 25 pictures and you charged 25 cents.

Lowman & Hanford trusted me for the penny picture camera. I reminded them of how much stuff I had bought from them when I had the finishing business in Port Angeles. They were leery but sold it to me; the whole outfit, developing pans and all for about $300.

We couldn't make payments on the house, so we moved to West Seattle. Business was slow at first taking penny portraits, but the Depression was on and people found they couldn't afford expensive portraits like they were accustomed to. Word got around that you could get baby and other pictures made cheap. People lined up when we advertised to photograph children around Christmas.

The Depression got worse and business at Newberry's slumped. I moved down to a dime store in Tacoma and worked for a while until business ran out also.

I had been up to Port Angeles to see Verne Samuelson. Verne gave me an old coupe he'd taken in trade and couldn't sell. I got back to Seattle with that. While I was working in Tacoma I rented a little room cheap, coming home on weekends.

One weekend I came home to find that Hazel Goodwin, my former secretary, had been out to see Muriel. Muriel mentioned that the Tacoma business was getting bad, and that I was going to have to find something else. Hazel told Muriel that I might do all right taking portraits in Tenino, where she had a lot of friends. We called Hazel and she came out and brought a picnic dinner.

We didn't have a garden that year and hadn't had many fresh vegetables. I remember she brought fresh tomatoes and they hit the spot. In Tacoma I had been living mostly on day-old bread because it was cheap.

We decided the Tenino idea was all right. We rented a little studio. I traded the penny portrait camera in on a regular portrait camera. We did pretty good for a while, with Hazel's friends and their friends. But Tenino was a small burg and by the time we'd taken pictures of everyone interested we'd worked ourselves out of business and had to close up shop.[3]

But Herb's troubles weren't over. In fact, his biggest hurdles were only beginning.

Notes & Sources, Beyond The Trails, Chapter Four

1. Albert Crisler insists the airplane was a Stinson A Trimotor, with a capacity of about ten passengers, although other sources claim differently. If so, according to Victor Davis, only 31 Stinson A Trimotors were built. The only remaining model is at the Alaska Aviation Heritage Museum in Anchorage, Alaska. Albert estimated such a plane cost between $25-50 thousand.

2. Herb Crisler Reminiscence, "The Wreck of the Stinson-Detroiter," as told to Ruby El Hult (1971)

3. Herb Crisler Reminiscence, "After the Plane Wreck." as told to Ruby El Hult (1972)

5

Crisler's Wilderness Conversion

The annual dinner of the Seattle Rod and Gun Club, held in the winter of 1929, offered Herb a rare chance to eat a good meal.

After dessert, talk at Herb's table got around to the number of hunters who'd managed to get themselves lost in the woods that hunting season. The worst case had been Port Angeles hunter, Mr. Ulmer, who had shot up his shells trying to summon help, threw away his gun then wandered around the wet, cold timber for a week before showing up starved and half crazy from his ordeal.

Herb knew Mr. Ulmer. Muriel had worked for him. Herb had this to say about the incident:

> Getting lost doesn't need to be serious. If a hunter has a rifle and shells he should shoot
> something to eat, not wander around in circles. Even a man who is lost, without gun or provisions,
> can get along all right by using his head.[1]

Herb's statement created a lively discussion. Most believed that the inhospitable Olympic Mountains were no place to fool around. Crisler scoffed at their ideas.

Several men pointedly questioned how much experience Crisler actually had in the Olympic Mountains.

During this period of Herb's life, by his own admission, he was "a cocksure, know-it-all hunter and outdoorsman," who had seen the interior of the Olympics, had climbed Mount Olympus and had enough experience at roughing it to be confident of his ability to take care of himself.

"It's almost sure--if you go around making brash statements sooner or later you'll open your mouth and get yourself into trouble," Herb wrote many years later.

Herb calmly addressed those around his table, "I wouldn't hesitate to walk, alone, over a period of one month, across the Olympic Mountains without carrying either food or gun, and believe I could come out fat on the other side of the Peninsula."

This statement resulted in a bit of good-natured ribbing from his table mates. One, Steve Arnett, reporter from The Seattle Daily Times, listened thoughtfully. After dinner Arnett cornered Herb.

"Were you serious?" Arnett asked. "That would be quite a story."

Herb assured Arnett he meant what he said.

"Mind if I talk to the city editor about it?" Arnett asked. "I think he'd be interested."

Herb thought for a moment. At least such a trip would provide him with an escape to the Olympics, and a chance to shoot some motion-picture footage, perhaps enough to make another movie, which he could show, and earn money. Herb agreed.

Before Christmas Arnett approached Herb where he worked at a dime store taking penny portraits. Arnett said his editor was keen to do the story, and willing to pay big money for it.

City Editor Rudy Bloch leaned back thoughtfully and appraised the man who entered his office. He was not a big man, but powerful, athletic and had the calm demeanor and direct gaze of someone who had a lot of confidence in himself.

Bloch questioned Herb about his experiences in the mountains, then decided Herb was no blowhard, that he actually was capable of attempting such a trip. Bloch pointed out the value in demonstrating that if a lost person could live off the country, the story might save lives.

He offered the following deal. If Herb would go into the mountains without food or a gun, and survive for one month, The Seattle Daily Times would be interested in backing the venture.

Crisler ready to set out on the 1930 "Survival Trip." Notice pigeon cage on top of pack.

They talked specifics; rights to the story, first rights to the pictures Herb would take. Money? Well, Bloch had to consult with Colonel Blethan, who kept a tight rein on the Times purse strings. Bloch returned saying the paper would pay $500.

To Crisler, broke, earning pennies, the price seemed a windfall. One could buy a new car with such a huge sum.

Herb agreed, but added he couldn't make the trip until the passes were free of snow and the huckleberry crop, upon which he planned to partially rely for food, was ripe.

Bloch agreed. That would provide the paper time to work out the details and draft a publicity campaign. Tentative departure was set for August, 1930.

On August 3, two weeks before departure, The Seattle Daily Times broke the story about the planned trip: SEATTLE MAN TO BRAVE OLYMPICS WITH AX, KNIFE.

The following day Bloch ran a follow up: CRISLER MAKING FINAL PLANS FOR WILDERNESS TRIP.

The Times certainly grabbed their reader's attention. Bloch kept the story sizzling. For the next two weeks, with the exception of the eleventh, twelfth and thirteenth, readers were bombarded with daily feature stories about the trip. By today's newspaper standards, the articles were pretty wild.

Sensational journalism was in vogue. Readers had been thrilled by the humans/versus the raw wilderness Press Expedition of 1889-90 story. Perhaps it took their minds off the Depression. Remembering the successful story about the Press Expedition may have influenced Bloch to sponsor Crisler.

Following are more 1930 headlines and excerpts from The Seattle Daily Times :

August 7: OLYMPIC HIKER IN GOOD SHAPE FOR LONE TRIP. Crisler is by no means in danger of dying, doctor who examined him at Virginia Mason Clinic claims. [The story included a nice picture of Crisler, the doctor and a pretty nurse]

August 9. WILDS TO GIVE ADVENTURER FARE FIT FOR ROYALTY. Mushrooms, blueberries, venison, grouse, wild honey. Here's a menu few persons would scorn, Arnett reported.

August 14. TREASURES OF OLYMPICS TO BE PICTURED. Crisler expects to see scenery unmatched anywhere in the United States.

As if Crisler's pack wasn't heavy enough already, someone conceived the idea that he carry carrier pigeons so that the paper could keep track of his progress.

C.A. Yatzunoff, a Seattle carrier pigeon breeder, would provide three of his best birds. One, Big Tom, was a valuable northwest champion racer with uncanny ability to return home.

Bloch decided one bird should be released each Friday from the tops of the three most prominent peaks along the route. Mounts Carrie, Ferry and Olympus were chosen. Herb agreed to film each release. The motion-picture would include part of each peak in order to prove beyond doubt that the location wasn't faked.

Early Sunday morning, August 17, 1930, Big Bill Thornily, who was headed to the Peninsula anyway, drove Herb to the <u>Times</u> building where they picked up the cage of pigeons. Herb was photographed against the side of the <u>Times</u> building with his pack containing the pigeon cage on his back, then they left for the Peninsula.

That same day the <u>Times</u> broke the story of his departure:

PHOTOGRAPHER CRISLER OFF ON HIKE THROUGH OLYMPICS. Crisler left Olympic Hot Springs this morning. From the mountains of the Peninsula he will wrest his livelihood for the next thirty days, relying entirely upon his axe and knife, his only implements.... [the axe was an ice axe]

Olympic Hot Springs Resort was usually busy, but this day it bustled with photographers and reporters after Herb's story. Herb was dressed in trail clothes, typical logger attire, woolen long johns and shirt, stagged canvas pants, a broad-brimmed felt hat to protect his head and new, calf-high, logger-type leather boots with hob-nail soles.

Herb unloaded his pack and the cage containing three bewildered-looking carrier pigeons.

Olympic Hot Springs, discovered by Billy Everett in 1906

Herb's friends, Jean and Harry Schoeffel, managers of the resort, were apprehensive about Herb's chances of success. Jean especially was worried. She had lost her brother after he drowned in Cat Creek. Her father, Billy Everett had carried the boy's body home on his back. She tried to discourage Herb from going.

The Schoeffels, perhaps more than anyone else, were acutely aware of the dangers Herb faced on such a journey. Jean's father's adventures, although impressive, had never taken him so far into unknown wilderness as Herb proposed to go. And Billy had always carried a gun and a little food and had a dog or two along.

Jean had prepared Herb's favorite dinner, baked chicken, mashed potatoes and gravy, biscuits, plenty of freshly-cooked vegetables and a quart of cold buttermilk. Jean tried to talk him out of going.

Herb was photographed dining. With the attention, flash bulbs exploding, Herb's appetite suffered. He barely ate. Jean gathered up the uneaten food and placed it into a sack so Herb could carry it along, but he refused, saying that would be cheating.

Before leaving, Herb unrolled the tarp which contained his equipment for the benefit of reporters and cameramen present. It contained one 16-millimeter motion-picture camera, one 120 millimeter format still camera, a heavy wooden tripod, 3000 feet of black and white motion-picture film, enough roll film for the still camera to last a month, the home-made sleeping bag his mother had made, a coat, small bag of pigeon feed, and a rain poncho. He carried no medicine, matches, extra clothing, cooking utensils, maps or compass. The contents were rolled into a tarp, then lashed onto a wood-frame pack board. It weighed 74 pounds!

Herb tied the cage containing the pigeons on top, lashed the tripod on one side, the ice axe on the other, then swung the pack onto his back.

Flash bulbs popped. Herb turned his back on civilization and headed up the trail towards Appleton Pass.

He was relieved to be alone after the fanfare. The pure mountain air reeked of pitch, earth and lush, green vegetation.

The trail passed through stands of old-growth Douglas fir and Western hemlock, which provided welcome shade, then climbed steadily. Herb was soft from city living.

Herb planned to reach his old Windy Hollow camp for the night. Each bend in the trail was familiar. At a large red cedar Herb stopped and shaved off a supply of the fine, hair-like bark to use as fire starter, knowing it would not be available in the alpine country, where only Alaska cedar grew.

Weariness overtook him on the Appleton Pass switchbacks. He had hardly slept the previous night, and the automobile trip had been wearisome. His shoulder and leg muscles, unaccustomed to such abuse, began to cramp and the new boots hurt his feet. Thoughts about what he was getting himself into nagged him.

His diary entry for the day explains his misery:

> Made only six miles today. Fainted the last mile. Dare not stop and rest, for fall asleep the
> minute I stop. Was never so hungry in my life. Saw many bear today. Am so tired and dizzy I
> can't make much headway, but must forge on.[2]

At Oyster Lake, with the sun dipping behind the high mountains, he flopped down with his pack against a tree, too weary to continue.

He awoke to the sound of cooing. His arms were asleep; muscles stiff with cold. Pale, gray light filtered through the trees. Herb assumed it was evening and got up to look for a campsite. Then he noticed the light was coming from the east! He had slept through the night with his pack on his back!

His stomach rumbled with hunger. Filling up on water helped. What for breakfast? He left his pack and set out with his hands full of stones looking for small game. He threw at small birds and pine squirrels until he wrenched his shoulder.

Disgusted to be in such poor condition, he headed southeast along the ridge.

Herb now entered an area beyond any trails, except those made by elk. Early day explorers, the Clallam Indian Boston Charlie, Billy Everett and local dentist Dr. Keith Thompson had followed these same game trails, aware that elk and deer knew the best routes.

In a small basin was Windy Hollow camp, his old hunting headquarters. As he expected, nothing to eat remained in the badly neglected camp. Matches were stored in a fruit jar on a shelf but Herb decided if he was foolish enough to live like a Caveman, he might as well use Caveman's tactics. He made a bow and drill stick, set the drill point into a small block of dry fir, then twirled the drill vigorously with the bow until smoke emerged. He fed shredded cedar bark into the embers and blew. A tiny flame shot up. He left the matches in the jar.

Desperately hungry, he dug a handful of avalanche lily roots and ate them raw. Replenishing the boughs in the makeshift bed inside the lean-to, he fell into a deep sleep.

He awoke in the night nauseated, got up and vomited, poisoned by the lily roots. He had noticed deer eating the flowers, and assumed the plants were all right. He had much to learn about living off the country.

At dawn he went searching for anything he could stuff into his stomach, huckleberries, small game--anything to stop the pain.

The delicious low-bush, blue-leaf huckleberry Vaccinium deliciosum grows in the alpine country. The berries are large, dark blue and sweet, but often do not ripen until September. Herb had relied upon them for food. Ordinarily the bushes would have sagged with berries, but most bushes were empty! Probably killed by a late, spring frost.

A doe black-tail deer sprang from her bed beneath a wind-blown cedar and stood watching. Herb instinctively lifted his arms as if he had a gun, squinted through imaginary sights and said, "boom!" If he had a gun, this deer would have been breakfast. He could have jerked the meat over a fire and obtained a supply of food lasting for days.

Without a gun, he felt apprehensive, uneasy, vulnerable, and realized that he had to sharpen his wits, and his throwing arm.

Herb Crisler, the famous hunter, he now realized, was nothing without his gun. He returned to camp and slept on an empty stomach.

Day dawned with a murky sky and light rain showers. Out hunting, Herb saw his first rabbit. He dropped his pack and stalked as close as he dared, then made a run and tried to kick the rabbit. His foot missed. He fell sprawling, landed on his sore shoulder and scratched his face. The rabbit disappeared into thick brush.

Defeated, Herb threw himself prone, face down, and beat at the ground with his fists, crying out in utter frustration. For the first time he realized it was possible that he might starve to death! He considered giving up and sneaking back to the Hot Springs, but realized that was impossible. He would be the laughing stock of the country after all that fanfare by the newspaper.

He'd trust the Lord to provide. If He didn't, starving served him right for making the boast. Herb had always relied upon a gun. Now he had to learn to think like primitive man, to become a scavenger.

That afternoon he threw a stone at a grouse, hitting the bird in one wing. The crippled grouse ran uphill, with Herb panting far behind. Before he could catch up with the bird a circling hawk swooped down and snatched up the grouse and flapped onto the top of a dead fir snag.

Herb was still using Windy Hollow camp at night. The following day he planned to leave and head for the High Divide.

Herb's diary fails to mention meeting two prospectors on Wednesday, August 20, day four on his trip. He left his pack and descended into Cat Creek Basin looking for food. In a muddy pond he noticed several frogs. Removing his boots, he waded in. After a lively, wet chase, Herb finally caught them all. He built a fire and roasted the frogs, reporting later that they were delicious.

Harold Everett, no relation to Billy, of Port Townsend and George Ohmert of Port Angeles were in the area prospecting for gold. They noticed someone above them on the mountainside. Since few people ever ventured into the area, they climbed the mountain to see who it was. They were astonished when he told them his plans. They offered food. Herb refused.

Later that day he came upon a covey of grouse in a thicket and killed three. He ate one and saved two.

He continued towards High Divide, upon which four drainages, the Elwha, Hoh, Bogachiel and Sol Duc rivers head.

From the head of Cat Creek, Herb struggled slowly along the steep mountainside on the south slopes of Cat Peak for about two miles, a route pioneered by young Boston Charlie and Billy Everett in the late 1800's.

Herb had been to Cream Lake before. In 1923 with Jack Howser and 1924, with Ed Halberg, Verne Samuelson, Al Knight and Reverend Stuart Goude. So he knew of the difficulties he faced.

The first was Wildcat Ridge, better known as the "Catwalk," a narrow, saw-toothed arete, the divide between the Hoh and Elwha watersheds, the only feasible route from the High Divide into the Bailey Range. There are places along the Catwalk where a person can look down, without moving one's head, and peer into both the Hoh and Elwha River drainages. Here a slip could result in a deadly fall. It is not an easy place to carry a load either. There are numerous, wind-blown, twisted fir and hemlock trees to grab at ones pack, slippery rocks to clamber around and windfalls and brush to dodge.

At the east end of the Catwalk, where the crest of the razorback ridge widens out to fifty feet or so, lies a surprising puddle of murky water. Curiously, the pond has no inlet or outlet. Why it exists on top a narrow ridge is a wonder of nature.

Here, on a tiny level place barely large enough to accommodate two or three tiny tents is Boston Charlie's camp.[3] He reportedly had a gold prospect near the camp.[4]

A story worth repeating occurred here.

Boston Charlie was camped here when an early snow storm struck. His feet froze. Unable to walk, facing certain death if he remained, he began crawling. He crawled across the Catwalk, around Cat Peak, through Cat Basin, along the rugged mountain ridges towards Oyster Lake and was crawling down the Boulder Creek trail when Billy came searching for him. Billy carried Boston Charlie on his back down to Olympic Hot Springs![5]

The next day, Friday, dawned clear and calm. Herb left his pack, stuffed Big Tom under his shirt, put the tripod-mounted motion-picture camera over his shoulder and climbed Mount Carrie, 6,995 feet elevation.

At the top, he set up his tripod and camera and pointed it at the cairn. He wrote a note on the parchment, placed it inside one of the aluminum leg capsules, strapped the capsule on Big Tom's leg, started the camera rolling, then released the pigeon.

To Herb's astonishment, the bird flew only a few yards, perched on a rock and began preening its feathers. Ten minutes went by. Herb threw snow at the bird. Big Tom lifted off and disappeared west, towards the Pacific Ocean!

A short distance below the summit Herb built a fire and photographed himself cooking and eating two of the birds he had killed the previous day. He placed a bouquet of wildflowers beside him for an added touch. Splendid views of Mount Olympus are in the background. This picture was one of the first published in The Seattle Sunday Daily Times upon his return.

That night was spent at Boston Charlie's. As he prepared to depart the following morning Herb picked up a lard can, which he had left there on a previous trip, thinking to use it to carry live coals.

 The route east from Boston Charlie's camp follows the contour of the range at about 5,500 feet elevation. The route crosses numerous steep-sided, gut-busting gullies which have been scoured by snow and rock avalanches, creating some very treacherous crossings. Rockfalls are common from above.

The wise old cow elk, which leads the herd, knows the best routes. During a traverse of the Bailey Range in 1990, the writer didn't see any elk tracks along here. Perhaps the animals know a better way. The terrain is often steep, the grassy slopes slippery and numerous cliffs can force a detour, down, then up again, hard work while carrying a heavy pack.

The distance from Boston Charlie's to Cream Lake, as the crow flies, is about five miles, but it's a miserable, slow, difficult sidehill scramble.

Only two places exist where water and a spot level enough to camp exist. One, a tiny level bench where spring water trickled, was where Herb spent the night of August 23.

He awoke during the night to the whine of wind in the stunted trees and the splatter of heavy rain beating upon the poncho over his sleeping bag. The storm had caught him in an exposed position. The wind was cold. The little poncho provided totally inadequate shelter.

At dawn Herb peered out of his sleeping bag. Mists and clouds, filled with rain, swirled by, running before a fierce southeast wind which blew up the steep slopes of the Hoh River Canyon. Rain blew under the poncho onto his sleeping bag. Visibility was near zero. Route finding was impossible.

Herb Crisler cooking grouse on top of Mt. Carrie, 1930.

It promised to be a long, cold, miserable day.

Herb stayed inside the sleeping bag as long as his aching back would permit, then crawled out. Since the campsite had little wood, and the wind prevented building a fire, Herb had to walk to keep warm. The only direction he could walk was down out of the storm.

He left his camera gear and sleeping bag rolled up beneath the pack tarp and began slowly descending the steep mountainside towards the distant Hoh River. It was, Herb remembered later, " a terrible trip." Slipping and sliding, he reached the Hoh, thinking he might find frogs or some kind of fish to spear or catch, but was disappointed.

The climb back, just before dark, kept him warm but robbed his strength. Crawling into the cold, damp bag on an empty stomach was an ordeal. He lay shivering, thankful for his wool underwear. Rain beat upon the tarp. It was a miserable night.[6]

The Bailey Range (left), Steven Peak and Mt. Ferry with snow patch (center left) and headwaters of the Hoh River. The Bailey Range Traverse, or Chrisler Route, lies along the flanks of the Bailey Range at about 5,500 foot elevation. Herb's 1930 trek took him across the Hoh River at the extreme right of the photo.

The storm died with the dawn. Visibility improved enough to travel. Getting up, pulling on wet, cold pants, and starting out, with no breakfast, no chance of starting a fire, was torture. Herb vowed he wouldn't be caught without means of making fire after this. He would carry coals.

Monday, August 25, day nine. Weak from hunger, Herb continued along the range, scrambling up and down steep, slippery ravines and across treacherous, rocky slopes. Several times he missed the route, found himself confronted by cliffs and had to backtrack. Late in the afternoon, on the flanks of Stephen Peak, he looked down upon Cream Lake and saw a thrilling sight.[7]

About 100 head of elk were scattered throughout the meadows surrounding the lake. It was too late to photograph, so Herb sneaked down through a strip of timber and watched. Several mature herd bulls, with six or seven antler points on each side, had gathered harems of cows and were attempting to keep rival bulls away.

Other bulls, known as "outriders", hovered about, bugling defiantly. Without cows of their own, they frantically attempted to steal cows from the larger herd bull's harems.The evening air vibrated with bugling as maddened bulls defended their harems of cows.

Fascinated, Herb watched until it was too dark to see, then returned to his pack in a clump of large alpine fir, crawled under some overhanging limbs and slept.

During the night he was awakened repeatedly by bugling, grunting, braying, chirping and squealing elk.

The following morning he took the rope off his pack and set a snare in a nearby deer trail. Visions of venison steak, with sizzling fat dripping into red coals, almost drove him mad.

Unable to shoot anything, Herb became, of necessity, a wildlife observer, an activity that had important influence upon his future.

Herb describes this change eloquently:

> The basin was as beautiful as it had been described--a veritable garden of Eden. Heavy precipitation caused the basin to be draped in a patchwork of waterfalls and green meadows with water trickling over wet rocks.
>
> The moisture also made for a good crop of huckleberries. And, O, happy day, I killed two grouse! With my strength partly restored, I built a bark shelter which would serve as a base camp. I would use it while exploring the area, would return to it after climbing Mount Ferry and would venture out to photograph the herd of at least 100 elk I found living on the bottom lands of the basin. The actions of the huge herd fascinated me; the crying and playing of the calves; the graceful grazing of the cows; the sparring and bugling of the bulls.
>
> It was while I lived amongst the elk herd photographing it that I came to grips with the strange things that had been happening inside me.
>
> I, who had thought myself so great---what was I? Standing alone, I was a puny, naked creature, not even a good scavenger. The power, the expertise of which I had been so proud was not mine at all. It had come out of the barrel of a gun. The animals were self-sufficient and self-contained. How unfair that man should come among them with such lethal power. All my years of hardly looking and certainly without caring I had destroyed lives such as these.
>
> With newly observant eyes I began to watch the nature dramas around me. I saw a bear cub pester its mother till she gave him a disciplinary swat of the paw that sent him rolling downhill like a rubber ball. I saw a cougar stalk a deer, and the deer jump aside at the crucial moment.
>
> When the grouse meat was gone, when the berries failed to stick to the ribs and I was hungry again, I looked around at my wilderness companions and thought poignantly, "The deer, the bear, the elk, they are all smarter than I. They flourish while I starve."[8]

It was August, but here, in this mountain fastness, the snow had melted only weeks ago. Silky phacelia, glacier lily, American sawwort, bluebells, broad-leafed and Lyalls lupine grew in the meadows. Green false hellebore grew as high as Herb's belt. Olympic mountain aster and American bistort swayed in the breeze. In shady places beneath the trees, delicate bunchberry, with four-petal, snowy-white flowers, escaped the sun. Each flower's insets of pollen and nectar in the center attracted honey and bumble bees and butterflies. The dainty flowers were in sharp contrast with the broad, flat, green leaves.

Queens cup, a delicate beauty, with its pure white, five-petal blossom and three, long, green leaves, also grew in shady areas. The higher, drier slopes were carpeted with patches of white and yellow mountain heather and spreading phlox. Hummingbirds and bees flitted from blossom to blossom, pollinating the flowers. Delicate bristles of purple Indian thistle's blossoms glowed with diamond-hewed drops of morning dew. Herb longed for a way of capturing the vivid colors on film.

Thursday produced some of Herb's best elk footage yet. If he was careful to keep his long trail of man scent away from the elk, and by staying concealed, he could approach close enough to obtain pictures with his long lens.

On August 28, The Seattle Daily Times ran the first mention of Crisler's trip since his departure:

> Fears for the safety of H.B. Crisler, Seattle photographer and mountaineer, who, for the past twelve days, has been alone in the wilds of the Olympic Peninsula, and from whom no word has been received, were being entertained here today.
>
> Virtually unarmed, Crisler entered the Olympic Peninsula country at Olympic Hot Springs August 16. (sic) With him he carried three homing pigeons which were to have been released at intervals. The first of these birds, known as Big Tom and valued at several hundred dollars, was

due in Seattle August 22. He has failed to arrive and no word concerning him has been received by his owner, C.A. Yatzunoff, bird fancier.

It is well known Crisler would have guarded the safety of Big Tom with great care. The two other pigeons, less valuable, would also have been guarded carefully. The fact that none of the birds have returned gives added weight to the fear that some accident may have overtaken Crisler.

Friday, August 29, day 13, the day the second pigeon was scheduled to be released, dawned bright and clear. A few puffs of white, fleecy clouds drifted in from the ocean, then dissipated beneath a deep, blue sky. Carrying only his camera, tripod, film and one pigeon, Herb left the bark shelter at dawn and headed up the little creek which fed Cream Lake.

The route to Mount Ferry was along a well-used elk trail, up past little Reflection Lake, then past the beautiful alpine lake that Herb would later name Lake Billy Everett, across a beautiful, level bowl with a crystal-clear brook, carpeted with wildflowers, then up snowfields to the pass between Mounts Pulitzer and Ferry. A glacier spilled down the west side of Mount Pulitzer, better known as Snagtooth. A frigid lake lay at the glacier's snout.

From here to the top of Mount Ferry was steep, loose scree. From the top of Mount Ferry Herb was treated to a dazzling, bewildering panorama of mountains and valleys in all directions.

He wrote a message with the date, his location and that he was okay, placed it in the capsule, then set up the motion-picture camera and pointed it at the peak.

A pair of red-tailed hawks circled curiously overhead. Herb waited until the hawks moved off, started the camera and flung the second pigeon into the air. The bird flapped its wings, then coasted down to a nearby rocky crag and began preening, exactly the way Big Tom had acted. Herb waited ten minutes then chased the pigeon off the rock. It circled the peak several times, then flew south. Since Seattle lay to the northeast, Herb decided being cooped up so long in the cage had disoriented the birds.

Herb returned to his bark shelter at Cream Lake late the evening of the 29th. He was tired, ravenously hungry, totally without food. He checked his deer snare. Empty! Somehow, he had to obtain fat meat. That night he tossed restlessly, awaking several times to hear deer feeding nearby. The elk had moved off. Visions of fat venison ribs roasting over the fire disturbed his sleep.

That same day the Times ran a story about two prospectors having seen Crisler in Cat Creek basin, August 20. This was the first confirmation that Crisler was still alive.

Saturday morning, August 30, Herb awoke at dawn and headed eagerly towards where he'd set the snare. A deer had became entangled but escaped.

Terribly disappointed, he walked around the lake where he'd noticed some ponds. Removing his boots Herb waded in and captured 40 little green frogs. Skewered on a willow stick and held over the fire to broil they were delicious. He charred the bones over the fire and ate those also.

He described later how a full stomach cheered him from a deep depression: "Then I sat back satisfied, thinking, the wilderness is beginning to accept me. I am learning its secrets."

Sunday, August 31, day 15: Herb was surprised, after eating the frogs, to wake ravenously hungry. Evidently the meat had awakened some latent longing in his shrunken stomach. Looking for grouse, or anything he could eat, he wandered into the upper basin again.

Herb found nothing to eat that day but berries. Back at camp he brought the last bird out of its cage, tied a string to its leg and offered tender shoots of greens. The bird eyed him warily, shied away, ignoring food, wondered, perhaps, the fate of its mates. Herb had become fond of the pigeons and often talked to them. Two weeks had passed since he'd left Olympic Hot Springs.

The next part of the trip was through country unknown to Crisler, and most likely anyone else. The Hoh River canyon, a great, steep-sided gash in the earth, lay directly between Cream Lake and Hoh Glacier, the only route to Mount Olympus. He was apprehensive about descending from Cream Lake because the mountain dropped away so steeply he couldn't see the bottom. No doubt massive cliffs lurked out of sight to stop him. Directly across the Hoh was

Mount Mercury, 6950 feet elevation and Mount Mathias, 7168 feet elevation. Looking up the Hoh he could see a tiny slice of Hoh Glacier. He decided to explore farther up, towards Mount Ferry.

But first he had to find something substantial to eat. Once he crossed the Hoh and ascended onto the glacier there would be nothing to eat or fuel for a fire.

That same day, August 31,

Cream Lake, Bailey Range. Mt. Mathias, 7,168 foot elevation at center, northeast flank of Mt. Olympus with glaciers at left. Herb's Cream Lake shelter was located in lower right foreground prior to the avalanche that destroyed it.

while Crisler was pondering his chances of crossing the Hoh Valley, C.A. Yatzunoff called the Times. Big Tom, released on Mount Carrie, one week overdue, had homed! Crisler's note said:

Mt. Carrie, August 22, 1930: So much to say and so little space! First two days had nothing to eat but some roots and a few berries. Berries are scarce in most places this year, so grouse are too.

One day had frogs for breakfast. They are small but very good. Third day killed a grouse with a stone, but arm grew so tired I wasn't able to throw any more. I realize now that the average person eats enough for two or three. Scraps that people consider garbage and junk in civilization would be luxuries for me.

I was very lame and sore after the first day's hike, but am getting more accustomed to it now.

Have seen six bear, several wolves' tracks, and 14 deer. Got within 100 feet of a small deer on a rock slide. Took some pictures.

Only beginning to get into wild country. Haven't seen an elk yet but plenty of fresh tracks. Expect to see elk any time now.

I really fear for the safety of the pigeons. Hawks are numerous and their natural food is scarce. This country is beautiful and rugged beyond description. Mount Olympus with its many glaciers and jagged peaks looms up above the others and looks very forbidding. Crisler.

On the reverse of the parchment was a note from boys in Yamhill, Oregon, dated August 24:

We caught your pigeon in our barn weak and hungry. Fed and watered it. Will put note back and turn pigeon loose again.[9]

Editor Bloch sent a photographer and reporter to pick up Big Tom, with orders to drive to Crisler's place and get pictures of Mrs. Crisler and Bobby, together with the pigeon.

On September second, the paper ran the photo and another story about Big Tom, and how this gallant bird, by returning home with a message, had "calmed the heart of a 4-year-old and assuaged the anguish of a fear-crushed wife and mother."Big Tom, the story claimed, had dodged hawks and encountered fog and smoke from forest fires, reasons for diverting into Oregon."

On Monday, September 1, day 16: Herb began planning his assault upon dark, foreboding Hoh Canyon. Above Cream Lake, in rock slides on the shoulder of Stephen Peak, were several Olympic marmot colonies. He decided a fat marmot was his only source.The marmot's natural enemies were coyotes, wolves, bobcats and cougar, so they are very attentive to their surrounding, and seldom far from a den in which to take refuge.

Herb spent the greater part of a day before he finally outwitted a marmot, and caught it diving into a shallow den and killed it with his club:

> As I stood there looking at him I was sorry I had killed him, but my craving for fat soon overwhelmed me again. I picked him up, went to a rock, and skinned and dressed him. Thick layers of creamy fat covered his body. I cut a green pole and peeled it, then gathered dry limbs and built a fire against the side of the boulder. After the wood had burned down I drove a forked stick on each side of the coals, threaded the marmot on the stick, laid each end on the forked sticks and adjusted them so the marmot was about six inches from the coals. Then I sat at one end of the pole turning it. As the carcass began to brown, fat dripped into the coals and sizzled. Saliva began running down my chin. I took my knife and sliced off a chunk of meat, and then the saliva began flowing the other way.[10]

The marmot weighed six or seven pounds. It was only with superhuman effort that Herb saved most for reserve. He limited himself to about a half pound a day, a piece the size of a candy bar.

September 2, day 17: At dawn, the sky was a pall of gray and it appeared as if a storm was approaching. The Hoh and Quinault River areas are the wettest places on the Peninsula, sometimes receiving 175 inches of rain per year. Herb hoped one of those storms wasn't approaching.

Just in case, Herb decided to carry live coals, a technique that has all but disappeared, but at one time, before sulphur matches, was used extensively. The gallon can he'd picked up had a tight lid, a wire handle and was just the thing. With his knife he poked small holes in the bottom and lid of the can. He put in a layer of gravel, coals from his fire, then covered them with a thick layer of grass. He packed up his gear and carried the can by its wire bail. He had enough cedar bark in his pockets to last him through the Mount Olympus part of the forthcoming trip. Herb explains how the coals can be used:

> If you put cedar bark on the coals and fan it, it will come to life. You can put a coal in a wrapping of cedar bark, place it in the palm of your hand, then whirl the arm windmill fashion (this is a boy scout trick) and the rushing air will fan it up, and just as it is about to blaze, you drop it quick into a pile of tinder you've already prepared. A whittle stick is good for fire starting--with your knife you make a kind of little Christmas tree of shavings.

> Also you could make a little fire in the can if you didn't want to start a camp fire. Before I took the lid off I set the can on three big rocks--that way it got plenty of air through and the coals would start to get red. I would then drop in some cedar bark and twigs--could cook over this little fire in the can. Or, if I was starting a campfire, would get the coals to glowing before I took them out with sticks. And I always got some good new coals before I put the grass over them and covered up the can again.[11]

> The south rim of Cream Lake Basin was bound by a series of ridges that came down off Mount Ferry and spread out to form the mountain's lower flanks. There were a couple lakes along those ridges. I had seen them the day I climbed Mount Ferry. I wanted to investigate the lakes if I could find

them, and leaving Cream Lake early that morning, carrying my pail of coals, I headed up the steep, partly timbered slope towards the rim, contouring to the level where I thought the lakes were. I found them all right, a ridge apart, both blue-eyed pockets in the rock walls, the first much larger than the second, and both hard to get around. Over the next ridge I came out above another large lake, one I had no idea was there. It was the prettiest of the three, being on a flat, with rock formations on two sides and gravel bars on the other sides. I made my way out to the level shores and found an easy way out.[12]

Herb found neither deer or elk tracks as he probed along the canyon's rim looking for a way down. Since elk and deer cover almost every square yard of their range while feeding, this was a bad sign and usually indicated extremely rough country. He recalled later: "Even wild animals had sense enough to stay away from such a dangerous area."

Finally he found what appeared to be a route down:

On beyond, the hillside was rockier again where a stream tumbled down into the lake. I kept to the south for half a mile or so. There I came to a good spot to rest, with a fine view across the canyon to Mount Olympus, the Hoh Glacier being central to my field of vision. I took off my pack and turning it so the pigeon had the same view, I gave him a long talk about what we were up against.[13]

The remaining pigeon and Herb had been companions for 18 days now. He had gotten into the habit of talking to the birds.

Herb talked. The pigeon only stared back. Patiently, Herb explained to the bird what was likely in store for both of them:

'Now, it looks so close you might think it's easy, but don't fool yourself. We are a mile higher than the river and we will find some very steep places to get over, and some dangerous, but don't worry. If I fall over a cliff and don't wake up and you are not hurt you will still have a chance. See that string? It's been dipped in marmot fat and the mice like it so well that I have to keep it in my pocket at night. So, if I leave you alone with your cage tied with this string and a little mouse comes along and eats the string, be as quiet as you can and don't scare him away. Didn't I tell you I'm your pal?'[14]

What I was looking for, as I hiked around the flanks of Mount Ferry, was a way down into Hoh Canyon that was not as impossible as the one I'd descended from my camp in the grass basin. Never was I going to get into a situation like that again. And from where I stood, lecturing the pigeon, I thought I saw a way. Off a little south was a big rock cliff with a slide chute down one side, and below, evidence of a flat area beside the river. I decided to chance the way I saw below.[15]

Herb took the plunge. He came upon some terrific cliffs, with great slide areas in places too steep to either keep his feet or walk down. So he sat down, placed the precious can of coals in his lap and skidded down on the seat of his canvas pants, using the tin-covered lower ends of his pack board as a brake. One slip and he could have broken an arm or leg, without any chance of getting out, or his remains ever being found.

The weather turned cold and rainy. The going was made worse because he had only one free hand, the other grasped the precious can of live coals, which he dared not leave behind or place inside his pack. Later, he would say:

That was the wildest, wildest country down there. I wondered if anyone had ever been there before. For there was no reason anybody would venture down all those cliffs and slides. The ordinary ways to reach Mount Olympus were by the way of the Elwha Basin, Queets Basin, then up Humes Glacier, or, alternately, by the Soleduck or Hoh Rivers and Blue Glacier. Only some fool intent on doing everything the hard way would pick such a punishing route.[16]

Herb reached the Hoh in the late afternoon. The river bank was lined with gravel bars. The current was very swift. He walked a ways and decided he had to cross, so cut a staff. The icy water was way over his boots. On the other side he removed his boots, poured out the water, wrung out his socks and put them back on again. He continued upstream until a steep, brushy bank forced him back across the river. He built a fire, dried his socks and clothing, warmed up, then went exploring.

A side stream contained swampy places where he thought he might find a frog. He discovered a well-used elk trail and followed it up to a meadow. A dozen cow elk and a few calves were grazing on lush grass. He found no grouse, berries or frogs.

That night in his sleeping bag, his stomach complaining, he had visions of juicy elk steaks broiling over the fire. He laid awake thinking about how he might kill an elk. He decided upon the following plan:

Towards morning I awoke and heard elk feeding above me in the draw. They had apparently moved in from the meadow during the night. The way they were situated, I thought I had them penned in. The canyon ran up towards the Bailey Range, with the meadow area so steep-walled by rocks and cliffs, no way out, except the nearby elk trail.

I figured that if I could whistle or something to frighten them they would rush out of the draw along the trail towards the river. No where else to go it was so steep. I had them hemmed in.

I cut a pole about 10 feet long from a green spruce sapling. It was about the size of my wrist. I took some twine and tied my hunting knife securely to the end of the pole. I'd hide along the trail, scare them, and when they ran by me, I'd stick one with the knife.

It was after daylight by the time I rigged up my elk spear. An hour later, after the light was good, I climbed the steep elk trail to near where the elk were feeding, and hid behind a big spruce. They were feeding down towards me and when they got about 100 yards away, I gave a loud, shrill whistle. I was right. The sound scared them. The elk started pounding down the trail towards me. When they seemed almost on top of me I jumped out. They were coming single file and close. I raised my spear ready to strike the lead cow in front, but before she got in range, she suddenly wheeled and jumped down the slope where it was so steep I assumed they couldn't go. The one behind the lead cow wasn't so quick and kept coming towards me. She was about five feet from me when I lunged at her and she also jumped off the trail and sailed by me with huge, powerful muscles flashing. When I suddenly realized how huge and powerful she was, I was plenty scared!

I knew if I had managed to stick that knife into her, well, she would have been 600 pounds of hurtling weight on one end of the pole, with hungry little me on the other end, and I knew right then which one of us would have been gutted. The pole would have gone right through me.

I was so relieved not to have come to disaster I saw the rest of the elk band jump down the slope without any regret. I'd definitely rather have a hungry stomach than no stomach at all.

This was such a narrow escape I forgot for awhile how hungry I was. I went back, poked up my fire, got warm and sat around being glad I was still all in one piece. But later the hunger pangs returned. Two or three times I made circuits around hoping to find frogs or grouse or berries, but nothing. Fog and bad weather continued. This was a dismal, hungry day.[17]

September 4, day 19: The morning was dark, foggy and damp, but I decided I had to continue. I did up my pack, wrapped myself in my poncho, took fresh coals from the fire and headed upriver carrying the pail.

Had to get above the steep bank which had forced me across the river the previous day. The cold weather had retarded the melting of the glacier and the river had dropped, so I made another crossing with no trouble.

Up a little side stream I saw a frog hopping across a grassy place. The frog stopped and I caught it easily. I stopped, set my pail on some rocks, opened it, let the coals brighten up, dropped in a little cedar bark and roasted the frog. I'd had no breakfast, deciding I'd better keep the remaining marmot for the glacier, so I chomped the frog down as if it were manna from heaven. Refreshed, I went on.

There was some brush and down timber, but the way wasn't too bad. But it was wet! All the brush was loaded with rain drops and I was soaked to the skin. Because of the black timber and fog I couldn't make out any landmarks, just groped along. The danger was falling over cliffs or into a ravine I couldn't even see.

Now and then I could see glimpses of white glacier ahead. About noon I came out above timberline and saw the glacier's edges directly above. Those edges looked entirely different from what I'd thought they would be from seeing them from a distance. I hadn't realized the glacier would lie high above its surroundings and I would have to find a way to climb up onto the ice.[18]

As I passed above timberline and came out onto the glacial moraine, the rain suddenly turned into blowing, howling sleet. This was a dangerous turn of events, for my wet clothes would freeze and my body inside them. I would have to find shelter quick and get a fire going.

At the base of some rocks at the side of the snow field I took refuge in a low, shallow cave on the lee side of a wall of rock. I removed the pack and detached the cage and pushed it as far back under the rock as it would go. The poor pigeon was a sorry sight. The rain had blown right through its cage and the bird was soaking wet. He had been thrown against the sides of the cage so many times while traveling on my back that his tail looked like a worn-out feather duster that had been stood on its end too often. I felt the same way.

I pushed the pack containing my cameras and film under the rock too, and began gathering armfuls of crooked limbs and piling them beside my newly acquired den for firewood. It kept raining, blowing, sleeting and snowing. I was wet to the skin, but gathering kept me warm without burning any precious wood supply and I kept gathering for a long time.

There was no timber at this elevation, only a few twisted, gnarled, wind-swept small trees that clung to rock cliffs for dear life. Many had given up the ghost and their bleached and broken skeletons were scattered over the terrain like a bone-yard. I crouched back under the rock and started whittling frizzle sticks to start a fire. I felt a tense moment as I dug the layers off my coals. Yes, they still smoldered. Every so often the wind would whip back under the rock, bringing a clattering of sleet. After patience, effort and fanning for long intervals with my hat, I got a fire going and lay down, propped on my elbow, to enjoy my comforts.

I soon found I had no comforts. The wind blew the smoke back under the rock, stifling me and causing my eyes to water until tears ran down my cheeks and I developed a sniffle. Steam boiled up from my wet clothes on the fire side, and if they happened to touch my skin it would almost blister me, while on the other side it felt as if I were lying against a cake of wet ice. The cave was so low I couldn't sit upright. After a couple of hours if I went outside I would walk around as if I had a broken back, and it felt like it. But any haven in a storm, and believe me it was storming. It looked as if winter had set in for good, and as if it had no intention to stop.

That evening I ate, very slowly, a piece of my marmot fat, the size of A five-cent candy bar. I knew that if this wild storm kept up I would not get off the mountain alive. I fed the fire and chased smoke all night, when it wasn't chasing me.

Anyway, the trip was on its last lap. I could tell by the feel of my bony cheeks and smaller legs and arms, protruding ribs and sunken stomach that I had lost considerable weight, but I didn't feel the pangs of hunger any more. The ground and rocks did not feel hard or uncomfortable to lie on, and I really was beginning to love the Olympic wilderness and its dwellers.

I realized new values. I had two five-dollar bills in my pockets and they were worthless. People placed a false value on money, using it as I had used my gun, ruthlessly destroying as I had done with my gun. It gave them a feeling of power. Values had re-shuffled themselves in my mind. What was most important to contribute to life and contentment was love in my heart, not hate; good black bread to eat, not white slices of fluffy nothing; a shelter that would keep out wind and rain, not a fancy castle; pure cool water, not whiskey, beer, wine, pop, coffee, or even tea; a real friend to love me as I was, even if I didn't have anything to eat or offer him.

This is what I wanted. This, I thought, is a little of the spirit of the Olympic wilderness. To all of its wildlife it is their shelter. They have been driven from the broad plains, from the fertile valleys, and from the useable forest. This is their refuge, in those worthless piles of rock, deep, narrow valleys and barren slopes. They have established a home in the last bit of wilderness that is left. Do I want to take it away from them, or want to take them away from it? Nobody would if they really understood. To man this was only scenery. To the animals this was home with all its joys and sorrows. If man would only think, he could preserve all this and still use the scenery, which is all this country is good for to man, and the animals could still have a home. But if man doesn't try to understand, this will all disappear from the face of the earth.

I knew I was a different man from the Herb Crisler that went into the Olympics. It might take a long time before my friends realized it, but the change was there and it was bound to grow.[19]

That night, as I shivered there at the edge of the glacier, the crazy, freezing winds lashing around me, and my life in the balance, I made a vow. Should I come out of this predicament alive I would never hunt again. Instead I would act upon my new consciousness of the world. I would put my energies to work showing others the wilderness world I had discovered.[20]

Friday morning, September 5, day 20: Dawn broke reluctantly, Herb's surroundings a dismal, dripping, muddled gray. Fortunately the wind had abated and the rain and snow stopped. It had been only a little storm. [More than three feet of snow has reportedly fallen on Mount Olympus during the month of August!] A fog bank filled the glacial valley. The wood supply was exhausted. While his hands were still warm he wrote a note and placed it in the leg capsule. Carefully he placed a bed of coals into his can and dampened them down with moss.

Stiff and weary, Herb struggled to the glacier's snout and found he could not climb to the top. He was forced to detour, along slippery cliffs of glacier-polished rock, and piles of debris. Finally Herb found a slide which he descended onto the surface of the ice.

Much to his relief, the surface was bare of snow and consisted of glittering white and blue ice. He jumped the many small cracks and skirted the large crevasses. Many extra detours were required to avoid the crevasses.

Visibility kept lowering as he climbed until it was near zero by the time Herb reached a portion of the mountain which he estimated to be the summit ridge. Clouds swirled about, obliterating everything. Climbing to the top of Mount Olympus was impossible in such weather.

Herb gave a parting pep talk to the pitiful-looking, bewildered pigeon, who had likewise spent a miserable, smoky night. Herb wondered if the bird could make it home.

He offered the pigeon a little grain as a parting gesture but the bird refused. Herb placed the grain on his own tongue and kept the rest. With some regret, he decided to launch the bird:

I decided I would give him a chance to try and tossed him into the air. He tried to catch himself on his wings. It took a few moments for him to get his sense of balance and find his new center of gravity. His front end went up and he started backwards in a tail slip. His wings began clawing the air like a dog trying to crawl out of the water up a slippery bank. He finally made it and flew over and lit on a rock and started preening his feathers.

I threw his cage over a cliff and watched it roll and slide out of sight.[21]

The bird finally took off and vanished in the swirling mists. Herb experienced terrible loneliness. The birds had been one last vital link with civilization. Now the last pigeon was gone, he was truly alone in the very heart of the Olympic wilderness.

Setting a course through the maze of peaks was impossible. He decided to wait and see if the clouds lifted and still attempt to climb the West Peak of Mount Olympus, which was close by somewhere if he could only see.

Herb probably camped at Camp Pan, a good location at the 6000 foot level, north of and below Blizzard Pass. A few dead snags provided enough wood for a small fire.

For two days, September 6 and 7, he stayed put. Rain, snow, fog and low clouds swirling about in a frightening manner. He had plenty of time to make notes in his diary, but his entries were terse indeed:

> Diary: No food but a few berries. Very cold and hungry. Very cold and stormy. Am soaked and very tired. Will not attempt to climb Mount Olympus but head for headwaters of Queets River. Heavy fog.[22]

On the morning of September 8, the clouds disappeared and the sun came out. Instead of freezing, it became almost unbearably hot. This allowed Herb to dry his sleeping bag and clothing. He headed east, again carrying coals, and proceeded through country unknown to him.

Photo of Hoh Glacier taken by Herb Crisler during his 1930 "survival" trip across the Olympic Mountains. It was near here he spent a night during a blizzard before heading up the glacier.

The normal mountaineering route east from Mount Olympus is via Blizzard Pass, so named because the Mountaineers party were caught there in a terrible blizzard, August 10, 1907, then down Humes Glacier. Treacherous but possible for a man alone.

Between the head of Humes Glacier and Athena, a 7,350 foot elevation spire, lies the Circe, a basin at elevation 6,874, located at the junction of three rock ridges which separate the Hoh, Humes and Jeffers Glaciers. Below the three rock ridges which form the Circe, lies an almost vertical drop of several thousand feet to Humes Glacier.

Entries in Herb's diary became spasmodic. Yet he still shot footage for a movie about his trip every chance he got. Herb's route off the complex maze of Mount Olympus remained a mystery, even to him. There were so many unnamed peaks[23] jutting out of ice, snow and perpetual cloud cover he couldn't determine exactly where he was.

We assume he crossed Blizzard Pass and descended Humes Glacier. Blizzard Pass, in particular, can be a windy, stormy place.

Herb planned to cast a wreath of wildflowers into a crevasse on Jeffers Glacier in memory of photographer Joseph C. Jeffers, a commercial photographer from Olympia, Washington, who had fallen to his death in 1924.[24]

His route off Mount Olympus presents the following mystery. Jeffers Glacier is southwest of the normal route down Humes Glacier. Assuming Herb did descend Humes Glacier into Queets Basin, it seems inconceivable that he would attempt to negotiate very difficult terrain to reach Jeffers Glacier, which lies in another separate high basin below Hermes and Athena peaks.

However, a direct route from the head of Hoh Glacier to Jeffers Glacier may be possible. Roy Muncaster and another University of Washington student were reported to have ascended Mount Olympus this way in 1914. About this confusion, Herb would later write:

I knew it [Jeffers Glacier] lay somewhat south, but there were so many snow and ice fields and glaciers that I did not know which was the right one. I sat down on the snow to rest and ate the last of my meat, chewing each bite until it practically disappeared from my mouth. I put a little of the pigeon's grain in my mouth, got up and walked on, chewing as I went.

Away out over the Pacific there was a long fog bank. I thought, I must get off this mountain tonight. As I walked, the sun was shining in my face. It was very bright and my eyelids were sore where they had got burned while shielding my eyes. I will be glad, I thought, when the sun gets lower and it's not so hot.

A dull roar like distant thunder began to echo from the mountainsides. At first I thought it was thunder, but there wasn't a cloud in the sky anywhere. The snow was getting soft and I could hear water running down through crevasses. The hot day had started ice slipping and it was breaking up inside. I started down steep snow and got onto what I took to be Jeffers Glacier. There were great rock walls on what I judged was the southwest side. I felt awed and strange as if I were going down into an ice-floored valley of death. Whether from the heat, bright light, or what, I was in a trance. The whole trip seemed unreal to me. I could remember the last pigeon I released but I couldn't seem to get time straightened out. It could have been last week, last year, yesterday, or a thousand years ago. I dimly remembered where I was and what I now intended to do. I heard a crack, a thunder and a roar. I opened my squinted eyes a little wider and there before me was a large gaping crevasse. I had not seen it before, or it had not been there. This is where my wreath of heather goes, I thought. It opened up especially for me.

I took the wreath from my pack and with a prayer tossed it into the crevasse. 'Don't be lonely, my friend, I am with you,' was the message my mind sent down with the wreath. I had a close, reverent feeling. We two were alone there on the mountain, the living man and the dead. And he was my friend.[25] There were no words but he spoke to me. 'I was held here. Men with crampons, ice axes, ropes and trained skill couldn't find me. But with your heart you have. This has released me. The spirit of the Olympics has been found and you have found it. Your ego has left your heart. It is empty. Now is the time to take the spirit in and it will grow and never leave you. Your ego will be in your head, but the spirit of the Olympics will be in your heart.'

There was another crash and rumble. I regained some of my natural sense. The ice is breaking up, I reasoned; I will never get off alive. The crevasse must have closed, for as far as I can remember, I walked straight ahead. I remember sliding down steep rocks and clinging to cliffs that looked as if it would be impossible to get down. It seemed like a nightmare. If I got stuck on the side of a cliff I just let go and let my dream take care of me. "The spirit of the Olympics will never leave you" kept sounding in my ears.

Where I went, what I did or what I ate, if anything, after that, I don't remember. I think I was sometimes in the Queets Valley, but I am not sure. I have gone back into this country several times to see if I could recognize any of it and it all seems familiar but I can not pin down one single spot and say for sure I was here.[26]

Herb was clearly suffering from the accumulated effects of exposure, anxiety, starvation and over exertion. He had already had several narrow escapes from certain death, but the following experience, which occurred during this particular part of the trip, so terrified him that he never forgot it:

> I had my camera set up to film myself crossing the ice. I came upon a crevasse. Not wishing to ruin the sequence, I decided to leap across. It looked safe enough. But my boots struck loose ice on the other side! I slipped and hung onto the lip of a deep crevasse with my ice axe, and only after some hair-raising moments was able to claw my way out of danger. Had I fallen I would have became famous as the man who took a motion-picture of his own plunge to death.[27]

The marmot meat was gone. Herb found a few handfuls of huckleberries, his only food for several days. On a meadow between two glaciers he caught grasshoppers, pulled off their wings, and munched them whole. 'Believe me, they were not good!' he reported. When the sun occasionally appeared, he almost died of heat prostration. At night the wind off the glaciers threatened to freeze him to death.

On September 7, Mr. Yatzunoff reported that another bird had homed. This was the third, released on Mount Olympus on the fifth.

On September 11 and 13, <u>The Seattle Daily Times</u> ran stories about the third pigeon. The second pigeon, released on Mount Ferry, was considered lost.

Was Crisler out of his head? One sentence in Herb's diary does sound as if he could have been far enough south of Queets Basin to have reached Jeffers Glacier:

> Across the Queets Valley looks like good blueberry country--but between me and it was a jumble of rocks, cliffs, ravines, all covered with vine maple thickets so packed by winter snow I couldn't crawl under them, through them, or over them. I had to thread myself through them like a needle. [28]

On Day 27, September 12, Herb's diary states:

> Took a bad fall on the ice. Injured hip, but not seriously. Had close shave going through ice tunnels on the Elwha.[29]

Later, reminiscing with Ruby El Hult, Herb provides us with a terse explanation of Day 27:

> That morning I started for the Elwha Basin. Crossed Queets Basin. Went by way of Dodwell-Rixon pass and down the Elwha Snowfinger to the headwaters of the Elwha River. Ice tunnels are part of the Snowfinger. Ice and snow. Some places could travel on top, some places had to go through tunnels. Snowfinger is not a glacier. Bad fall on ice. Slipped, fell, hurt hip and limped. Close shave: came out of an ice tunnel just as a block of ice came down from overhead--barely saw or heard it before it hit. Just missed me.
>
> On the Snowfinger about a half mile up, came to a narrow place. Rocks on one side, a few trees on the other. Vine maple thickets--bad going--when you get through thickets there is a camping site. A creek comes down from Mount Seattle. I stayed that night at the camp site.[30]

A horse trail had been constructed to Queets Basin for the Seattle Mountaineers Club expedition to attempt the ascent of Mount Olympus in 1907. After almost a month in steep, rugged country it must have felt wonderful to walk on a maintained trail.

On day 28, Herb hiked three miles down to Chicago Camp where the trail from Elwha Basin joins the main Elwha-North Fork Quinault cross-Peninsula trail.

At Chicago Camp he found discarded tin cans and evidence that men on horses had camped recently. He found mouldy, discarded potato peelings, carefully gathered them up and placed them in a can. By the river he found a discarded leader and a fishing fly lodged in a tree. He cut a willow for a pole, and caught 12 rainbow trout. Nine were laid on sticks over the coals. With the boiled potato peelings the meal was delicious.

The following morning he roasted the remaining three trout for breakfast, then began the three-mile hike to Low Divide Chalet.

48

His diary for the day states it was a difficult hike, because of his worn-out condition and lame hip. He was, "Cold, hungry and sleepy."

Much to Herb's surprise, as he reached the Chalet, a man wearing a huge backpack came down the trail. He introduced himself as Bill Woerner, end-coach of the University of Washington football team. He was carrying 90 pounds, and explained that he was trying to get in shape for the coming season. This was the first human Herb had seen in 26 days, since the prospectors in

Olympic chalet, Low Divide, photographed by Herb Crisler on 1930 "Survival Trip."

Cat Basin. On September 14, day 29, Herb reached the newly-constructed Chalet.[31] The doors were locked for the season. Herb was desperate. Inside were temptations; firewood, warm beds, food, a telephone.[32] Here's what happened:

Hand-sawn rough board shutters were fastened over all windows. It didn't look like I was going to get the warm welcome and good eats I had expected. I tried the back door. It was bolted. I went around to the front. It was locked with a big padlock.

What to do? It was only a day's [18 miles] trip by good trail to Lake Quinault. [Herb means the old trailhead at the junction of Graves Creek road and North Fork Quinault road] Should I start out now, or should I stay under the woodshed tonight and go out tomorrow? I couldn't make up my mind. Were the 30 days up? There was a forest telephone inside if I could only get in. I tried the shutters, prying them with a stout stick, trying to find a crack so I could see inside.

Finally I found a shutter with an inch crack down the center. I looked through and could tell I was looking into a storeroom. Rows of canned goods stood on the shelves--canned tomatoes, corn, all kinds of canned soups, corned beef, roast beef, stacks of condensed milk, canned peaches, pears, apricots and fruit cocktail. I was drooling. Canned pineapple, canned butter. I can't stand it any longer, I thought. if there had been iron bars on the window they wouldn't have stopped me. I hunted through the woodshed until I found an old axe, and through the window I went.

I connected the phone, got the owner of the chalet on the phone and told him who I was, where I was and how I got in. [33]

Next he called Editor Bloch. Bloch said that his month was up, that they had received the message from the third pigeon, and expected him at Quinault trailhead the next day. Bloch also instructed him to take some pictures of himself eating his first meal and to be sure he had lots of food piled around on the table.

He then called Dr. West. Dr. West was relieved to hear from him, and agreed to bring Muriel and Bobby to the trailhead for a grand meeting. Then it was time to feast:

I built a fire in the range and began to prepare my first meal. I made biscuits--lots of them. [He made 50] so there would be a large platter sitting in front of this biscuit-loving southerner. Then opened cans of corn, spinach, roast beef, asparagus, and two cans of peaches. I love peaches.

I had a big dinner all right. The paper couldn't say I skimped on my first meal after I got out. Finally I got it all on the table and after piling on my plate all the food that would stay, and arranging the other close around, I set up my camera, opened the shutter, and ran back to the table, grabbed a biscuit in one hand and the knife with a big chunk of butter on it in the other and froze. The light was poor and I had to hold this pose for 10 minutes. During this 10 minutes the aroma from the hot biscuits continually floated up to my nostrils. I wanted to eat so bad I thought I could never hold out. But now I had my "public" to think of. This was what the Times wanted, so I suffered for my public.

Finally the 10 minutes was up. I walked over and closed the shutter and started eating. I knew I shouldn't eat very much in my condition. I intended to eat a little and stop, but those hot biscuits tasted so good I couldn't. It wasn't long before I began to get sick. I stopped eating but that didn't help. I got so sick I was afraid I would die. Then I rushed outside and lost my dinner. It didn't taste bad coming up. I was still hungry. So I went back to the table and ate only a little, but my stomach was so upset I lost that. Realizing now that I would have to be very careful, I opened some clear soup and ate that. It stayed down. Now I can say I enjoyed five meals for my first dinner--three going down and two coming up.[34]

The next morning, feeling much better, he cooked a big breakfast, crammed the left over food into his pack and started down the trail.

Herb practically ran down the North Fork Quinault trail, eating leftovers on the go. He made it all the way out to the trailhead in one very long day. Herb met Dr. West carrying Bobby on his shoulders, Muriel tagging behind. Dr. West pulled a quart of buttermilk from his pack. Herb drank it down in almost one gulp, then talked all the way out to the car.

On September 19, The Seattle Daily Times carried the first of a series of stories about Crisler's trip. The lead photo was a picture of Herb, still in his trail garb, with a month's beard, drinking his third quart of buttermilk.

The doctor examined Crisler and found him to be in excellent health, although he had lost 20 pounds, instead of "coming out fat" as he had at first suggested.

The paper ran two consecutive week ends of special coverage in their Sunday Edition. The first, October 5, had full page, one-inch-high headlines, A SEATTLE TARZAN CONQUERS THE OLYMPICS, a long feature article and a rotogravure page including 14 photos by Crisler. His diary was included. The story was syndicated and picked up by newspapers as far away as the East Coast, where The New York Times ran a special Sunday Rotogravure Section.

The Atlanta paper also ran the article and pictures. Herb's sister Vara read the story, went running to Adora and said, "Mama, Mama, Herbert's gone plum crazy."

The following Sunday, October 12, The Seattle Times Sunday Magazine ran another special Rotogravure Pictorial Section, with eight pictures taken on the trip. Some were eight by ten format.

Besides the $500 cash, and payment for the pictures used, what did the trip accomplish? As Editor Bloch had said, Herb proved that a person could survive for a long time without food in the wilderness. Second, the survival trip established the name Herbert B. Crisler as a mountain man and photographer extraordinary. Crisler became a northwest legend.

Actually the trip both enriched and changed Crisler's life. His experiences eventually enabled Herb to begin what he had always dreamed of doing: a career as a professional natural history photographer.

Before the word environmentalist came into mainstream use, Herb was one. He became acutely concerned about the environment and determined to preserve the wild Olympic wilderness. Forever after Herb considered himself on a one-on-one basis with the animals which lived in the Olympics. Herb explained what happened to him:

I kept the vow I made on snowy, freezing Mount Olympus that night I didn't know whether or not I would live or die. I remained "converted" and like all persons who have acquired a new gospel, I wanted to spread the word. My ambition was to become an ambassador for all the wild creatures of the Olympics.

I was determined that my camera should become the eyes of millions who would never be able to travel into the Olympic Mountain wilderness to learn first hand of its inhabitants.

The next time I returned to the mountains, it was as a guest to the creatures who live there, not as an intruder. As a guest, I spent every summer for the next 20 years, 1931 through 1950, photographing the Olympic Mountain high country and its wildlife.

Through the motion-picture film Lois[35] and I produced in those 20 years we became, first, the eyes of hundreds of thousands of people who attended the lecture-circuit showings we gave all over the United States, and later, the eyes of millions when we sold the film to Walt Disney Productions. It became one of the True-Life Adventures Series, under the title, The Olympic Elk. So, the dreams I dreamed came true.[36]

Before these dream became a reality, Herb suffered through a great many challenges. Difficulties much harder on his soul than the survival trip across the Olympic Mountains. A time would come when he longed to be back on his survival trek, to escape his misery in the city.

The Great Depression still gripped the country. Herb was soon to find himself in such miserable circumstances his experiences on the survival trip seemed of little consequence.

Notes & Sources, Chapter Five.

1. Seattle Times Sunday Magazine, Aug. 5, 1973

2. Herb Crisler's Diary of the 1930 trip, courtesy Ruby El Hult.

3. Boston Charlie (18??-1927) was a Clallam Indian. The Clallams' homeland is in the vicinity of the Elwha River.
    One of Boston Charlie's cousins married Clallam County pioneer John Everett. John Everett had crossed the Straits of Juan de Fuca in a canoe from Victoria, British Columbia and homesteaded at Freshwater Bay.
    Boston Charlie's wife Mary, a Clallam from the village at Pysht, gave birth to several children but they all died. Mrs. John Everett gave birth to William in 1868, then died in childbirth.
    Since John Everett was away hunting most of the time, he arranged for Boston Charlie and Mary to raise the child Billy, which they delighted in doing. The boy lived with his relatives until he was old enough to accompany his father.
    Billy was a small, powerful man, who loved to hunt cats with his hounds. As a young man he explored far into the wilderness, discovered the Catwalk, which provided access into Cream Lake Basin. This was without fanfare and prior to the Press Party's first crossing of the Peninsula.
    Billy Everett developed Olympic Hot Springs, and later owned a farm just below the lower Elwha bridge, on property now owned by Harold Sisson. Harold Sisson was born in Port Angeles in 1916, and has lived most of his life on the Elwha River. Starting in 1908, his father, Dewitt C. "Dewey" Sisson, hauled supplies for Billy Everett to Olympic Hot Springs with his pack train from his Mountain Inn on the upper Elwha River near the covered bridge. D.C. Sisson was also a pioneer in several Olympic Mountain explorations. Source: Interview with Harold Sisson, 12-27-91.

4. Lois Crisler, Olympic Trail Talks, No. 75, Port Angeles Evening News. 17 Nov., 1950

5. Ibid.

6. Later Herb built a lean-to shelter here and named it Eleven Bull basin.

7. Cream Lake, discovered by Billy Everett, was so named because glacial water caused the lake to be milky colored. The glacier which contributed to this discoloration no longer exists. The lake is now clear.

8. Herb. B. Crisler, The Seattle Times, 5 Aug., 1973

9. <u>The Seattle Times,</u> 31 August, 1930

10. Herb Crisler, "Western Wildlife Photographer," courtesy Ruby El Hult

11. Herb Crisler Reminiscences, "Transporting Coals," as told to Ruby El Hult, Ventura, CA (1978)

12. Herb Crisler Reminiscences, "Survival Trip-South Rim and Lakes," as told to Ruby El Hult

13. Ibid.

14. Herb Crisler, "Western Wildlife Photographer," From Cream Lake to the Headwaters of the Hoh, courtesy Ruby El Hult

15. Herb Crisler, "Survival Trip," as told to Ruby El Hult (1978)

16. Herb Crisler Reminiscences, "The Survival Trip", as told to Ruby El Hult, (1978)

17. Herb Crisler, "The Survival Trip". Spearing Elk by the Hoh River, as told to Ruby El Hult, Ventura, CA (1978)

18. Herb Crisler, "Diary, account of 1930 trip", Courtesy Ruby El Hult, (1978)

19. Herb Crisler, "Western Wildlife Photographer", The Night Under the Rock, courtesy Ruby El Hult

20. Herb B. Crisler, <u>The Seattle Times</u> <u>Sunday Magazine,</u> 5 August, 1973

21. Herb Crisler, "Western Wildlife Photographer", Releasing the Last Pigeon, courtesy Ruby El Hult

22. Ibid.

23. Seven peaks over 7000 feet elevation exist in the Mount Olympus complex. Many, many more over 6000 are in the immediate area.

24. See Chapter eight for accounts of Winona Bailey and George Welch. Both suffered injuries after falls in the same area.

25. Actually, Crisler had never met Mr. Jeffers, but his friend E.B. Webster had, and had spoken to Herb about the Olympia photographer.

26. Herb Crisler. "Western Wildlife Photographer," courtesy Ruby El Hult

27. Ibid.

28. Ibid.

29. Ibid.

30. Herb Crisler Interview, Ruby El Hult (1973)

31. Low Divide Chalet was a new building when Herb visited. Construction was completed in 1930 by members of the pioneer Olson family from Quinault. They built the lodge for use by hunters and tourists. The Depression was on and business was bad. Eventually the lodge fell into disrepair and became the property of the National Park Service. An avalanche later destroyed the building.

32. A Forest Service telephone connected Port Angeles with Elwha Ranger Station, Dodger Point, Deer Park and Hurricane Hill fire lookouts, Humes Ranch, Elkhorn Ranger Station and other ranger stations along the Elwha River trail and Olympic Chalet. The telephone was used by fire lookouts, trail maintenance crews and national forest rangers. The old wire and insulators are still much in evidence today. During most of the decade the Crislers resided at Humes Ranch, they had use of this telephone. The line was abandoned about 1950, after the use of two-way radio came into use.

33. Herb Crisler Reminiscence, "At Low Divide Chalet," courtesy Ruby El Hult

34. Ibid.

35. Lois Brown Crisler, Herb's future wife

36. Herbert B. Crisler, <u>The Seattle Times Sunday Magazine,</u> 5 Aug., 1973

In the Grips of the Depression

The crash of the Stinson-Detroiter was only the first of a series of calamities which affected Herb's life during this difficult period. After the survival trip he was unable to find work, and in dire financial condition, with no income.

During the fall of 1932 Herb suffered another humiliating setback. He was thrown into jail in Port Angeles for killing deer without a license. He had made himself a promise during his 1930 trip across the mountains never to hunt again, but old habits die slowly. Hard times placed him out hunting again.

This story has several versions around Port Angeles, but hopefully, this true version will present the correct facts about Herb going to jail. Some of the people involved are still alive, so to protect them from any embarrassment, I'll not mention their names.

An old friend, who had hunted with him many a time, and had helped when he was down and out, collared Herb and said he had two fine nephews who had never been hunting. They both had new rifles and badly wanted to get a deer. He asked Herb if he would guide the lads. How could Herb refuse?

Herb explained he didn't have enough money to even get to Port Angeles, let alone outfit a trip or buy a license. That was no excuse, his friend said. He'd provide everything, including a license.

Needing a shelter for such a hunt, Herb and a friend, Chet Goodwin, went to the Boulder Creek area shortly before the hunting season in 1932 and put up a split-cedar lean-to structure on the ridge between Boulder and Cat Creek, only about an hour's hike from Olympic Hot Springs.

Herb packed in a pressure cooker, a tin can sealing machine, a supply of tin cans and a big copper boiler so he could can venison on the spot so the meat could be taken back to Seattle.

The boys were picked up at Port Angeles and brought to camp. Because of some foul up, neither Herb nor Goodwin had a license, although the men had already gone out and shot a buck for camp meat.

The boys were eager, too eager, as it turned out. They sneaked out from camp, without Herb or Goodwin knowing about it, saw two deer and started shooting. They shot a doe and her yearling fawn.

The frightened boys covered the deer with brush and returned to camp. If discovered, they were sure they would be arrested and go to jail. Herb noticed something was wrong and the boys admitted what they'd done.

After reprimanding them for their poor judgement, Herb promised he would take care of the matter. But first they had to leave and return home just in case the law found out about it.

It was against Herb's principles to waste meat. He and Goodwin retrieved the two deer, gutted them out and hung them to cool.

Both men were in camp the next day when they spotted the game warden and his deputy coming. Herb quickly hid his rifle, but both men were caught with the meat and no licenses. Both were arrested. They helped the officers carry out the evidence. Ruby El Hult adds what followed:

> Port Angeles was at the time a small town where everyone knew everyone else. The consensus among the law enforcement officers and the general public was that Herb was shielding some Seattle sportsman. If he would confess who made the illegal kill, he was told, he'd be let go.
>
> Herb felt the boys already had learned a hard lesson, which would last them a lifetime, and he was determined to protect them. He refused to change his story. On October 14, 1932, Herb

pleaded guilty to hunting without a license and killing three deer illegally. He was fined $250 and sentenced to 90 days in jail. Goodwin got off with a small fine for hunting without a license.[1]

After his 1930 survival trip, Crisler was always good copy for the local press. The story was placed on the new services wire. It appeared in both Seattle and Port Angeles newspapers. After the story came out in the papers, the friend who had asked Herb to guide the boys paid Herb's fine. The jail sentence was something else. Herb became the guest of Sheriff E.O. Norton at the Clallam County Courthouse jail.

Herb was aghast at the condition of the jail. "This jail is a disgrace," Herb told Sheriff Norton. "Bring me soap, scrub brushes, paint. No one wants to live like this, even the fellows thrown in for only one night. We'll have this place spruced up in no time." Herb and the other prisoners went to work, scrubbing, scraping and painting.

Crisler was well known in Clallam County as a talented photographer and improvisor. He hadn't been in jail long until the sheriff showed him a catalogue. The object of interest was a "mugging machine", a camera which could take pictures of people who had been apprehended, or who the law wanted to place on record. The list price was $385, out of reach of the sheriff's budget.

The sheriff asked Herb if he could make such a machine. Herb assured him that he could. He was provided free run of the jail, courthouse and shop, and the town also if he needed something. Herb rummaged around the basement of the courthouse and located a collection of old copper stills which had been confiscated from local bootleggers. The dome of one still became a large, polished reflector for the photo light.

Herb knew someone in Port Angeles who had an old twin-lens camera which he would sell for two dollars, so he bought that. An old iron stand was resurrected from the junk pile and used to support the camera apparatus. An abandoned, office swivel chair became the seat, and a background was built from beaver board and old water pipe. Herb built the switches. A coat of paint and the "mugging machine" was ready. The sheriff tested it and was delighted. It worked perfectly every time.

The local paper published a story about Crisler's "mugging machine", concluding with this paragraph:

> For the county it was rather a lucky mistake that Herb Crisler made when he knocked over a couple more deer than he was entitled to, for the commonwealth secured the services of an expert photographer, who, out of the sweepings of the courtroom basement built a "mugging machine" listed for $385 in the catalogue.[2]

With the jail spic and span and the mugging machine built, Herb had still served only a third of his sentence.

The county was out of money. The sheriff was hard pressed to feed inmates. It was decided to release several who were not criminals. The sheriff called Herb into his office and said, "It's nonsense keeping you in here. I'm going to let you go--just lay low, keep your mouth shut and no one will know the difference."

That night the sheriff let Herb slip out, handing him some of the money he'd saved the county on the mugging machine as a parting gesture to help him return to Seattle.

After all of the hard work building and stocking the Boulder Ridge shelter, Herb never returned to it. He sold his guns and never hunted again. Chet Goodwin and some friends improved the structure and used it for years.

When Russ Dalton of Port Angeles visited the site, late in 1989, he reported finding the copper boiler, a handmade wooden shovel and some kitchenware. The shelter roof had collapsed.

The airplane crash, the Depression, losing his house and being thrown into jail were only the beginning of Herb's troubles.

During the fall of 1933 his marriage collapsed. The marriage had never been a happy one. Herb had been raised as a strict Southern baptist. He believed once one made a commitment, he was bound to it. Divorce was practically unheard of during the 1930s; unthought of in the atmosphere in which he was raised. It never occurred to Herb that there was a way out of his miserable marriage, until he could no longer make a living for his family.

Muriel had been a schoolteacher, then later when Herb met her in Florida, a bookkeeper. During the time the Crislers operated the photo business in Port Angeles, Muriel kept the books and managed the business. During those years he never had a dime of his own because Muriel begrudged giving him money. If he so much as asked for any there was unpleasantness. They fought about this. Herb hated domestic fighting, so he went without.

Muriel had protested when Herb sold the photo business, mortgaged property, moved to Seattle and bought the airplane.

She became even more bitter after the wreck and blamed Herb for their poverty and his decision to get into the air transportation business.

Herb was touchy about their poverty, disregarding, perhaps, the bankrupt national economy and the fact that millions of other bread-winners were also unable to provide for their families.

The situation deteriorated even farther after being forced into using the rent money to buy fuel oil for the apartment, although oil only cost four or five cents a gallon.

Herb walked back and forth from West Seattle to downtown looking for work because he didn't have carfare.

Franklin D. Roosevelt had taken office in 1932 and his promised relief program, the Works Projects Administration (WPA) was finally available.

To many, the program was welfare. Herb was too proud to consider signing up for it. Muriel wasn't. She insisted that if Herb wouldn't sign up, she would. Herb said if she did, he'd quit her!

One day Herb returned home to find that she'd not only signed up, but had got boxes of food and other items and had made arrangements for him to go to work with a WPA crew the following morning.

Herb was stunned by this announcement. Instead of following through on walking out, as he had threatened, he agreed to give it a try. The work was cutting cord wood and hauling it to needy families.

Once on the job he became outraged to discover that the work crew loitered around smoking and talking beside a campfire and worked hardly at all. Herb was an experienced axe man and sawyer. The ten-man crew only cut a cord of wood that day, a job which Herb could have done alone. They resented the fact that he wanted to work, and encouraged him to loaf. His pride severely wounded, he returned home in an angry, desperate mood.

Muriel asked him how the job had gone. He announced that he didn't intend on returning to work. Muriel then became angry and offended. She insisted that he had no choice. They argued bitterly throughout the night. Neither got any sleep.

The next day was Sunday. Herb was sitting in the living room staring out the window, his mind in turmoil. Muriel started in on him again, insisting that when Monday morning came he was going to work. Herb simply got to his feet and walked out. He didn't even take a coat.

He began walking towards Renton, which was 15 miles away. The farther he walked the more resolved he was not to return. His inward thoughts powered his legs, and he kept going. It felt good to be walking, out in the open air, free of the influence of his wife and troubles.

A woman is better off without a man if he's no good, Herb kept reasoning. Because he was unable to provide, he assumed he was worthless. The Depression did that to people. So ended a marriage which had lasted 15 years.

By late in the day Herb was out in the country on the Cedar River drainage. He had been in this area once before and had found a little lake he had liked.

He walked until he found the lake. It was peaceful and calm. Several mallards paddled about happily. Herb squatted down and watched, enviously. Even the ducks are better off than I, he reasoned. They do not know what the Depression is.

A chicken farm was close by. He went to the owner, told him he was down and out, and requested permission to camp by the lake on private property. The farmer sized him up, saw that he was no bum, felt sorry for him, and gave permission.

Herb had not a cent, only a pocket knife. He didn't smoke so had no matches. He borrowed some from the farmer, built a fire, constructed a bough leanto which protected him from the dew and frost that night.

He sat beside the tiny campfire staring into the flames. His thoughts wandered over the course of events which had so cruelly placed him in such a predicament.

He was weary after the long walk. It grew cold. He piled wood upon the fire and sank down into his bough bed. He spent a long, cold, miserable, hungry night.

The following morning a man happened by, looked at Herb huddled beside his little fire and asked him if he had been cold last night? Herb admitted that he'd almost frozen. "Well, in Renton they're giving away blankets to the needy," the stranger announced.

Herb walked into Renton and received a government blanket and a frying pan. What he found to eat we do not know. Perhaps there were soup kitchens in Renton.

Back at camp he soon made arrangements with the farmer to cut wood in exchange for eggs. He also helped dig potatoes for a few of those.

Herb's friend, Mr. Meeker, who owned a meat market in Seattle, learned of his whereabouts and predicament. Herb had guided Meeker on hunting trips on the Olympic Peninsula. Meeker owned a cabin in the area where Herb was camped. Mr. Meeker and Herb's staunch friend Dr. Roy West had became acquainted through their association with Crisler. Dr. West learned of Herb's predicament through Meeker. Together they drove out and located Herb's camp.

Dr. West was amazed to find his normally cheerful friend, by nature an exuberant person, feeling totally depressed and emotionally drained.

Dr. West returned with a tarp, basic foods, warm clothing and blankets. The gesture brought tears to Crisler's eyes.

Herb arranged with the farmer to cut cord wood on shares and began earning a little money. He panned for gold in the Cedar river, earning a few cents for his efforts. For several months he remained in the make-shift camp, existing as best he could.

He didn't cut himself off from Muriel and Bobby entirely. Whenever he was able to take eggs or other food or got a little extra money he made the long walk into West Seattle and helped her out. He still used Muriel's address, and kept his camera gear stored there, but never lived with Muriel again.[3]

Early in 1934 Meeker told Herb he would give him a job driving a delivery truck. Herb returned to Seattle, thus ending one truly desperate phase in his life. But times were still tough.

While delivering meat for Meeker's Specialty Shop he met Marian Meeker, his employer's daughter. Marian kept the books for her father. An ambitious young lady, she also was an accomplished pianist. She had a studio in the Fischer Building on Third Street and gave piano lessons. She also owned the Mari Ann Yarn shop. She had recently returned from a trip to England and had been impressed with the quality and low price of English yarn and was importing and selling it successfully.

It was through Marian Meeker that Herb became a renter in the Fischer Building also. Herb fixed up a tiny room, hardly more than a broom closet, and paid $5 a month rent. This was to become his home for the next few years.

He had no telephone, but used Marian's office number and she took messages for him. He was trying to reestablish himself as a commercial photographer while working part-time for Meeker.

For her answering service he paid Miss Meeker $1 a month. She also typed an occasional business letter for him.

One day Herb mentioned to Miss Meeker that since she sold yarn, she ought to wear a knitted dress to advertise her wares. Miss Meeker allowed that was an excellent idea but she didn't have time to knit herself a dress. Herb said he had plenty of time, that if she'd teach him how to knit, he'd knit her a dress. A quick learner, he began knitting, an excellent way to pass the time while riding street cars, he claimed. He completed a two-piece dress which Miss Meeker sometimes wore. Herb's knitting, like most everything else he did, also received attention from the press.

Herb was still broke. He spent about $1 a week for food, mostly leftovers at Pike Street Market. He discovered if he went to the market about closing time Saturday night the farmers would sell off their remaining produce cheap, since it wouldn't keep until Monday. For five cents he could buy five or six heads of lettuce. One time he bought ten. Dark bananas were ten cents a dozen. For ten cents he could buy five or six loaves of day-old bread. A gallon of buttermilk was ten cents.

City living didn't agree with Herb. He ached to return to the Peninsula and do some photography, but photography was expensive.

Herb had become acquainted over the years with the head clerk at Lowman and Hanford's photography department. Whatever he purchased he got 25 percent off.

He desperately needed a new motion-picture camera to replace the old one he had carried on the 1930 trip.

Kodak color motion-picture transparency film had appeared on the market. Photographers were highly excited about it, but few had the opportunity to try it out, or the money to buy any, as it was expensive, compared to black and white.

Herb talked the clerk into selling him a second hand Cine Special, a portable motion-picture camera which would handle either color or black and white film, for $300. New, the camera sold for $600. He arranged monthly payments. He also rented a projector for five dollars a month, the rent to apply towards the purchase price. After it was half paid for, the clerk let him take it.

Eastman Kodak was searching for an experienced photographer to test their new Kodachrome transparency film in the Pacific Northwest. Since Herb had worked for Eastman Kodak in Florida, they chose him, and sent five rolls of their new color film for Herb to test. Excited, since

Herbert Crisler portrait by Thompson Studio. 1949.

he'd dreamed of using color film, Herb quickly arranged a trip to the Olympic Peninsula. Perhaps now people would see what his beloved Olympic Mountains and their wildlife were truly like.

This same summer of 1934, two Tacoma men announced that they were going to imitate Herb Crisler's survival trip across the Olympic Mountains. If he could play Tarzan[4] they thought they could also.

Things didn't go quite as they expected. They soon became so hungry they returned defeated.

Chrisler was interviewed by the press regarding the Tacoma Tarzans' failed attempt. Tongue-in-cheek, Crisler confided to the reporter that the reason the Tacoma men failed their ordeal was that they had not trained properly.

"And how should they have trained?" the reporter growled. "By knitting," was Crisler's reply. "Nothing like it for calming ones nerves in preparation for a mountaineering expedition."

The article appeared in the Seattle Times, titled "Tarzans Should Knit, Needle Expert Insists" and showed Crisler sitting on a stool, wearing only bathing trunks, busily engaged in knitting. The article states that the reason Crisler was knitting was because he also was in training for a trip into those same Olympic Mountains.

Evidently the Tarzania craze extended to mountaineers and newspapermen as well as movie goers. Everyone was weary of the Depression after several years of being broke and out of work. Later that summer the Seattle paper carried a second Tarzan knitting story, with a self portrait of Crisler and his companion, Dr. A.G. Schultz, a dentist, standing naked except for flour sack skirts around their waists, somewhere in the wilds of the Olympic Mountains.

The article was headlined, "So, Mr.Tarzan Looked Mr. Bear In Eye And Bayed Like Dog." According to the story Crisler had:

> Already taken pictures of bear, bear cubs, calf elk, elk, bull elk, fawns, herds of deer, etc., and still had 80 feet of the original 500 foot roll, then shot 60 more feet on deer and was looking for a marmot to complete the last twenty. At that moment a bear popped up in front of him with an insolent stare.
>
> He'd been eating berries, Crisler said. I trained the camera on him and kept sneaking up, sneaking up. He ate berries, rolled in the snow, and behaved as long as he heard the camera

clicking. The film began to run out. I was looking in the finder. The bear's head got bigger and bigger. I looked up and he was right in front of me. When the camera stopped clicking he started for me. I fixed him with my eyes. When I laid down the camera he charged.

I grabbed a couple of rocks and jumped on top of a boulder. He came to the rock, raised on his hind feet and spread out his front paws. I hit him right on the head. He was dazed and ran to the snow field. I wanted to keep the offensive, then get away gracefully. But I did the worst thing I could have done. I bayed like a dog, and the bear charged again. I went back onto the rock and threw stones at him. Finally he went away.

All this time Dr. Schultz, Crisler's Tarzan companion, was also having a "bear" experience. Two cubs were in the top of a tall tree. The one below wanted to get higher. His brother bit him to get his place, but never made it.

Crisler and the dentist wore practically nothing on their ten day trip. It was to have been a two weeks jaunt, but they ran out of film. When the Seattle Tarzans weren't wearing shorts they wore flour sacks, which are more primitive.

Unlike the Tacoma Tarzans, who lost their bet, Crisler and Schultz took along some food, but not much. Just salt, rice, sugar, raisins, dried apricots, dried figs, etc. But nothing civilized; not even a mushroom.[5]

Back in Seattle Herb sent the color film to Kodak. He had totally ignored reading the written instructions which accompanied the film before exposing it.

After Kodak processed and viewed the film they informed Crisler that he'd gone against all the rules of "color" photography and taken pictures of wildflowers <u>against the light</u>. The light shone right through the flower petals! Eastman was pleased. They'd learned something; the pictures were some of the most exciting color film they'd ever seen.[6] Using the new 16-millimeter color transparency film, Herb had instinctively discovered a technique widely used with color film, exposing certain translucent nature subjects, such as wildflowers or frost-reddened leaves, backlighted. It doesn't work with black and white film.

Herb's dream had come true: Color film, so he could show the beautiful Olympic Mountains and their wildlife to the public. He was convinced that color would revolutionize the motion-picture business. He wanted to get started but had no money.

A 100-foot roll of Kodachrome film cost about five dollars. Black and white half that. Earning enough money to shoot, process the film and edit the footage into a movie worth showing was a costly project.

Herb decided he had to make enough money so he could afford to stock up on film and shoot a color movie in the Olympic Mountains. But how?

Notes & Sources, Beyond the Trails, Chapter SIX

1. Ruby El Hult, <u>An Olympic Mountain Enchantment</u>. C.B. Publications, Inc. Port Angeles (1989)

2. <u>The Port Angeles Evening News,</u> 31 Oct., 1932

3. Herb Crisler Reminiscence. "Out in the Cold on Cedar River," as told to Ruby El Hult.(1971)

4. The "Tarzan" came about because Herb became known as the "Tarzan of the Olympics" after his 1930 survival trip from Olympic Hot Springs to the Quinault River.

5. Two newspaper articles, Crisler scrapbook, courtesy Ruby El Hult.

6. Herb Crisler reminiscences, "Back In Seattle-Lighting On His Feet." As told to Ruby El Hult.

7

The Spirit of the Olympics
Bringing the Olympics to the People. Herb Suffers a Bad Accident.

* * *

"That country up there is so wild, if you ever fell down one of those mountains,
nobody could ever find you but God." (Don McQuade, 1938)

* * *

Herb had made a black and white movie of his thirty-day solo trip into the Olympic Mountains in 1930. The story was well known in the northwest because of extensive coverage, including many Crisler pictures, in The Seattle Daily Times. and the New York Times.

Hotcake Camp. Herb cooking hotcakes.

Many theaters had been closed because of the Depression, so Herb didn't receive as much income as he had hoped. The movie was also shown at the Lincoln Theater in Port Angeles, where he was paid in silver dollars. When Herb's sister Phanoy married, he presented her with some of the silver as a wedding present.

In 1934 Herb decided to build a shelter below Appleton Ridge. He named it Hotcake Camp. It was located one day's hike in from the trailhead on Boulder Creek. Herb had originally favored the area for hunting so thought it would be a good base for wildlife photography. The Elwha elk herd frequently lingered in the area both spring and fall.

Hotcake Camp became the first of eight major line camps he eventually built across the Olympic Mountains. It was a Crisler tradition that all camps have appropriate names.

Herb began thinking how effective it would be if he could play sound with his color movies. If viewers could only hear the bugling of a bull elk, the roar of the waterfall, the babbling of a brook and the cry of a red-tailed hawk as they watched his color films, perhaps they could more easily feel the spirit of the Olympics, the feeling he was trying so hard to convey to people through his photography.

Herb kept eating by doing photography for the Carnation Company and other commercial accounts. Carnation had one of the largest and most modern dairies in the world on the Tolt River east of Seattle. The company had just acquired Albers Milling, which specialized in pet food, an expanding product at the time.

Like many other free-lance photographers, Herb struggled to find enough money to buy as much film as he wished and to upgrade his equipment.

The snow-free season in the high country was short, August and September being the only months when it was feasible to travel during most summers.

He frequently went as far as Cream Lake Basin. Although he had the big hollow fir to cache supplies in, and could sleep inside if it was storming, he wanted to build a lean-to there for photography purposes.

In 1935 he was showing TEN DAYS IN THE OLYMPICS. By 1936 his movie, WINTER WONDERLAND was available. In 1937 he offered SEVEN LAKES OF THE OLYMPICS, a film about Seven Lakes Basin, a popular place for fishermen and backpackers.

One day in 1937, Herb Crisler appeared at KOMO Radio offices, mentioned he was a motion-picture photographer and wished to talk to someone who might help him match sound with the new color films.

He was referred to Don McQuade, sound engineer. McQuade kept wondering: who is this man? I know him. Then he remembered this was the mountaineer who had crossed the Peninsula without food or a gun a few years before. McQuade had seen the film Crisler made of the trip and had never forgotten it.

McQuade and Crisler, it turned out, had common interests. McQuade was interested in producing motion-pictures, since he'd once worked in theater. They discussed the problems of sound. Don outlined what he thought could and what couldn't be done. He told Crisler that if he didn't find what he was looking for to come back, that he would work personally on the problem.

Herb did come back. He was determined. McQuade explained that in the meanwhile he'd researched the subject. Although sound tracks had been incorporated onto black and white film strips for years, technical reasons existed why the same process wouldn't work with 16-millimeter color film. Brilliant engineers were exploring the problem, so far without success. The idea was a good one, but a solution didn't appear to be forthcoming in the immediate future.

Herb explained one reason he wanted to put sound with color film. Carnation was willing to pay him big money for a promotional color film, with sound, of their dairy operations so they could show it to customers and clients all over the country. McQuade told Herb that he had contact with sound engineers at the University of Washington, and agreed to talk with them.

Sound engineers at the university claimed the only solution, at present, was to record the audio on thirty-three and a third discs, then play the records with the film. They warned of two problems; synchronization and duration of a disc, which limited audio to approximately 10 minutes. If a longer film was desired, and more than one record required, an annoying interruption was unavoidable. This meant the projector had to be shut down while a disc was changed, something no projection operator wished to do.

McQuade and Herb agreed to a "handshake" partnership. As a pilot project, Herb spliced together some color stock footage and Don produced a sound track on a disc.

Synchronization, they discovered, between sound and film was indeed a problem. It was embarrassing for the audio to be describing a bull elk while a wildflower bobbed on the screen, or commenting about a landscape when pictures of a circling hawk was shown. This problem was partially solved by placing a hand-operated rheostat in the feed wire to the projector. The projector operator listened closely to the audio, with which he had to be familiar. He then either speeded up or slowed down the projector to match the audio.

If the projectionist became distracted and lost his place, and didn't know whether to speed up or slow down to get back with the audio, pandemonium occurred!

Their first commercial production was a ten-minute color film with sound. They tested it by showing at Rotary Clubs and businessmen's luncheons in Seattle. Few viewers had ever seen nature and wildlife on color film and no one had seen color with sound. Viewers were enthusiastic.

But the short duration records presented serious limitations for what they wished to do. Carnation's public relations people could hardly describe their empire in ten minutes.

Sound engineers at the university solved this by building a large, special record player which would hold two records at a time, side by side, so that continuous sound was possible. Viewers did not realize that the sound track was run separately, and was not an integral part of the film. [1]

Pioneering talking color motion-pictures was exciting and challenging, but also took time and cost money. Money was always in short supply.

Muriel had sued for divorce in 1935. Herb was under court order to pay $35 a month child support for their adopted son, Robert.

Herb soon became bored with the aspects of business. His ambition was to be out shooting in the field. Sometimes he'd simply vanish into the wilderness for a few weeks. When he returned he would be his old enthusiastic happy self. Then the tediousness of business would drag him down again.

Herb and Don produced several medical films for surgeons and dental surgeons and an animal husbandry film for the Carnation Company.

Later they also produced a wildflower film, which the State of Washington bought for $500.

In 1937 something happened which brought national attention to the Olympic Peninsula: The possibility of a new national park.

President Franklin D. Roosevelt, on a tour of the West, purposefully made a side trip to the Peninsula because of the controversy which had been raging about creation of a national park.

Both conservationists and lumbermen had been nervously eyeing the rapidly diminishing supply of what, only decades ago, had been seemingly inexhaustible stands of old-growth Douglas fir, western hemlock, red cedar and Sitka spruce forests throughout the Pacific Northwest.

Stands had now been significantly reduced, especially at lower, easily accessible areas. The only places where significant forests remained were in the high Cascade Mountains, where snow and steep terrain prevented train logging, except for a few short, snow-free months each summer, and the Olympic Peninsula, which still had large tracts of forest.

The Peninsula became the last battleground, so to speak, between those who thought cut-it-all and those who believed some stands of old-growth should be preserved for future generations.

There had never been much of a dispute over whether or not the Olympic Mountain high country should be set aside as a national park. The issue was how many acres should be included. Timber interests, heavy-weights in politics, argued that the forests were over-ripe. They were doing the <u>trees</u> a favor by chopping them down, bucked them into saw logs, and making lumber, or pulp.

Trees were not the only thing which fueled the fires of controversy over a park. Another ingredient in the stew was the noble Olympic elk, now officially named Roosevelt elk, <u>Cervus elaphus roosevelti</u> after President Theodore Roosevelt, who's eleventh-hour pen had created 610,560 acre Mount Olympus National Monument, in March, 1907, shortly before the President left office.

Conservationists wanted both the elk and their old-growth forest habitat protected. Unbridled market hunting for elk, both for their delicious meat and ivory teeth, had decimated the herds to alarming numbers by the turn of the century. Elk had been placed on the protected list by the Washington State Legislature in 1905.

As early as 1904 Congressman Francis W. Cushman of Tacoma had unsuccessfully introduced a bill to have the Olympic Mountains set aside as a national park.

Congressman W.E. Humphrey of Washington State had also lobbied unsuccessfully to establish a game reserve to protect the elk on the Peninsula.

There was little middle ground in this struggle. Battle lines were clearly drawn. People were either for or against. [2]

Meanwhile, the National Park Service quietly placed a four-man investigating team into the area. Their report concluded that many areas were indeed unique enough to warrant creation of a national park. They also claimed that homesteaders, especially their packs of dogs, on the Hoh River had prevented elk from reaching some of their traditional winter range.

Elk numbers had increased, after being protected, until over-browsing was occurring. The U.S. Forest Service, Olympic National Forest Division, in conjunction with the State Game Commission, successfully obtained permission from the legislature to open the elk season for four days in the fall of 1933.

About 150 elk were harvested. Again, in 1936, 1937 and 1938 controlled elk hunts were allowed, and 1200 elk were taken.[3]

In 1935 Representative Mon C. Wallgren of Washington State introduced a bill which provided for the establishment of Mount Olympus National Park of 728,360 acres.

Lumbering interests screamed bloody murder and rallied their forces. Public testimony on the bill was heard for nine days in April, 1936. A considerable amount of pulpwood (converted into newsprint) was consumed by the press carrying arguments for or against the Wallgren bill.

The Aberdeen World, a pro logging paper if there ever was one, bitterly opposed the bill, but reluctantly admitted it would be sympathetic to a "sane and reasonable-sized" park. Timber people were of the opinion that any "reasonable" sized park should contain few, if any, marketable trees. Which would have meant the park would have been only above timberline, an area of almost perpetual snow and cold.

Into this turmoil stepped President Franklin D. Roosevelt, a man who, like President Theodore Roosevelt, believed in the value of national land set-asides. The president came ashore at Port Angeles from the destroyer U.S.S.Phelps, on September 29, 1937, the first American President to ever visit the Peninsula. Excitement ran high as thousands gathered to watch his entourage pass along First Street then turn south on Lincoln.

In front of the Clallam County Courthouse the entourage stopped. President Roosevelt climbed the courthouse steps and made an impassioned speech supporting creation of Olympic National Park. A large banner hanging over the courthouse doorway implored, "Please, Mr. President, we children need your help. Give us our Olympic National Park."

American and Washington State flags were much in evidence. The president spent the night at Lake Crescent Tavern, where Washington senators and representatives, Forest Service and National Park representatives gathered for a conference. Roosevelt was known as the "persuasive president". He expressed a strong desire to see approximately 680,000 to 860,000 acres, depending on which of Representative Wallgren's bills passed, set aside during the forthcoming session of Congress.

Even the bill's opponents agreed that the central core of the Olympic Mountains should be set aside as a park. They disagreed with environmentalists only on the park's size.

This visit to the Peninsula by the president, and prospects of an impending park, invigorated proponents, including Herb, who was adamantly in favor of the park.

Rosalie Edge, a nationally-known Eastern environmentalist, also threw her considerable influence behind the creation of Olympic National Park.

Opposed was the governor of Washington, timber companies, railroad interest, miners, chambers of commerce, mayors and others whose desire was unbridled exploitation of all natural resources.

Remembering the vow he'd taken that night, at the terminal of Hoh Glacier in 1930, to become an advocate for the animals, concerned about whether or not the area would be set aside as a park or not, Crisler decided to do something to try and sway people towards support for a park. Experience had taught him that few people, besides Peninsula residents, had the slightest idea what the proposed park looked like, since few roads entered the area.

Herb decided to film a color movie which would show people what the Olympic Mountain interior looked like. Herb thought most people, including skeptics, once they saw such a color movie, would be swayed into supporting a park.

Although six of the eastern snow peaks of the Olympic Mountains, Fricaba, Deception, Mystery, Warrior Peaks, Inner Constance, and Hal Foss, all over 7000 feet elevation, were plainly visible any clear day from Seattle, Bremerton, Tacoma and many populated areas around Puget Sound, few people had even been to the Peninsula.

The trip was not a simple one. Car ferries or a steamship ride were necessary to even reach the Peninsula, unless one considered driving all the way around Hood Canal on a very narrow, crooked road.

Don McQuade concurred that such a film could sway people's opinions.

This was an ambitious, expensive project, with little time before the issue was to be decided. Using some of Herb's recent color footage of the Olympics, as well as film shot special for the project, they set to work. Their goal was to produce a 90-minute color film. The film's name was Beyond The Trails. Writers from KOMO Radio and sound engineers from the University of Washington assisted in various parts of this production. Don had access to professional recording equipment at the studio.

Three showings were advertised, on November 20, at Fischer Studios on Third Avenue. Tickets were $.27, including tax.[4] The film was also shown at Port Angeles.

The film was well received, but attendance was disappointing. It undoubtedly enhanced support for the park. Many viewers told Don and Herb they had no idea how unique and beautiful the area in question was until after seeing the movie.

The next national park hearing was held at the White House the following April. Representative Wallgren had introduced a third bill into Congress, which provided 860,000 acres for a park. Washington State's Governor Clarence Martin and Benjamin F. Kizer, Director of the Washington State Planning Council bitterly protested. They countered with a park only half that size, containing 450,000 acres.

President Roosevelt's charm and powers of persuasion went into high gear. In a brilliant move, he suggested a compromise; an amendment to the third Wallgren bill, reducing the size of the park to 680,000 acres, with a provision that would subsequently allow any president to expand the area to 892,000 acres by proclamation, after consultation with the governor of Washington and National Park and Forest Service representatives.

All present agreed. The Third Wallgren bill, so amended, passed the House and Senate with little comment and was signed into law June 29, 1938.

The Peninsula had itself a national park. Opponents, after having time to consider the sneaky clause where any president could increase the size, blew their stacks! They diligently set to work attempting to undermine and change that clause.

Crisler and McQuade were ecstatic. Their film hadn't made them much money, but thoughts that it had helped rally last minute support for the creation of Olympic National Park made the long hours of work and expense seem worthwhile.

They didn't suspect that the controversy over the amount of acres included in the park was only beginning and that the battle to maintain the size would be ongoing for many years.

Now that Herb's beloved Bailey Range and the heartland of the Olympic Mountains were protected by park status, he itched to do more photography there, believing that once people saw what the park offered they would help to retain its size:

> I started going into the Olympics each summer, taking a few pictures of the animals to show people what there is in the Olympics. I observed the habits of the animals and watched them live their natural lives while they did not know they were being watched, and the more I found out about them the more I loved them. I wanted other people to know the animals and beauty of the Olympics as I knew them.
>
> Then came the development of color 16-millimeter film and improved 16-millimeter cameras. This looked to me like a good way to bring the wild interior of the Olympics to those that would never see it any other way and it would still leave the wilderness undisturbed. I put all the money I could rake together--and that wasn't much--into cameras, film and a projector.[5] Color film was as yet in the experimental stage, and the results would often be disappointing. But the spirit of the Olympics was

still in my heart; I couldn't stop. I would spend my last dime, go without for a long stretch at a time, live on a dollar a week, in order to buy film. As I got better pictures, I could charge five dollars for showing them to clubs and other groups.

Sometimes these people irritated me. Some thought so mechanically, that they did not get the feeling I wanted to put over. I wanted them to feel the Olympics, love their living creatures, and enjoy the mountain flowers. Instead, they would come up after the show, compliment me on the fine photography, ask what kind of camera I used, how close was I to that bear, my weren't you afraid, shouldn't you have had a gun, what stop did you set your light meter?

Some camera hounds are trophy hunters. They like to have their cameras and all the gadgets to brag about to their friends, like hunters with their mounted elk antlers.

Why did they always ask me those silly questions? I didn't know. I wouldn't sit and listen to a concert artist playing the violin concerto, then go up after the program, compliment him on his fine performance, and then ask if he minded telling me whether he used a black cat's guts or a white cat's gut on his violin.

One arty lady inquired about my art background. "You have mastered composition. Whom did you study under, may I ask?" I told her how I got my composition. If I were going to photograph, say, a flower, I would first look it straight in the face then squint one eye. [A camera has only one eye] Then I would walk around to its back and squint the other eye. I would go around the flower squinting at it at different angles. When I found one that made me say, "Ah," from that angle I took the picture. She walked away haughtily.

Not all people lacked understanding, and my heart glowed to see those who had the real feel. It always made me ache to do a better job of bringing the Olympics to the people. If there were some that couldn't see what I saw in the pictures, it was my fault. I must get better pictures and more of the natural things the animals do in their daily routine of living. I must get better flower pictures, that show the struggles of the alpine plants to survive under the severe conditions they must grow in.

So, I continued to save, and buy better equipment and more film. I was getting set for my biggest trip yet. I had the most film that I had yet possessed. I had bought a good camera and better lenses, but they were only tools.

I got enough food together to last for two weeks and started into the Olympics on my most ambitious photographic expedition yet. The weather was good. I was in good physical condition and everything was coming along fine.

In the fall of 1938, Herb talked Don into accompanying him on a trip into the Olympic interior. "To see what I was made of," Don admits.

On September 1, they went to Olympic Hot Springs. After a soak in the mineral springs and a visit with Herb's friends, Jean and Harry Schoeffel, they shouldered full packs and headed up the Boulder Creek trail. Both men packed cameras. At Hotcake Camp they settled down to do some serious nature photography.

They didn't have good luck. The wind blew and rain poured down. Finally, after several days, they saw a large herd of elk at a distance, too far away to photograph. The elk disappeared before they could get closer.

Don's allotted time was almost up. That night, Herb asked, "Don, do you think you can find your way back?" Don admits his stomach did a flip flop but he said he supposed so, why?

"I think I know where that herd of elk are, and we've still got enough grub for a week or ten days. I know you have to go back. If you can go out alone, I'm going to trail that herd and try and get some close-up pictures." They parted company September 12. Herb went on alone.

A week went by. Ten days passed, and Don still had no word. More time went by. Don was sick with worry. "You know," Don says, "that country up there is so wild, if you ever fell down one of those mountains, nobody could ever find you but God."

Finally, two weeks later, the phone rang. It was Herb, calling from Quinault, clear on the opposite side of the Olympic Mountains.

"Where in God's earth have you been?" demanded Don. "I've been worried sick!"

"Well," Crisler drawled in his southern accent, "I had a little accident. Delayed me some. But I'm all right now. I'll see you when I get to Seattle."

Four days passed. No word from Herb. Again Don began to worry. Then, into the KOMO studio came an almost unrecognizable figure. His clothes were torn to shreds, face unshaven, bandages here and there, an arm in a sling. "He looked like a bum--except Cris being Cris, he managed to be more picturesque than that," Don recalls.

"I forgot I didn't have any money on me," Herb said lamely, "and I had to hitchhike to Seattle--and the way I looked, you know, people just didn't want to pick me up."[6]

What happened was, the second day after parting from Don, about nine o'clock in the morning:

I had been traveling along a steep heather slope so long my ankles were tired. They wanted just one level place to step. Below me about a hundred feet the heather slope broke over a crag about 20 feet high, at the base of which was a 20-foot-wide, boulder-strewn flat and a small stream flowing among the boulders. I started down to see if I could descend into this stream-bed.

Then I did something I knew one should not do in the mountains. There was a stick about as big as my wrist and ten feet long lying on the ground. It was bleached the common weathered gray that is usually the sign of sound wood. I wanted so badly to step on something I could straighten my ankles on, that I took a chance. The second I put my weight on it there was a sharp snap and I lost my balance and fell over on my side.

I started to roll, but this did not worry me. I thought I could easily stop myself. But the weight of my heavy pack rolled me over on top of it. While in this position, there was nothing I could get hold of.

I could only paw the air. Then the rounding pack rolled over on top of me, and as I came over onto the ground, I grabbed a handful of heather. But with the momentum and the weight of the pack combined, the heather tore out by its roots. I continued to roll, gathering speed at each turn and the heather I grabbed now would jerk out by its roots the moment I seized it. I saw that tactic was useless and tried to get the pack straps off my shoulders.

I almost succeeded, but as soon as I stopped pulling heather I gathered momentum fast. As I went over, the strap would come back into place and it wasn't long before I was bounding and rolling down the mountain side like a loose rock.

I was helpless now to do anything to stop myself. I was sure that I would be dashed to pieces on the rocks below but I was not frightened. I didn't mind dying. It even went through my mind the trouble and hard work it would cause my friends and others that might come hunting for me, and the toil of packing out my dead body.

I wished there were some way I could let them know that I would rather be left here. I thought of Mr. Jeffers.[7] Maybe we could make contact again. Maybe I wouldn't be alone up here after all. I thought that I would say to him: Had I done the right thing? I had tried to carry the spirit [of the Olympics] in my heart. Now maybe I am the spirit!

These thoughts ran through me like a speeding panorama. Then they blended out in nothingness. I never hit the ground consciously. I just drifted off in darkness. For how long I don't know. Then a dim light. Was I in the hereafter? I couldn't tell, but thought I was. (There is no pain in the next world.) I had no pain. Then a little more light.

I opened my eyes a wee bit and I saw miles of boulders as high as my head. They ended in a blackness as far away as across the sea. 'There's no place on earth like this,' I thought. I must be dead. But I was rigid as stone. I saw a hand lying in an unnatural position, limp against a rock. Could this

65

be my hand? I wiggled my fingers. Those out there did not move. It must not be my hand. At a distance I saw the sole of a shoe with a leg in it. That was my shoe. I recognized the rubber crepe sole I used, so as to be able to travel noiselessly and get closer to animals. But I couldn't tell whether the feet were still attached to the body. I couldn't focus my eyes. I am still in this world, I thought, but I am broken all to pieces. I don't want to live this way. I won't live anyway. Then everything was dark again.

The next time I woke up I had more use of my senses. I realized I was lying on an arm and that it was aching. I was able to pull it out and it was all right. I could raise the other arm that the hand hung to. Some of the fingers were at an odd angle. My head was wedged between a boulder and my pack, but I was able to get it out and was somewhat relieved to find my neck wasn't broken. I dragged myself over to the stream and dropped my head in the cool water.[8] This revived me a lot.

My arm and wrist were broken, I knew, but although my foot was at an odd angle there did not seem to be any broken bones. I examined it thoroughly and decided it was only twisted out of joint. But with only one good hand I couldn't think of how to get it back into place.

Finally an idea came into my mind. A small alder stood on the bank. I dragged myself to the pack and removed the rope I used in tying the pack to the pack board. Then I got over to the alder tree and got the rope over a limb. One end of the rope I tied around my foot. I lay flat on my back and raised my leg as high as possible, at the same time pulling on the other end of the rope. When I got my foot as high as I could, I tied this end of the rope to some large, exposed roots. Then I swung as much of my body weight on the rope-tied foot as I could. By twisting and pulling, the ankle finally snapped back into place, with great pain.

For a couple of minutes I was so exhausted with pain I could not untie the rope and when I did get it untied I just laid on the rocks and suffered for a while. Finally I got to my feet and though it pained me, I could walk some.

Next was the broken arm to take care of. I had a small axe. With my good hand, I managed to flatten two pieces of wood about a foot long. I had some cloth sacks, so I tore them into strips and took them and my improvised splints over to where I got my ankle back into place. I tied the rope around my hand, swung my weigh onto it, and worked the bones until they felt even. When my hand looked fairly straight, I held the splints together with some adhesive tape and started wrapping the strips of cloth around them. When I had to tie a knot I helped with my teeth.

When I got this all done, I felt quite patched up. Now what to do? I could have started back right then--though a little later I couldn't have--but if I tried to carry my pack I could not make it, and if I didn't take my pack I might get so weak without food and sleeping bag that I would perish. I had come to get pictures. I had everything to get pictures with. Even if I still had a broken arm, I still wanted to try.

Up the stream the ravine spread out into a small rock-strewn, grassy meadow. I decided to try and get my pack up to it, make camp for a few days, and see how I got along. I managed to get everything up and to erect a lean-to with my seven-by-nine silk tarp.

After the shelter was completed, I dragged all the dry limbs I could find into camp. Then I fixed myself a little rice soup, set a pail of water near, and crawled into my sleeping bag, leaving my shoe on my left foot. It was swelling fast and I was afraid if I took the shoe off, I would never get it on again.

I rolled and tumbled all night. I developed a fever, couldn't sleep and couldn't find a comfortable position to rest my broken arm, and it ached all the time. It seemed like days before day broke, but daylight didn't give me any relief from the pain.

My body was covered with bruise spots and every muscle and bone ached. Now I thought night would never come, but when it did I was still in pain. I found that lying on my stomach was the most

66

comfortable, but in this position there wasn't enough room in the sleeping bag for my broken arm. I solved that problem by cutting a hole through the side of the sleeping bag so the arm could protrude outside. The arm got cold and I couldn't sleep. I finally put some extra sacks over it and went to sleep.

The next day I felt much better. I cooked my meals and exercised a bit, although it was painful to walk.

By the fourth day I decided to continue my photographic trip. I had broken one of the tripod legs and mended it with sticks and tape.

I continued across the Olympics, taking pictures and following approximately the same route I took while living off the country [1930]. Although I now had food I sometimes thought I would rather have two good hands.

It was hard getting over rocks and glaciers with only one hand. I could not afford another slip, not even once. Setting up my tripod was one of my worst problems. Have you ever tried setting up a tripod with a camera mounted on it in a hurry on a rough hillside? It's not easy. I solved this problem by tying a forked stick to my broken arm, one prong cut off three inches long, the other one a foot long, so that it gave me a kind of hook. I used this hook for many things. I could even carry a pail of water with it.

I had to ration my food. I even drank the rinsing from the pail I mixed hotcake batter in. It was going to take longer than I had planned. I didn't want to have to live off the country. I wanted my time for photography.

When I was traveling on the rarely traversed south side of Mount Olympus, the country all looked as if I knew it, but I could not pin it down. I finally came out at Lake Quinault with a wonderful collection of 16-millimeter colored motion-picture films of the Olympic Mountains of which I was very, very proud, thinking now I could really show people the spirit of the Olympic wilderness, and I was pleased and happy. But after I got back to Seattle I was to be disappointed again. There was not the interest shown in the pictures that I had hoped. The public talked about me and my broken arm-- how I had set it myself, how I could stand the pain, how I had the courage to continue across the mountains.

Yes, it takes courage to go across the Olympic wilderness, was my answer. But it takes more courage to hold the spirit of the Olympics.[9]

Herb neglected to mention several interesting things which occurred on this trip. A few days after leaving his recovery camp, during his stay at Cream Lake, Herb found a pair of shed elk antlers near camp. They were huge, so he dragged them over and propped them up against the wood pile:

Suddenly a bull elk burst into the clearing. He saw the antlers, let out a bellow and charged. I was right in line. I grabbed my camera and started shooting. I think I got the tip of his horn. Suddenly, just a few feet from me, he stopped. He saw that the antlers on the ground weren't attached to anything. Without displaying any fear, the elk examined the antlers carefully, then trotted away.

All night long however, he kept circling my camp, trumpeting and snorting at me. The elk are having their fighting season now and he wanted me to come out and battle him, I guess. I stayed inside my sleeping bag.[10]

As if the trip so far hadn't had enough excitement, Herb also had a scary, close encounter with a black bear. He managed to drive off the aggressive bruin with a rock.

Back in Seattle, Herb's first stop was at KOMO Radio. He knew Don would be worried, as recounted earlier. The Seattle Times heard about Herb's adventure and published a photo of Herb with his arm in a sling, his broken tripod under one arm and a pith helmet on his head. An accompanying story was headlined: Photographer Breaks Arm, Faces Bear, Elk in Wilds.

One of the joints was healing crookedly. For an account of Herb's operation, we refer to a story by Ruby El Hult:

Next stop was to Dr. Roger Anderson, for whom he had made surgical films. Anderson was the man who invented the bone pin (a layman's term for inserting a steel pin into a broken joint while it heals). Though Herb's arm was okay, one of his knuckle joints had set crooked, so he couldn't bend it. Dr. Anderson told him it would have to be broken and reset or he'd never have proper use of the hand. He wanted to give Herb an anesthetic so that he wouldn't have to suffer pain when it was re-broken. Herb said, 'No, he'd rather take the pain than to be sick from the poisons.' The doctor warned that the pain would be intense, but quick. 'You sure you don't want anything to kill it?" While the doctor talked he was feeling the joint with Herb's hand over his knee and, when Herb reiterated that he wanted no anesthetic, with a very quick motion, before Herb knew what he was doing, he chopped the hand down over his knees and broke the joint. The pain was so excruciating Herb nearly passed out. At least it was over quickly!

Then Dr. Anderson set the hand and put in a bone pin at the end of the finger. He said Herb must remain in Virginia Mason Clinic for a week so they could take his temperature regularly and make sure he had no complications.

Herb was placed in a special room. When lunch was served he thought it awful. He decided a week of such food would kill him, so he determined to leave. A nurse came in, took his temperature, and said she'd be back in an hour. As soon as she left he found his suit, dressed, and with his coat over the arm that was in a sling, simply walked out. No one paid any attention.

He went to the home of friends connected with the Carnation Company, for whom he was still doing promotional films. Herb was made welcome and told he could stay. He cautioned his friends against revealing his whereabouts. He was without a temperature and doing okay.

After a week, he headed for Dr. Anderson's office. On the way he ran into a Seattle Times photographer which recognized him.

The photographer said, 'Crisler, where in the hell have you been? Dr. Anderson has been wild, trying every way he knew to locate you. He was sure you'd developed complications and was so damned stubborn you'd die of them before coming back into his office!'

Herb said he'd been just fine. The photographer took Herb's picture with his arm in the sling with the bone pin at the end of one finger. That evening the Times carried an item about his disappearance from Virginia Mason Clinic, and used the picture to illustrate the story. Herb went back to Dr. Anderson, the pin was removed and the knuckle joint was as good as new.[11]

Herb was broke again. He badly needed income so he could buy more film and supplies. But how?

Notes & Sources, Beyond The Trails, Chapter Seven

1. Interview with Don McQuade, 04 Jan. 1992

2. Lois Crisler, "Logger's Loot in the Olympics." Island of Rivers. Pacific Northwest National Parks & Forests Association, Seattle. (1988)

3. Murray Morgan, "The Great Elk Shoot of 1937", Island of Rivers, Pacific Northwest National Parks & Forests Assoc., Seattle. (1988) A "tongue-in-cheek" account of early-day elk hunting.

4. Interview with Don McQuade, 04 Jan. 1992

5. At the time, Herb owned a Cine Special motion-picture camera, various 120 millimeter reflex still cameras, a Bell & Howell auditorium-grade, 1200-watt projector and a large, beaded screen designed especially for color films.

6. Interview with Don McQuade, by Ruby El Hult. (1971)

7. Joseph C. Jeffers, photographer for whom Jeffers Glacier is named, died August 24, 1924 in a climbing accident on Mount Olympus.(See Smitty Parratt, Gods & Goblins C.P. Publications, Inc. Port Angeles (1984)

8. In this regard, Herb was fortunate. Many large sections of the high country are without water during the late summer after the snow has melted.

9. Herb Crisler, "Western Wildlife Photographer", (unpublished) Courtesy Ruby El Hult

10. The Seattle Times, 26 Sept. 1938

11. Herb Crisler Reminiscence, "The Finger Pin--1938," as told to Ruby El Hult (1972)

8

Herb Marries Education

> I love the storms, big and small--
> The roar of summer, the howl of fall,
> The sting of winter blizzards,
> The breeziness of spring--
>
> I love them all.
> It must be the love of wilderness in me.
> Herb Crisler

Herb found a job. It didn't pay much, but the fringe benefits suited his every desire. Olympic National Park was his work place.

The stage for this unlikely episode of Herb Crisler's life is wild, secluded Elwha Basin. The time was a balmy day in August, 1940.

Crisler, alone, dressed in stagged khaki pants and flannel shirt, with a sweaty red neckerchief tied around his head, carrying an 85 pound pack, arrived at the basin late one evening.

He watched from afar, a smile on his face, while a large party of Seattle Mountaineers Club members scurried about like ants, pitching tents, gathering wood and unpacking gear.

Wood smoke spiraled through the trees. Tired backpackers sat rubbing blistered feet. There was not much talk. People were not only exhausted, they were overwhelmed, by the near-vertical mountains surrounding their campsite.

Herb found a level sleeping spot, no small feat in this rugged place, slid out of his pack and pulled out a packet of mail. He asked for the club's secretary, and handed over his bundle, which he'd carried 30 miles, from Whiskey Bend.

Then he withdrew quietly to the sidelines, uncertain exactly how his presence, as a park ranger, would fit into this rather motley crowd, a number, which he noted with satisfaction, were attractive females.

Miss Lois Brown, a slender, tall brunette with a long, thin neck and large, haunting brown eyes noticed the stranger in their midst, and that he chose to remain isolated from the group. He wore a park ranger's badge but certainly didn't fit the stereotype. Obviously one of those nondescript, part-time rangers the park service hires each summer on a temporary basis, she assumed correctly.

However, anyone who had walked this far carrying a heavy pack was a welcome guest of the Mountaineers. Miss Brown left the group, wandered aimlessly, drawing closer all the while to the stranger, then approached Herb politely.

Her rangy, swinging gait had caught Herb's attention. He recognized the stride of someone who not only enjoys walking but is good at it.

She made polite comments about the spectacular setting of Elwha Basin, nestled in a primeval-looking gulch at the bottom of six-thousand foot mountains. She politely inquired if he had ever been in the mountains before?

Herb pursed his lips thoughtfully. "Not with such a large party," Crisler drawled, his soft Georgia accent flowing as surely, and slowly, as honey on a crisp morning.

Miss Brown liked the accent, and was captivated by his glittering blue eyes, so "full of light." She began discreetly pumping her friends for more details about Crisler. She stopped after they began joking about her "maidenly" interest. No one seemed to know anything about him anyway.

Herb had been asked by his employer, Olympic National Park Service, to head up the Elwha River, deliver mail to the Mountaineer party, wherever they might be, then take motion-pictures of the group's activities for park use. The party was assembled at Elwha Basin in preparation for an ascent of Mount Olympus. Such an expedition was an important event, for both the club and the park. The park was interested in encouraging more public use of the back country. Policies quite opposite from modern thinking!

Heavier camp supplies and tents had been carried in on pack animals by Grant Humes and deposited at Elwha Basin--the end of the trail for horses. Club members carried their own personal effects, a little food, sleeping bags, enough equipment to spend a couple of nights, since the distance from Whiskey Bend to Elwha Basin exceeds what most people care to cover in one day.

After the evening meal a large bonfire was built and the club's evening social hour started. Most members joined in, but Miss Brown decided to go to bed and rest up for the strenuous climb up the Snowfinger, the snow bank that fills the nearby canyon below Dodwell-Rixon Pass, then the steep trek down to Queets Basin.

After Miss Brown climbed out of her sleeping bag the following morning and began circulating amongst her women companions she regretted her decision's to retire early. Everyone was gushing about the evening fireside. Her friend Helen said, "Oh, Lois, you should have been there last night..."

Lois' eyes opened wide as she learned that handsome, blue-eyed Mr. Crisler had captivated his audience with a thrilling two-hour fireside talk about his extensive mountaineering experiences! Which included climbing all three peaks of Mount Olympus with Tom Newton, in 1920, and a solo 1930 survival-type traverse of the Olympic Mountains without food or gun, on which he saw not another human for 28 days. They had listened in amazement while Herb described how he'd become so hungry he'd eaten frogs and grasshoppers.

Lois was chagrined. To think she had judged him a novice in the mountains. Hadn't he adroitly avoided her question about even having been in the mountains before?

Helen rambled on and on. Mr. Crisler was from Georgia. He'd been sent to the Peninsula in 1918 during the war, had started the first photo-finishing business in Port Angeles, sold out to start an airline in Seattle, crashed the plane, lost everything, made a second solo trip across the Olympics in 1938 during which he had broken his arm, and many other fascinating experiences.

Clearly Crisler had become the darling of the group, at least to the unattached females, while Lois slept. And, Helen added, looking pointedly down her nose at Lois, Crisler was single!

Mentally kicking herself, Lois began getting ready for the ascent up the Snowfinger. Her thoughts bubbled over with repressed curiosity about this man. Crisler was nowhere to be seen.

Large groups are seldom early starters. It was almost ten o'clock by the time the party lined out with their heavy packs and began struggling through dense stands of alder and willow between the campground and the end of the Snowfinger.

To Lois' surprise, someone had already been through and had cut out some of the brush with an axe. Who could have done this, she inquired?

Oh, that was Mr. Crisler, she was informed. He left with his pack at four o'clock. Lois pursed her lips thoughtfully.

The climb up the Snowfinger was grueling, sweaty and sometimes dangerous enough they considered roping up, but didn't. The snow had been undercut by the stream below. Occasionally they were forced to walk through caves beneath the snow, which was scary, since chunks frequently fell from the overhead.

Near the top they met Crisler with an empty packboard. He had already made one trip to Queets Basin and was enroute to Elwha Basin for a second load.

He told the group that if they would cross Dodwell-Rixon Pass quietly, they might observe a herd of elk on the other side. As he passed by Lois he completely ignored her, but flashed smiles at each of her lady companions, the ones that had stayed awake and listened to him the previous evening. Lois bit her lip in despair.

The herd of elk were still grazing on the lush, flower-covered meadow. A few were bedded down on a snowfield, chewing their cuds. The group spent a thrilling hour observing the beautiful tan colored, black-trimmed animals.

Lois divided her thoughts between this gorgeous, elusive mountain man and the herd of fascinating wild elk.

The following night they met again at Queets Basin. Herb was fixing something to eat over a tiny, smoky fire. Lois and several of her lady friends came over and asked if he'd mind if they watched an experienced mountaineer cook.

Herb, with southern politeness, bowed gracefully at the compliment. He explained his "cooking" techniques in great detail, demonstrating politely how he selected a particular can from his pack, how to attach the can opener, which way to twist the crank, how to avoid being cut by the lid, measures to avoid burning the can's contents and other trivia, which consisted of heating or cooking something simple, then eating it out of the same pan, or can.

His performance delighted the ladies. Everyone had a good laugh, followed by some good natured banter. The ladies left, including Miss Brown.

Later, Miss Brown found some excuse to wander by Herb's campsite again. He announced that he was going along on the climb up Hume's Glacier the next morning to photograph. If he returned in time, and it would please her, he would take her out stalking game in the basin.

Lois felt a rush of blood to her pale cheeks. Maybe he had noticed her after all. She regretfully said she hadn't been selected by the group leader and wouldn't be going. She gratefully accepted and left, telling no one about Herb's offer, staking everything on the evening private foray with Crisler. Wouldn't her friends be surprised and jealous?

The day dragged on. She had no idea when he would return, if it would be with the climbing party, or alone. Finally she got restless and went on a long hike in the basin.

Queets Basin is a rugged piece of landscape, but a delightful place to explore. Men sent to the basin by Lieutenant O'Neil in 1890 named it the Garden of the Gods.

The basin has several levels, the main ones at 3300 and 5500 feet elevation. The basin is mostly open, rolling heather meadows. One is constantly reminded that this area was recently glaciated, as the basin is dissected by a rollicking stream of milky snow melt which emerges from Humes Glacier. Tiny clear brooks cascade down from hanging snowfields. Far below one can hear the dull thunder of Queets River as it roars through an impassible canyon.

Rocky, glacier-polished outcrops are fringed by scraggly, twisted clusters of mountain hemlock, bent grotesquely by wind and tremendous annual loads of snow and ice.

The basin is wildflower paradise. Lois was fond of wildflowers. She found beargrass, paintbrush, avalanche lily, alpine yellow monkeyflower, Jeffrey shooting star and a dozen other flowers attempting to soften the raw harshness of the newly exposed land with gaudy blossoms. The drone of honey and bumble bees filled her ears.

Lois became unmindful of time in this fairyland. When she returned to camp the cook said that Mr. Crisler had returned looking for her, inquiring if Miss Brown was present, then went off into the woods with his camera. She pointed out the direction.

Dismayed, Miss Brown blundered madly into the woods in an attempt to find him. She was embarrassed, chasing a man through the woods like a school girl. But she couldn't help herself.

Suddenly she broke out of the woods onto a bluff overlooking a little meadow with a pond in its center. In the woods on the other side of the pond she caught sight of Crisler carrying his tripod-mounted camera over his shoulder.

Suddenly a black bear emerged from the brush, walked deliberately to the pond, jumped in and began splashing and wallowing.

Miss Brown shouted and waved her hat, trying to call Crisler's attention to the bear, which he apparently did not see. Without either hearing her call or recognizing her presence, he stalked off in the other direction and disappeared.

Miss Brown sank down, bitterly disappointed. She watched the bear enjoy its bath. Was she ever going to get this man's attention?

Back at camp Lois told her story about the bear, neglecting to mention Crisler.

At the campfire that night Lois purposely hung back. She wanted to tell Herb what happened, but was too embarrassed to admit that she had been stalking him.

It was just as well. A lady friend of Lois' told Herb about Miss Brown's experience with the bear, and that she had tried to alert him so he could capture this rare scene with his camera.

"No, I didn't see her or the beah," he drawled.

His eyes found Lois. "I've always wanted to photograph a beah in a wallah," he drawled. He really looked at Miss Brown for the first time.

"I didn't fall in love with him the first time I saw him. It was the next day," Lois was to write years later.

A 7x7 Bull Elk in the Bailey Range.

Herb stretched out that night on his bough bed under the stars in his sleeping bag and pondered his future. Was he destined to spend it alone? Like an old, outcast bull elk, kicked out from both the bachelor groups and the main herd? Could he expect to find a woman who would go into the mountains and live the rugged life necessary to photograph? Not likely, he reasoned.

Impossible, he concluded. Still, Miss Brown obviously wasn't afraid of the wilderness. But an English teacher? What if she discovered his schooling ended at the third grade ....?

Crisler's film of the Mountaineer's trip to Mount Olympus would be shown at the Club's annual reunion dinner in Seattle that fall. Lois secretly counted upon that as an excuse to see the elusive Crisler again in perhaps a more civilized situation.

The film brought enthusiastic response from club members. Miss Brown's duties at the dinner included toastmistress. She toasted almost no one else--except the fabulous Mr. Crisler, a fact which didn't escape every lady present.

Later that evening she did have a chance to talk briefly with Herb. He said he would be returning to Olympic National Park. As soon as his work was completed, probably in October, he would look her up.

October came and went without a word from Crisler. Miss Brown, although busy teaching at the university, was bitterly disappointed.

Herb didn't return to Seattle until near the Christmas holidays. Much to his surprise his answering service had a message from Miss Lois Brown. "I waited a month for you to call," the message read. "I decided if I ever wanted to see you again, I would have to call you!"

If a story involves two people and romance, it will likely have two versions. Here's Crisler's version of how he and Lois Brown met:

Now that the Olympics had been made into a national park, park officials wanted some color movies of its rugged scenery and wild animals. I was not making enough money to be able to buy film and keep up my work. It looked as if working for the Park Service might be fitting for someone like me.

Here was an organization trying to do just what I wanted. My ideas about conservation paralleled theirs. I felt I had unusual ability to get the pictures they wanted. Besides, I was especially in love with the Olympic wilderness and perhaps had seen more of it than any other man. I should fit into this organization like a well-formed key into a lock.

After it was arranged that I should take pictures for the Olympic National Park Service, I was very happy. I felt that I had really found my niche in life--nothing to do but the thing I wanted to do and felt called to do--and I started out to do my best.[1]

But flaws began to show up. The Park had an account for film, but there was no appropriation for a photographer's salary unless he had passed civil service. That was got around by putting me on as a temporary ranger. A park photographer is in a much higher salary bracket and the government furnishes his cameras for him besides.

Since this was what I wanted to do, the salary did not matter. But there was another catch. A ranger is supposed to clear park trails and do other maintenance work. My cameras and camping equipment weighed 65 pounds without food and I was planning to be gone from sources of supplies for as long as three weeks at a time, which would add another 20 pounds. That much I could carry with me. But the orders were that I must work some on the trails.

I was provided with a seven-foot cross-cut saw, two wedges, an eight pound sledge and an axe, so that I could cut out logs I found across the trails.

That was not all. The Park Service must know where their rangers are all the time. The service could not afford the publicity of having something happen to their rangers without their knowing at least where they were. So I must take a portable radio phone. They had a very light one, just out, the very thing for me--weight, 30 pounds!

With all this weight to relay across the mountains, for every 10 miles I moved forward I would have to walk 50 miles and could have my camera with me only one-fifth of the time. On my own, I had five times the chance to get unusual pictures as I had now.

But don't think that is all. A ranger must make out reports on everything that he does, and that is most important of all. What the big shots in Washington go by before they sign your paycheck is your report. If a ranger is smart, for every hour's work he will take two hours to make out a report. This would cut my photography time so short it would not pay me to pack along my camera. I can't spell so anyone can read it, and I can't write very plainly. Besides, I did not want to be a report maker. I wanted to take animal pictures. And come what might, I was going to take them. So I ditched everything but my camping outfit and cameras and took pictures.

In spite of no reports I continued to receive my check from the Park Service, and that fall delivered some good pictures to the superintendent. He was pleased, having a real feeling for the value and beauty of wilderness himself, and wanted me to take more pictures for the park. He suggested that I take the civil service examination.

I got the forms. Whoever figured them out could have been very smart about some things, but he surely did not know anything about taking animal pictures in my rugged Olympics. And if he did not know anything about it, how could he tell whether I knew anything about it or not? He couldn't. According to my answers to his questions, my head wasn't even fit to hang a hat on.

It seemed what I needed to get a job was education, not ability to do the work. I thought if I had to have education to bring the spirit of the Olympics to people, why I would get education.

So I went to the University of Washington. Looking over the different courses and points required, I decided this point system would be nearly impossible for me. But over at Parrington Hall, in the English department, was one complete unit of education that took my eye. If I could somehow uproot this unit and transplant it without it wilting, this would be my best chance of getting an education. This unit was called Miss Lois Brown.

I struck up a conversation with Miss Brown. To let her know of my skills and physical fitness, I remarked that I had climbed the highest peak in the Olympic Mountains. She was impressed. She said, "It must be wonderful to be able to climb mountains. Go on. Tell me more. You must live such an interesting life." I told her more.

In fact, when we parted, she knew practically everything I had ever done or said. I hadn't found out one thing about Miss Brown. She seemed so glad to have someone to talk to that I felt sorry for her. Poor woman, she must be very lonesome.

Later, I was informed that Miss Brown had not only climbed Mt. Olympus, but also Mt. Rainier, Mt. St. Helens, Mt. Hood, Mt Baker, and all the other major peaks of the northwest. [An exaggeration, perhaps, but Miss Brown did have considerable mountaineer experience.]

Everyone, it seemed, told Miss Brown about themselves but no one knew much about Miss Brown. I have known a lot of women that knew all the answers but here was one that knew all the questions.

I decided to skip all other subjects and start right in to get my Master's Degree, and to do my thesis on the life of Miss Brown.

My thesis research proved very interesting. Seventeenth century Pennsylvania pioneers branching off to Ohio proved to be her mother's side of the family. Her mother had been a school teacher. When still a young woman, she came west [to the Dakotas] and proved up on a remote homestead while living in a sod house. Her father, of English descent, was a circuit-riding Methodist preacher with a good brain. Preacher meets teacher. Results, Miss Brown.

Her mother decided she really had something there, and started spending a lot of her time to try and make her a super-intellect. She was so busy trying, she forgot to have any brothers or sisters for little Miss Brown.

By the time she reached school age, she was ready for the fifth grade, but for reasons of morale, they slipped her back a notch or two. Most of the family's income that was left over after the grocery bill was paid was spent on Miss Brown's education. That wasn't enough, so Mother Brown went back to teaching. Before Miss Brown was old enough to teach, she too was teaching, by a simple method of addition when filling out the application forms.

All this didn't impress me too much. I decided that I would reconsider and go back and major in love making. It looked to me that what education needed was not mechanical loving but a romantic lover. This behavior didn't agree with Freud or behaviorism. That barred me from the psychology class, so I had to set up my own course.

I almost flunked the first session. It was to be at Miss Brown's house, not far from the campus. Concrete steps led up through weeds, brush, shrubbery and trees that closed on all sides on an old two-story, vine and rose-bush-covered house. Wooded steps led to a railed-in front porch that extended half around the house. I rang the door bell and waited. I heard steps inside. The door slowly opened for only a little way, and there stood Miss Brown in her bathrobe, looking as unkempt as the old place.

'Go away,' she said. 'I have the flu. You might catch it.'

'Oh, is that all,' I replied, relieved, and walked right in, holding a corsage out to her. 'If I must catch it, I would rather catch it from a friend.'

'But I am going to the hospital. My neighbor is coming to take me soon.'

'I will stay until she comes.'

'But there's nothing to eat in the house.'

'I will take care of that. You lie down here on the davenport and don't tell me where anything is and we will see if I can get a meal.'

I stepped into the kitchen, turned on the light, and closed the door. My first impression was that I had made a mistake in trying this. I wondered if even Miss Brown knew where anything was in this kitchen. Frying pans, tea kettle, coffee pot, and kettles were strewn over the top of an old coal range. All had been used next to the smoky fire and were as black as soot on the outside. Over in the corner of the room was a little worn-out dirty sink with an assortment of cupboards around it. Five doors led out of the room. I opened one. It led to the front porch. I tried another. It led to the back porch, the next to the bathroom, one to the living room, of course, and the last--well, that was what I was looking for--the pantry.

There was clearly a place for everything and everything was in its place--the pantry. Here were rows of bottles of milk, minus the cream, in all stages of sourness; assorted home-canned fruit and homemade jams and jellies; empty glass jars, empty cans. Everywhere were empty pasteboard cottage cheese cartons and paper milk-bottle caps. I kept looking in boxes, bags, drawers, and cupboards until I accumulated enough groceries for a meal and went about preparing it.

As well as I could, I tidied up the kitchen, which was also the dining room. A faded curtain on a wire could be pulled across the room to cut off the view of the sink and stove.

With the table set with clean linens and the dinner hot on the range, I was all ready to surprise my bathrobe-draped hostess. I opened the door quietly and looked in, expecting her to be asleep.

What I saw was a complete surprise. There stood my hostess in a smart, white-trimmed, black and velvet dinner gown, smiling and looking as if she had never been sick a day in her life.

While we were eating dinner, joking and laughing, Miss Brown's small, kindly, dark-haired neighbor entered without knocking, to take her to the hospital. She stopped speechless, her eyes looking like Eddie Cantor's. Grade on first lesson--an "A".

The next few lessons were not so good. I began to find out that Miss Brown was not so lonesome after all. Every time I reported for a lesson, someone was either there or three or four would drop in later. Students, former students, friends, former friends, by ones, twos, threes, sometimes a half a dozen at once would pop in.

Some wanted advice--my boyfriend ditched me, my girl goes out with other fellows, that boy you said was all right tried to kiss me last night. Some had other troubles. Some just came to visit and talk art and literature. They would discuss Tennyson, Beethoven, Shakespeare, Virginia Woolf, or Hemingway.

I didn't know Virginia Woolf from Lydia Pinkham. Maybe the civil war was accurate after all. I realized I might be flunked out of such a class if I didn't do something, and quick.

Dropping by the old house one Friday morning to see if I might find some clue to why she had me for dinner only on Fridays, I was a little surprised to hear someone inside. I was sure Miss Brown was at the university. I rang the bell and a stout middle-aged woman with a very pleasant smile opened the door.

'Is Miss Brown at home,' I inquired.

'No. Won't you come in?' was her reply. I told her I would love to come in and rest a while. She said she was Miss Brown's housekeeper, and came every Friday. She went about her work.

After sitting a short while I went into the kitchen and told her that I would love to do the dishes. At first she demurred but I persuaded her, and started washing them. Now I realized why Friday only was dinner night. The same dishes we had used the week before were still unwashed, along with a week's accumulation.

Mrs. Reed and I worked hard almost all day. After everything was as neat as a pin I arranged a vase of flowers in the front room. 'Miss Brown will like that,' remarked Mrs. Reed. 'I think she is going to have company for dinner. She had me buy some extra groceries.'

At dinner I explained to Miss Brown that I had come by that morning to leave some flowers, found the housekeeper, and stayed to help her. This I did every Friday thereafter.

The second time I arrived to help Mrs. Reed told me that most of Miss Brown's boy friends just sat around talking and she thought Miss Brown should marry someone like myself. Soon she found out I was the one who came for dinner Friday nights. She became my sales woman. Miss Brown began coming home for lunch on Friday, and I began to get A's again.[2]

Meanwhile, Herb was working at whatever commercial photography he could find. He still lived in the tiny cubbyhole in the Fischer Building.

He bought a used typewriter and presented it to Lois, encouraging her to write something. She did make several attempts, and let Herb read what she had created. He made no comment.

One Friday night, while some of Lois' students happened to be at her house, Lois asked Herb's opinion about what she had written.

Herb asked her if she wanted his opinion with students present? She said yes.

"All Right. This is what I think. You don't have anything worthwhile to write about."

Herb had learned enough about Lois Brown by now that he thought he had found the coup de main, something which might eliminate unwanted academic competition, and decide her, an academic, to say "Yes" to an uneducated mountain man. He had discovered she was crazy about flowers, especially wildflowers, and that soft music put her into a romantic mood.

Herb fine-tuned his strategy. His record player, projector and film in the back of the car, he headed for Miss Brown's for the usual Friday night dinner:

Dinner was over, the screen was up, film threaded in the projector and all was ready to roll when the doorbell rang. The worst of luck! I was all set for my most important lesson with my best movies of the Olympic wilderness. I was working for an 'A' plus this evening.

In walked three girls. 'Oh. We are just in time to see a movie!' I snapped off the lights and turned on the projector, sat back in a sulk, and let it roll. Before the reel ran out I got an idea. My final reel they should not see.

At the finish I snapped on the lights. 'Show's over,' I said and sat down determined to out-sit all comers this evening.

Finally, after talking about almost everything I knew nothing about, they went home.

'The conversation was so interesting I forgot I have one more short film I would like you to see.' This was my very best wildflower picture, with soft background music. All the delicate coloring was well registered with lots of columbine and red heather. 'I call it a poem without words,' I remarked.

Near the last, two thumps turned into one rhythmic beat. I stopped the projector and walked over to where Miss Brown sat in the dim light, at first gently brushing her flushed cheek with my lips.

'But I want to write a book,' she protested.[3]

Herb had expected exactly such a ploy. He handed her a package. Brown eyes wide with surprise, Miss Brown opened it. Out rolled a supply of pencils and notebooks.

'Marry me. You will have something to write about,' was my reply.

That night I graduated.[4]

Yes, it was true. Although Miss Brown had taught creative writing at the University of Washington for years, she had never written anything for publication herself. Her time, and her considerable talent, had been directed towards her students. A few, including Irvin Petite, would become well-known northwest writers.

Miss Brown's composition class had, on average, about 18 students. Irvin Petite, after he became a professional writer, wrote the following:

The best thing that happened to me at the University of Washington, 30-odd years ago, were three teachers: Lois Brown, Trevoir Kincad and Edward G. Wagenknecht.

Miss Brown would come into class in a floor-length black dress, her arms full of books. These she piled on the work table at the front of the room. From their edges protruded dozens of strips of paper and cloth, old envelopes and strings. They sometimes included the Bible, Webster's Dictionary and books by the likes of Bertrand Russell, Aldous Huxley and Virginia Woolf--all of them writers I was to "meet" through her introductions.

Although Miss Brown craved writers-philosophers who were for their day independent thinkers, she was most circumspect in discussions of her own life. She reminded me of a Quaker maiden--but, also one who knew about Morgan le Fey.[5]

While Herb was courting Miss Brown he had the opportunity to closely observe the attitudes, actions, and reactions of the students at this designated and more or less desecrated spot of accepted higher learning.

Herb was unimpressed. He once wrote that, "It was encouraging to see the many serious-minded students who are studying and planning so they can contribute to the world of better living. To accumulate knowledge for yourself is a good thing, but knowledge for knowledge's sake is a parasitic luxury and gives one a pot-bellied brain."

At the beginning of their partnership Herb had told McQuade, "If I ever find a woman that will go into the mountains with me, our partnership is ended."

McQuade thought this over and decided their partnership would likely continue for a long, long time, if that was the excuse Herb Crisler was looking for to end it.

What woman would subject herself to such a vigorous, dangerous, hard life? Where would he ever find anyone who would, or could, follow him?

When it came to planning the wedding, Miss Brown was as elusive as ever:

Miss Brown was so busy teaching and correcting papers that there was no time to plan our wedding. I didn't see the need of all this fuss to find out student's grades anyway. I can tell an "A" student by their thick-lens glasses, callouses on their elbows and their mouth putting their chins in parentheses. You don't have to worry about an "A" student. He can get a gas station that a "C" student owns. That only leaves the "B" student to worry about. The poor "B" student is too smart to make money and too dumb to be an intellect. For them there is always social work.

`You should be ashamed of yourself,' someone may think. `You shouldn't talk that way about education. What about the scientists? This would be a dull world if it wasn't for them.' You are right: We wouldn't have the atomic bomb to worry about. The psychiatrist will say that my resentment is caused by me having no education myself. As if I didn't know! But psychiatrists are popular because people like to have other people figure out what they themselves already know.

However, I am going to marry education, and maybe I won't be resentful any more.

I could tell by Miss Brown's actions and remarks that being married wasn't going to make much change in her life. She planned to stay on and teach at the university, and of course the old house was close to her work but I could move in. That would be all right with her. She is a very generous person. She probably figured she could attend seminars in the summers while I carried on my photography in the Olympics.

This did not jibe with what I figured our married life would be. But how to win Miss Brown over to my way of life was a problem I had to solve. It worried me quite a bit. Then I got an idea. The next time I had an opportunity to talk with Miss Brown I put it into operation.

`You want to write,' I said. `How would you like to live in a log cabin in the mountains for a whole year? Then you could write all you please.'

`I would like that,' she said with an air of entering into the game of fairy-tale.

`Then take a year's leave of absence. I know just such a cabin and we can move in as soon as we are married.'

This silenced her for a moment. Miss Brown had lived in a world of thoughts, not actions. But her romanticism got the best of her. `I will,' she cried.

I asked every time I saw her if she had applied for her year's leave yet. She always said no. I kept prodding her and finally she asked and received it. But I could see that she felt as if she had been swung over a bottomless black chasm on a rope.

Others around the university felt the same. They started a movement to show Miss Brown how foolish she would be to marry someone who was out of her world, to move away from the center of culture and live a trapper's life in a log cabin with a hill-billy that went around with a camera shooting skunks. All this pressure from the brains, brought to bear on Miss Brown, complicated things for me, but romanticism is a great lever, and the wedding day was set.

Two days before the wedding I had to go to Spokane, Washington, so I did not have an opportunity to rehearse the ceremony, get my suit pressed, or do any of the other things a bridegroom is supposed to do before his wedding. A friend of mine promised to rehearse the ceremony with Miss Brown, then instruct me just before the wedding. I needed to have my suit cleaned and pressed, but as it would be Sunday morning when I arrived from Spokane it would be a problem for me to get it from the cleaners. But since we were being married at the home of a friend who lived out in the country, and Miss Brown planned to stay with them the night before the wedding, she suggested I have my suit delivered to her place and then just come there to dress.

I had seen the material for her wedding dress, a snow-white satin. I could see how beautiful and graceful Miss Brown with her soft brown eyes, and properly made up, was going to look, and I planned to make some color movies of her in her wedding gown.

While in Spokane I called her but was answered by one of her neighbors who told me that Miss Brown had laryngitis and was unable to talk. I hung up, disappointed in not being able to talk to her. Then it dawned on me that if she couldn't talk, she couldn't say Yes! This looked bad. I wondered if the university psychology professors had been talking to her?

It was about seven o'clock Sunday morning when I reached Seattle. As soon as I had breakfast, I went out to Miss Brown's house to dress. After shaving and taking a leisurely bath, I combed my hair before dressing in order not to leave any loose hairs on my clothes. After putting on my trunks I donned my white shirt, then collar and tie, then socks, sock supporters and shoes. I was keeping my suit newly pressed as long as possible. I looked at my watch. It was eleven o'clock. We were to be married at two. I had 20 miles to drive. I must hurry to get there in time to receive my friend's instruction and find out if Miss Brown was able to say Yes.

I looked in the closet for my suit. It wasn't there. I looked in the spare bedroom. No suit. I was getting desperate. It was my wedding day and I had no suit and this shirt-tailed, garter-legged outfit would be more appropriate in a burlesque show. I was

Herb & Lois Brown Crisler in Seattle about 1941.

79

wishing our country friends had a phone, when the front doorbell rang. That's the tailor with my suit, I thought, and rushed to get it.

When I opened the door, instead of a boy with my suit, there stood a sweet-faced, plumpish young lady. She blushed and stammered, `You have no suit!'

`Yes, I know,' said I.

`Where is Miss Brown?' she inquired.

`She's getting married,' I replied. The girl turned and walked away as if she thought it was about time.

I went into the bathroom to wash the perspiration off my face and when I turned to get a hand towel there was my suit.[6]

At two o'clock, when the music started, I took my position and watched the door at the far end of that strip of white leading from the evergreen-banked alter. Soon the folds of the snow-white gown appeared, tapered up to a superb waist and shoulders.

Miss Brown walked gracefully to where the white canvas turned to lead to the altar. I timed my actions as my friend had instructed me. But Miss Brown became self-conscious doing the skip-step glide of the wedding march and struck out walking at her natural gait. I turned as soon as I could and hooked my arm for her hand but she was too quick for me, and I had to run to catch her hand and pull it gently through my arm, and so we got to the altar together. And she could say Yes!

On Sunday, December 7, 1941, Miss Brown became my wife. That day a war started.[7]

The Japanese, of course, had struck Pearl Harbor only hours before.

Herb was 48. Lois Brown Crisler was 45.[8] Lois's friends at the university, who had tried diligently to discourage her marriage to this "ignorant" mountain man, gave the union six months to a year. So much for "educated" guesses!

Notes & Sources, Beyond the Trails, Chapter Eight.

1. Herb had turned over his commercial photography accounts to his partner, Don McQuade.

2. Herb Crisler, "Western Wildlife Photographer," Courtesy Ruby El Hult

3. Ibid.

4. Ibid.

5. Irvin Petite, The Seattle Times Sunday, 23 Jan., 1972

6. The lawn wedding took place in Kirkland, at the home of a former student of Lois Brown's, Edna Fagerberg.

7. Herb Crisler, "Western Wildlife Photographer," courtesy Ruby El Hult

8. Lois Brown was born in Spokane, Washington, August 8, 1896. She received her BA degree from the University of Washington in 1920, and her Masters in 1925.

Elkhorn Ranger Station

Donna Caldwell and 500-year-old
Sitka Spruce

Lake Billy Everett

Promise Creek Pass, Skyline Trail

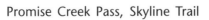

Olympic Harebell, endemic to Olympic National Park

Purple Lupine and the peaks of Mt. Olympus, from Hurricane Ridge

Spreading Phlox, smooth Douglasia, Martindales Lomatium

Avalanche Lily

Black-tail Deer

Blue Heron

Olympic Marmot, endemic to
Olympic Mountains

Mountain Goats

Cougar

Whiskey Bend Trail Sign

WHISKEY BEND
ELEVATION 1273 FEET

RICA CANYON	1.7	ELKHORN R.S.	11.5
MICHAEL'S RANCH	1.8	HAYES RIVER R.S.	16.8
HUMES RANCH	2.3	HAYDEN PASS	25.2
DODGER POINT	13.5	LOW DIVIDE	28.4
DOSEWALLIPS RD.	40.5	N. FORK, QUINALT RD.	44.0

Humes Ranch

Backpackers at Reflection Lake,
Bailey Range

Herd of Roosevelt Elk crossing the Hoh River

Black Bear in the Bailey Range

Group trekking in the Bailey Range,
Mt. Olympus behind.

Bobcat

Spotted Owl

Blue Grouse

Bull Roosevelt Elk in the rain forest

Herd of Roosevelt Elk in the rain forest

Subalpine Firs plastered with snow

Aerial, looking across the top of Mt. Carrie, Carrie Glacier, Mt. Olympus behind. Hoh Valley lies in between.

Boston Charlie's Camp, East of the Catwalk

Queets Basin, foreground, Mt. Olympus and Humes Glacier.

The author at Kimta Basin

Norma Sanderson negotiating the Catwalk

Castle-in-the-Cat in Cat Creek Basin

High mountain meadow, wildflowers, Mt. Ferry

9

Hume's Ranch. A Winter on Hurricane Hill

HI BEAUTIFUL
Tra la la lee-tra la la lu,
I'm so happy I don't know what to do--
I could sing a thousand years,
Or a century or two,
Couldn't stop singing just for you.

Where have you been all this time?
Now I've seen you, I've changed my mind.
Wanna be with you wherever you go,
And I promise to sing forever and ever more.

I'll sing a short song just for you,
And the lyrics will be only a word or two:

Hi, beautiful!
I'm so happy I don't know what to do.
Herb Crisler

The "log cabin" in the mountains Herb had referred to was Hume's Ranch,[1] a homestead located on the Elwha River, eighteen miles southwest of Port Angeles. The ranch could be reached only after a 2 1/2-mile hike from Whiskey Bend, a dead-end road above the Elwha Ranger Station. Because the Humes Brothers, and Ranch, plays such an important part in the history of the Elwha River Valley and the life of Herb and Lois Crisler, some description of its beginnings are in order.

The homestead's origins came about as follows: In the fall of 1897, three New York men, William E. "Will" Humes, his brother Martin and

Elwha Ranger Station, Elwha River Valley, Olympic National Park.

81

a cousin, Ward Sanders arrived in Seattle, with intentions to head for the Klondike gold fields. In July, two ship arrivals, the **Excelsior** at San Francisco on 15 July and the **Portland** at Seattle on 17 July, broke electrifying news of fabulous gold discoveries in the Klondike.

The nation, in fact the world, was suffering from a terrible depression, so such news resulted in an immediate stampede for Seattle and Alaska. Few people knew where the Klondike was, and for a time, it was assumed to be somewhere in the Northwest Territories, instead of the Yukon Territory.

Personal letters written by Will Humes, dated from 1897, on file at Olympic National Park, indicate the following scenario:

Once the Humes party reached Seattle they received two disheartening, but up-to-date, news items straight from people arriving from Skagway, Alaska: 1) The good ground in the Klondike had already been staked. 2)It was too late in the season to head north.[2]

Like many other bewildered stampeders in Seattle, the Humes party were victims of hype from untruthful promoters and press. They were also unaware of the stringent stipulations on supplies imposed by the Royal Canadian Mounted Police, stationed at the summit of Chilkoot Pass. Before anyone was allowed into Canada, each person was required to have a year's supply of food, plus ample tools and clothing to survive a year in the Arctic, or they were turned back. Since there was no place in the vicinity of Dyea, Alaska to buy such enormous amounts of supplies, the supplies had to be bought before sailing for Alaska.

The Humes brothers had been fur trappers in the Adirondack Mountains. They were no strangers to rugged, wilderness living. But they didn't have much money, so the news they received in Seattle changed their plans of heading north, at least for that year.

Instead, they inquired if there was someplace they could spend the winter trapping, hunting and living off the country until spring. They were assured there was, plenty of it, especially on the remote, wild Olympic Peninsula.

Only seven years had passed since James H. Christie, John Sims, Harris Runnals, Charles Barnes, John Crumback and Christopher Hayes, accompanied by their three dogs, Daisy, Bud and Tweed, known as the Press Expedition because they were sponsored by the Seattle paper by that name, had made a six-month-long sensational first north to south crossing of the Olympic Peninsula during the winter of 1889-90. The Expedition had made national headlines, and was still being talked about around Seattle. The party had entered the wilderness along the Elwha River near Port Angeles, which may have influenced the Humes brothers to select that city as their destination in search of a place to winter.

They arrived at Port Angeles on a steamer in October, 1897, and checked into a hotel. After inquiring around for some place to winter, they headed up the Elwha River on November 9. Their destination was a level bench along the river where they had been told they might find an abandoned log shack.

Here they spent the winter, hunting, trapping cougar, bobcat and other fur-bearing animals. For food they had trout, perhaps salmon, elk, bear and deer.

They tanned elk hides to make sleeping robes in preparation for the Klondike. William wrote letters attempting to borrow money from friends and relatives in New York to enable them to head north in the spring. They still entertained ideas of heading for the Klondike.

As the winter wore on, news from the Klondike became more discouraging. More than 70 stampeders had been killed on Palm Sunday by an avalanche on Chilkoot Pass. Tales of starvation, frostbite and death were common. River steamers heading up the Yukon had become trapped by ice, etc.

Especially of concern were rumors that many stampeders who had actually reached the Klondike in 1897 had been unable to locate claims and were destitute for a way to return home. A terrible famine was reported in Dawson City. Each paper they read on infrequent trips to Port Angeles had stories by disgruntled stampeders who felt lucky to have escaped the frozen north. Although the Humes boys were good woodsmen and hunters, we can also credit them with brains. They gave up going, which was wise, as only a tiny fraction of the tens of thousands of stampeders that actually reached Dawson ever found gold.

Their brother Grant joined them in the spring of 1899. The four men built a small, sturdy log cabin, bought pack horses, cleared hay meadows, built a hay barn and planted fruit trees. They also built another cabin on a mining claim farther up the river.

Besides hunting and trapping, the Humes brothers began outfitting and guiding big game hunters and transporting freight for Forest Service crews and mountaineers.

Both William and Grant explored and climbed in the Olympic Mountains prior to 1907, at which time they contracted to outfit The Seattle Mountaineers Club first expedition to climb Mount Olympus.

Will pioneered several mountaineer routes, and was rewarded by having Humes Glacier named in his honor.

Will returned to New York in 1914, married and remained in the East. The other two men also drifted away. By 1915, Grant Humes was alone on the Elwha River. Grant became well known, and lived at Hume's Ranch until he became ill in 1934. He died April 20, 1934 at Port Angeles.

Grant Hume's old barn on a meadow beside the Elwha River. Note cabin on bench above big hay meadow.

At the time the newlywed Crislers moved into Hume's Ranch, the sturdy log cabin had long been deserted. The homestead was owned by Peninsula Plywood Corporation. Herb obtained permission to use the place for a very small monthly rent.

Back to Herb's account after the wedding:

> The next week, as soon as Lois got all of her term papers graded, we loaded into the old two-door Hudson all the bedding and cooking utensils we thought we would need for living a "year" in the wilderness, and started for Hume's Ranch.
>
> We left Seattle early in the morning, crossed Puget Sound to Port Townsend by ferry, drove to Port Angeles where we bought beans, salt, rice and a pair of rubber boots for each of us.[3]

Port Angeles buzzed with news. Everyone was talking about the bombing of Pearl Harbor. Rumors flew: Japanese soldiers had already landed at Neah Bay; Japanese aircraft were reportedly seen through the winter mists; Japanese submarines were lurking around Port Angeles harbor to attack naval shipping, etc., etc.

The war wasn't the only headline news item in Port Angeles. The "Lady of the Lake" murder,[4] the most sensational horror story in Port Angeles' history, almost overshadowed the war news. The murderer had been apprehended and brought to Port Angeles in the fall of 1941 to await trial. With all the hysteria Herb was delighted to leave town and head for the hills.

As the Crislers drove west out of Port Angeles, they were stopped at several main intersections by sentinels and asked to show their credentials. Japanese soldiers were expected to invade the Olympic Peninsula momentarily. With such disastrous thoughts on their minds, Herb and Lois headed into the comparative tranquility of the wilderness.

They stayed the night of December 20 at Wamilla Inn[5] with Rhea & Art Shellenberger, five miles from Whiskey Bend. They made arrangements for the Shellenbergers to receive their mail.

The following morning, with gloomy, gray storm scud hanging over the moody, dark forest like a wet, woolen blanket, they bucked snow drifts up a narrow, winding road through old-growth forest to Whiskey Bend, the Elwha River Trail trailhead.

Daylight only lasted about eight hours, less beneath the towering, moss-covered forest on an overcast day. They got out of the car and peered around. A wet chill immediately seeped through their city clothing.

Drifts of snow, covered with wind-blown debris, limbs, needles, mosses and big-leaf maple leaves, lay strewn about the forest floor. The forest loomed dark and somber. A cold rain, mixed with occasional flakes of wet snow, slanted through the forest canopy. Each gust of wind shook down wet snow from the boughs, creating sounds like the pattering of tiny feet. Wind moaned through the tops of the tall, swaying fir trees with an eerie wildness.

What went through Lois' mind? This was zero hour! What would her life be like after this? Lois finally managed to sum up the courage to write about this bittersweet time of her life, but not until years later.

Undaunted, Herb selected what he thought they would need from the car and loaded both packs. Fortunately Lois was no stranger to a loaded packboard. They headed up the snowy trail.

Herb's thoughts were upon reaching Hume's Ranch, seeing the condition of the place and getting the cabin dried out before nightfall. Many years later he also would write about this particular time:

> I had a problem to select enough bedding, warm clothing to withstand the rain, and food to make my new bride comfortable. No one had lived in the cabin for years. The skunks and pack rats had taken over. Most of the moss chinking was out from between the logs, and the roar of the Elwha River was so loud you couldn't hear yourself think. The sheet iron, air-tight heater, was burned out, and the forest, including all dead wood available, was sopping wet, as well as ourselves. Lois never said much--but I could tell she was doing a lot of thinking!
>
> I finally had a fire going and was able to keep ourselves in a "no man's land" between comfort and misery. It took me several days of hard work to establish even this survival stage: get together enough wood to keep the fires going while we went to the car and packed in enough bedding, clothing and beans to maintain this standard of living.
>
> The first day I noticed a bit of wilderness "newspaper" on the cabin window, which I hoped Lois couldn't read. It was the mud prints of a bear's paws and nose. He had looked through the window that first night to see what was going on. In about a week I had shifted our position from a primitive survival to the comfortable side, and I could start planning what I wanted to do.

The following is a quote from what one of Lois' former English students wrote about Lois at this stage:

> Lois Brown Crisler was not the type for the role of wilderness wife. Highly educated, sensitive and shy, she was out of place in the log cabin to which Cris took her following the wedding. Used to the conveniences of city living, she could not cope with a place where heat, light and cooked food all evolved from hard, human labor. She smiles now at how she hugged the stove, or went outside between rain storms to "admire nature" while Cris cut wet logs for fuel, packed the necessities of life from the car parked three miles away--and even did the washing.

Herb's writing continues:

> What I hoped to accomplish was to accumulate enough film to be able to produce a movie that would give people the same feeling towards the wilderness that I had while living off the country. [The

84

1930 trip] Our first problem was to be able to live in the wilderness with other living things without infringing on their rights. In our hearts was a written bill of rights for the wild animals and all living things. All enforcement laws must first be written in the hearts of the majority, and Lois and myself were the majority here at Hume's Ranch. With only a few dollars accumulated, and no income whatsoever,[6] we had started a project that should have had eight thousand dollars a year allotted for expenses, and yet we spent nine years in this manner.[7]

From Lois we get yet another version:

Cris brought me to this old log cabin in the wilderness on a December day [the twenty-first] in 1941. It was the day after I finished reading bluebooks and turned in the final grades for my fall classes at the U.

It was a gray, wet day. As we left the forest and entered the clearing I had my first view of Hume's Ranch.

Cris opened the door and we came into the cabin. My heart sank. The puncheon floor was pitted with caulk marks and littered with knee-high piles of trash brought in by pack rats.

The furniture was a couple of home-made wooden benches and a long table under the little windows on one side. In the two dark corners opposite, stood a rusty jumbo heater and a sagging bed spring propped on apple boxes. The air smelled of mice, dust and skunks.

Cobwebs and dust covered the log walls. From between the logs half the moss chinking was gone.

We had one of our wedding presents with us, a Coleman(R) gas lantern. From outside at night the cabin looked like a house built of jackstraws. Streaks of light ran between the logs.

All our supplies were out at Whiskey Bend, except what we had brought in on the packboards on our backs.

My first night at Hume's Ranch I was half scared anyway. I had noticed a tan smudge in the middle of each lower pane in the six-pane windows. What made that? I asked Cris.

It was the bear, he explained. He took me outside and pointed out paw marks on the log below each smudge.

A creek runs under the apple tree at the corner of the porch. The bear had got his nose muddy picking up apples. Then he had stood up and methodically inspected the inside of the cabin.

The logs didn't feel very thick to me that first night. I wished the river would stop its rush for just one minute, so I could listen for stealthy footsteps outside.

The next morning it turned cold. I was a hothouse plant. I nearly froze.

There was no wood. Cris rigged a box on his packboard and began backpacking some old wet chunks left from Grant Humes' time, from down in the stump pasture.

I huddled by the stove in ski clothes and sweater. I didn't know how to take hold. It looked to me as if I would freeze long before I learned.

Cris had everything to do at once. We made a daily five-mile run to and from the car before breakfast. Cris brought home 100 pound loads, as I found out later. I trustingly accepted his statement that my own loads weighed about 25 pounds.

But the day we got down to where the spring scales were, in the car pack, I learned differently.

The scales only weighed up to 50 pounds. After we got home, I took Cris' pack apart to weigh it. I put my foot down right then about 100-pound packs. (My foot slipped. It took me about five years to make that edict stick. Or any other for that matter!)

Cris grinned. 'Did you weigh yours?' he asked. Mine weighed 45 pounds.

Cris washed the logs in the living room with suds and hot water. He scrubbed the hand-hewn puncheon floor. For days afterward it was wet and cold. With lye he broke down the black grease on the ancient utensils hanging on logs behind Grant Hume's cracked stove in the kitchen. In every spare second he backpacked more wood.

Now, looking back, I can see what a stranger in a strange land I was. My education was just beginning.

City girl, schoolmarm, bookworm--shy, modest, sensitive--no wonder I was nervous. It was going to be years before I learned to wipe my nose on my cuff and my pocket knife on my trail pants.[8]

"I want us to have our first Christmas alone at Hume's Ranch," Herb had announced one day shortly after they were married. That was the reason they rushed to the ranch before Christmas.

Lois describes that first Christmas together:

On Christmas afternoon Cris took me along to get the tree. Down by Idaho creek he found a young white fir.

In the dark little cabin there was no room for the forest tree on the floor. Cris cut off its tip and set it on the new oilcloth on the table. Its flat fronds looked varnished on top and white underneath. It looked very formal and graceful.

I was thankful to string popcorn and silver the cones. It gave me a pretext to sit down.

Cris hung red India prints in a bower around the bunk, and decorated the cabin with cedar and fir boughs.

The cabin smelled of new oilcloth, soap and the wild fir still wrapped in ozone. The gasoline lantern hissed. Outside the river rushed. The window panes looked dark and bright.

I announced to Cris a complete new discovery in my life. This was fun, to work like a beaver, cleaning this little old cabin away in the wilderness! It was actually--I could hardly believe this--actually more fun than going to some ski lodge for the holidays.

We put our presents around the base of the tree, then opened the door. It was snowing. I wondered if it would get so deep we couldn't go out to the car for more grub.

We read the story in Matthew and sang 'Joy to the World' a little bashfully.

The next morning we 'had the tree.'

We had agreed to give each other only 50 cent presents. Cris had five presents for me, including a Chinese lantern of powder puffs, a box of incense, lily bulbs and a jew's harp.

I gave Cris a pair of glittering black castanets. (They cost $3.50)

Evidently we both had the same idea--the big silence up here. No radio, no phone, no newspaper. Just the mountains, the great forests--and us, starting a new way of life.[9]

Years later, while on lecture circuit, stuck in some hotel at Christmas time, with horns blaring and people pushing, the Crislers would fondly recall their first, very special Christmas together at Hume's Ranch.

Soon after arriving Herb stopped whatever he was doing at the moment and said to Lois: 'Let's not ever get so busy we don't have time to drop everything and ramble.' Hikes they could afford:

That first winter up here at Hume's ranch we rambled almost daily. The five-mile morning run out to Whiskey Bend to retrieve supplies from the car and back didn't count.

But in the afternoon we put on our parkas and went out circling the trails to see what was going on.

To Cris a muddy patch in the trail was a newspaper. I could read Einstein and Infeld's "Evolution of Physics." But I couldn't figure out this Hebrew script of the wilderness.

Sometimes Cris chuckled and stopped to read a whole paragraph. Sometimes he caught the headline at a glance and strode on.

To me the book was closed. Like a city person I just noticed if things were "pretty."

Cris was surprised when he discovered that his wife was 'forest illiterate.' He began to teach me the alphabet. The doe's track, the fawn's, the buck's. A walking track, a running track with the toes splayed out and sometimes the fetlock mark showing. Wildcat tracks. The difference between skunk and rabbit tracks, between squirrel and mouse. Elk tracks--bull, cow and calf.[10]

Herb describes how they set up housekeeping:

Hume's Ranch was located on a "divide" between civilization and a living wilderness. In order to exist, we had to bring in some civilization. We could not forage, so we had to grow as much of our subsistence as possible. We did not have sufficient means to buy all our groceries. Our vegetable garden had to be fenced with pickets split by hand. All things had to be done without money.

All through the first winter I worked long, hard hours: cooking, washing, cutting firewood, fixing up the old cabin. I split six-foot palings, and erected a high paling fence around a 100 by 100 foot plot of land for a garden. This high fence was to protect the garden from the wild animals that came into the clearing--elk, deer, bear, coyotes, cougar, wildcats, and numerous other small game such as squirrels, weasels, skunks, etc. All were welcome, as were many species of birds and insects--even ants. I wanted to live with them. Not as a scientific observer, not as an invading tourist, but as a fellow inhabitant in their wilderness home. I felt no fear nor superiority. While there are some things I can do that they can't, there are many things they can do that I can't. Most of them can outrun me. They can travel and live off the country easier than I, and, as a whole, they have healthier living habits than man. For example, their coat is far superior and man will even murder an animal for his coat--and then give it to his wife or girl friend, so she can feel superior to other women.

I spent most of the first spring and summer at Hume's Ranch spading and planting the garden, setting out raspberry and strawberry plants, and pruning thirty-year-old apple trees that the Humes brothers had planted. They never tried to grow anything in the vegetable line except potatoes. I did some filming of the inhabitants of the living wilderness around the ranch and made a photographic trip into the Interior.[11]

On this 1942 trip, Lois' first to Cream Lake, Bob Crisler, now 15, came over from Seattle and went along.

They first went to Hotcake Camp. Lois had been this far in 1941 before they were married, and had returned to her car alone while Herb went on into the Bailey Range.

They added a lean-to guest shelter at Hotcake Camp, so they could take visitors there from Hume's Ranch on overnight trips.

Hotcake Camp had received its name years before, during the 1930s, because of a cast-iron stove top. One of the buildings had burned at Olympic Hot Springs. Thrown out was a wood-burning stove with a commercial-sized cast-iron griddle top. Herb decided the griddle was what he needed at his camp on Appleton Ridge. Never mind that the piece of cast iron weighed over 100 pounds! He tied the stove top onto his pack board and carried it in. Later Herb admitted, with a grin, that this was the heaviest pack he ever carried into the mountains.

He built a rock fireplace in front of the lean-to, complete with stove pipe, and set the griddle over the top. Many memorable flapjack feasts were cooked on that Paul Bunyan-sized griddle.

After leaving Hotcake Camp, they went on to Cat Basin where Herb showed them where he intended to build a shelter. They crossed the Catwalk, Lois' first of many, many crossing of this razor-back, difficult access to the Bailey Range.

At the east end of the Catwalk, Boston Charlie's camp, they stopped to rest. Herb said, 'We could camp here. I have a cache.' He astonished Lois by diving into the bushes and coming out with a frying pan.[12]

Lois looked into the brackish water and saw tadpoles and larva swimming around, thankful when Herb announced they were going on. The frying pan went back into its hiding place. They continued, traversing the west part of the Bailey Range and camped at what they would later call Eleven Bull Basin.

The following day they went on to Cream Lake. On the north shore, with a view across the lake and of the mountains, Herb started building a shelter cabin.

On an earlier trip to Cream Lake, Herb had been looking for a dry place to sleep beneath a clump of large subalpine fir.[13] He noticed a rotten spot on the side of one huge fir and struck the scar with an axe. The tree sounded hollow. He chopped through into a large, dry area, pushed his pack through, crawled in and spent the night. For decades he used the hollow tree as a cache and covered the opening with a hinged door to keep animals out.

This fir, six foot nine inches in diameter and 130 feet tall, is the largest known of its species in existence, according to the national park service.

Out of grub, they returned to Olympic Hot Springs, then drove Bob Crisler into Port Angeles to send him back to Seattle. When Lois picked up their mail she found two letters from her dean at the university demanding to know if, and when she was coming back. There was also an offer to raise her salary.

She agonized all night over the decision. She appealed to Herb. 'Do what you want. I'm staying here,' he said briskly.

Lois felt as if she was out on a limb. She was not a decision maker. Finally she wrote a letter of resignation. She realized that Herb had waited a long time for the opportunity to spend as much time as possible photographing the Olympic Mountains and their unique, beautiful plants and wildlife. The thread linking her with the academic world finally severed, she decided to apply herself to what they were attempting to accomplish.

To celebrate Lois' decision, Herb worked 18 hours a day getting the garden in shape then took Lois back on a second trip to Cream Lake!

Herb's garden kept them from going hungry. He raised almost everything they needed, except potatoes. He earned a winter's supply of spuds by helping Billy Everett dig his annual crop on his farm down on the Elwha, near where the old bridge now stands.

Herb hauled humus from beneath the alder and big-leaf maple trees in the nearby forest in his wheelbarrow to build up the soil for his garden. The fertilizer worked wonders and was free:

> We bought a tin can sealing machine, and canned lots of corn, tomatoes and peas from our garden.
> We also had lots of apples for applesauce, and wild blackberries. After the first summer, we had an
> abundance of raspberries and strawberries, more than we and our many guests could eat, so we were
> able to can these also.[14]

The Crislers often had visitors, both two-legged and four. The number of two-legged visitors would swell the longer they remained at Hume's Ranch, especially after their films were shown each winter nation-wide, until the numbers became a tidal wave of people who wanted to meet the Crislers and see where and how they lived.

A few were Lois' friends from the university--curious, no doubt, to see how she was making out as a wilderness wife. Perhaps encouraging her to return to a "civilized" academic life in Seattle. We have no indications that she considered doing so.

Herb was well known and liked, although he cherished his privacy also. People respected the fact that, although not making any money, he was making films of their beloved Peninsula and its wildlife.

Lois, from all accounts, was a gracious, considerate hostess. However, she had a tendency to remain aloof at times. Ruby El Hult claims Lois frequently had the capacity to "shut people out" for long periods. Hazle M. Chapman, who knew the Crislers well, also remembers that Lois sometimes withdrew like a turtle hiding beneath its shell for long periods of time.

Hume's Ranch was, and still is, a favorite destination for overnight week-end campers, trout fishermen and day hikers.

Sometimes a dozen guests would arrive for the weekend. Leaving a comfortable home in the city to backpack into the wilderness to visit friends in a log cabin held a certain allure. Many probably yearned for what they assumed was the "simple" life.

Some bedded down in one of two other split-shake buildings which adjoined the old cabin. Others camped beside the river, down by the hay meadow.

Herb eventually built a lean-to shelter near the cabin for guests to sleep under. Lois named it the "bothy", which meant guest shelter in another language. The "bothy" would sleep twelve. Later, wishing to expand the garden, the "bothy" was torn down and another smaller one built farther up the hill.

Crisler writes about other bounties from Hume's Ranch:

The bothy, located just above Hume's Ranch cabin. A place for guests to sleep.

Besides the berries and vegetables, we had fresh rainbow trout from the river and in the fall, fresh apple cider. Not only did I raise enough produce to feed our guests and ourselves summer and winter, but throughout the growing season, I would take backpack loads to friends in Port Angeles. In late fall the bears would come to get what apples were left after the cider and apple sauce making. One time I had an unusual experience in this connection.

A bear let me get within six feet from him while I was filming him standing on his hind legs, gathering apples with his front paws. By talking softly to him, he relaxed and actually laid down and went to sleep near the apple tree--after he got his belly full of apples.

In the winter elk and bear could often be seen in the meadow or swimming the river. The big cat never swam the river if he could help it. The animal would go miles to find a log to cross on. Half a mile up the river from the ranch was a trail bridge across the river with a three-foot-high guard rail on each side, built out of six-inch poles. The cougar preferred to walk the guard rail, although the bridge was across a narrow canyon, and the roaring Elwha River was 25 feet below.

The cougar has a large circuit hunting route which takes him about 10 days to cover. One cougar included Hume's Ranch on his circuit. If there was snow on the ground, we could count on seeing his tracks across the rail of the bridge, in the forest beyond the fence or near the root cellar where we kept all our canned produce, apples and potatoes. This root cellar was dug out of the side of the mountain, and the back end was covered with logs and dirt. The front outside was a shake roof, overhanging to keep snow from banking against the door.

One evening Lois went out to the root cellar to get some things for supper. When she came to the overhang at the door of the cellar, she had a strange feeling that something was watching her. She said her first impulse was to run for the cabin, but she gained control of herself and went about her chore. Next morning I went out to the cellar, and there were big cat tracks on the roof, where he had stood watching. It is hard to say what might have happened if Lois had run.[15]

Herb had a more intimate introduction to this, or another cougar. He was several hundred yards behind the cabin hauling leaf mould with his wheelbarrow when he noticed a cougar calmly watching his activities from a forest glade only a few yards away. The cat's eyes stared at him without expression.

Herb set down his wheelbarrow and began backing down the trail, wishing for his camera, but also curious about what the animal might do. The cat followed at a distance of about 75 yards.

When Herb was 50 yards from the cabin he ducked behind a tree then sprinted for home. Herb's dash ended abruptly as the cougar sailed past him, then bounded back into the path ahead of his astounded playmate:

I put on the brakes and skidded to a stop. The cougar calmly sat there, with those beautiful big, golden eyes looking at me, as much as to say: what do we do next? At this time I would like to know too, the answer to that question. I knew that I couldn't win in a foot race. After a few seconds that seemed hours, I decided to scream at the top of my voice, as if I were badly hurt. This, I hoped, would bring Lois running to see what had happened, and in some way might solve the problem. But it didn't work as I hoped. Lois happened to be lying on the grass in front of the cabin, taking a sun bath, and when she heard me scream, she thought something was coming down the trail, and she ran into the cabin and closed the door until she could put on more suitable clothes.[16]

The big cat solved my problem in a very simple way. When I let out that awful scream, he bounded into the air as if his whole body was made of springs, then took off up the mountain like a scared cat. He went about 20 yards and then assumed a leisurely gait, stopping two or three times to look back at me as much as to say: what got into you? Now that I have had more experience with wild animals, I think that cougar had seen me working in that glade many times, and he thought, of course, that I had seen him. Maybe he wanted to get better acquainted--maybe he did want to play--who knows?

One thing for sure, he didn't want to kill me. He could easily have done that.[17]

The Crislers were so busy they didn't often get out to collect their mail from a box at Wamilla Inn. War occupied everyone's minds and actions. Much defense construction was underway to build large artillery bunkers and military installations along the Straits of Juan de Fuca and the Pacific Ocean. Only when they went to town for supplies, or when visitors came by, sometimes bringing several newspapers, did they learn the latest war news. People who normally never planted vegetables were starting victory gardens, to help the fresh produce situation, so service men could have what was available through regular distributors. It wasn't unusual for the Crislers to return home and find a few packets of seeds left by some thoughtful visitor.

Expecting a Japanese aerial attack on Port Angeles, the government instructed the U.S. Forest Service, through a civilian program called the Aircraft Warning Service, to man strategic fire lookouts on the Peninsula to watch for enemy aircraft. Hurricane Hill Lookout, on Hurricane Ridge, a few miles south of Port Angeles, west of the present day national park visitor's center, was usually manned only during the fire-season. The government decided the lookout should be manned year round as an observation point guarding the Straits of Juan de Fuca against possible carrier-based Japanese war planes. The isolated job was deemed suitable for a married couple.

Herb suggested they could do their bit for the war effort by volunteering for the job. Lois agreed. The job paid a small salary and food. Herb and Lois needed the income. Herb had sold his guns and given up hunting, so he couldn't supplement their larder with game.

Don McQuade tells of paying the Crislers a visit about that time, noticed their limited cuisine, and invited them to go into town with him for dinner. He ordered steak, hoping this would serve as an example. The Crislers poured over the menu for a long, long time. Lois ordered steak, but Herb ordered beans, laughingly insisting his stomach might revolt at steak, since they would be returning home to a steady diet of beans. Herb never lived that down.

Hurricane Hill was eight miles, by trail and road, from Whiskey Bend, four thousand feet higher in elevation. If it hadn't been for the bulge of the mountain they could have probably looked up from Hume's Ranch and seen the lookout. To reach this lofty peak and lookout, the Civilian Conservation Corps constructed a road, called the Wolf Creek Trail, from Whiskey Bend, near the present-day Elwha River trailhead, to the peak during the early 1930s. The term "trail", instead of road, stuck and was appropriate, as it was a narrow, winding road with several frightening switchbacks.

Hurricane Ridge Lookout, 1942. "The Lookout was a spun-sugar house when powder snow fluffed deep." (Lois Crisler)

The present 18 miles of road from Heart of the Hills to Hurricane Ridge was started by the Park Service in 1950. A lot of dynamite was used to blast a road out of solid rock, and construction engineers, workers and equipment alike were severely tested. The initial road, called Govan's section, was opened to the public in 1958, but the road as we now know it wasn't completed until 1970.

An interesting note about construction of the Hurricane Ridge Visitors Center. All the timbers and materials for the lodge were hauled up the Wolf Creek Trail by Arvie Smith with his West Coast logging truck, a remarkable feat because of the hairpin curves. The Visitors Center opened, summers only, several years before the new road was completed.

After the new road opened in 1970, the Wolf Creek Trail reverted back to exactly that, and is maintained by the National Park Service.

Living on a mountaintop, for the Crislers, turned out to be a memorable adventure. Most people would have thought it an unbearable ordeal.

Herb, of course, took along his cameras. Never to be without fresh vegetables, he also took garden seeds! Garden seeds in the fall? To the top of a mountain? Yes, wherever Herb went, if he planned to stay long, a garden would soon be sprouting. Later, while photographing wildlife north of the Arctic Circle, he raised a few chives and parsley, possibly the first (and perhaps only) garden on the North Slope. Herb wrote about the Hurricane Hill experience many years later:

From the last of October we were snowed in for seven months. Our lookout was a 13 X 13 foot building, with windows all around. It was bolted to solid rock. There was a five-eighths inch steel cable stretched from all four corners of the building and anchored to the rock several feet away. This gave the lookout additional protection to prevent it from being blown off the top of the mountain. On each side there were two shutters hinged at the top so they could be closed to protect the windows if unoccupied, or propped up on struts to give an unobstructed view if occupied.

The first month was a peaceful, leisurely existence. Then the storms came. No one had ever spent the winter on Hurricane Ridge, but whoever named it made an understatement. The strong winds lasted for days, and were so powerful I had to stretch a cable along the crest of the ridge to hold onto, in order to get in and out the door. The window shutters broke their struts, and flapped in a storm like a bunch of grouse taking off. I was afraid they would be torn from their hinges, and be hurled through the windows. I wanted to get them closed and bolted down, but when I grabbed one I would be thrown around like an old rag hanging on a clothes line in a high wind. By hanging on until there came a short lull, and with Lois' help, I managed to get them all bolted down, but it took most of the day. Inside, it was like living in a flat bottomed boat on a rough lake. The building had worn its anchorage until it wasn't snug to the rock any more. It would roll, jump up, then come down with a slap on the rock like a boat against a wave. At first we expected it to take off any minute, but after a few exceptional storms, we could console ourselves with: Oh, well, it has been lots worse than this.[18]

Lois described the interior of the lookout:

The 13 X 13 foot space was occupied with a table, bunk, stove, water storage cans, lockers, and easy chair, and the fire-table pillar filling the center, as well as Cris's three-by-six-foot garden bed in one corner. This left only a narrow isle around three sides of the fire-table.[19]

Herb continues:

These winds created some unusual effects. They blew the wet snow on the trees which became a solid mass, like white marble statues. This snow was unlike dry snow that builds out on the lee side of an object. The snow here builds up in the teeth of the wind, shot on like arrows.[20]

Christmas was approaching. They were sleeping in another building, actually the wood shed, 100 feet below the lookout. The wood shed, being more protected, didn't receive quite the full impact of the hurricane force winds as the lookout did, so sleeping during storms was less interrupted.

On the morning of December 7, 1942, their wedding anniversary, Herb had been on watch since midnight. He had baked a pound cake, using the last butter and eggs in the lookout.

After Lois woke up she went up to the lookout for breakfast. Herb held up the cake. He was, Lois would write, "pleased with himself", because the cake had turned out beautifully. He went down to their storehouse in the woodshed to get eggs for breakfast. They had 36 dozen stored in waterglass. When he returned, the sparkle was wiped off his face. "Lois, we got no eggs. We got an omelet. A 36-dozen egg omelet." He led her down and pointed to a frozen mass of broken eggs.

A park ranger had promised to snowshoe up with their mail about the third week in January. On December 24, a gray, dismal day, Herb called Lois to the window and pointed. Black dots on the snow were creeping towards the lookout. We're being invaded, but not by Japanese, he muttered, lowering the binoculars. After a while the door burst open. In crowded a red-haired, burly sergeant and four soldiers.

Importantly, without even saying hello, the sergeant asked to use the phone. According to Lois, "He nearly swamped the lookout with his sense of importance." He called his major down in Port Angeles. From the conversation, something equally as important as a Japanese invasion had taken place. The sergeant concluded his call by saying, "The men are in pretty bad shape, sir." He urged that relief trucks be driven as far as possible with hot coffee, food and medical supplies.

What alarmed the sergeant so? His men, "trained" as they might be, were not prepared for the deep snow and steep climb up Wolf Creek Trail to Hurricane Hill. They were scattered up and down the snowy slopes in various stages of collapse!

Fifty soldiers, most from New York, had been in a training camp down by Wamilla Inn. This was their last day before moving out. Their company commander explained there was a lookout on top of the mountain in back of camp. To "celebrate" their final day of training, they were to drive up the road until the snow stopped their vehicles, hike to the lookout, then have the rest of the day "free!"

Without snowshoes or skis, floundering in soft, wet snow to their waists, the men began to collapse. The mountainside was now littered with "casualties".

But that was not all. Rhea Shelleberger, from Wamilla Inn, upon learning the men were going to the lookout, sent along several weeks accumulation of Crisler's mail. The mail had been distributed between the men. Consequently, the mail was also now scattered up and down the mountainside!

Slowly the tired soldiers straggled in. One was a lieutenant. Another lieutenant was somewhere below. Each soldier, if he had any, handed over his packet of soggy mail upon arrival.

Since there was only room for a few at a time in the lookout, Herb went down and built a fire in the woodshed. The Crislers made kettle after kettle of hot cocoa and served up boxes of pilot bread. After each group was fed, Herb led them down to the wood shed to thaw out.

Eventually everyone was fed and accounted for except the other lieutenant. They could see him lying in the snow, a tiny black speck in the distance. Worried, Herb strapped on his snowshoes and went down, thinking the man might be hurt. He had made the mistake of wearing hip boots! Eventually this officer also made it to the top and sprawled on the bunk. It took seven cups of hot cocoa before he revived.

The rest of the winter's happenings seemed an anticlimax after feeding 50 soldiers in a 13 X 13 foot cabin, a truly "loaves and fishes" experience, which they never forgot.

Herb and Lois alternated so that each was on watch 12 hours a day. Many days they were unable to see between wood shed and lookout because whirling, swirling snow-packed clouds enveloped the mountain top in complete white-out.

To pass the time they read until their eyes gave them trouble. With cabin fever threatening, the skies would suddenly clear.

Dawn would reveal surroundings so glorious the storm was soon forgotten; Mount Olympus and the Bailey Range loomed, draped with majestic new tapestries of white, to the south. Subalpine firs, soldier-straight and trim before the storm, were transformed into white, often hunchbacked blobs and grotesque shapes without form. The subalpine firs have adapted to alpine regions and deep snow. It's slender, short boughs, and upturned needles discourage the bough from collecting heavy loads of snow like most evergreens. Some became so loaded their tops bent almost to the ground, as if bowing for mercy before the power of winter. Magical drifts, of every conceivable shape, spiraled off amongst the trees.Trees and rocky outcroppings, familiar before the storm, became unrecognizable shapes by the fickle whims of wind-driven, powder snow.

The azure, sometimes tranquil, often stormy Straits of Juan de Fuca were visible to the north. Across the Straits, through binoculars, Victoria's buildings were white periods and brown exclamation marks against the distant mass of Vancouver Island.

Birds and small animals, having disappeared into some shelter during the storm, reappeared, desperately searching for food and water. Water warmed on the stove and set outside for the birds soon turned to ice and had to be reheated.

The Crislers enjoyed their avian neighbors. The birds served as a reminder that life was possible in this inhospitable place on top of a rugged mountain. A pair of sharp-shinned **Accipiter striatus**, the ultimate, forest-dwelling raptor of the hawk family, circled overhead, or perched statue-like in dead snags, patiently waiting for movement that might mean dinner, if only they could catch it. A cottontail rabbit nibbled fir boughs by the snow-covered outhouse. Outside their window a mottle-breasted pine siskin and a male red-breasted nuthatch, with white and black bars alongside his head, vied with a bossy, noisy Steller jay for a handout of crumbs, seeds, and a dish of water.

In a nearby hemlock, a pine squirrel ignored the threat of hawks and scrambled gallantly amongst snow-covered limbs in search of cones, wisely saving his cache beneath the snow for even harder times.

Imprisoned on a mountaintop, with no renewable source of reading material, and thoughts of students and school far away, Lois' mind slowly began a transformation. For the first time she really had time to observe the stark beauty of her wilderness surroundings and the mini-dramas unfolding outside her window. She began to write about nature, hesitantly at first, unfamiliar with the subject, especially the outdoor jargon, then more boldly as she gained confidence.

Pleased, Herb encouraged her, aware that writing about her wilderness neighbors might open her eyes to the splendid drama surrounding their perch on the mountain.

Lois read everything she wrote to Herb, seeking approval. He was conservative with his comments, an uneducated person criticizing someone with Lois' credits. Herb, however, was a much better observer of natural history than Lois. He was an excellent writer also, but only if he voluntarily chose to do so.

Encouraged, Lois began to relax and let the words flow naturally. It took time, actually years, but eventually Lois found her own, terse, unique, entertaining and often humorous style. It was to change but little during her long career as a columnist, lecturer and book author.

Their marriage had already survived one winter at Hume's Ranch. It would be further tested here in this tiny, wind-blown shack on top of Hurricane Hill. Strangely enough, instead of causing friction, the isolation bound them closer together. Later, especially during the rigors of surviving in large cities while on tour, they would recall their winter on Hurricane Hill with fondness.

Lois was astonished by her husband's powers of observation about wilderness creatures. Other people saw only a thrush on a twig. Herb noticed that the thrush was a mature male, in the act of defending his territory in preparation for mating and nesting.

By late February Herb's thoughts were already upon the inevitable garden. He began planning for spring:

> In one corner of the lookout I constructed a three-by-six-foot greenhouse seed bed. In it I grew wheat, lettuce, onions and radishes for salads. I also grew some tomato plants. In the spring I would go down the mountain on skis as far as the snow lasted, then cache my skis and snowshoes, which I took along to use in climbing back. Then I hiked to Hume's Ranch and planted my garden, and set out the tomato plants that I had grown in the lookout. By the time I returned to Hurricane Ridge, I knew I had done a day's work.[21] Spring came with a rush. Swift mountain streams and waterfalls appeared overnight. Marsh marigolds formed their buds under the snow banks, coming into full bloom a couple of days after the snow was gone. Often they were in the path of a rushing brook, formed from melting snow. Then these golden flowers could be seen in full bloom a foot under the crystal-clear water. In other places, avalanche lilies would impatiently force their bent, budded, slender necks through the snow banks.

> My most interesting experience on Hurricane Ridge was getting acquainted with a true mountaineer, the "whistling" marmot. The animal is seldom found very far below timberline. Here in the Olympics, about two thirds of a marmot's life is spent in hibernation.

> The Olympic marmots are hoary marmots, the largest of the three American woodchucks.[22] The color of Olympic marmots is variable; tawny or gray or brown. The year we were on Hurricane, the marmots came out of hibernation the second week of May. Each marmot had its own "lookout" spot; most of them on rocks by their burrows but if there were no rocks close by they used the mound of dirt formed by digging the burrow. One marmot emerged from hibernation right by our door. A large rock covered with lichen was her lookout. At night she slept in her burrow, but for siestas, she chose the rock. In sunshine she flattened over it like a fur rug. When the weather worsened, she stayed out as

long as possible before going underground. She hunched like a cat, with the wind riffling her fur and the fog drifting into the blue abyss below. We called her Molly Grumpy. In order not to startle her when opening the door, or coming up to the lookout, I would always call: 'I'm coming Molly.' Thus forewarned, she would let me pass without disappearing into her hole.

Marmots have a rangy voice, and utter only one sound, the famous "whistle". It can stop your heart when a startled marmot rips it out near your feet. Usually the whistle is a danger sound uttered for the species' safety.

I think the Olympic marmot, both old and young, are the most playful animals found anywhere. They are free, and rich enough to be both peaceable and playful. I quote from Lois' writings, `Waves of flowers followed the receding snow fields and over them dragged the lustrous brown marmots, nibbling like crazy, but meanwhile relaxing, bellies to ground, luxuriously. They dragged in this way over rocks, nibbling lichen. They rippled through the grasses, mowing off phlox, miner's lettuce, rosy douglasia, and still the meadows looked as flowery as ever. Later, where tall lupine bloomed, you would see some big gray marmot stand up picturesquely to pull down stalks of blue flowers to eat. Marmots must surely be among the prettiest feeders in the world.'

[Again, Herb quotes from something Lois wrote:]

One evening Cris did not come for supper and I went to look for him, cautiously--the sun was low but he might be filming--I looked through the fringe of alpine firs into a small, shadowy meadow. Level sunlight chinked the west fir with gold. The camera stood idle on its tripod. Cris and the marmot twins were playing. The marmots rushed towards him. He made a little jump at them. They veered and raced past him, their feet thumping like a deer running. They turned and ran back and he jumped at them again. Mostly they chased each other but they accepted the man, they included him in.

Again, Herb's writing:

The Olympic marmot, by their selection of terrain and developed habits, have acquired for themselves a perfect Utopia. They are active the most beautiful four months of the year. With plenty of food, pure fresh air and water, they literally live in a bed of roses without thorns. Instead of packing and going south for the eight cold winter months, they crawl into a dry burrow with their warm coats, and go to sleep. It's as peaceable as a private room in a Miami hotel, and lots cheaper.

During May and June I spent only six hours a day on my twelve hour watch. Lois was on 18 hours. I used 12 hours either filming or at Hume's Ranch working in the garden. We each had six hours sleep. I had come to the conclusion that the Japanese were too busy now protecting their homeland to try to raid the U.S.A., and felt the aircraft warning was "busy work", and wasn't necessary anymore.

I had something that was much more important: the picture I had filmed of the storms, the top of the mountain encased in snow and ice, the coming of warm sunlight, turning the bleak land into a carpet of green, on which there were many designs in multiple colors. There was a network of crystal-clear rushing brooks. All this made it into a living wilderness for it was the home of graceful deer, the singing birds, and the playground for marmot. A wilderness without its animals is as dead as a boarded-up house.

The Wolf Creek Trail was cleared of its last snow July 13, 1943, and we moved back to Hume's Ranch.[23] I edited my film of the winter and spring down to a ten-minute short, and called it "After the Storm--A Poem Without Words." This, I thought, was a most important venture. [24]

Herb's plans had been to stay with the lookout job until it was finished, then use the money to buy film and supplies so they could start serious motion-picture filming in the high country. However, Lois developed serious health problems.

Temporary replacements were found so the Crislers could return to the ranch and so Lois could seek medical attention and Herb could tend and harvest his garden. They expected to be absent from the job only two or three months.

It didn't work out that way.

Their plans to spend the summer photographing in the high country, as well as returning to work on Hurricane Hill, had to be canceled, through 1943 and 1944.

Notes and Sources, Beyond The Trails, Chapter Nine

1. The original log cabin, built by the Humes brothers about the turn of the century, reached by walking from Whiskey Bend trailhead, has been restored by Olympic National Park, and is listed as a National Historic Site.

2. Although the letters indicate this information was what the Humes party thought was true, there is an inconsistency with the known facts. Approximately 30,000 stampeders gathered at Dyea during the fall and winter of 1897-98, crossed Chilkoot Pass, and built boats at Lake Bennett in time to head down the Yukon River to Dawson after spring breakup. Anyone headed across Chilkoot Pass for the Klondike in 1897 either had to backpack their ton of supplies, or hire Chilkat Indian porters.

   Two tramways were constructed across Chilkoot Pass, one, an endless rope tram, dragging sleds up the Golden Stairs, was built by Peter Peterson in 1894. Other crude affairs followed, including one powered by two horses going round and round on a treadmill at the Scales, which also dragged loaded sleds. Two steam-powered aerial trams, starting from Canyon City and ending at Crater Lake, began operations in April, 1898. An alternative was to hire horse packers at Skagway, then travel across White Pass on a rugged, horse-killer of a trail. Either way, this was only the first phase of a very rugged, expensive trip to Dawson.

   I relate the above to indicate that the Humes Party simply either didn't have the money, or got cold feet.

   The White Pass & Yukon Railroad wasn't completed until July 29, 1899, by which time the Klondike Gold Rush was in decline.

3. Herb Crisler, "Western Wildlife Photographer", courtesy Ruby El Hult.

4. Actually the trial was delayed until February 24, 1942. What caused all the excitement was, in July, 1940, an unidentified, murdered female body had been found floating in Lake Crescent. The body was eventually identified as Mrs. Hallie Illingworth, who had been missing since before Christmas, 1937. Her husband claimed his wife had deserted him. Actually he had murdered his wife, wrapped her in blankets and ropes, weighted the body and threw it into the lake. The cold, pure waters of the lake had preserved the body until it resembled a cake of soap. Eventually the ropes rotted and the body floated to the surface after 31 months! Monty Illingworth was brought from California to Port Angeles to stand trial and received a second degree murder sentence.

5. Wamilla Inn was located near the present Elwha Ranger Station.

6. Not exactly correct. Lois received $20 a month from renting her house in the University District. According to the Public Records Archives Department of the University of Washington, Lois received a reduced salary until officially dropped from the staff almost a year later. Herb was under a court order to pay $35 a month child support for Bob.

7. Herb Crisler, "Western Wildlife Photographer," courtesy Ruby El Hult.

8. Lois Crisler, "Olympic Trail Talk--24," The Port Angeles Evening News, 4 Nov., 1949

9. Lois Crisler, "Olympic Trail Talk--80," The Port Angeles Evening News, 22 Dec., 1950

10. Lois Crisler, "Olympic Trail Talk--25," The Port Angeles Evening News, 11 Nov., 1949

11. Herb Crisler, "Western Wildlife Photographer," courtesy Ruby El Hult.

12. Lois Crisler, "Olympic Trail Talk--," The Port Angeles Evening News.

13. The subalpine fir, Abies lasiocarpa, is one of the most widespread, as well as attractive, of all western firs. Like its close cousin the grand fir, Abies grandis, which is similar, but tends to grow at lower elevations, the subalpine fir's crown is tapered and spike-like to better resist the heavy loads of snow common to its range. The beautiful evergreen needles, dark green above and silvery white beneath, have also adapted to resisting heavy loads of snow by pointing upwards, instead of flat, as are the needles of other firs growing at lower elevations, such as Douglas fir. The limbs of subalpine fir are very short for the same reason.

14. Ibid.

15. Herb Crisler, "Western Wildlife Photographer," courtesy Ruby El Hult.

16. Herb, in his version of the story, fails to make it plain that his "run for it" was an attempt to reach the cabin to get his camera, not fleeing for his life. By yelling, he hoped to get Lois' attention and ask her to bring the camera.

17. Ibid.

18. Ibid.

19. Lois Crisler, "Olympic Trail Talk #31." The Port Angeles Evening News, 23 Dec., 1949
    A "fire table" is the device, like a huge compass card, with a means of sighting across the card and reading the degrees, which lookouts use to pinpoint the location of a forest fire. If compass bearings from two lookouts pinpoint the smoke, the fire's location is triangulated and plotted on a map.

20. Herb Crisler, "Western Wildlife Photographer," courtesy Ruby El Hult.

21. If Herb stuck to roads and trails the round trip would have been almost 22 miles. Elevation difference would have been about 3000 vertical feet. Since the road to Hurricane Hill looped alongside the mountain directly above Ludden's Cabin, he may have had a shortcut directly up the hill, saving many miles.

22. The animal Herb was observing has now been classified the Olympic marmot Marmota olympus, endemic to the Olympic Mountains.

23. Herb neglected to mention that the main reason they left Hurricane Hill and the job was because Lois was very ill.

24. Herb Crisler, Western Wildlife Photographer, courtesy Ruby El Hult.
    Editing motion picture film requires electricity. Since Hume's Ranch didn't have any, Herb stored his equipment at Wamilla Inn, near where the Elwha Ranger station now stands. Later, after the Inn was removed by the park service, he did his editing at the Methodist Church in Port Angeles. In return, he often showed his films at church social gatherings. During the last few years at the ranch they edited at home with a portable generator.

10

Improving Hume's Ranch
The "Ravens" Lend a Hand (1943-45)

Herb's plans to spend several months in the high country, starting in the late summer and fall of 1943, were hampered because of Lois' illness. Her trouble had started while at Hurricane Hill Lookout. She wasn't strong enough to make trips into the interior, and sought medical attention.

There was plenty to keep Herb busy. Many trips were made to Whiskey Bend and Port Angeles for supplies and to Seattle to see a doctor. Lois' problem persisted.

Herb took this opportunity to enlarge and improve the garden. Birds and rodents were a constant threat, especially to the berry patch. Herb cut long poles, rigged them across the top of the berry patch fence, then draped chicken wire over the poles. Around the bottom he placed small-meshed wire to keep out mice and other small rodents. Eventually the enclosed garden was 80 feet long.

He repaired the cabin roof, fell snags and sawed wood, did the cooking and washed clothes by hand.

An increasing number of visitors arrived. Many helped in the garden, cut wood, picked apples, helped make cider or other tasks. Guests enjoyed working at Hume's Ranch. Herb had a way of making jobs fun. Some brought gifts of food, fresh oranges, lemons, green peppers, bananas, ham, fresh buttermilk which they knew Herb loved, fresh cream specially for Lois, and items which the Crislers couldn't get without making the long trip to town. The latest newspapers were always welcome. No one was turned away without a dry place to sleep if they wanted one. With all the activity, the summer of 1943 passed quickly.

By the spring of 1944, it became obvious that Lois needed major surgery, which was performed in Seattle.

After being released she wanted to return home to recuperate. Since she was unable to walk, Herb built a platform on his wheelbarrow, spread sleeping bags and blankets and wheeled Lois up the trail.

With Lois recuperating, Herb stuck close to home most of the spring of 1944. Once the garden was laid by, he was anxious to begin construction of the line of shelters and camps, some of which he had already started.

He wanted to begin filming several new movies about Roosevelt elk, which seemed to be the most popular animal in his previous movies. Herb intended to show the films during the winter to earn badly needed money.

Herb bought a large supply of waxed, square, wide-mouth five-gallon cans, the kind used for coffee beans, fish livers and other products, from American Can Company in Seattle. He also bought several dozen army surplus sleeping bags at $1 each. The cans were ideal for storing sleeping bags, film and food at the caches. Equipment and supplies would be protected from animals and weather. Two of these loaded cans could be carried crosswise on a pack board, or three to a pack horse.

One balmy summer day two husky, live-wire young women from the University of Washington arrived at Hume's Ranch. One was Carol Preston, studying to become a professional clinical psychologist. The other, Hazle M. Chapman, was working on her Master's degree. Her thesis; Planning a Community School Camp.

The two women had been intrigued by the closeness of Olympic National Park. On clear days they would gaze towards the beautiful, snowy peaks of the Olympic Mountains west of Seattle and speculate about what it would be like to visit the area.

They decided on a backpack trip. Neither had any experience, but that didn't discourage them. Winter evenings were spent consulting hiking maps and making lists of food and equipment they would need. After someone told them Lois Brown Crisler, a former university faculty teacher, lived along the Elwha river in a log cabin, they chose that location for their adventure.

The girls prowled First Avenue's army surplus stores. Clerks, realizing the girls knew nothing about equipment, plied them with rucksacks, sleeping bags, heavy army-surplus boots, mess kits and an army-surplus pup tent of questionable vintage.

Like most novice backpackers, they took along far too much gear. Pots, cookware and cups clanked and bulged from their packs as they staggered to the Greyhound bus depot.

They received wide-eyed attention after leaving the bus at Port Angeles. Female backpackers, especially if strangers, were a rarity in those days. They hitched a ride to the Elwha River. The kind soul that picked them up deviated from his course along Highway 101 and drove them up the Elwha Valley, and then up the old road to Whiskey Bend Trailhead.

Hazle Chapman & Carol Preston ready to head out for backpack trip to the Olympic Peninsula, 1944.

Chatting merrily, to keep up their spirits (and perhaps to scare away bears and cougar) they started up the trail. A gray sky hung over the forest like a wet blanket. The old-growth forest closed around them, mysterious, unfamiliar. The wind moaned, rain splattered down through the boughs and their packs already seemed too heavy. They were both determined and plodded on, tired, apprehensive about where they were going to spend the night and frightened, although neither would admit it to the other.

Hazle, "Chappy" to her friends, at the time of this writing, lives in a retirement home in Lacey. Although she has heart trouble, she is still interested in the outdoors.

During our first interview, Chappy brought out a battered, green Swiss alpine hat, complete with feather, cocked at a rakish angle, which she had worn half a century earlier while backpacking with the Crislers. She recalls that on this first trip into Olympic National Park they were so inexperienced they carried canned goods and cooked oatmeal in a thermos bottle!

By the time they reached the fork in the Elwha Trail that leads down to Hume's Ranch the girls were in bad shape. They were badly overloaded, their clumsy boots had worn blisters on their feet, and the ill-fitting rucksacks, intended for male soldiers, had worn raw places on their hips and backs.

For a time they stood at the gate, staring at the old, weathered log cabin, wondering if they would be welcome. Smoke rose in fragrant blue wisps from the stovepipe. A large, fenced garden, several fruit trees, a shed behind the cabin, although picturesque, looked pretty crude. Would a former faculty member dare live here, they whispered? Bravely, they opened the gate, crossed the yard and knocked.

A tall, spindly woman opened the door. To the girl's relief, she smiled at them and insisted they come in. They dumped their packs on the porch and entered the crude, one-room cabin. To their immense relief, Lois welcomed the girls warmly, as the Crislers did all visitors. Seated at the table, they were offered cool mountain water from a nearby stream. Lois politely neglected to inform them that deer, elk, bear and an occasional cougar frequented the pool from which the water came. That would come later, after they became acquainted.

Herb was off somewhere, looking for wood. Lois was delighted after discovering the girls both attended the university. A lively dialogue about people they knew, and what was happening at school, began.

Suddenly the door burst open and Herb Crisler walked in. He sized up the visitors boldly, and also made them welcome. They thought he was a romantic-looking person, dressed in rough, woodsman's clothing.

By the time the visiting slowed, long shadows reached dark fingers into the nearby forest. Lois lit a coal oil lamp. The girls asked if they could camp nearby for the night.

Lois assured them they were welcome. Herb brought a large pan of vegetables from the garden and prepared a steaming dinner. All four got along famously well.

After dinner they offered to wash the dishes, but Herb declined, saying it was no bother, that they should just relax and rest. The girls listened wide-eyed while the Crislers told about adventures with wildlife around the cabin and described spending a winter in the fire lookout on Hurricane Hill. To their amazement, Herb beat on an empty pan and coaxed a black and white skunk out from under the cabin floor. He fed it bread from his hand.

Herb Crisler displays produce from his garden at Hume's Ranch.

Skunks lived beneath the floor of Hume's Cabin.

"This is the skunk's home," Lois said, "The skunks were here under the cabin when we came, so we feel they have more right to the place than we do."

The girls asked where they could pitch their tent. The Crislers insisted they stay in the cabin. Herb and Lois took sleeping bags and went outside to guest's quarters.

Chappy still remembers that first, long night at Hume's Ranch. The mattress was so lumpy she hardly slept. The strange roar from the river kept her awake. Carol tossed and turned. Her blisters hurt and her back ached.

The next morning Herb cooked enormous stacks of delicious hotcakes smothered with butter, with a choice of apple butter, jam and syrup. The girls were surprised that Herb did the cooking.

After breakfast the girls taped up their feet, thanked the Crislers and continued on up the trail to Lillian River. They were told a camp site was located there. They planned to go to Elkhorn Ranger Station the following day.

Before they reached Lillian River a steady rain began. The camp at Lillian River is not a pleasant one, being in heavy timber. Finally, with some slivers of fir pitch Herb had provided, they got a tiny blaze going. Dry wood was nonexistent. The fire sputtered, died, then spewed acrid smoke.

Supper was cold and dismal. The girls retired early. The pup tent leaked. The ground was hard and full of rocks. Their backs ached from the lumpy mattress the night before. They tossed and turned. Every time they fell asleep, a gust of wind shook the tall trees, dumping a deluge of water on the tent, threatening to capsize the roof. Water seeped into the tent and soaked the bottom of their sleeping bags. Leaks from above soaked the tops.

At dawn they emerged, discouraged, stiff and cold. An upward glance through the dripping forest canopy disclosed a leaden sky with no let up in sight. Efforts to start a fire failed. Breakfast was cold, left-over oatmeal out of the thermos. Discouraged, they packed their wet equipment, even heavier now, and headed back down the trail.

Back at Hume's Ranch the Crislers took one look at the soggy clothes, and hustled them inside by the stove. Dry out, have supper and spend the night, they were told. Herb found two dry sleeping bags. The girls politely refused the Crisler's bed a second time, and insisted on sleeping in the bothy, the lean-to shelter built for the benefit of guests. Herb took them out and showed them a deep pile of moss and ferns they could use for a bed. A few playful wood mice might scamper around, he said, but they were harmless.

The front of the lean-to was open to the night. Herb had reported that both cougar and bear frequented the ranch, but the girls were so tired they fell into a deep sleep.

Herb & Lois Crisler operating the drag saw at Hume's Ranch, 1946.

The next morning, after another hearty breakfast, Herb mentioned that he had much work to do. The weather was still rainy. The girls enthusiasm for camping had chilled. They offered to help.

Herb produced two pair of cotton work gloves, a splitting wedge and maul and led them into the woods. He had already sawed stove-wood lengths off a Douglas-fir log. The two girls went to work splitting wood.

The sledge struck the iron wedge with a report like a pistol shot, sending sparks of hot steel shooting every which way. The fir split easily into stove-sized chunks. The odor of pitch filled their nostrils and pitch stuck to their gloved hands. They enjoyed the work, taking turns with the sledge, until blisters forced them to stop.

Reporting to Herb that they now had blisters on both ends, Herb, grateful for a split and stacked supply of wood, invited them to remain as long as they wished.

It wasn't all work. Herb taught them to catch fat rainbow trout in the river. They listened attentively while Herb described trips into the Olympic Mountains. They learned tips on how to travel and survive in the wilderness. They marveled at Herb's powers of observation while walking in the woods. Lois thrilled them with her descriptions of the beauties of Cream Lake Basin. They shuddered as she described the Catwalk. They listened attentively while Herb described Billy Everett, and his exploits exploring the heart of the Olympics with his dogs and gun, before anyone knew what lay hidden behind the Bailey Range. They vowed to meet Billy sometime. Their wish came true after being invited to join the Crislers and Billy on a backpack trip to Cream Lake.

The girls stayed for a week. Come back anytime, Herb invited, the woodpile would always be waiting. The friendship developed into a lasting one.

Back in Seattle, their academic pals were jealous after learning they had become friends with Herbert and Lois Brown Crisler and had actually been guests at Hume's Ranch.

Chappy and Carol would return to Hume's Ranch many times during the next few years. They learned woods lore and backpacking from the Crislers. They were invited along on some extensive backpack trips into the Bailey Range, and on an attempted climb of Mount Olympus from the Hoh River, aborted because of bad weather on Blue Glacier. Chappy

Carol Preston and Helen Rupp splitting and hauling wood.

owned a 120 millimeter Kodak reflex camera. She took many black and white photos around Hume's Ranch and on backpack trips. Herb gave her tips about exposure and composition. Many of Hazle's photos are included in this book.

Carol and Lois became life-long close friends. Chappy started her own wilderness guiding and camping business and eventually became so busy she lost personal contact with the Crislers.

During the summer of 1944, while Lois was still unable to rough it in the mountains, a youth from California came to stay with the Crislers. Herb took this opportunity to start a shelter cabin in Cat Basin. Loading themselves down with a froe for splitting cedar shakes, a buck saw, shovel, nails, axes, grub and camping supplies, they headed up Boulder Creek Trail.

The location of this shelter was chosen to be a day's trek from Hotcake Camp. The latter was the first of a string of shelters on what is today known as the Crisler Traverse. The log and shake cabin was located on the mountainside, in a grove of sub-alpine fir, on the west side of Cat Basin. A little spring-fed stream provided water. Herb chose a spot with a splendid view of Cat Peak.

During the previous winter on Hurricane Hill, Herb had learned to ski. Lois was already an experienced skier. Several Seattle friends, including Chapman and Preston, also expressed a desire to come to the Olympics and ski. The difficulties of skiing on Hurricane Ridge were rather daunting.

The Crislers tried to keep the road between the Elwha Ranger Station and Whiskey Bend open during snow by driving over it frequently, but the upper portions of Wolf Creek Trail became blocked with snow early in the fall.

To ski, the Crislers, and their friends, drove up the Wolf Creek Trail as far as possible, then snowshoed or walked the rest of the way. This made for a long, tiring day, too strenuous, even for Herb. He built a split-shake lean-to shelter about halfway up the Wolf Creek Trail and called it Halfway House.

Storms are frequent and violent on Hurricane Ridge. Some campers complained when they awoke to discover their sleeping bags covered with several inches of snow.

Herb discovered a well-hidden, snug log cabin, in the timber below Hurricane Hill Lookout. According to Norma Byers of Port Angeles, the cabin had been built in 1924 by her father, W.W. "Winnie" Calkin, her brother Glen, herself, her sister Alta, and the two Calkin girl's husbands, the brothers Clifford and Wallace Smith.

Herb Crisler and Carol Preston fishing on the Elwha River.

W.W. Calkin, while hunting along Hurricane Ridge, found a vein of manganese and staked a claim, recorded as the Lady Norma, Location Section 30 (30-6W). A creek crossed the property then, but doesn't exist today.

Calkin cut shake bolts for the cabin far down the road, split them, then packed the shakes up the mountain with horses. Norma remembers one of the horses falling over a cliff, scattering shakes down the mountain. Hurricane Ridge was popular for deer hunting. The Calkin and Smith families also used the cabin for hunting, but by 1941 had abandoned using it altogether. Crisler fixed up the cabin and named it Ski Lair. A supply of food was hauled in while the road was open. A wood supply was cut and they were set for some cozy nights and days of skiing. Hazle and Carol were frequent visitors at Ski Lair. Hazle remembers it was a beautiful place, especially when the subalpine fir were smothered with loads of snow.

Norma claims the Forest Service took over the cabin later on and kept it stocked with emergency supplies.

Calkin's Cabin, visited and photographed in 1992 by Warren Hilt of Port Angeles, had been smashed flat by snow. In October, after Lois was able to carry a load, they completed the new shelter in Cat Basin. Instead of leaving the front open, as originally designed, they enclosed it with logs and chinked the cracks with moss. Complete with bunks, home-made table, a few boxes for cupboards and a sheet iron stove with oven, it was a cozy, favorite camp.

They were looking out the open door one evening when Herb drawled, "Why, this's no shelter. It's a castle. What shall we name it, Lois?"

Lois looked east, towards Cat Peak. The last rays of the setting sun burnished new snow on the peak to a golden copper color. She peered down into the darkening, green meadows of Cat Basin. "Castle-in-the-Cat," she said. The name stuck.

Carol Preston, foreground, and Helen Rupp at Ski Lair, the old Calkin's cabin on Hurricane Ridge.

Hotcake Camp was Camp One and Castle-in-the-Cat was Camp Two in their line of shelters. At this writing, 1997, the cabin has collapsed from the heavy snows of 1996-1997. (See color section for photo)

That late fall of 1944, with their summer's take of film, the Crislers went to Wamilla Inn, along the Elwha River road, where electricity was available. The editing process was satisfying, but painstaking work. Scenes which they needed most usually seemed to be missing, were still at Humes Ranch, or couldn't be retaken. In trying to conserve film, Herb often neglected to shoot fill-in material which he later needed.

After the laborious task was completed, four short films, WE SPENT A WINTER ON HURRICANE; A PACK-TRAIN FISHING TRIP IN THE OLYMPICS; BIRDS OF OLYMPIC NATIONAL PARK and AFTER THE STORM were ready to show.

They drove down to Billy Everett's to show the movies. Also present was Mrs. Everett, their son Carl and neighbors. The Everetts and guests enjoyed the films immensely. But Herb decided the films lacked something.

Billy, now 76, told Herb he wanted to make one last trip to his beloved Cream Lake. Herb agreed he could accompany them the following summer.

Several days later, back at Hume's Ranch, Herb came into the cabin, removed his coat, placed his hands on the table and looked squarely at Lois:

'Lois,' I said, 'the pictures need music. We're going to Seattle and buy music.'

Lois offered her voice of reason. 'We haven't enough money to even get to Seattle and back!'

I said stubbornly, 'We're going. Anyway, we'll start.'

We made up our packs, went out to Whiskey Bend and drove down the hill to one of the most amazing experiences of our lives.

We picked up our mail at the box, six miles away. Lois sorted as we drove. One envelope had an odd return. In pencil, in the upper corner, was written the word "Love, from the Ravens."

'This is funny,' Lois said. She thought it was a joke. Then she opened the envelope. When she saw what was inside, she sat silently for so long, I glanced at her. 'What's the matter?' I asked.

She held it up for me to see. Three sheets of empty paper. Not a mark on them. Folded inside was a hundred dollar bill! Not a check. A bill.

'Who's it from?'

Lois searched the contents. Nothing. Except blank paper and the bill. She examined the envelope's hand writing. The address was not printed, but drawn like the hand writing of a child, so it was perfectly anonymous. There we were with a hundred dollar bill in our laps.

The music came to $96.00!

Our pictures cried for an audience. I went out and got one. Phil Jackson, of the University of Washington Campus, let me use his little 50-seat theater. We telephoned friends to come.

There was a terrible difficulty. I had ordered silent titles for our pictures from elderly Tom Guptil of Port Angeles. I had planned those captions carefully. Tom caught the flu and went to the hospital!

At the back of the little theater Phil had a sound-proof control booth with a tremendous bank of knobs and dials. Lois was to stand in the midst of those controls and regulate the music. Now she made a suggestion. There was a microphone in the booth. She would narrate the pictures.

That night another film lecturer sprouted.

No, the pictures did not support themselves, much less us. We supported them. We put all we had into them. We worked our heads off because we loved the films and thought they were important. But what really kept our project going was the Ravens.

Big Bill Thornily of the Black Ball Ferry Lines was one of my friends at the first showing. Afterwards he said, 'I don't want to ever see an artist without his brushes. If you get stuck for film, Cris, I'll see that you get a roll.' He did more. He stirred up the Olympic Peninsula Hotel and Resort Association to donate $300 to help.[1]

He also gave us free ferry transportation from the Peninsula to Seattle. Since the ferry would have cost about as much as the showings paid, we were lucky that he did. To save on board and room we stayed with friends while in Seattle, and chipped in on groceries as we could. A showing meant an absence from home of at least three days.

As for paying depreciation on the costly equipment we were using, that was out of the question. There was my Eastman Kodiak Cine Special Number Two motion-picture camera, a German 16-millimeter Arriflex, lens from 15 to 400 millimeter, tripod, the Bell and Howell auditorium-model projector, the amplifiers and public address system. The projector burned a 1200-watt lamp bulb. This gave brilliant projection for audiences up to 500. We even stretched it to 2,000. But one lamp only lasted about 10 hours and cost $10 each.

Lois' Hudson car, still hanging on from university days, we used free gratis for transportation.

Only a few of our friends had any idea how much film it took to photograph wild animals. We didn't have a script and go out and film what we wanted. We filmed what we saw and were lucky enough to have a chance at. When we came out in the fall and viewed our summer's take, we made whatever kind of story our film would cover. As for the actual filming, we could not predict when a wild animal was going to do what we wanted. If we tried to save film, intending to start filming when the animal did something interesting, he acted before we could, and the scene was lost. Or, at best, we got the end of the action and not the build-up. On the other hand, if we anticipated his moves and started filming while he was motionless, just eating or walking, we might shoot up all the film we dared expend and have to stop filming just the second before he snapped into the action we'd hoped for. We had to gamble and use all our knowledge and woodsmanship.

Ideally, a wildlife photographer would have all the film he wanted and shoot it freely. This would require about 25,000 feet each summer. On one of our lucky summers we exposed about 10,000 feet of film.

Our equipment was expendable. We didn't worry about it, although it appeared as if we were racing into a dead end where we would have no camera, projector or car. Sometimes I felt ironic when some school superintendent handed us $10 with patronizing liberality, as if we had greatly enriched ourselves at his school's expense. Actually, if we arrived back at the ranch without spending more than the cost of gas and grub, we were lucky.

But film we had to have. The Ravens took over. There was one spring when it looked as if we were stuck. I went on getting the Ga'den ready to lay by, planning to go into the high country as usual.

'What are we going to use for film,' I asked. The Ga'den fed us while we were at home, winter and summer, but did not provide proteins, butter or milk. They came from McGlenn's Grocery down in Port Angeles. In summer, up in the high country, all our food had to come from the grocery. Canned butter, expensive powdered eggs and powdered whole milk, and so forth.

Then one of the Ravens came. We found a big package in our mail box out by the Elwha River bridge on the main highway. 'Looks like film,' I said. Lois cut the strings while I drove. It was $300 worth of 16-millimeter Kodachrome for the Cine-Special. There was no return on the box. After Lois removed the wrapping paper, on the inner wrapping was scrawled, 'Ask me no questions and I'll tell you no lies.' Signed, 'Robin Hood.'[2]

Living at a remote location made arranging their film showings a nightmare. At the time they had no phone at Hume's Ranch:

Finally, we had a little film library company in Seattle arrange our showings for us. We got our mail so seldom that by the time we received our mail the dates were past when they wanted our pictures. Then there was the time we wrote to a school executive offering a certain block of time for bookings in their school system, received no reply and booked the time elsewhere. Then the school expected us to show!

The company tried to arrange several showings on each trip. Our little $10 bookings looked important to us. To the company they must have looked like a big nuisance. But Frances Rarig, wife of the owner, believed as we did, that the pictures were worthwhile and meant something to people. So patiently the company arranged our bookings.

We would work like mad for a week, then race home with a little money before it got used up on expenses. Sometimes we had four showings a day. Two at one school in the morning, two at another school in the afternoon. Thirty dollars in one day! It took about an hour to set up. I would ask the principle what she would like me to show. I had my pictures in 400-foot reels; bears, fishing, marmot, elk and so forth. She would order one sequence for the first hour, another for the second, the $5 hour.[3]

Gradually we learned. After each reel everything paused except the children's tongues, while I removed one reel and threaded the next.

After a year or so of booking through the Rarigs, we received a letter from another Seattle booking agent inquiring if we would accept a booking at $75, less 15 percent commission.

Accept it! This lofty transaction was above anything we had ever dreamed of. This was Sam Hurok, who also booked the ballet. We still did not realize that there was a "lecture field." I think it developed while we were away from the world, during our first period at the ranch.

On this booking something happened which changed our minds about how we were showing our films. We were to show six times at an army camp near Seattle. Four were at camp schools and two at the recreation hall for soldiers. A top Hollywood feature followed our wildlife show. The day turned into a bedlam.

The sweat, tension and anxiety of packing our heavy equipment around, finding outlets, setting up, and testing the sound equipment wore me down.

Soldiers crowded into the hall. Patiently the soldiers watched our first 400-foot reel of chipmunks, or what-not. Then the lights came on. I changed reels. When the lights went out again, what did they see? Not the feature. More elk or chipmunks or something. They began booing. Once more lights, change reels, then darkness. More elk, chipmunks. More boos and groans, louder this time. Doggedly, we plowed through the routine of our first showing. The projector was located in the center of the room and Lois sat on a high stool. After our show was finally over and the feature was on, Lois sat immobilized on that high stool, too embarrassed to move. Her cheeks were aflame and she felt as if she was a petrified pillar.

But that wasn't all. We still had the second show to suffer through. A superior officer was present this time, and just before the lights went out, he stood up and peered around deliberately. The soldiers weren't any happier than the first bunch, but they weren't as demonstrative.

Lois lost a year off her life that night.

After it was over, Lois bared her lacerated heart to me. `Maybe I bettah splice the reels together. No lights between. Probably hold the audience bettah,' I said mildly.

Lois stared hard at me. `You mean you could tie them together? All this time we could have had just one threading instead of a three minute wait between each 400-foot reel?'

Frances Rarig dreamed of hiring a downtown auditorium in Seattle and putting on our pictures. But frankly, she and I both realized that though people would like our pictures once they got there and saw them, there was no advertising point about them to bring people out. I said what I needed was to film a bull elk fight.

Frances Rarig died. The new agent expanded our range east of the mountains and south to Portland. We felt that our work was very important. We felt a missionary zeal about bringing the wilderness to people who otherwise could not see it. But our income was still minus zero.[4]

By 1944-45, the Crislers were finally receiving the attention necessary to place them into a more lucrative circle of viewers than schools and garden clubs. Their hand bill for the period lists two main features, THE KING OF THE LIVING WILDERNESS, 50 minutes. THE WEB OF THE WILDERNESS, 60 minutes, and three shorter films, THE

WHISTLING MARMOT, THOSE BLOOMING MOUNTAINS and BIRDS OF OLYMPIC NATIONAL PARK, each which ran about 12-15 minutes.

Notes & Sources, Beyond the Trails, Chapter Ten

1. Mr. Thornily, a businessman, recognized the publicity value of the Crisler's films for the North Olympic Peninsula and Olympic National Park. During this period, most people, while they may have heard of the Olympic Peninsula, had little idea what Olympic National Park was like. It wasn't visited by many people.

   Later, after their illustrated lectures were presented nationally, people from all over the United States came to see Hume's Ranch and the park, inspired after viewing Crisler's films.

2. Herb Crisler, "Western Wildlife Photographer," courtesy Ruby El Hult.

3. The Crislers, through their nature films, a rarity at the time, were alerting a whole generation of young people to the values of wildlife and wilderness. We can thank the Crislers, and other pioneer motion-picture and still wildlife photographers, as well as writers such as Osa Johnson, and others who followed, for a present generation, who are comparatively well educated about the requirements necessary for the conservation of nature.

4. Herb Crisler, "Western Wildlife Photographer," courtesy Ruby El Hult.

<h2>16 mm. Motion Pictures
In Color</h2>

The King of the Living Wilderness

(Running Time: 50 Minutes)

This picture shows a little of our pioneer life; then goes into the interior of the wilderness to show a little of our supply depots or caches, and of ourselves in the mountain scenery in which the pictures were made; some just pure beauty; a sequence of the re-balancing of nature, in which the bear plays an interesting part; and the life cycle of the elk or wapiti, the largest and stateliest deer in the world.

The Web of the Wilderness

(Running Time: 60 Minutes)

This includes:

OUR PIONEER LIFE—Showing our life in our old pioneer log cabin, three miles from a road, seven miles from our nearest neighbor.

A PACK-TRAIN FISHING TRIP—A fishing party that passes our log cabin on their way up the Elwha River after rainbow trout. And do they catch them!

WE SPENT A WINTER ON HURRICANE—Where, as air-craft warning observers during the war, we were snowed in for nine months. Shows the storms of winter, the break-up of winter, and the coming of the flowers and the deer to the high country.

TRAILING THE KING OF THE OLYMPICS—Good elk portraits and herd activities.

THE BLACK BEAR—Good portrait shots of black bear and the story of a little cub that climbs a tree to escape the photographer, much to the distress of his mother.

● Either program is best prefaced by about ten minutes of comment by Mrs. Crisler.

Shorter Films For Fillers

THE WHISTLING MARMOT. Interesting story of the large, western Whistling Marmot, now apparently becoming extinct. 15 minutes.

THOSE BLOOMING MOUNTAINS. The story of a girl who climbs the mountains to see the scenery and discovers the wild flowers of the alpine meadows and talus slopes. 15 minutes.

BIRDS IN THE OLYMPIC NATIONAL PARK. Portraits of a variety of birds found in the Olympics, including the water ouzel or dipper, a bird of the mountain streams, the hermit thrush, and Clark's nutcracker, named for a member of the Lewis and Clark expedition. 12 minutes.

All of these pictures are filmed, edited, and narrated by Herb and Lois Crisler, who live in the Olympic wilderness. There are two complete shows.

A lecture film for churches, clubs, schools, and all who love the out-of-doors.

The web of many strands—animals, birds, and the grandeur of mountain scenery—large and small things that form a complete web of a living wilderness.

Filmed in one of the largest wilderness areas left in the United States, the Olympic Mountains, in the northwest corner of the State of Washington.

For further information write

*Herb Crisler
Rt. 1, Port Angeles
Washington*

11

The Crisler Traverse
Caches and Camps. High Country Cuisine.

During the spring of 1946, Herb worked long hours to prepare the garden and get things ready so they could spend as much time as possible in the high country as soon as the snow melted.

Of all the scenes shown in their motion-pictures the previous winter those of Olympic elk brought the most enthusiastic response. Applause and recognition are balms which sustain and encourage any photographer. Herb decided elk was what they must concentrate on during the forthcoming season.

June was a busy month, with almost constant visitors. They had told everyone who planned to come that June was the optimum month, since the weather would be nice and they would be in the high country after July.

Herb had built a hot house in which to start plants for the garden. The garden had been planted in April and May, with several plantings of sweet corn so that it would come into ear over a period of weeks. Herb still found time to take visitors on trout fishing trips and short explorations of the area.

Carol Preston and Hazle Chapman arrived. Herb had cut down a large Douglas fir snag on the hillside above the big meadow and sawed it into stove-wood lengths with a drag saw. The air soon rang with the sound of sledge against steel splitting wedges. As the woodpile grew, so did the girl's appetites. Herb was hard-pressed to keep them fed.

Carol Preston & Herb Crisler falling a big fir snag at Hume's Ranch.

But it wasn't all work. They sneaked down to the river in the gray dawn to catch trout for breakfast. Sometimes they wandered off exploring and game watching. Deer, bear and elk often appeared around the ranch. The girls thought being there was paradise.

One golden spring evening, with twilight settling over the ranch, Herb called the three ladies outside. They watched a band of 11 elk, four of them calves, struggle across the swift Elwha, shake the water out of their tan coats and begin cropping fresh, green grass in the old hay meadow below the cabin. The river was exceptionally low so the spring calves had little trouble crossing.

A blue grouse boomed its mating call in the timber behind the ranch. Far off in the timber across the river an owl hooted.

The girls bedded down in the bothy. During the night a black bear circled the yard fence, then walked within a few feet of where the girls were sleeping. They didn't know about their visitor until morning when Herb pointed out the bear's paw marks. Before the high country became snow-free, Herb and Lois began the herculean task of stocking their various camps and caches with food, film and equipment necessary to photograph without undue interruption after the high country was open enough to travel through.

From Chicago Camp cache, they carried loads to Lake Beauty and Queets Basin, often walking over snow fields. Sometimes Herb had to chop footholds across steep places where hard-packed snow and ice blocked the way. Sometimes snow cover made walking easier because it filled in the rough features of the land and covered windfalls and brush. Downhill descents could often be made in record time, if the terrain wasn't too steep, simply by sliding on their rear ends, dragging the bottom end of their packboards for a brake.

From the South Fork Quinault they carried loads up the Big Creek trail past Three Lakes, spending the night at Three Prune Shelter, then on through snow, slush and ice to Kimta Basin where Herb had decided to establish Far Camp, the last in the chain.

On the return trip, getting an early start from Kimta, packs empty, they made the trailhead, 14 miles, in one long, exhausting day. At trailhead they spread sleeping bags they'd left in the car under a spruce tree, ate some extra rations and turned in for the night.

Between trips, Herb laid by the garden so they would be free in July to head "upstairs" to film the elk herds as the animals worked their way to the timberline basins in search of the first green grasses.

After several years of following Herb and living the rugged outdoor life, Lois began to blossom as a keen observer and talented writer--although nothing much had been published yet.

She even summoned up enough courage to go to the outdoor privy at night without flashing the light into the nearby apple tree and on top the root cellar to check and see if the cougar was watching.

She learned to decipher the meanings of tracks in the snow, to read where a tiny Townsend's chipmunk's life had suddenly ended by a bloody splotch, victim of the swooping talons of a swooping, sharp-shinned hawk. To marvel at frost patterns on dead alder leaves, budding Oregon oxalis and other subjects which surrounded her. Sometimes she'd lie down on the forest floor and closely examine the mosses and lichen that grew in profusion in the rain forest.

Lois Crisler's academic friends, the ones who had given the marriage six months to a year, misjudged this remarkable woman badly.

Lois' upbringing shouldn't have been conducive to the outdoor life. Far from it. Her father, the Reverend M.R. Brown, once had a parish circuit in Waterville, Washington, near Wenatchee. The Browns separated while Lois was about 12. Lois and her mother moved to Spokane.

Her mother, a courageous, ambitious girl, had left Ohio and homesteaded on the Great Plains. She had lived alone in a sod hut while proving up on her land, then later moved to the Columbia River Basin, where she attended the Ellensburg normal school, now Central Washington College of Education.

After the separation, Lois' mother's desire was to educate her daughter to become an intellectual. Having learned the value of an education the hard way, Mrs. Brown encouraged Lois to read and devote herself to an academic life. To pay for her child's education, Mrs. Brown went back to teaching school.

Pampered and dominated by her mother, Lois was blatantly ignorant about cooking, housekeeping and the "drudgery" of ordinary life. She was a bookworm, reading everything she could get her hands on.

Because of this, many of Lois' friends assumed she wasn't cut out for the rugged life necessary to follow Herb Crisler.

According to Hazle Chapman, Lois Brown Crisler could be a tough-minded, competitive person if she chose. She was capable of much hardship without whimpering or flinching.

Ms. Chapman claims Lois loved the wilderness. But what really drove her to stay with it were animals and wildflowers. Perhaps that was one reason why, at age 45, she was willing to give up her profession at the university, and a steady paycheck, in favor of the uncertain, but perhaps more romantic, life as the wilderness wife of a penniless photographer. Later she would write about her values of wilderness:

Elbow room--usable elbow room--is going to become one of the scarcest, most priceless of our national resources--if only it isn't all recklessly squandered before we realize it's gone. The adult personalities of today were shaped on the last of the wilderness. When wilderness goes, the psychology of a country changes from free to slavish. And, there is no such thing as a small wilderness.[1]

Lois' was no stranger to roughing it. Before she married, Lois had met Bettine (Elizabeth) Huelsdonk, daughter of the famous "Iron Man of the Hoh" John Huelsdonk and his wife Dora. John was a legendary hunter, trapper, logger and one of the first white settlers to penetrate and homestead the remote upper Hoh River Valley on the south Olympic Peninsula.

Bettine invited Lois to visit Huelsdonk Ranch. To reach the ranch Lois claimed she, "walked 18 miles by the old puncheon trail from the nearest road. It used to be 25 miles."[2]

Lois walked into the yard to find Bettine splitting cedar boards to build a new house for her and her new husband, John Fletcher. But Bettine wasn't too busy to consider what she described as, "a little vacation trip."

Bettine's idea of pleasure was to climb Mount Tom, 7,048 foot elevation, a remote peak at the head of the South Fork of the Hoh southwest of Mount Olympus. With Bettine's husband Johnny Fletcher and Ed, a Huelsdonk hired man, they set out, walking through old-growth forest, following elk trails, from Huelsdonk Ranch, up the South Fork Hoh and onto the rugged mountain.

This was not a trip anyone not accustomed to roughing it would likely accomplish.

The life the Crislers led in the high, rugged Olympic mountains was uniquely different than the way people lived elsewhere. Herb describes a trip:

On these trips I would plan on being gone for two weeks, following approximately the same route I had taken while living off the country.[3] Everything we needed for the two weeks would have to be carried on our backs; camera and film alone weighed 75 pounds. There were sleeping bags, a tarp for shelter, a few extra clothes such as socks, coats and rain clothes.

Rainfall averages over a hundred inches a year in this country.[4] All one summer I had only four days of sunshine, the rest of the time with the camera in a waterproof bag, fastened to my pack board, which I carried under a poncho.

We made two-week trips on a regular schedule. That was, two weeks on the trip, and one week at Hume's Ranch, then another two-week trip. All during July, August and September, although I had only four photographic days, we made regular scheduled trips.[5]

One reason for the strenuous schedule was because the Crislers were expanding the number of their caches and camps. From Castle-in-the-Cat they tried to make Cream Lake in one long day. With a heavy pack that is a tremendous amount of work.

If they found wildlife and stopped to film, or if they got a late start, reaching Cream Lake was out of the question. Boston Charlie's was not a good substitute, being too close to Cat Basin, exposed to the wind, with no timber available for a lean-to type shelter or a wood supply.

To fill in the gap, Herb built a shelter at Eleven Bull Basin, a small level place with one of the only dry-weather stream along the flanks of the Bailey Range. A tarp was carried in to place over a frame work of poles. This became Camp Three.

Cream Lake Shelter was a log affair, with an excellent view across the lake and of Mount Mathais, 7168 foot elevation. Herb split cedar shakes for the roof from an Alaska cedar windfall. The remains of this log with saw cuts can still be seen about half a mile up the inlet stream in a splendid stand of timber. He backpacked the shakes to the shelter.

I estimated the saw necessary to cut off the shake bolts would have had to have been at least four or five feet in length. The only acceptable method of carrying such a long saw is over one's shoulders, with one's fingers through the teeth or around the handle to balance it. How he carried this saw along the steep grades and across the mean little canyons and washes of the Bailey Range is beyond comprehension. In addition to the saw he would have needed a brace and bit, froe, axe and nails. For a hammer to drive the froe to split the shakes he used a wooden mallet made on the spot out of Pacific yew **Taxus brevifolia**, an extremely tough, but poisonous to humans, wood which grows along steep, high mountainsides.

The Crisler Traverse from Cream Lake to Queets Basin (Cream Lake is described in more detail in Chapter Five) continues through the natural pass between Mounts Ferry and Pulitzer, then along the crest of the divide between the Elwha and Hoh Rivers, past the famous Lone Tree, a wind-blown solitary specimen of subalpine fir. The roots must be embedded in solid rock to prevent it from being blown down by hurricane-force winds. Lone Tree stands without the company of other trees, on the bleak divide between Mount Pulitzer and Mount Childs. Its only limbs, tortured by buffeting winds from the southwest, point to leeward.

In a small clump of subalpine fir and mountain hemlock, **Tsuga mertensiana**, on the east side of this ridge, Herb established one of his most exposed and spectacular camps, called High Camp. Never more than a framework of poles, a tarp and cans containing supplies, this site affords breathtaking views, if one is lucky enough to be there when the sky is clear. Otherwise it is a lonely, isolated and exposed location which one wouldn't choose to suffer through frequent prolonged storms.

From High Camp, the route meandered along the divide, first on one side then on the other to avoid obstacles. Near Mount Childs several spectacular peaks, nameless at the time, rise to about the 6000 foot elevation.

The Crislers called these rock spires the Prophets. The narrow passageway through which they passed Lois called the "Defile of the Prophets." Both names were known only to them. Practically no one else traveled this remote area.

Crisler told several close friends that if anything in the Olympic mountains was ever named for him, he would be delighted if it were these ragged, jagged rock spires.

Although no one man accomplished as much towards promoting and preserving the Olympic Mountain wilds as Herb Crisler, his name does not yet officially grace any mountain, although a lake near Steven Peak does, according to Smitty Parratt, Gods & Goblins, bear the Crisler name. The Crisler Traverse, also unofficial, through the Bailey Range, also bears his name, although it was probably established by Billy Everett and partly by Boston Charlie, who had penetrated as far as Cream Lake decades before Crisler came to the Olympic Peninsula.

These peaks were later named the Ragamuffin, Hoodlum and the Urchin by climbers Kent Heathershaw, Doug Waali and Robert Wood in 1961. Only one name stuck.[6]

The Crisler Traverse then continues along the divide, through Bear Pass, then down heather slopes and snow fields into Queets Basin. Queets Basin shelter, Camp Six, was located on the rim of the basin, at the base of Mount Queets, on the brink of the abrupt drop-off into Queets Canyon.

Crisler described the shelter as a "wonderful one, against a big rock which reflected campfire heat back into the living space." It was later destroyed by avalanche.

The next section of the Crisler Traverse was the most formidable, hugging the western flanks of Mount Queets, Meany and Noyes, all about 6,500 feet elevation, then crossing the worst obstacles on the entire route--Saghalie Canyon. Therein lies a mystery.

Remember, while on the survival trip in 1930, Herb tried to reach the Quinault/Queets divide from Queets Basin and was rebuffed by alder and vine maple thickets and cliffs? We do not know exactly the location, but it is believed to be on the east side of the Queets River Canyon. One can descend through thickets of Sitka alder, the true bane of mountaineers, with difficulty, true, but climbing up is almost impossible, as the trees have been smashed level to the ground by snow.

The alternate route, a detour down the Elwha Snowfinger, up the main Elwha trail to Low Divide then around Mount Seattle on the northern portion of the Skyline Trail is long and strenuous, with much elevation loss and gain.

Therefore, Crisler continued, over a period of years, exploring for a shorter route between Queets Basin and Lake

Beauty. A route around Saghalie Canyon, a formidable, deep gash in the mountainside, the upper end which terminates against the jagged cliffs of Mount Noyes, would have saved much labor. From Queets Basin, as the crow flies, it's only 5 miles to a hairpin curve on the Skyline Trail north of Lake Beauty.

One day Herb and Lois were exploring south of their camp in Queets Basin when they discovered an unknown, but well-used elk trail leading south. Aware that elk knew the country, they followed. The trail became more and more difficult as they went south, in strange country they'd never seen before. As they neared the gaping chasm at the headwaters of Saghalie Creek, they were amazed to learn that elk had discovered a secret crevice, or ledge, along the cliffs. In places the crevice was so narrow they wondered how a mature bull elk with large antlers could pass without his antlers striking the cliff and unbalancing him. Did they turn their heads sideways? After observing some of the places elk have traveled, I wouldn't be surprised.

The route was more like a mountain goat trail, than something an elk would use, but the Crislers had seen elk use places they didn't think they could go previously. Only after snow had melted would this route be passable, but being on the west side of the mountain, the sun would melt the snow early in the spring.

Eventually the elk trail reached small meadows containing tiny lakes, on the south side of Saghalie Canyon. Then the trail disappeared as elk spread out to graze. Herb took bearings and blazed a few of the scrubby trees. Elated, they returned to Queets Basin. The next day they packed up their gear and followed the elk trail and were soon at Lake Beauty.

They continued to use this secret route between Queets Basin and Lake Beauty until they quit the country in 1950.

On a solo trip in 1966, starting from the Quinault, when Herb was 74, he suffered a bad fall while looking for the south end of this trail, in the vicinity of the Skyline Trail. Seriously injured, Herb remained in camp for several days until he was able to walk again. He again spent several days searching for the shortcut, failing to locate it. No elk tracks were in the vicinity, and looking over the head of Saghalie Canyon, Herb decided a tremendous rock slide, perhaps during a severe earthquake that shook Western Washington during the late 1940's, eliminated the trail.

Herb completed the 1966 trip, by a difficult route down across the Queets River, then up Mount Athena until, in the vicinity of the terminal of Jeffers Glacier, where a well-used elk trail between the Queets Valley and Queets Basin traverses the mountainside. Herb arrived at Sol Duc Hot Springs 16 days overdue. He'd been gone 30 days.

On the south side of Saghalie Creek canyon, Herb and Lois had built a camp below Lake Beauty in a dense clump of fir. The cache consisted of a lean-to shelter of poles with a tarp to place over it during the summer. A rough board cupboard was nailed in a tree. A splendid, well-used elk trail passed near the camp. It wasn't unusual to hear the clatter of elk hooves passing during nights spent here in this wild, remote spot.

After leaving Lake Beauty their route continued uphill, intersected the now practically abandoned Skyline Trail, then meanders back and forth along the divide between the Queets and South Fork Quinault. Deep snow lies here, on the north-facing slopes, occasionally until August.

The trail crosses Hee Haw Pass then swings to the Quinault drainage and winds around, as well as up and down, some devilishly-steep little washouts and ravines. This trail is impassable for horses and seldom used by anyone, since it's free of snow only a short period of the season. The park service does practically no maintenance on the high portions of this trail.

A mile south of Hee Haw Pass one comes suddenly, and surprisingly, in this land of near-vertical geographical features, onto a pretty little bench with a level place for camping. A spring, the only water during late summer between Lake Beauty and Kimta Peak, is bordered by yellow mountain-heather, varileaf cinquefoil, sub-alpine buttercup and mountain monkeyflower. Several old campfire rings, some no doubt used by Crisler, although it wasn't one of his stocked camps, indicate use. It's sometimes referred to as "high camp" by backpackers.

From "high camp" the route angles upwards along barren slopes over glacier-polished rock outcroppings. This section is known as the "cairns" because several were built on likely places to guide the traveler. The cairns lead to Promise Creek Pass.

The trail then plunges down switchbacks into immense Kimta Creek Basin, which has several arms, all precariously steep. The trail hangs by its toes along the Quinault side of the divide, passes through a recent burn and windfalls, then snakes up through large patches of luscious huckleberry on the slopes of Kimta Peak, a favorite hangout for black bear during the fall. The trail traverses the east side of Kimta Peak, where there is a tiny level place, room for several sleeping bags, and a trickle of water in late summer. One clear night, during a full moon, I laid in my sleeping bag and watched a black bear eating berries near camp.

A splendid 7 x 7 Roosevelt bull elk in Kimta Basin.

The trail then zigzags along the divide and finally breaks out onto level, open meadows at the headwaters of South Kimta Creek. Kimta or Far Camp was located here on a tree-covered knoll with excellent visibility into the meadows below. The cache was in a grove of fir. The only trace I found in 1991 were a few blazes, nails in trees for hanging clothing and fire-blackened rocks.

This camp was supplied by backpacking from the South Fork Quinault. Far Camp wasn't completed until the late 1940's and, being so far, wasn't used much.

Why did Crisler bother to travel as far as Kimta Basin to photograph? Because one of the largest herds of elk anywhere in the Olympics spent summers in this vicinity during that period.

The large herds no longer exist. Probably due to heavy hunting pressure in recently clear-cut logged areas adjacent to the national park and an abundance of cougar, a major predator of elk and deer.

The most beautiful, and largest, Roosevelt elk bull I've photographed was down the mountain half a mile below the trail in this area. I had been exploring along the Skyline Trail, carrying only camera gear, sleeping bag, a bit of food and tent fly. It was late afternoon. I was already weary, having walked ten miles, and out of food when I spotted two 7X7 bulls fighting far below the trail. I went down and began photographing. They broke off the engagement, and one bull kept moving slowly down the mountain. He was an ideal model, fascinated by my cow chirp, and allowed me to photograph him several times. Suddenly I realized the sun was setting. I had a long, sweaty climb back up to the trail. It was getting dark by then, and I carried no flashlight. I hurried towards Three Prune, where I had cached tent and food, but didn't arrive there until long after dark. Fortunately there was a full moon, or I would have been forced to spend a hungry night in my sleeping bag on the trail.

Some of Herb's most productive filming took place near here. If no elk were present, and this was often the case, they retraced their steps, taking two and a half or three days to reach Cream Lake.

Frequently the Crislers discovered animals they wished to photograph, but were located so far off the route they set up temporary "prop" camps, a tarp and a couple pots, using supplies from the nearest main camp.

One of Herb's most famous still photographs was made at a prop camp southwest of Mount Ferry, with an excellent view of Hoh Glacier. He is squatting down beside a campfire with a skillet in one hand. Several pots and pans are strewn on the ground nearby. Filling the background is immense Hoh Glacier and the jagged peaks of Mount Olympus. The camera caught Herb flipping a hotcake high into the air with the skillet. The hotcake is outlined against the glacier ice, and blots out Athena's Owl, a sharp pinnacle northeast of Mount Olympus.

Another lean-to shelter was built near Chicago Camp along the Elwha River Trail. Herb hired a horse packer to carry supplies to this camp so they could be relayed into Queets Basin and up the Skyline Trail to Lake Beauty.

One of the hazards of traveling light between camps was being detained by weather, such as low, blinding clouds and fog. Frequently they found game, and photographed until it was too late to travel, and had to spend the night, known in the jargon of mountaineering as "siwashing." Spending a night in the open with no food, sleeping bag, and perhaps no fuel for a fire, was something to be avoided, if possible, because weather in the Olympic Mountains is so changeable.

At least the Crislers had the luxury of a fire during their years in the mountains. Fires are now prohibited above 2500 feet. It seems unlikely the Crislers could have spent long periods in the high country without fire to dry clothing, cook and keep warm through long spells of rainy weather. Lightweight backpack stoves were unavailable.

How did Herb carry all those tons of equipment? At first he used an army rucksack, then a surplus Trapper Nelson-type pack board. Carrying the Pathe newsreel camera, which with tripod weighed nearly 100 pounds, on such a board was impossible. He built his own in 1921, using Alaska cedar for the framework, a canvas cover and hooks along both sides to lash the load to.

After he decided to make a career of wildlife photography in 1934 Herb built another version. The previous canvas-covered board caused excessive sweating. The new frame was long enough he could grasp the lower ends, which helped support the heavy loads while removing the pack and made it easier to rest the ends on the ground while taking a break. The long packboard ends also allowed one to dig them into the snow when sliding on their butts down snow fields. Instead of canvas, he covered the part which rested against his back with strong commercial fishing cord so his back could ventilate.

Two inches of the lower ends of the frames were covered with tin to prevent them from splitting when dropped or dragged over rocks or hard-packed snow and ice on steep downward descents.

Herb Crisler with heavy pack load of supplies, Appleton Pass, headed for the Bailey Range.

On one side was a strap for his tripod and on the other a strap for his axe. This new pack board served for over 20 years and was later used in Colorado and the Arctic.

What was the heaviest pack Crisler ever carried? He was asked this question often:

> Probably the iron stove top from Olympic Hot Springs. Schoeffel couldn't believe I'd packed that all the way to the Hotcake Camp--said it must have weighed 125 pounds. Maybe it did. I remember resting a lot going up those switchbacks toward Appleton Pass. [7]

The logistics of supplying seven remote main camps, plus another nine caches, was expensive, complicated and involved:

After I located the seven campsites, the weight we had to carry decreased, but it took more capitol. On our return trip the system was to leave our sleeping bags and all extra film and grub at the last camp. Here the sleeping bags stayed the rest of the time, along with the shelter tarp. The following trip we would leave them at the next camp, and so on, until when we left Hume's Ranch [1951] we had 16 camps and 32 sleeping bags in the Olympics.

Many of our shelters were bark or shake lean-to's. I knew this country well before I took Lois through it. I had discovered possible ways of getting over impossible places; sometimes by swinging around a cliff by the limb of an alpine tree, or feeling for a handhold back of a rock that I couldn't see around. It always tickled Lois when I had felt for some time for a place I knew was somewhere near, but hadn't been able to find. I would say: 'Somebody moved my handhold.' I delighted in showing how much I had learned about the Olympics and the animals.

The Olympic elk is not the most productive herd animal in the U.S.A. (About 3000 at the time I was filming them) But elk has become the mountain goat of its species. In winter they browse along the rivers and low benches, but with the coming of spring, they start up for the high mountain meadows. During the summer, a herd's range may include a dozen basins or watersheds. They feed along the top of knife ridges, going from one basin to another. At this time the cows and calves form large bands. The young bulls stay together, but some of the younger are seen with the cows. The old bulls have bachelor clubs. Elk are a sociable animal, with the exception of the "hermit" bull. He is always found alone, and never mixes with the others. The hermit bulls were once herd bulls, but have been whipped-out by stronger, younger bulls.

The Olympic elk is a very silent animal until about the first week of September. At this time the bulls begin to communicate. Bulls have a variety of sounds: the bugle, the squeal, grunt and a combination of all three. The cows have only one, a "startled bark." Most bull's voices differ from each other. I could tell from the voice which bull it was; whether it was a certain herd bull or a mature outrider who was aspiring to become a herd bull, who felt strong and mature enough to challenge the herd bull to a showdown. The last of September is the mating time. Bugling is the signal that the rut is approaching.

Elk have developed a system of selective breeding that evolved them into the largest species of red deer in the world. In early September one of the more aggressive large bulls, often the herd bull of the year before, will start rounding up cows and keep them together, running away any other bull that comes near. By this time the elk's antlers are mature, and the velvet begins to shed. They help this process by rubbing their antlers on alpine trees, stripping off the bark and polishing their antlers until they gleam in the sunlight.

As September days go by, the mountain sides turn crimson and gold. Bugling increases. Tension builds until the very atmosphere is electric. At any time now one of the outrider bulls may seriously challenge the herd bull to fight, and the winner takes all. Many times I have seen this happen, but was never lucky enough to get movies of it. I wasn't at the right place at the right time. It was either too dark, too stormy or I was too far away. I had learned to tell by the voice of the challenging bull and the actions of the herd when a real fight was about to occur.

The first time Lois was with me at this challenging time, one of nature's mysteries unfolded before our eyes. We were resting in a meadow, and the camera on its tripod stood near. Three hundred yards up the steep mountainside was a herd of elk. The herd bull and about half the cows were lying down. The others were feeding nearby. No other elk could be seen but outriders could be heard bugling all around.

Soon I heard a challenge I knew. 'Lois,' I said, 'there's going to be a fight.' The herd bull and cows stood up. 'He is going to round up his harem in a tight formation,' I said. He rounded them up. The outrider challenged again, much closer now. 'The herd bull will move towards the challenger and wait. The cows will stay where they are,' I predicted. That was confirmed. Another bugle from the challenger.

I said to Lois, 'He will soon appear opposite the herd bull through those trees, and when this happens there will be some of the fastest maneuvering and footwork you have ever seen. The bull that is highest on the mountain when contact is made will have the best chance of winning.' The action started when the challenger broke through the alpine trees and each bull ran up the mountain, angling towards the cows, which were standing rigid as a statue.

The next few moments were the most exciting I have ever witnessed. The challenger was gaining elevation faster than the herd bull, but, the old herd bull was a quick thinker. He whirled around and started to climb at an angle, in the opposite direction, before the challenger figured out what to do. Then the herd bull switched back to his original direction, and in making the switchback maneuver he was able to travel faster, and thereby out-climb the bull that was going straight up the mountainside. The challenger saw his mistake too late. The herd bull had gained enough elevation to be able to turn and meet him head on, running down the mountain before contact. This monstrous punch knocked the challenger sideways, and scrambling down the mountain he seemed to have difficulty keeping his balance. He seemed glad to just back up and stagger through the trees without a harem.

After the excitement was over, Lois looked at the camera standing on the tripod--unused. She gave me a knockout punch: 'Are you a farmer, or a photographer?' she asked. I felt like following the defeated elk back into the brush.[8]

What did the Crislers eat while in the wilds? People asked that question frequently. Remember, this was long before freeze-dried backpack food and many other lightweight dehydrated foods which are widely available today. Lois answers the question of what they took, and what they didn't take:

On a ten-day or two-week vacation you can survive on almost anything. But we are out almost all summer. Besides, we want to keep our strength so we can do this kind of thing for years to come.

We prefer naturally dehydrated foods like beans and rice. We take lima beans or kidney beans because they are said to be higher grade proteins than navy beans. We take brown rice because we cannot afford to backpack the vitamin-deficient white rice.

Dehydrated proteins are hard to get. Two years ago we had a spree of amino acid preparations. They were dehydrated proteins that set us back two bucks a can and tasted like drugs.

Then we discovered "multi-purpose" food at 35 cents a can. It tasted like onions, combines with other food and is said to be equivalent to steak, peas and lettuce.

We take lots of powdered milk. Every day I make up two cups of powdered milk into liquid. That's equivalent to two quarts. We drink this milk plain and hot, seasoned with a little butter and salt. We put lots of powdered eggs into hot cakes and camp bread, as well as making scrambled eggs.

We take good old "rat trap" cheese because its said to be richer in protein than the processed kind. For fruits we use mostly apricots and prunes. Apricots require very little sugar and prunes none.

One thing we don't do that many campers do. We don't eat a lot of candy. We have practically eliminated chocolate bars and other candies from our diet.

We have found that if we have enough good protein we have no desire for chocolates.

After a ten-day or two-week trip most backpackers come out famished, with canker sores in their mouths and talking about what they're going to eat first when they get "outside."

We used to be like that too, till we discovered that most of the "hidden hunger" was due to a lack of raw vegetables and fruit. Now we supplement our camp diet with one lemon a day between us, one small orange apiece daily and one raw green pepper between us daily.

We selected green peppers because they are light and richest in vitamins for their weight. Besides, they are in units and keep well in a moist plastic bag.

Since adding these to our diet we haven't experienced that ravenous craving, although we may be on camp diet for as long as three weeks at a time.

If there's anything we do long for it's freshly picked fruit. One of our most frustrating experiences occurred once when we came home after a long trek in the mountains, expecting to have a big dish of fresh strawberries right out of Herb's Ga'den.

A couple of guests had arrived at our cabin from Seattle the day before. They had eaten all the strawberries and for a homecoming treat for us had cooked split pea soup and a big dish of chocolate pudding.

To us, even in camp, pea soup and chocolate pudding are at the bottom of the list of "dead" unliked foods.

For us, even in the mountains, we have gelatin made with fresh, raw lemon. [9]

Making do with trail food which had been laboriously packpacked into the wilderness, while a garden of fresh vegetables went unused at Hume's Ranch was one of the frustrations of spending summers in the high country. They mentioned it often.

The Crislers had what many might consider odd trail eating habits. On arising, Herb drank one quart of warm water spiked with two tablespoons of apple cider vinegar, one tablespoon of Fruit Fresh(T) and two tablespoons of honey. For breakfast they liked hotcakes, oatmeal with chipped beef or dried whole milk, honey, butter and applesauce.

For lunch they sometimes had cornmeal mush with cheese and prunes or apricots.

Supper consisted of all the hot, powdered whole milk they wanted, seasoned with butter and salt. Herb insisted he slept better if he went to bed without a lot of solid food in his stomach.

The first trip into the mountains each summer to examine the condition of the caches was always a time of suspense. Especially after winters of unusually heavy snowfall. Avalanches were always a hazard for most of the high camps, especially the ones located in basins such as Cream Lake and Queets Basin.

The loss of a cache in their line of camps was a serious matter. They might stagger into a camp late in the evening, worn out, looking forward to a dry bed, shelter and food, only to find the camp swept away, with the next a long day's march away. Such a loss would mean backpacking in tools, rebuilding, then trips to resupply, all during precious, snow-free photographing time.

Occasionally, they entered the Bailey Range from Dodger Point. The route, after leaving the dead-ended abandoned trail on Ludden Peak, is a difficult one. Ludden Peak forms an obstacle which must either be scaled, or traversed.

The traverse is a seldom-used, difficult to find way trail which meanders along the side of a cliff face on the east side of the rugged peak. One nasty little rock cliff and steep rock slide has to be traversed where ropes for security are a good idea. Then the route continues down a snow-filled gully to the upper edge of a vertical cliff, where one is forced to make a right turn and clamber up the side of the gully through a tangle of twisted, yellow cedar trees flattened by snow.

Retired Park Ranger Robert Baldwin of Port Angeles, who has made many trips into the Bailey Range, says Crisler built a ladder and kept it positioned where one must climb up the steep bank out of this gulley.

From there the way trail traverses the mountain, then climbs a very steep pitch, if you're carrying a heavy pack, to the Scott/Ludden Saddle where there's an ideal camp spot in a tiny, level meadow. An elk trail angles up the mountain and along the divide between Goldie River and Long Creek, south of Ludden Peak to another camping spot above a little lake. Next the very summit of Mount Ferry, elevation 6,157 feet, has to be climbed. There is no other way as cliffs on either side block progress. As usual, the elk know the best, and sometimes only route between ranges.

After the strenuous labor of backpacking supplies into the rugged and remote Bailey Range, some items might be considered too precious to use. This was the experience Lois had the very first time she went to Cream Lake with Herb:

He opened the cache [in the hollow tree] and lovingly laid out each object on the mountain meadow while I watched.

I was very tired and hungry and one object made a profound impression on me. It was a two-and-a-half pound can of ham. Tonight, I thought, we eat well.

Then Cris started putting things back into the cache. He put back the ham. 'Lois', he said, 'you betta hurry and get that dried onion soup started or we won't have a thing to eat.'

Two years later the ham spoiled. Uneaten. Poetic justice.[10]

Lois used sarcasm like a fencer uses his sword.

Notes and Sources, Beyond The Trails, Chapter Eleven

1. Lois Crisler, "Olympic Trail Talk--85." The Port Angeles Evening News. 2 Feb., 1951

2. Lois Crisler, "Olympic Trail Talk--3." The Port Angeles Evening News, 24 June 1949

3. He refers to the 1930 survival trip. On the trips referred to here they did not cross the upper Hoh River and go onto Hoh Glacier, but continued around the Bailey Range to Queets Basin.

4. Some years much more than that. In 1997, the official rainfall at Hoh Ranger Station, before Ranger Martha Hutchinson closed the station temporarily because of the road washout, was 190.42 inches, a new record. According to District Ranger Bill Rohde at Kalaloch, the unofficial record may have been an astounding 200 inches, or 16.66 feet!

5. Herb Crisler, "Western Wildlife Photographer," courtesy Ruby El Hult.

6. Only the name The Ragamuffin stuck. The peak they named The Urchin, is now un-named. The peak they christened The Hoodlum is now known as The Urchin. Smitty Parratt, Gods & Goblins, CP Publications, Inc., (Port Angeles, WA 1984)

7. Ruby El Hult, Herb Crisler in the Olympic Mountain Wilds, 2nd Edition, Swallowtail Press. (Puyallup, WA 1992)

8. Herb Crisler, "Western Wildlife Photographer", courtesy Ruby El Hult.

9. Lois Crisler, "Olympic Trail Talk--6", The Port Angeles Evening News, 6 July, 1949

10. Lois Crisler, "Olympic Trail Talk--7", 22 July, 1949.

12

The First Tour
The Frogs Lend a Hand. The Crislers Meet Walt Disney.
To Cream Lake with Billy Everett.

During the winter of 1946, after a long, tiresome session of editing film in a breakfast nook at Olympic Hot Springs, the closest electricity, and several try-out showings around the Northwest, Herb decided to drive to Georgia to visit his mother. Lois was incredulous. A little angry, perhaps. How could he even consider such a thing? They had little money and figured it would cost at least $1,000. The old Hudson coupe wobbled on its last legs, barely able to make trips to Seattle, let alone Georgia. Suppose it broke down?

But Herb was capable of lightning-swift decisions, unafraid of plunging in, sometimes against odds which might turn another man's hair white. He thought it would be worth while testing the waters of a more sophisticated audience for their films and lectures. He steadfastly refused to allow a lack of money to prevent him from following his hunches. Lois threw up her hands in despair.

One tiny thread of hope dangled within their grasp. Lois had met the wife of Alan Hunter, author and pastor of Mount Hollywood Congregational Church in Hollywood, California. Lois wrote and asked if they might show at the church for half the donations. The showing was confirmed. This might produce gas money--if anyone attended? If those who did come emptied their pockets of change into the hat!

All other bookings they would have had to be arranged while on the road; difficult, with no mailing address or phone number for prospective customers to use.

The Hollywood showing looked big to them, as they set out in Lois' old car, simply because it was the only hope they had.

Before they left, Webster, publisher of the <u>Port Angeles Evening News</u> suggested Lois send back frequent reports relating their travels for the local paper. It was the break Lois needed to begin writing in earnest. Into the already overloaded Hudson, on top the projector, photo equipment, cans of film, screen, camping gear, personal possessions and winter clothing, went Lois' typewriter.

This would be the very first time they had ever shown to an audience outside the Pacific Northwest. Would sophisticated southern Californians boo their "chipmunk" pictures?

This possibility passed through their minds as they chugged along Highway 99 through rain-drenched Oregon. Rivers were flooding, windblown limbs were across the roads, people were desperately trying to get home, and the Crislers were traveling!

They pinched every precious dollar, eating store-bought food, looking for the lowest gas prices. At Grants Pass they left Highway 99 and went down the Pacific Coast Highway through the Redwoods, rather than dare snowy Siskiyou Summit, 4310 feet elevation, with their worn tires.

Lois, who had worried herself sick about financing the trip to begin with, eventually began to relax and enjoy herself as gigantic redwood groves appeared alongside the road. She was astonished to discover that each grove had been bought and preserved by groups or individuals. She read the names on the signs as they passed: Arnold Grove, Cedarville Garden Club Grove, Huntington Grove. Which led Lois to observe:

I wished our own Indian Valley, as stately and thrilling back in 1926 as these California redwoods, could have been saved this same way by Port Angeles and Seattle businessmen, if not for nature lovers, at least for tourists.[1]

This was her first trip to California. And she had a writing __assignment!__ She provided her readers with a visual feast, observing and note-taking with incredible lucidity:

> California, dank, cold, but kids playing in the streets. A girl in a studded sombrero. Mud-colored streams and rivers. Mud-colored sheets on the line. [Then, as they got farther down] The faint stink of fertilizer from the fields. History-dripping San Luis Obispo was just our first pepper trees and purple vines. Beyond it, speeding towards the ocean, we came to the interesting part, flat, brown velvet fields slanting to the sea, red tomatoes that never froze, and tender, green-clad hills.[2]

In Ventura they were successful at booking at the Museum of Natural History in Santa Barbara for the return trip. Then they headed for Los Angeles.

San Francisco they had taken with gaiety. Los Angeles crushed them. "It was so vast, so impersonal, so greedy," Lois wrote.

They drove into North Hollywood on Sunday, December 7, the worst possible day of the entire year for bumper-to-bumper traffic. This was the day of the annual Christmas tree lighting, several miles of fantastically-lighted Christmas trees and yard displays, which most of the local population drove to see.

Although the highway was six-lanes wide, it was locally considered "Christmas Tree Lane!" The traffic was crushing, the drivers rude and the air was thick with stinking, stifling smog, a term the Crislers had never heard before. Herb describes how they felt:

> Driving in this strange, hot, fast, hazy tumult we were the most lost, discouraged mountain mice in the world. We were both thinking the same thing. In this vast, arid uproar, what could anyone ever care for our pictures? I was first to put it into words. `Us and our little chipmunks.'
>
> We had never been as discouraged or overwhelmed as we were that evening in our motel. It never even occurred to either of us that this was our wedding anniversary.[3]

Despite a hunch no one would attend their film and lecture in this sprawling, strange city, they found the church, set up and were astonished when a large, enthusiastic audience arrived. The film was applauded over 100 times! Applause so spontaneous Lois had a difficult time getting her narration across! Hollywood people loved the films.

After the lights came on, people crowded around the Crislers to shake hands and congratulate them on their film. For an hour they fielded questions about the Olympic Peninsula, Olympic National Park and Hume's Ranch. To the Crislers' total surprise, several people announced they intended to come and visit such a beautiful, unusual place.

Most important, famous, influential people were in the audience. People like Larry Trimble, who trained Strongheart, and other celebrities. People who not only appreciated their work but were willing to help the Crislers show their pictures elsewhere. They stayed that night with Reverend Alan Hunter.

The bewildered, yet elated photographers decided perhaps there was an audience in the cities who thirsted for exactly the type of product they had to offer. Who could blame them, considering the crowded, foul-smelling conditions in this sprawling city? Viewing, even on a screen, the green, lush Olympics and its abundant wildlife was like a breath of fresh air.

One couple who attended, Mr. & Mrs. Paul Granger, invited them to visit, and stay as long as they wished. They accepted with some misgivings: the Grangers were total strangers. When they reached the Granger place the following night they discovered it was dream castle:

> A concrete, stucco, and oak house with big balconies, as stately and romantic as a Romeo and Juliet stage-setting, in the Chisleshurst District below the Griffith Park planetarium and overlooking the city. In our bedroom the tall window draperies and the covers on the beds were of slipper satin in palest apricot cream; the chaise-lounge and chairs were in cream satin. You could track a person in the nap of the carpet. When we were alone I told Cris, 'Now you mustn't sit here or here or here.'
>
> A minute later I looked around and he had spread his jacket neatly on the floor and sat down on

it.

'Don't want to get any of that satin fluff on my pants,' he said.

Nothing so vulgar as one bathroom. Mine was cream color, with tub and shower. Cris' was in cream and delft blue.

However that wasn't so much. We have a two-seater at Hume's Ranch.

What we do not have at Hume's Ranch is a maid to bring us breakfast in bed, a luxury I took advantage of just for the experience. The first time, I felt as silly as when Cris rolled me up the trail in the wheelbarrow. We ordered our meals when we pleased. When we had them in the sunny breakfast room and our host and hostess were absent, the maid kept popping in to ask us if we wanted anything. We could not figure out why she was so attentive till we discovered that Cris was tramping on the little call button under the table.[4]

Paul, an inventor, showed them his pride and joy, a well-equipped machine shop where he pursued his hobby of manufacturing things. His private garage contained several expensive, shiny cars.

Granger explained his wealth. His father had struck it rich in the Colorado mining fields, and had left his fortune to his only child, Paul.

The Grangers listened to stories about the Crislers' experiences in the Olympic mountains with avid fascination. They seemed especially interested in Hume's Ranch, and how they managed to live in such a place. They marveled to think people actually lived where they had to carry everything on their backs two and a half miles by trail to reach home.

While watching the motion-pictures of Hume's Ranch, Paul had noticed Herb pushing a heavily-loaded old wheelbarrow up a steep trail. He inquired about that. Herb told how he had found a wheel and built the home-made wheelbarrow to haul some of the heavier items such as stove wood, lumber and decayed vegetation for the garden. Herb explained that pushing the wheelbarrow up a steep hill from the lower field to the cabin loaded with wood almost caused him to rupture himself.

To their total amazement they discovered that some of their newly-found friends, without even being asked, were already arranging showings for them when they came back through in the spring.

The Grangers also mentioned if they ever wished to visit San Diego, they kept a house there, with a maid and gardener, and the Crislers were welcome to use it for as long as they wished.

Staying with the Grangers gave Lois a chance to unlimber her typewriter. Her first column, "Crislers Have Series of Adventures While On Journey Into South to Show Their Films," was published in the Port Angeles Evening News 15 January 1947.

The column became an instant success. The war and gas rationing were over. People were anxious to go motor traveling again. The Crislers had many, many admirers on the Peninsula, as well as elsewhere. Subscribers licked up Lois' home-spun style and clamored for more. The circulation department was mystified after receiving several subscriptions from southern California.

With her academic background and experience, Lois was certainly capable of writing for intellectuals. Instead, with instinctive knowledge of her potential readers, she chose to point her literary pen at the common people, the type she might encounter while shopping at McGlenn's Grocery or Ben Franklin's.

As they prepared to leave, they extended an invitation to visit Hume's Ranch, not really expecting the sophisticated Grangers would be interested. The Grangers accepted enthusiastically, promising to come the following spring.

They drove away in awe, wondering what the Grangers, accustomed to living in a palace in Los Angeles, would think of their little log cabin, the two-hole outdoor privy, no electricity, no running water and a family of skunks living beneath the hand-hewed puncheon floor? Lois hoped they'd change their minds and not come. Herb though they'd love Hume's Ranch.

They drove on east, stopping to visit Lois' cousin in Claremont, a college town out in the desert east of Los Angeles. The cousin arranged for them to show their films at Scripps College, where she worked, on their return trip. Unknown to the Crislers, this and the other spring showings in Southern California would provide unexpected, long-term benefits.

They headed east across the Mojave desert. They stopped beside a dingy motel in Indio late that night. Herb went looking for a room. He stomped back. "They want $4 for a dirty little room," he growled, driving on.

Later, out in the desert, with stars glittering overhead, they flung their sleeping bags and air mattresses on the hard ground, undressed by the light of the moon and hung their clothes on a creosote bush. They were lulled to sleep by the yapping of coyotes. When their money ran low, they stopped at churches, asking if they could show a wildlife movie. More often than not, they met with curt brush-offs.

They prayed they didn't have car trouble. They ate frugally, camped out whenever they could.

On the Peninsula, the Ravens had stepped in and helped when their finances ran low. Now, in the arid southwest, they discovered another group which appreciated their motion-pictures:

> What kept us going was our discovery of the "Frogs." We use this term with all humility and respect. It came from my experience when I lived off the country for 30 days in the wilderness. My `bread' proved to be the little frogs in the mountain lakes. Our `frogs' were now one of the few religious denominations, so close and brotherly across the continent that the recommendation of one group automatically lets you in with groups a thousand miles farther on. This denomination was the Seventh Day Adventists. They paid us a fee of $25. It looked big to us. It kept us eating and gas in our car. We could arrive in a town, call up the leader and have a showing scheduled two days later.[5]

Lois was enthralled with the desert. She couldn't get enough of it, wishing to touch things--until Herb had to pull cholla thorns out of her fingers with tweezers!

They experienced unusually cold weather, until they reached Phoenix:

> It was in Phoenix that we crawled out of the old red flannels into warm sunshine and discovered the first place that competed with the Olympic Peninsula as a bit of God's country. It was the price of fruit that won us. Tangerines picked each with the fresh green leaf on it for 11 cents a pound, heavy grapefruit for three, oranges as big as a baby's head for nine. 'You know, Lois,' said Cris thoughtfully, 'I wouldn't mind a little place here to live, in the winter.'[6]

Lois' eyes missed very little:

> A red-cheeked Mexican young woman driving a high yellow tractor. Her black hair shone in a neat American-girl pompadour, her three-year-old baby clung to her side as they bounced along.[7]

Working their way east, they were disappointed by the dirtiness of El Paso, on the old Butterfield Trail. At every gas station Lois had questions for the attendant: "What is that brush spotting the hills?" "Cedar, Ma'am." "But wasn't it greasewood a few miles farther back?" Her articles were filled with intricate detail.

Did Herb ever remind Lois: "I told you if you'd marry me you'd have something to write about." Yes, he certainly did.

Their first stop in Herb's home state of Georgia was Savannah, which Lois described as, "An old ugly city, through slums of tumble-down gingerbread near rich mansions of pre-Civil war days, where now black negroes swarmed."

At Herb's sister Gladys', they enjoyed southern home-cooking, a turkey dinner served by a negro maid.

They turned north, visiting Mother Crisler and Herb's brothers, Albert and Lester in Charlotte, North Carolina. It was a tearful reunion.

A more tearful parting. They bent their route back west towards Herb's old birthplace, near Athens:

> The deep beautiful red mud that coated cars like rust as high as the door handles prevented our driving out to Grandfather Bruce's farm, Cris's birthplace. We slewed out two miles though, the car going crab-wise, to the Jarrett mansion. In every district there is one big old house that once dominated the whole country, its former owner raising cotton in every bottom between the hills and floating it down the river to Augusta.[8]

They explored one of the old abandoned mansions, rotting into eternity now, with a little clap-board kitchen-house out back where negroes had sweated and cooked over wood fires to keep the heat out of the mansion. They found huge dugout oaken troughs in the musty old smokehouse, troughs where hams and bacon had been salted and seasoned before smoking. Lois looked wistfully at the size of the logs. There were no trees anywhere that large now, she commented. Tin cans littered the back yard, having been pitched out the window:

      'Pity it couldn't have been kept up and preserved,' Cris said. 'Up north that would have been done.'

      'Yes, the way we're preserving the unique old Ludden cabin,' I said ironically, 'with its deer-skin furniture.'[9]

They had proudly showed their films of green-clad Olympic mountains to 2000 people while in the South and received many exclamations of surprise and delight. Few had even heard of the Olympic Peninsula. When they mentioned Washington, several people mistook their meaning for Washington D.C.!

Back in California, they showed their film at Scripps College. After the show, a beautiful lady invited them to her home for dinner. The gracious woman said maybe she could get Wendell and Lucie Chapman to come out from Los Angeles on the spur of the moment to join them. The Crislers had never heard of the Chapmans.

The Chapmans were writers and photographers who loved the wilderness also. They agreed to come. It turned out like a fairy story. The dinner was extravagant. The home was a splendid castle. Everyone was very friendly and polite.

The Crislers listened attentively while the Chapmans explained how they had "educated" their three children by camping for several months on Great Barrier Reef, Australia, toured New Zealand, and later included the children while photographing animals on safari in Africa.

Herb was fascinated by the Chapmans. He gladly accepted an invitation to visit them in Los Angeles.

The Chapmans had never even seen the Crisler pictures. They had only their host's word that the pictures were extraordinary. When Herb and Lois next showed the film at a Hollywood church the following Friday, the Chapmans not only came, but brought 20 guests of their own. It was a warm, crowded and appreciative showing.

Also present were two associates from the nearby Walt Disney Studio. They invited the Crislers to the studio for lunch.

After the showing, Lois asked Mrs. Chapman how she had liked the pictures. "Wait till you come and stay with us," she said.

So the Crislers in their mud-spattered old Hudson followed the Chapmans to a big apartment perched on a steep hillside. They were shown to a comfortable room with bath.

Without asking, the Chapmans got busy on the telephone. Two days later the Chapmans and the Crislers stepped out of the car at the Pasadena Civic Auditorium. To meet them were two men, the operator for the arc projector and an important-acting man, a prominent booking agent. He was the "key to the back door of all the important Southern California bookings," according to the Chapmans.

Lois and the agent had a falling out right away. The agent insisted Lois stand on stage. Lois explained that wasn't the way they did it. She sat on a high stool back amongst the audience, where she could watch the pictures.

At last the agent capitulated. Five people sat down. Lois and the agent sat side by side, "But like two cats on the back fence, with their fur straight up," in Lois' words.

As scenes of the Olympic Mountains appeared, the fur gradually fell flat. When the blue sky and snow-capped Olympic Mountain vistas taken from Hurricane Ridge filled the screen, the agent, suddenly less important, turned and said softly to Lois: "We'll have to tell folks these aren't painted."

Lois overheard Wendell whisper to Lucie, "They're in."

They were. At the end of the preview they were booked for the Pasadena Civic Auditorium for January and February for the Adventure Series.[10]

Still the Chapmans were not satisfied. They arranged one more preview, this time in a luxurious home near the Planetarium. Lucie baked cookies and Wendell called all the program chairmen of the most important clubs in Hollywood, Los Angeles and the University of California.

After this showing, in a gigantic living room, they had refreshments. One by one the club's chairmen signed up for the following spring.

Why did the Chapmans do all this? Wendell was a busy writer. When the Crislers tried to thank them the Chapmans said, "People were nice to us when we came in from the wilderness with our beaver and moose pictures and our book, **Wilderness Wanderers**. We've just been passing on what we received."[11]

Herb and Lois were euphoric. They floated out of the apartment and drove off suspended on a magic carpet of future, good-paying engagements. Truly, southern Californians were the epitome of appreciative audiences. But the most thrilling was yet to come.

Next they visited the Disney Studio for the lunch appointment. Lois was gawking at wall racks full of books from the Fantasia program to Br'er Fox, when she realized she was not alone. "Walt, this is Mrs. Crisler," someone said. She looked up:

> At a Roman nose and filled teeth above a misty blue and green striped sweater with a russet line and a brown tweedy suit, looking into that face and the gray brown eyes for the genius that dreamed up animation.
>
> `As soon as I get out from behind the eight ball I'd like to do something about your pictures,' Mr. Disney said.
>
> We didn't tell him we were not interested, at least at this time, for our fairy story had already happened.
>
> Then we ran into the man next in authority to Mr. Disney, his producer, Ben Sharpsteen, a tired little man with a kind, brown face, who held out his hand to me. `I understand you have good animal pictures.' `We have good animals,' I replied.[12]

The Crislers hadn't the slightest idea that Walt Disney and Ben Sharpsteen would someday play an important part in their lives. That chapter of the fairy story hadn't been written yet.

Their hosts took them through the studio, where ordinary visitors were not invited, including tiers of narrow little "cells", with paint pots and thousands of cold cream jars sitting by, where young artists were painting hundreds of five by seven celluloid.

Then they entered the film cutting room, where men sat at $5000 editing machines. "That's the way it's supposed to be done," Herb drooled.

Lois threw him a, 'You'll have to be satisfied to work at the breakfast nook at Olympic Hot Springs,' look.

Before leaving southern California, they received a travel-worn letter:

> In February, we received another milestone-marking letter. It had been addressed to Port Angeles and had been seeking us through forwarding addresses for weeks. This letter was from George Pierrot, one of the leading lecture managers in the country, offering us an appearance the following year on his World Adventure Series in Detroit, along with two other nearby showings. All within three days of each other. 'This will at least pay your way east,' he wrote. 'Anything else you can secure will be velvet.'
>
> George's sister and brother-in-law had chanced to see our pictures at a church in Seattle and had written to him about them. On their word, he had taken a chance on perfect strangers.[13]

The Crislers drove out of Southern California in a much more positive mood than they'd had when they arrived. They headed north and put on a show at Reed College, one for the American Camping Association at Gearhart, Oregon, another at Grand Coulee Dam and a final showing in Spokane, Washington, before heading home, arriving in March, 1947. The final travel column from the trip was published in the <u>News</u> on March 7, 1947.

Lois was kept busy maintaining correspondence links, not only with many wonderful people they had met while on the trip, but details with agents regarding the forthcoming bookings.

The ever-growing, demanding audience for their pictures weighed heavily on their minds. Their new network of viewers were sophisticated, well-traveled, educated people who expected a lot from their pictures. Their films were already good, but being true professionals, they resolved to do even better during the summer filming season.

Hume's Ranch seemed like heaven for the two weary travelers. The merry twitter of a winter wren, sitting in a tall

Herb loading "Step 'n Fetch it", the gas powered wheelbarrow.

Douglas fir behind the cabin, welcomed them home. The silence surrounding the ranch seeped into their travel-weary souls. Slowly they unwound, appreciating the calm, tranquil, healing effects of their stock-in-trade, the wilderness and neighboring wild animals.

The family of skunks still resided beneath the floor. No one had bothered anything, but heavy snow had wrecked havoc with the wire mesh over the garden.

The Crislers didn't forget their local fans. They occasionally showed their pictures to Peninsula schools and clubs. It was the school children they enjoyed showing to most--inserting the "value of wilderness message" into receptive young minds.

The fruits of their labor were responsible for the growing interest in the environment during the next several decades. At least this was their goal.

An excellent example of this occurred while doing research at the local library for this book. This writer was scanning microfilm of old newspapers. A lady was waiting to use the machine and asked if I'd mind if she watched how the machine worked. She sat down beside me. I found the column I was looking for and began to read. The lady said excitedly, "That's Lois Crislers' column."

"Did you know the Crislers?" I asked.

"Of course. They came and showed their films to us children at the Sequim elementary school every year. The films were wonderful. Herb wore a beard, which us kids used to joke about. We teased him and told him he looked like the black bear in the film."

Four decades later she recalled scenes from Crislers' pictures: Shots of chipmunks quarreling, Olympic marmots eating wildflower blossoms while lying flat on their stomachs and the bull elk fight!

"Dad took us kids to see The Olympic Elk," she said. "Those wonderful pictures of Crislers turned our family on to Olympic National Park," she said tenderly. "Before that, my dad thought the park was just a waste, all those trees not being used."

Herb hurried to start his garden. Snow in the mountains seemed deeper and lingered later than usual. With prospects of showing to larger audiences in the east, they prayed for good weather and lots of pictures during the late, short summer.

One evening Herb was working in the garden when he heard a strange noise. He put down his hoe and listened. It sounded like a small gasoline engine.

He went to the cabin and alerted Lois. She heard it also. The sound came closer and became louder. What in the world? they wondered.

Down the trail came Paul Granger and his wife. He was driving a motorized wheelbarrow, powered by a two-horsepower, air-cooled engine!

Mrs. Granger, dressed in the latest fashionable hiking clothes, tagged along behind. The wheelbarrow was loaded with suitcases and boxes of food and gifts.

To the Crisler's astonishment, Paul stopped the engine and showed off his invention. "Thought maybe this would ease your work load," he said proudly. [14] Paul explained how to run the machine. The front wheel was driven by a belt attached to the flywheel of the engine. Power could be applied by adjusting a hand lever on one arm of the wheelbarrow.

A gasoline engine at Hume's Ranch? Well! Powered drag saws to cut wood had been used also.

Herb was quick to see the advantage of a powered wheelbarrow and was delighted. They named it Step'n Fetchit.

Instead of being repulsed by the crudeness of Hume's Ranch, the Grangers were captivated. Everything was so simple and uncomplicated they relaxed and enjoyed nature. Their eyes bugged out in astonishment when Herb leaned down outside the cabin and beat on an old pan with a spoon. A skunk appeared from beneath the floor. Herb then fed the animal.

They caught beautiful rainbow trout from the bright, sparkling-clear waters of the river and made an overnight trip to Hotcake Camp. The Grangers' biggest thrill was watching a herd of sleek, brown-and-tan elk slip cross the trail.

At the ranch, Paul tackled the endless task of splitting wood with vigorous gusto. His inventive mind no doubt trying to devise an easier way to split blocks of Douglas fir four feet in diameter. He promised to come back next year and cut a big supply. This pleased Herb. Getting in the wood supply was one project he scarcely had time for.

After obtaining a promise the Crislers would stay with them again when they came to Hollywood that fall the Grangers departed, to tour more of the Peninsula.

Chappy and Carol made their annual appearance at Hume's Ranch in June. First they limbered-up by working on the woodpile. Next they helped Herb rig a cable across the Elwha river so he could drag a raft back and forth, to bring red cedar from the other side. He needed cedar for shakes, and there were none left on the north side of the river.

The girls hinted that they'd like to do some serious mountaineering. How about a trip to the Bailey Range? Herb had promised Billy Everett another trip to Cream Lake, so it was agreed that Carol, Chappy, Billy, Lois and Herb would go. The date was set for late August.

June brought a steady supply of visitors. Some were strangers. A few were from the California audience. Others were long-time friends. All were made welcome. On weekends 20 or 30 people might appear. Despite the fact they were busy, the Crislers managed to spend time with each person, a graciousness people appreciated.

Snow lingered later than usual in the high country. Mount Fitzhenry, a 6000 foot elevation peak across Long's Creek, west of Hume's Ranch, was their weather barometer and snow-pack indicator. By walking out into the big meadow and looking at the mountain they could judge how much snow still lay in the high country.

The weather stayed wet, cool and cloudy. Rain fell almost every day. The garden was up and growing, but they began to wonder whether or not they would get any photography accomplished this season.

They attempted to reach the Bailey Range in late June, by way of the Catwalk, but were forced back to Castle-in-the-Cat by deep drifts, too soft to walk across, on the High Divide. They cached the contents of their packs and returned to wait a few more weeks.

Finally summer burst forth. Warm sunshine and chinook winds melted the already rotten snow in the mountains almost overnight. It was time to go "upstairs."

In Cat Basin, glacier lilies, their blossoms enveloped in protective leaves, still entombed in snow when the Crislers' went to bed, were upright and blooming by morning.

Elk calves frolicked beside attentive cows. A doe deer stood licking her fawn. They watched a mother blue grouse act out her "broken wing" drama to lure them away from her brood.

They spent the next month and a half photographing elk, deer and bear along the steep crags of the Bailey Range. If they

Dodger Point, Lois Crisler facing camera, Billy Everett in light-colored hat at right.

discovered a herd, they followed, if possible, sometimes for days at a time. Usually the elk caught the human scent and disappeared. It was exhausting, frustrating work, but they enjoyed every minute of it. Especially they appreciated solitude and being surrounded by extraordinary beauty.

Their only regret was not being down at the ranch to enjoy the fresh vegetables they knew were coming on. Occasionally Lois would make a solitary trip down to the ranch to water the garden, get the mail and bring back vegetables. Sometimes Herb accompanied her. Other times he remained at one of the camps to film, not wishing to waste a precious day of the short season.

Late August, the date for the trip to Cream Lake with Billy, Carol and Chappy arrived. Herb made arrangements to have their gear carried up the Long Ridge Trail on borrowed horses. Two former students of Lois' agreed to go along as far as Dodger Point, then bring the horses back.

Carol and Chappy were excited. At last they were going to see Cream Lake, which they'd heard so much about. They had refined their backpack equipment since the first trip to Hume's Ranch two years before.

Chappy carried a supply of 120 millimeter black and white film for her Kodak reflex camera. They camped beside the tiny lakes below Dodger Point. The next day the two students took the horses and headed back towards the trailhead at Whiskey Bend.

The five shouldered their packs and set out along the old, abandoned, dead-end trail which terminated on the rocky cliffs on the east face of Ludden Peak.

From the end of the trail on around Ludden Peak is a steep, dangerous traverse, no place for a person with rubber legs and a tipsy balance. Herb used a security rope on the worst pitch, a rock cliff, where a fall could have been serious. Then they had to climb out of the deep gulch, up a home-made ladder to avoid a tangle of Alaska cedar. The girls were astonished at the ease with which Billy negotiated such places. [15]

They ate lunch beside a tiny trickle of water in the saddle between Mount Scott and Ludden Peak, then followed a meandering elk trail to the top of the ridge south of Ludden Peak. They camped above a charming little alpine lake with a view of Mount Ferry. The lake was surrounded by fresh elk tracks.

Carol and Chappy went for a swim in the lake, although it was bitter cold. They returned to camp with glowing cheeks.

The trail then leads up the side of Mt. Ferry, with one dangerous place, where a slip could end in disaster. Once on top, the group were treated to superb views of the Upper Hoh River, Cream Lake Basin, Mount Olympus and the nearby peaks of the Bailey Range.

Billy had been quiet so far on the trip. A slender, slightly-stooped man, 79 years old, Billy had no trouble keeping up and doing his share of the carrying. Now, with his beloved Bailey Range and Cream Lake Basin in full view, his tiredness from the climb disappeared. He became animated, talkative and proudly pointed out beloved places he'd discovered years ago.

Hazle M. Chapman, Billy Everett & Carol Preston on 1947 trip through the Bailey Range.

Hot Cake Camp, Carol Preston on left, Herb Crisler at griddle in the shelter and Billy Everett sitting with eyes closed.

He described the country fondly: "There, by that rocky knob my dogs treed a big tom cougar in 1900. By that little pond a bear maimed Howdy, one of my dogs, in 1914. In that high saddle beside Steven Peak the fog caught me away from camp one evening in 1922. Blinded, with cliffs all around, we didn't dare move. Me and the dogs curled up and shivered until dawn. The fog lifted and there was our camp, only a few hundred feet away." Billy laughed uproariously after telling this.

To descend Mount Ferry, Herb led them almost to the toe of the glacier spilling down the west side of Mount Pulitzer, 6,200 feet in elevation. Chappy still remembers, half a century later, their walk across the alpine basin west of Mount Ferry. A hanging paradise of glacier-polished granite outcrops, purple lupine and paintbrush growing profusely in closely-cropped green alpine meadows. Elk were nature's lawn mowers here. Their tracks and droppings were everywhere. A charming little crystal clear mountain stream tumbled slowly across the meadow, then fell tinkling over a little waterfall. Surrounding snowfields and peaks reflected in a shallow blue pond. Billy led them to a secret, shallow pond, his favorite, private bath in the Bailey Range. Sweaty, they waded in and bathed in the warm water.

The girls now understood Billy's love for this secluded, mystical wilderness valley, one of the most remote in the Olympics.

Herb led, following a crystal-clear meandering brook bordered with purple lupine, two varieties of Indian paintbrush, mountain asters and alpine monkeyflower. They stepped carefully to avoid the flowers.

Suddenly a large, beautiful alpine lake appeared. The lake, surrounded on two sides by meadows, was fed by a little stream which tumbled over a waterfall. Wildflowers and moss grew profusely along the stream. Wood

Carol Preston & Hazle M. Chapman sit inside Eleven Bull Basin Shelter. Crislers used this as a halfway point between Cream Lake Shelter and Castle-in-the-Cat.

Billy Everett stands beside the lake named after him by Herb Crisler on the 1947 trip through the Bailey Range.

fern and wildflowers vied for space in the cool shade below the waterfall.

Billy Everett sank down and feasted his eyes upon this magical place. He had discovered this lake half a century ago, decades before anyone else had ventured into the area. When he tried to describe this beautiful valley to others they only laughed and thought he was daft. Except his uncle, Boston Charlie. He had taken the old man there. Boston Charlie had taken one long look, then claimed the lake was the resting place of mountain spirits. It held special meaning for both of them.

Herb slid out of his pack and found a chunk of wood six feet long. Silently he withdrew a wooden sign from his pack. Chiseled into the wood were the words, LAKE BILLY EVERETT.

Herb nailed the sign across the pole, scooped out a hole in the gravel, set the post, then beckoned Everett to come close.

"I proclaim this beautiful place Lake Billy Everett, in honor of the fine man who first discovered it," Herb said.

Billy was totally surprised. He stared at his name on the sign and his mouth opened with a wide grin. With much ceremony he slowly removed his battered old felt hat, made a gallant bow and said with great dignity, "I accept this honor."

Chappy walked around the lake and took pictures of the lake with Billy standing by the sign. It was a delightful experience. They felt honored to have known and traveled with the old pioneer.

They went on to Cream Lake shelter. Herb built a fire in the stove and baked golden brown biscuits. Served with honey, they were a special delight. Billy told hunting stories after dinner, waving his arms, jumping like a school boy during exciting parts, pointing excitedly. He looked younger than his years.

Lois Crisler had suddenly become quiet and withdrawn. Chappy and Carol noticed, but didn't know why she was acting this way. Since human behavior was Carol's forte, she tried to talk privately with Lois, but learned nothing. She talked to Herb. He said nothing was wrong. It was just one of Lois' frequent melancholy spells.

A storm crept stealthily up the Hoh River Valley from the sea under the cover of darkness and rain began to drum on the shake roof. They were thankful for the shelter and the ladies all remained in their sleeping bags. Between rain showers Herb and Billy went exploring with Herb's motion-picture camera. They returned saying they found no elk in the area. Chappy and Carol listened while Billy spun stories about hunting and exploring. They thought Billy someone special. His dark, lively eyes sparkled like live coals. They admired his profound knowledge and respect for the wilderness.

A few years later, after Billy died, Lois Crisler eulogized this pioneer mountain man:

There was a touch of greatness about Billy Everett. I think there was about Pa Huelsdonk too. Pa was the famous pioneer of the Hoh.

I often ponder these two men, trying to fathom that touch of greatness--so different in each. The whole world goes one way. There was something in Pa and Billy that went the other way. What was it? What was that touch of greatness?

For one thing they were both allied with a big country--the Olympic wilderness. Most people turn their noses away from nature and burrow into towns. Those two always kept the wall down and wide open between them and the wilds.

For several years Cris annually took Billy to Cream Lake Basin, beyond the trails.

I was worried the first time. Billy was in his seventies. One hand was crippled from blood poisoning. There would be places where you could use both hands to hang on with.

Billy Everett with blueberries, aged 79, on trip through the Bailey Range with Herb Crisler.

Cris laughed at me. 'Billy will get along better than you will,' he said.

He did. He jaunted up rock walls, along cleavers and over the Catwalk like a gentleman on a boulevard. That was Billy's old-time skill.

On that first trip with us he told me a bit about his philosophy. 'It is not right to get hurt in the mountains,' he said. 'Back in, this way, it would mean a lot of trouble to the others in the party.'

That impressed me. That was the courtesy of the wilderness.

Billy had the courtesy of the camp, too. He never crowded to the good places by the campfire. He never acted eager for his food, or hungry.

Billy had a wonderful physique. He treated his own health with a kind of reasonable courtesy too.

He was supple and lithe. People have the notion that all great mountaineers must be tall. Billy, like Pa Huelsdonk, was rather short. Pa had a stocky build. Billy was built like a traveler.

He was camping alone, far beyond Cream Lake Basin once, when he felt that first storm of winter coming.

Next morning as soon as he could see to travel, he set out for Olympic Hot Springs. Ordinarily it would take two long days to make the trip. There was not one inch of man-made trail the whole way. No trail down Boulder Creek even.

Billy ran wherever he could. By dark he reached the hot springs ahead of the storm.[16]

There was a kind of poetic justice in Cris taking Billy to Cream Lake when he was old. Billy had taken an old friend of his own to Cream Lake when he himself was young. The place was beautiful and he wanted old Boston Charlie to see it.

To Billy the beauty was not just the scenery but the life. 'Nearly 300 head of elk around the lake the first time I saw it,' he said. 'Some lay in the edge of the water, some in the meadows. Some were

131

walking out of the forest. It was the most beautiful sight I ever saw.'

Billy had the power of being happy. I think that is a very remarkable thing in an old person.

Billy acted out his stories. His dark eyes flashed and laughed. They focused far away or close as the animal he told of moved.

Billy was 78 when he told us the famous story of how he knifed the bear. He lunged. He leaped back. He must have jumped backward four or five feet!

It was to save his dog that he had done that bold and dangerous thing. Cris repeated the story to Pa Huelsdonk. Pa nodded. 'Of course,' he said. 'Of course a man would risk his life to save his dog.'

Billy and Pa were both lonely sometimes for someone who could say 'of course' at the right places. They missed the men of the old big days who accepted each other's dangers and courage.

I think that touch of greatness about Billy Everett came in part from his feeling of oneness with nature.[17]

After 10 days of scrambling around the Bailey Range, including stops at Eleven Bull Basin, the party reached the Catwalk. Herb had cut steps through some of the worst places.

They reached the west end, on the flanks of Cat Peak, and were nibbling cheese and taking a break before descending down to the old, dead-end abandoned trail along the High Divide. The two girls were relieved to have safely negotiated the famous Catwalk without trouble.

Carol Preston turned to Lois and said thoughtfully, "A woman would have to really love a man to follow him across there more than once."

Already overdue, they stopped at Castle-in-the-Cat. While they were lazing around camp the next morning, a small airplane appeared over the High Divide. They paid little attention, until the plane began circling.

Someone mentioned it would be funny if the plane was searching for them! Who could be worried about them, though? They argued about what day it was. They had lost track of time. Getting out to the trailhead on any certain day seemed of little importance.

Traveling along the ridge towards Appleton Pass the next day, they were surprised to meet a party of a dozen people wearing backpacks. They stopped to visit. Herb asked where they were from. They replied Michigan. They were visiting the Olympics getting a little background for the Crisler lecturers on the World Adventure Series scheduled for Detroit the following winter!

When Herb told them he was Crisler, and introduced Lois and the others, the visitors were so astonished they could think of little to say.

When they reached Olympic Hot Springs they learned that indeed the plane had been searching for them. They were four days overdue!

Notes and Sources, Chapter Twelve

1. Lois Crisler, Port Angeles Evening News. 15 Jan., 1947

2. Ibid.

3. Herb Crisler, "Western Wildlife Photographer," courtesy Ruby El Hult

4. Lois Crisler, Port Angeles Evening News, 29 Mar., 1948

5. Ibid.

6. Lois Crisler, Port Angeles Evening News, 14 Feb. 1947

7. Ibid.

8. Lois Crisler, Port Angeles Evening News, 03 Mar. 1947

9. Ibid.

10. Lois Crisler, Port Angeles Evening News, 07 Mar. 1947

11. Ibid.

12. Ibid.

13. Ibid.

14. Lois Crisler, <u>Port Angeles Evening News,</u> 29 March, 1948

15. For a more detailed description of this route, see the end of chapter 15.

16. This would be a distance of more than 15 very rugged miles, as the crow flies, with no trail, not counting the ups and downs across gullies. A remarkable achievement.

    An even more remarkable trip through the Bailey Range was made by Robert Baldwin, a retired park ranger living near Port Angeles. He departed from the South Fork Sol Duc trailhead at four o'clock in the morning, traveled by flashlight until dawn, went over the Catwalk, along the spine of the Bailey Range, over Mount Ferry, then down the Long Ridge Trail and met his wife waiting for him at Whiskey Bend, all in one 18-hour-long marathon day!

17. Lois Crisler, "Olympic Trail Talk"--72" . 27 Oct, 1950

13

The Second Tour
Northwest Winter Weather Follows the Crislers Wherever They Go

The Crislers' out-of-state bookings during the winter of 1947-1948 were scheduled for after the first of the year. They spent Christmas in Washington. They felt entirely different about heading south than they had the previous winter.

With friends to visit, confirmed engagements for their films, knowing how much Californians appreciated their pictures, gave them something exciting to look forward to.

With high optimism they headed south in Lois' veteran old gray Hudson on a stormy New Years Day.

In Oregon they encountered high winds, torrential rain and flooding rivers as storms marching east from the Pacific Ocean swept through the Willamette Valley.

Their first appearance was scheduled in San Francisco. They had the usual jitters as they entered the city and were engulfed in bumper to bumper traffic. Finally they reached the address and set up, thinking the show might be a hurdle:

> It was for the Town Hall Lecture Series, our first showing on a regular lecture series. Well, it was a big friendly audience. Half of Port Angeles seemed to be there. But I think it was the Californians who started the applause at intervals all the way through.

> Our next night's showing was one we had our hearts set on. It was for 76-year-old Charles Kellogg, the man born with one of the wonders of nature in his throat--the syrinx of a bird as well as the larynx of a man. If you ever heard the old record, "Listen to the Mockingbird," sung by Alma Gluck, it was Charles Kellogg who was the mocking-bird, singing through his nose, mouth closed, without any mechanical aid.

> Charles Kellogg himself came out to meet us--a handsome, white-haired man with a beautiful physique and clear, brilliant blue eyes. He held out his arms to us sightlessly.

> 'Oh Cris,' he said, 'my eyes! They're gone. I can't see your pictures. But I can listen to Crissie tell about them.' (He calls me Crissie.)

> Travel-rumpled, we were led around the circle of bankers, doctors, artists, in the immense living room, and halted before one 80-year-old lady, 'Mrs. Achilles,' they said.

> The Achilles' had financed George Eastman and she named the Kodak. Last year she and her son divided sixty million dollars of their profits among Eastman Kodak Company employees.

> Our suite that night was downstairs in one wing of the big house. It spreads in a hospitable semi-circle around the tiled patio on whose outer edge grows an oak with 20-foot branches. Below us is the misty space and shine of the whole Santa Clara Valley.[1]

Next, sprawling Los Angeles and appearances at those haughty, exclusive clubs which had signed last spring. They showed at the University Club, the Los Angeles Breakfast Club, the Friday Morning Club, even the super-elitist Ebell Club.

The Friday Morning Club was the most dignified and exclusive of all Los Angeles women's clubs, a "sea of beautiful hats." Herb stepped out to make the opening introduction, smiled sweetly and said:

`For some reason I don't feel so nervous here as I did over at the Breakfast Club. Perhaps it's because I feel more at home amongst the furred and feathered creatuahs.'

Standing behind the fold of velvet curtain in the wing, waiting for my turn, I heard the soft ripple of laughter from the house.

Then Cris went on. `Because they're so cuddly.' There was a startled titter from the dowagers in the audience. If only Cris had stopped there. But no, `And regardless of what the naturalists say, the wilder they are, the cuddlier they are.'

Furtive giggles from the stately audience. I could have wrung Cris's neck.[2]

The cream of all clubs was the Adventurer's Club. Only 200 men belonged. In order to be a member, one had to have distinguished himself by some unusual adventure on either land, sea or in the air. No women were allowed, not even to lecture.

However, this rule was relaxed when it was discovered that Lois was the narrator. During its 36 years, only five women had been allowed inside. One was Osa Johnson, author of the successful books about Africa. Although the club showing offered various mechanical difficulties, members loved the pictures.

Since there were no showings for a while, the Crislers decided to accept Paul Granger's offer to use his house in San Diego. Paul kept the San Diego house for sentimental reasons. It was his place of birth.

The Crislers drove up to a big, beautiful old white house on a hill with an ocean and town view in an old district of good homes.

The housekeeper showed them to their room, handed them a key to the front door and departed. Lois describes the luxurious accommodations:

An old-fashioned bedroom, with high ceiling, gold brocade over the chairs, broad tapestry bell-pulls, a private lounge-porch, and an immense bathroom with a marble wash-stand and a tub long enough for me or Abe Lincoln. We felt like two kids who had accidentally rubbed Aladdin's lamp. [3]

Their main reason for visiting San Diego was its famous zoo. They planned only a short visit, as caged animals didn't excite them. However, this was the most nearly humane zoo they had ever seen. They rounded a corner and ran slam bang into something with which they were very familiar:

What fascinated us was the ledges of rock where Hyas Puss-puss, as Billy Everett calls the cougar, stalked and talked. We actually watched the cougar utter again and again the strange bright, bird-cries that we have heard occasionally on the trail to Hume's Ranch and up in the mountains and that we have stood and listened to, looking at each other with the surmise that this was no bird we were hearing, but the big cat of the mountains.[4]

They stayed all day and left only at closing time.

Next they headed over the mountains east of San Diego, and had an experience which confirmed their belief that northwest weather followed them, regardless of where they went:

We left the main highway and to Cris' immense satisfaction we drove straight into a snowstorm in extreme southern California. Just to show them, [people back in Port Angeles] he got out and rolled snowballs for us to suck. [while Lois photographed] Then California showed us--by easing us down over a seldom-used road into the desert of the Salton sea.

That night we slept among the date-palms beyond Indio at Thousand Palms, where we rolled in on the Bovees, formerly of Lake Crescent Inn.[5]

Next they drove back through Los Angeles and took the Pacific Highway north, reporting no traffic. That night they spread their sleeping bags on a high, sandy spit beside the ocean with the crash of the surf lulling them to sleep.

They stayed overnight in Santa Cruz, then headed over the mountains for an appearance at Oakland. Along the highway over the mountains hundreds of cars were parked, their occupants out building snow men and laughing excitedly. Others were piling snow on the trunks of their cars, then driving off towards home to see if they could make it to the valley before the snow melted.

The showing at Oakland was for the Sierra Club. The club's president, Bestor Robinson, welcomed the Crislers warmly. They had met the previous fall when Robinson had come up for the congressional hearings at Lake Crescent regarding the reduction in the size of Olympic National Park.

They appeared at two churches in Berkeley. The first went smoothly. At the second everything went wrong. First, they spent too much time deciding upon the correct tint of pink camellias for the corsage on Lois' gray-blue dress. They argued back and forth and finally let the sales lady make the selection. Then they missed their way and were late arriving. While setting up, with the church already nearly full, Herb suddenly discovered he'd left the film at their motel. He left Lois to hold the crowd while he raced off for it.

When he returned, in the dark, he got lost. Frantic, he drove around the neighborhood. Lois had the church's address in her purse. He noticed a church surrounded by a great crowd of people, stopped and rushed in to discover it was the wrong church!

Now, really worried, he drove around and around, looking for the right church.

Finally he located the correct church. Lois was badly shaken, nearly hysterical. She assumed either the car had broken down or he'd been involved in an accident.

Then, near the climax of the first reel, the sound went dead and the pictures continued unexplained. "You'd need the lives of a cat to live through many showings like that," Lois was to write.

Their hosts, the Robinsons, insisted that the Crislers could not think of leaving the Bay area unless they visited Yosemite. They found Yosemite Valley deserted. They were disappointed. After the Olympics, the sheer rock walls of Yosemite seemed not so impressive as they did to most people.

The next booking was at Santa Barbara at the Museum of Natural History. Just before reaching the city, the old Hudson began to buck and lurch. They became hopelessly stalled at a busy intersection. Herb struggled to restart the engine. Finally, they worked out a plan. Lois held her foot on the gas while Herb drove and braked. They finally reached the location. Herb parked and the engine gave a sigh, a gasp, then died.

After the lecture, Dorothy and Walter Hirt, airplane lookouts who had relieved them on Hurricane Hill, came backstage to congratulate them. Also Donald Culcross Peattie, the noted author, was present. "You have both done a beautiful job," Mr. Peattie said.

The Hudson refused to start and had to be towed to a filling station.

Repairs were made, but the mechanic's diagnosis was bad. They coaxed the Hudson along until it carried them to a showing on December 11 at Thatcher School, an exclusive boys school in the Ojai valley.

After the show, the car refused to start again until the boys lined up behind and pushed it down the hill. Herb headed for cousins of Harry and Jean Schoeffel's at Oxnard, hoping they would know a good mechanic.

The Diedrichs owned 200 acres of rich Santa Clara farmland. While the car was being repaired, they toured the farm, and put on a showing of their films in a drying shed for 50 neighbors and friends.

The next appearance was at the Pasadena Civic Auditorium. They stayed with Mr. & Mrs. Paul Granger. They were mysteriously tense about the Pasadena showing. After the responsive farmers in the Santa Clara Valley, they decided Pasadena could be a cold, unresponsive audience.

When they arrived they were handed numerous telegrams of encouragement from friends in the northwest, which broke the tension. The show went well and they were stormed back-stage with well-wishers after the performance.

The final showing in California was at the Sunday Evening Forum at a church in Fresno, a "first-rate lecture series." Afterwards, the manager said, "The church has had this series for twenty-five years and I've been here for seven, and this is the best program we've had."

Next they headed for Denver. Severe storms were reported in the mountains. They called the American Automobile Association and were routed through Tucson, Arizona. The first night they slept out in the Mojave desert. The following night, between Tucson and Phoenix, they had a scare:

> Cris parked beside the highway and obeyed his hunch not to sleep by the car but to drag our
> sleeping bags under the sheep-tight fence and out into the cactus behind a greasewood bush. Hunches

are the most valuable thing anyone does have. No sooner had we lain down for the night than a car shot up purposefully and stopped across the highway from ours, about a hundred feet from it, facing it. Their lights went out almost before they stopped.

Behind our bush Cris and I sat up electrified, in the dark. Then perfect silence. If a car passed we strained our eyes to see by its passing light. After about half an hour, probably less, in reality, when the highway was dark and still in all directions, a door clicked softly. Their lights came on. Near the beam of the headlight stood one man. Another walked towards him from our car. Cris heard some of their brief words: 'Don't know where they went.' Both got in and the car shot off. We slept the rest of the night with both ears and one eye open![6]

Some of their friends back in the Pacific Northwest read about this harrowing experience in Lois' column and shuddered. The Crislers shouldn't have to subject themselves to such dangers, they reasoned.

Herb had always wanted to visit Carlsbad Caverns, New Mexico. They went to El Paso, Texas to turn north. They stopped at a store to buy groceries. The engine started, but the car refused to budge. Herb called a garage. The car was towed away and they went to a motel.

The following day Herb walked down to see how the car was coming. The transmission lay scattered over the floor. A complete overhaul would be required. They had barely enough money to buy food and gas!

The bill came to $130! The mechanic refused to accept a check. They wired home for cash, then waited and waited. Through some mistake the money didn't come for two days.

After heading out again they were running tight for time to reach the first showing at Colorado Springs, so passed by Carlsbad. Herb was disappointed.

Because of bad weather warnings ahead, they returned to Las Cruces then headed north on Highway 25.

Now it was Lois' turn to be disappointed. One place she had always wanted to visit was Santa Fe, but time did not allow more than a quick stop for stamps, then on north, headed for Las Vegas, New Mexico and snowy Raton Pass.

The radio was reporting terrible blizzards in the mountains. Many roads were closed. They drove through Wagon Mound and into a blinding wall of wind-blown snow. The highway was deserted, with only an occasional oncoming car groping along with their lights on. The radio reported several serious highway accidents and traveler's warnings. Herb continued on.

They arrived in Colorado Springs on time, much to their host's surprise. The temperature had been eight below zero the previous night.

While at the Springs, they stayed with the brother of the Reverend James Albertson of Port Angeles, Dr. Cyrus Albertson, who had arranged the Colorado showings for them. The First Methodist Church had rented an auditorium which would hold 1,200 people. To accommodate the crowds they put on two shows. An additional show was held at the local high school the following morning. All were full.

The following afternoon, at the Denver showing, the auditorium overflowed with 1,400. About 200 were turned away. News that good wildlife pictures were showing spread like wildfire by word of mouth. That night there was another big crowd and 400 were turned away.

After one showing, a man who worked for the state game department introduced himself to Herb and told him he should consider coming to Colorado to film bighorn sheep in the nearby Tarryall Mountains. Herb filed this away in his memory bank. They made a presentation in Pueblo, then, to avoid the high passes leading west out of Colorado, headed north through Wyoming, then west towards Salt Lake City. The high prairie across Wyoming was one long, continuous swirling snowstorm. There were no high passes to trap them.

Praying the car didn't break down again, they plodded on.

Lois was impressed with Salt Lake City's location. Brigham Young had chosen the site at the base of the snowy Wasatch Range and the Mormons had built a lovely city. She especially relished the splendid mountain views which reminded her of the Olympic Mountains from Port Angeles.

Again storms caught up with them. Lois ended her column of the season, by writing the following:

On the afternoon of our showing here, at the first Methodist Church, a snowstorm began that lasted into the night, blocking roads leading east out of the valley. But we had a very warm audience that evening at this, the last showing of our tour. Luckily our homeward road was not blocked and the next morning we left.

Floods in Oregon, drought in California, freezing in El Paso, blizzards in Colorado, snowstorm in Utah! We're coming home.[7]

March can sometimes be a harsh, drab month on the Olympic Peninsula. While indications of spring may be observed in lower elevations along the straits of Juan de Fuca, only a few hundred feet increase in elevation discloses quite another climatic zone.

Port Angeles lawns were green. Crocus and daffodils bloomed along the walkways. After turning up towards Whiskey Bend at the Elwha ranger station, all signs of spring disappeared. Limbs blown down by winter storms littered the road. Several huge hemlock windfalls across the road had recently been cut out. Patches of snow still lingered in shady places in the thick, dark rain forest and the drab effects of winter remained.

At Whiskey Bend they sat in the car, letting the fact sink in, that, despite all those thousands of miles of hazardous winter driving, they had arrived home safely.

Herb went into the woods where he had cached the packboards. They began loading their packs, taking only what they thought they had to have to set up housekeeping again, leaving the rest in the car.

A depressingly low, gray cloud ceiling blotted out the sky. Mists swirled and the wind moaned through the harsh sawtooth skyline of swaying evergreen boughs as they struggled and puffed up the trail under heavily-loaded packboards. Their muscles were soft from months of too much rich food and inactivity.

Halfway to the ranch Lois rested her pack on a convenient windfall and looked around. She could feel the damp cold seep through her light clothing and shivered.

A Townsend's ground squirrel emerged from under the log, saw Lois, let out a terrified squeal and dived back to safety. Lois laughed.

Ragged, tormented, slate-gray clouds of rain and fog swirled above the Elwha River. One moment a great puff of fleecy vapor shot straight up, the next down, then sideways, rolling and churning as if spewed from a geyser.

The strange geyser effect, Lois thought, was what Geyser Valley was known for. Lois recalled a stanza of a poem that described the area:

Trampin' yer man-made royas,
Dreaming of home sweet home;
Thinkin' of Ol' mountain zephyrs,
Back whar I love to roam.
There's somethin' up thar' at's callin'
Callin' in tones that thrills;
Come to the wide free open
Back in the Geyser Hills.[8]

Herb was far ahead, determined to make it all the way to the ranch without breaking his stride. The cool, dripping, evergreen forest engulfed him like a soothing balm. For the first time in months he could feel the old excitement of being in the wilderness coursing through his veins. The moan of the wind in the tall firs, the dull roar of the river through Rica Canyon and the familiar rain forest was medicine he needed after the icy highways and the hectic, uncertain rigors of the tour.

Lois suffered from a terrific anxiety hangover. With a nervous sigh she pulled herself to her feet and struggled on, the pack straps pinching the soft flesh of her shoulders.

Was it really worth it? She kept wondering. The stress of putting on shows, such as the "lost church" experience, where anything could go wrong? The rigors of travel? Some 10,000 miles of dangerous, wintertime driving? For what? Barely enough money to exist?

Now so much work needed doing they would not likely catch up. No, it certainly wasn't worth it, she concluded. She would mention the subject of giving up the tours to Herb as soon as she reached home.

But still, she reasoned, their work cried for an audience...?

She turned down the branch trail leading to Hume's Ranch. From somewhere amidst the jumble of rotten windfalls and lush rain forest came a distinctive, loud series of trills and tumbling warbles, ending with a sharp "kip, kip, kip."

Presently a dark reddish-brown winter wren appeared. It bobbed and flitted through the ground cover as if possessed. It dived into dark recesses in a rotten windfall, inspected the low, moss-covered limbs of a vine maple, hung upside down from a mossy limb then disappeared into the maze of boughs of the overhead evergreen canopy. From high in the firs the tiny voice trilled a second long, merry welcome.

Cheered by the familiar greeting, heartened to think such a diminutive bird had survived the winter in such a wet, hostile environment, Lois called back, "Hello little neighbor."

When the Crislers had moved to Hume's Ranch, seven years before, Herb had said, "Let's not get so busy we haven't time to ramble." That time had long ago passed. Winters, a period when they previously took time to "ramble" and catch up on odd jobs, were now absorbed by the hectic tours.

With the big-time eastern lecture circuit looming ever closer, they felt driven to produce additional outstanding film this coming summer. If for no reason other than they were weary of looking at the same pictures over and over again themselves.

Lois walked out from under the spreading evergreen boughs of the old-growth forest into the clearing. The familiar log cabin appeared exactly as they had left it. A wisp of acrid cedar kindling smoke spiraled from the chimney, dove low across the meadow and assailed her nostrils.

Lois breathed deeply. Memories of hundreds of campfires swarmed in her head. It had been months since she had smelled campfire smoke. Her pace quickened.

Fresh elk tracks in the soft ground outside the yard gate caused tingling up and down her spine.

Herb stood peering around the corner of the cabin. He placed his fingers across his lips and motioned her to join him.

She eased out of her pack and sneaked behind Herb. A herd of elk milled excitedly in the alder grove on the opposite side of the river. "They're thinking of crossing," Herb said.

The Elwha was running nearly full from spring snow melt in the mountains. Finally the lead cow plunged into the swift, deep water and began swimming across. Another cow followed. The larger, more experienced animals made the crossing without trouble.

Not the younger, last-spring calves. Almost fully grown but lacking courage and experience, several were swept down the river, banging against boulders and thoroughly frightened. A few turned back and straggled up the bank, mewing for their mothers. The few yearlings which made it across stood shaking water from their coats, staring back at their friends across the river, as if to say, "what a bunch of sissies."

The mature elk that had already crossed paid the ones lagging behind not the slightest attention. They trotted into the big hay meadow by the old barn and began cropping new shoots of tender green grass.

The yearlings across the river lost sight of the rest of the herd. Frantic at thoughts of being left behind, the calves plunged into the icy river again with renewed determination. Following the example of their elders, this time they headed upstream on an angle, swam frantically into the current, made it safely across, then sprinted, bucking and leaping with joy to join the band.

"Like watching Crisler movies," Lois said.

"Better. No people," Herb added.

They went into the cabin and sat at the table. Neither spoke. The cabin was icy cold and damp. They waited impatiently for heat from the stove to spread its warmth.

Dusk was descending. Rain splattered on the shake roof. A wood mouse scampered out from behind a box, peered at the invaders, then dived out of sight beneath the stove. Herb smiled with satisfaction.

They soaked in the familiar surroundings, glad to be home, listening to the dull roar of the river, the comforting crackle of cedar in the stove. Warmth slowly radiated through the dampness. The teakettle's spout began to steam. Herb got up to move it. He lighted a lantern.

"A winter wren called hello to me along the trail," Lois said.

"Someone stayed overnight. Probably several nights. Refilled the wood box, cut a big stack of cedar kindling and laid a fire before they left," Herb said.

Lois went to their bed in one corner, expecting to see it rumpled. Perhaps even muddy boot tracks. The bed was exactly as they had left it, except in the very center was a cardboard box with a ribbon around it. She took the package to the kitchen table.

Herb stared curiously while she slit the ribbon, opened the box and dumped the contents. Two dozen packages of garden seeds and a note slid onto the table.

The note was written on the back of the January page from last-years's calendar. Lois read the large scrawled letters: "Welcome home. We love you," was all it said.

Lois sank down onto her chair. Her chest heaved. Tears sprang into her eyes. Her head tipped forward. Being home released a tiredness of body and mind which hadn't been apparent before.

Herb Crisler filing an eight-foot bucking saw on porch of Hume's Ranch Cabin.

Herb gently took the note from her fingers and stared at the message, considering who's handwriting it might be.

No five words could have been more appropriate, or a better homecoming. To know they had been missed and were loved by someone made the winter's travels seem more worthwhile. People appreciated their films and their efforts. True, their bank account was exhausted, as usual, but money wasn't everything.

"We love you too, whoever you are," Herb drawled ever so softly. They never discovered who had stayed in the cabin and left the seeds.

Lois placed her head on her arms and began to sob. Herb gently massaged her shoulders and neck muscles.

"Back there, on the trail," she sobbed, "I decided it wasn't worth it. All the work and travel and tension, just to show a few pictures. I intended to suggest we quit the lecture circuit."

"Us and our chipmunks," Herb drawled. "Sometimes I feel the same way." He opened the lid and shoved dry fir into the stove. "But 40,000 people who saw our pictures think it's worth it."

"The winter wren, the elk, the note and the box of garden seeds changed my mind. I suppose it's worth it, after all."

"You're just exhausted. I'll make supper." Herb lighted a second Coleman lantern and headed for the root cellar.

When they awoke at dawn the elk had disappeared from the meadow. But three black-tail deer stood outside the garden fence nibbling on a few sprigs of green berry buds protruding through the wire. The scraps of leftover supper Herb had left on the porch for the skunks were gone. Herb went to the root cellar and brought out a few apples to treat the deer.

Also gone were feelings of doubt about the forthcoming summer's work. Lois pinned the "Welcome Home" note to the curtain where it would serve as a reminder that someone thought they were important.

They set to work with a renewed zest, preparing for a busy summer. There was plenty to do.

To add to the urgency, the Eastern engagements were booked for late October. They would not have the normal long, languid fall to finish chores, edit film, can produce from the garden and make apple cider as usual.

The old Hudson was in terrible shape. How would they drive east?

So many friends, many of them new, wished to visit Hume's Ranch they had again set June aside for visitors. During this month, before they must start for the high country, they hoped to accommodate visitors and accomplish much needed work at the same time.

The Grangers were the first to visit. Paul had been captivated during their previous visit by the relaxing atmosphere. He offered his company executives a deal: If they would vacation on the Olympic Peninsula, instead of going elsewhere, he would allow them three weeks, with pay, instead of the normal two. He decided the calm surroundings would relax them after the hectic pace of living and working in Los Angeles and start their creative juices flowing again.

Hazle Chapman and Carol Preston arrived. They put in their usual stint on the wood pile, sometimes getting up and slipping off at dawn to catch a breakfast of trout from the river.

They tried to talk the Crislers into another backpack trip, but Herb and Lois were too busy to go at such an early date.

July found the Crislers again freighting supplies on their backs and lugging camera equipment amongst the high peaks and alpine meadows, working their way back and forth between the high camps, wherever elk and other animals could be located.

The flab of winter fell away. Their health and mental outlook improved. The wilderness and exercise does that to people. The old motion-picture camera was giving Herb trouble, worn out from years of rough use.

Every two weeks they made trips down to the ranch to tend and water the garden, get the mail and pick up a supply of fresh vegetables. Summer sped by.

The first snows hit the alpine areas in late September. They closed their camps, edited their summer's take of film and prepared to head east. How they were going to get there was a question which had plagued them all summer. The old Hudson would never make it.

Notes & Sources, Beyond the Trails, Chapter Thirteen

1. Lois Crisler, Column of 25 March 1948, Port Angeles Evening News.

2. Ibid.

3. Lois Crisler, Column of 26 March, 1948

4. Ibid.

5. Lois Crisler, Column of 26 March, 1948

6. Lois Crisler, Column of 30 March, 1948.
    After reading this column, friends were horrified. Why, they asked, did such cherished people as the Crislers have to subject themselves to such risks while on the road? Clearly a more suitable vehicle was required.

7. Ibid.

8.   The fifth stanza of one of Mr. Ludden's poems found in his belongings after his death in 1927. Smitty Paratt, <u>Gods & Goblins</u>, A Field Guide to Place Names of Olympic National Park, CP Publications, Port Angeles, 1984.

"Doc" Ludden named his place near Humes Ranch "Geyser House."

The Press Party named this area Geyser Valley after they heard a curious drumming while struggling up the rugged country along the Elwha River. The noise sounded like steam escaping from a geyser vent. A look across the river disclosed what appeared to be steam swirling. This led them to assume a hot springs was located across the river.

According to some sources, the sound they heard was a blue grouse drumming. This is difficult to believe. For two reasons: 1)Experienced mountain man James Christie would not be so easily fooled. 2) The Press Expedition went through the Elwha Valley during mid-winter. Grouse do not begin mating until early spring.

Perhaps the drumming sound was caused by the Elwha River pouring through Rica Canyon with considerable force.

14

The National Lecture Circuit

In the fall of 1948 the Crislers faced several dire emergencies. They had exposed some excellent elk footage, and incorporated it into their new picture which they were scheduled to take east for the big national lecture circuit.

But they were broke. No one paid them to trek around the mountains, where costs skyrocketed for film, camping supplies, equipment and store-purchased food. Also, it took cash to purchase, then process motion-picture film.

McGlenns Grocery, on Lincoln Street in Port Angeles, understood the seasonal nature of their business, and ignored sometimes long-standing charges for groceries, knowing that Herb would pay when he could. But many things couldn't be charged, such as expenses while on the road. Herb disliked being in debt.

The old Hudson teetered, complained, sputtered and could be coaxed up the hill to Whiskey Bend only with the greatest persuasion. Herb decided it wasn't worth fixing.

Herb's motion-picture camera was worn out and not worth fixing either. It was a desperate time.

They mulled over what to do about the lack of cash while they canned produce from the garden and edited their summer's take of film. They made a few local film presentations to practice with the new film. But they were rushed for time and truly financially bewildered.

Word got around about their situation. Friends, probably the "chipmunks", alerted townspeople about the camera. "Big" Bill Thorniley of Black Ball Transportation swung a lot of weight with local civic groups. He was president of the Olympic Peninsula Hotel and Resort Owners Association, and a resort owner himself. After explaining, at a meeting with colleagues, about Crisler's financial situation, their forthcoming lecture schedule, their worn out car and how important Crisler's work was in bringing tourists to the Peninsula, an expensive new Eastman Kodak Cine Special motion-picture camera was purchased through donations and presented to the Crislers.

The Schoeffels, up at Olympic Hot Springs, where Herb sometimes edited his film, were staunch supporters, old friends and believed in what the Crislers were doing. For almost two decades, since Herb's 1930 survival trip, Crisler had provided more free publicity for the resort with his pictures and lectures than any paid advertising.

Schoeffel cornered Verne Samuelson in his office at First and Lincoln. Verne, a long-time friend and trekking buddy of Herb's, had became a wealthy Port Angeles business man. His Ford motor agency was booming and his banking investments thriving as the North Olympic Peninsula's economy grew.

They discussed the fact that Herb and Lois needed to drive east to show their films, and about the state of the Hudson. Both recalled having read in Olympic Trail Talks how Herb and Lois had slept out in the Arizona desert and been frightened when men stopped and looked over their car, with all its expensive camera equipment inside inviting theft.

They decided that people as valuable as the Crislers shouldn't have to do such a risky thing as sleep on the ground while on the road.

Schoeffel inquired what Verne's rock bottom price would be for a new Ford truck big enough to haul all their equipment? Something large enough they could sleep in? Samuelson suggested a panel truck. The price was $2900. Schoeffel supplied the money. We suspect that was a bargain price. Herb was to pay when he could.

This was, of course, before truck campers, or recreational vehicles were available. Encouraged by this unexpected turn of events, Herb worked long hours customizing the new truck. He built a plywood bed equipped with an innerspring mattress across the back, a tiny clothes closet, a grub box, shelves for storage and a long, wooden tube down the center in which to slide their big, professional-model beaded screen. With the addition of a Coleman(R) camp stove they could cook, eat and sleep while on the road, saving money and time while traveling. No longer would they have to take their chances with highwaymen, rattlesnakes, scorpions, black-widow spiders and tarantulas, although it was highwaymen they feared most.

More good news came by mail. Their California booking agent scheduled three additional bookings for January, including one in San Francisco.

Herb & Lois Crisler hiking past Reflection Lake, a tarn below Lake Billy Everett in the Bailey Range.

As soon as the truck was ready, they loaded up half a ton of supplies and equipment and headed east on October 13, taking the direct northern route through Montana, for a six-month-long tour.

Their first engagement was the Methodist Church in Sioux City, Iowa. From there they drove to Detroit and stayed in a twin-bed suite at the Hotel Fort Shelby. They showed at the Detroit Boat Club, one of the oldest boat clubs in the United States.

The next day they met their new eastern agent, George Pierrot, one of the leading lecture-managers in the country and manager of The World Adventure Series. Pierrot explained their busy schedule over lunch. Starting the following morning, they were to go on a half-hour breakfast club network broadcast at the Hotel Statler with hosts Tony and Dorothy Weitzel, who were known as Mr. and Mrs. Radio.

This was the big time. How did the "little mountain mice" respond? Lois reported:

She felt like a cross between Mme. Schumann-Heink and the Borden cow. Cris was just Cris, as always--unabashed, patient, quick, friendly, having a good time.[1]

They had no sooner returned to their hotel room than in popped a news photographer and reporter. The photographer flashed off a couple of pictures and left. The reporter whipped out a note pad and searched for a story:

I told him everything I could think of but he diddled his pencil. He had just one angle on his mind and we didn't connect with it. How much does it cost you to live up there in the wilderness? That was the angle of our lives we knew least about. I though of Cris's ga'den at Hume's Ranch on the Elwha and the muscle and sweat that made it. How could you translate that into dollars?

The reporter tried again. 'Do you like it here?'

I thought of the beauty of the Olympic mountains and the clean air--then the sprawling city here below our windows. 'Like it? In all this poverty?'

The reporter glanced around our mirror-shining room. He was stumped.[2]

Next came the Michigan State College at East Lansing. The dean invited them to dinner. Lois was tense and nervous. She wore a long dress, with gold belt and velvet cloak. Herb wore his usual boots, doeskin jacket and relaxed manner.

They couldn't get the sound through, even with the help of stage crews. Lois looked around wildly and began to sweat:

Cris looked distraught, with a warning, hush-hush look in his eye to me.

Cris got up over the tension, as he always does, and with his genial introduction before the mike in the hollow vastness full of people, wrapped the audience up in a little bundle and put them chuckling into the palm of my hand. [3]

But the worst was yet to come. When Lois snapped on the opening fanfare for the title, it went tick-tick. Someone had tested the sound and cheerfully left the needle on the middle of the record:

Okay, okay, the picture's the thing. Tell them where Washington is--Washington State, you know. My mike was dead. I sat in silence, admiring our map, which is not self explanatory, till with a loud pop and a whoosh someone suddenly piped sound into my mike and breathlessly I gobbled into my explanation, trying to overtake the scenes which were shooting by.

About two-thirds of the way through the first reel, the picture suddenly ran clear out of frame, then blurred to a stand-still and all four thousand and one of us sat in vast silent darkness.[4]

Lois filled in with stories about a bull elk fight while a replacement projector head was searched for. She switched to the story about how the cougar had played tag with Cris and the lights came back on. Then, while the head was being installed, Lois told about another elk fight, dreading the delays.

After it was over, the dean--along with many others-- came backstage and said, "That's one of the finest lectures we've ever had here."

The following morning they reported to television studio WXYZ in Detroit. They were to be interviewed by Mr. Pierrot. The subject was the World Adventure Series, on which they were appearing that afternoon. The television crew were almost as excited at the Crislers. Television was a new medium. The station had only been on the air five weeks!

They went to a make-up room. Lois wrote, "Now that Cris has worn lipstick, I expect ultimately to get him into a tuxedo."

After the television show, where 25 minutes of their pictures were aired, they went to the Institute of Arts for another showing. Lois wasn't impressed by the coldness of the situation:

They left the white bulbs off in the row of yellow footlights, to soften them, but still there was a wall of light between me and the auditorium full of people. I like better the Mt. Pleasant Grange, where you can read every farmer's lean face and if he likes your jokes it warms your heart right now.[5]

That evening they were dinner guests at Mr. Pierrot's big, beautiful home. Among other distinguished guests was Ben East, a field editor of <u>Field and Stream.</u> After eating, Ben and Herb were both inspired to show some of their films. Ben showed wild geese from Hudson's Bay to Louisiana.

Herb showed new footage from last summer's filming along the Bailey Range. Ben said, "That was the most wonderful animal picture I've seen, barring none."

At every major showing they met ex-Port Angeles people, or friends who had friends in the Northwest. People who had seen the Crisler's itinerary in the <u>Evening News</u> and written east to tell acquaintances to be sure to see the Crisler pictures.

After attending the first of their lectures, Mr. Pierrot, who knew a winner when he saw one, immediately set out to book preview engagements for them at as many places as possible. Most top bookings could only be secured after a highly critical staff had screened the performance.

The next appointment was in Cleveland, then on to New York for a preview at the American Museum of Natural History. On the way, they visited Niagara Falls.

At Watertown, New York they looked up Grant Hume's nephew, Captain Neale Humes, who had once visited Hume's Ranch, while the Crislers were not at home.

The Crislers hoped after the preview at the Museum of Natural History to be placed upon their regular lecture series for the following season.

Instead, they received an unexpected surprise. After previewing the films, the program director booked them for December ninth to fulfill a cancellation.

After the preview they were thrilled to meet Rosalie Edge, a noted conservationist, who had lent her support for creation of Olympic National Park.

She remarked that the battle over the park continued, reminding everyone that only last March, timber interests had tried to halve the parks' size, from 835,411 acres to 400,000 acres. In Alaska, Ms. Edge said, developers were after the Kodiak National Wildlife Refuge, set aside for protection of the Alaska brown bear. They wanted to build hydroelectric dams there.

Also complimenting them on the film was Patricia Casselman, wife of Bill Casselman, news editor of the <u>New York Daily News</u>. While waiting for the booking date, they had time to explore New York City. They were invited to lunch with Mr. and Mrs. Casselman.

To their astonishment, Bill told them he had once visited Hume's Ranch with Charles and Esther Webster! Mrs. Casselman accompanied the Crislers on a tour of Radio City Music Hall.

While waiting for the next engagement, they visited New England, including Walden's Pond, which Lois reported, to their disgust, was filled with garbage.

Stories were spasmodically sent to the <u>Evening News</u> about most of the highlights of their travels.

In New Hampshire, they unexpectedly were invited to appear on a half-hour-long radio show, Town Crier. They had to explain to their talk-show host where the Olympic Peninsula was located. A few days later they lectured at Bowdoin College in Brunswick, Maine. One of two western boys attending the college told them the president, in the chapel that morning, had announced motion pictures from the Olympic Peninsula in Oregon!

To remind them how small the world was, they met Dr. Gross, head of the biology department, who had been in the Olympic Mountains the previous summer while on sabbatical leave.

One of the films shown during this period, "After the Storm, a poem without words," reduced many mothers to tears. But all wasn't roses, as Herb explains:

Where our pictures were known our audiences built up. But sometimes in a new place Lois would look around beforehand with discouragement and whisper despondently, 'There's no one here.'

I would whisper back, 'If there's just one ten-year-old boy that gets something out of it, it's worth our while. Maybe he'll be another John Muir. You put on a good show for 'm.'

People liked the pictures. But our reward was not general approval. It was the look in the eyes of someone or some few people after the showings. Maybe they were the ones who said least but we knew it had meant something to them. We could even tell during the showing if someone like that was in the audience. Even if we didn't meet them, I would say afterwards, 'There was <u>someone</u> out there.'[6]

Herb's statement explains the Crisler's philosophy. Although they desperately needed money to live on and continue their work, money wasn't the object. During this particular winter their expenses were more than they took in.

Their message was subtle, but concise: Here folks is this beautiful wilderness, Olympic National Park, with all its unique flora and fauna. Although most of you have never even heard of it, don't even know exactly where it is, and will probably never visit, it belongs to you, the people of the United States. It's fragile, subject to exploitation, and its very size can be reduced by the stroke of an indifferent president's pen!

Even if you cannot visit, at least love and support Olympic and other national parks for the benefit of those who do care and keep them safe as you would any other natural treasure. Only through continued support, and eternal vigilance, will wilderness places be preserved for your children and grandchildren.

What courage! What determination! What sacrifice! The Crislers would soon be starting another filming season without enough money to even pay their debts or buy film. Even though discouragement haunted them, they never seriously considered giving up. Recognition often comes reluctantly, usually too late and sometimes not at all to most creative artists. Herb continues along this vein:

About the lowest ebb of all was a showing in Manchester, New Hampshire. It was the first year we traveled east with our pictures. The next year we showed these same pictures at Orchestra Hall in Chicago and turned people away at Constitution Hall in Washington, D.C. But this night we set up in the church basement among the tea towels and punch bowls of a ladies' bazaar. It was the dinner hour and deserted. Finally a few kids straggled in. One darling angel girl clamped her face on the mike and blew. We explained that might break the crystal. She watched vixenishly and every time we glanced away she tried it again, until Lois moved over and sat by the mike, holding her hand by it.

Four or five fat women, interested chiefly in the sale of punch, came in. Our friend, who had with infinite effort gained this opportunity for us to show, brought what crowd there was--a dozen of her friends.

Our mike did not break. Our hearts didn't either. But our pocketbooks did. We lost about $1000 that entire trip east.[7]

There were many other small disappointments. One night they set up their special beaded screen beforehand, then went out for something to eat. When they returned, they discovered a group had needed the space for a meeting, and had simply crumpled the screen and pushed it out of the way, ruining it. The screen cost $100. "That's all right," a man in the group explained, "you can't hurt a sheet." For a long time there were blank spots on their projected pictures until they could afford a new screen.

In January, 1949, they were scheduled to preview at the National Geographic Society in Washington D.C. For a lecturer, this was the top engagement in a very competitive field.

They were well aware that many glitches could suddenly materialize to spoil their program. The society insisted two of their own projectionists run the machine. This made Herb nervous. The air was filled with tension. Lois wrote:

First we showed our completed lecture. Then we were to show our new footage from last summer. Between the two, the staff members came up and shook hands with us. I was so relieved I could have hugged them.

Two times they broke the film, wasting precious scenes. If these were expert projectionists, I'd hate to have our film run by amateurs.

After it was all over the chief film editor said to Cris, 'I've been with the society for 35 years and yours are the finest animal pictures I've ever seen.'[8]

Back in New York they were invited to dinner at the Salmagundi Club in Greenwich Village. Its members were artists. The "big one" was next. Understandably, Lois was suffering "buck fever:"

> I had a sore throat. To save my voice for the lecture that evening in New York, at the American Museum of Natural History, I practically stopped talking, which did not bother Cris much...

> I braced up on coffee, "the drug," Kitch truthfully calls it. For most lectures I'm not even nervous but for some reason for this first big lecture in New York City I was so scared I was afraid I'd forget my lines.

> It didn't help that Cris had decided to change my introduction that afternoon, and had dictated a totally new one. I had snatched a glance at it while at the Salmagundi Club. But now, trembling alone in the dressing room, just back of the blue velvet stage curtains in the museum auditorium, I could not remember two words together. So I ditched the speech and tried only to hang onto the main points.

> The auditorium was full and people were standing around the back. Both during and after the lecture there was much applause.[9]

They raced back to Washington, D.C., and appeared for a Boy Scout-sponsored showing in Arlington. Then for a Sunday evening lecture at Grace Lutheran Church among the embassies:

> Both were well received, yet Cris and I felt a curious inner deadness. First we questioned our presentation. Then we questioned our pictures. Finally we questioned the audience. Perhaps it was something about the people who lived in this wilderness of stone and protocol.[10]

They showed their film to the publicity director of the National Park Service. He invited other park service officials. Here's what he said about their films:

> After the showing, Director Newton Drury rose and made an impromptu speech, saying, among other things, `These pictures are as near perfection as possible, both in story and in picture. They reveal to us the true meaning of what we are battling for here in the maelstrom of red tape in this wilderness of Washington, D.C.'

> With a feeling of content we left Washington in the afternoon sunshine on our way south.[11]

Their travels took them to Williamsburg, Virginia, then on to Charlotte, North Carolina, where they showed to a group of wealthy lumber mill owners, arranged by Herb's brother Albert, a private pilot for one of the mill owners.

In the mill owner's elaborate clubhouse Herb listened to the happy giggling of four negro women who were making sandwiches and salads. Herb called Lois' attention to the fact that those were happy faces. Those they had just left in the nation's capitol were definitely not!

Then on to Athens, Georgia, where the Crisler family got together for a good southern Christmas.

Their travels took them as far south as Key West, Florida. Herb had first arrived at this outpost of civilization on a fishing boat in 1915 after crossing the Everglades on foot.

The charming little Cuban village he recalled had disappeared. The town that replaced it was, according to Herb-- "subjected to progress."

Traveling north on the Keys Highway, Lois was driving while Herb sat attentively with the little motion-picture camera resting on the window. He'd seen a large fish jump, which he thought was a sailfish, and was ready in case another appeared. Suddenly he yelled, "Stop!" Lois explained:

> I glanced out his window and saw two birds milling in the air. One was an enormous bird with a long forked tail that looked like a creature from Mars. The other was a small white bird. By the time I could stop the car there was only one bird.

> `I saw the two of them chasing each other,' Cris said. `I didn't think the big one could catch the little one. In fact, for a while I thought the little bird was fighting him, the way little birds fight a hawk sometimes.

> `Then that long neck reached out and grabbed the little bird.' Cris' awe transmitted itself to me. `He swallowed it,' he said. `In the air! For a second one white wing hung out of his mouth. It gave

him a three-wing effect. Then he kind of gobbled and that gull rippled down his throat like a rat down a snake."[12]

Herb later insisted this was the most spectacular wildlife event he'd ever seen. Not even excepting an elk fight. He was so excited he forgot to use the camera!

They visited newly-created Everglades National Park and were terribly disappointed. Burning had reduced much of Florida's savannah lands to naked hummocks. The local Audubon Society had been fighting for years to get the burning and wanton roadside shooting of wildlife stopped, but the public were hard to convince.

They had wanted to film flamingos and alligators but the flamingos were gone and only a few dozen alligators remained, according to the rangers they talked with. They saw all the more reason to fight development in Olympic National Park.

The odometer on their new truck showed 12,500 miles as they turned north. They were as far as they could get from Port Angeles, without leaving the United States.

They drove through eastern Tennessee and stopped at Memphis. They called at the home of Faye Russell Wright. Faye had been one of the park telephone operators when the Crislers were air-craft warning observers at Hurricane. Faye had been known throughout the park network as "the voice."

Winter storm warnings were out for Arkansas. They drove up the Mississippi road through darkness and torrents of rain. They passed through Kentucky and Missouri, headed for showings in St. Louis and Kansas City. This was the dead of winter, with icy roads and sub-zero temperatures, but they had bookings to fulfill.

In Missouri they experienced an ice storm, trees covered with gray ice, their limbs swelled to giant proportions, bowed and broken from the weight. Beneath some trees were piles of ice-covered limbs which had broken off. "Fat pigs in silver fields skidded and sat down on their hind quarters," Lois reported. The highway was like an ice skating rink.

"Just try and remember," Herb consoled Lois, "that at this moment negresses in sleeveless, green cotton dresses are flipping bream out of the tepid canals of Florida."[13]

Despite icy highways and cold, they had good attendance at two showings in St. Louis. "Some of the people from Friday night appeared at the Sunday night showing too, with friends. We just had to see those pictures again, they said."[14]

The tour over, they drove back across the country, fighting winter weather until they reached the warm, wet side of the Cascade Mountains of Washington. They had logged 17,000 miles on the new panel truck.

On April 20, 1949, Peninsula residents had a chance to welcome the travelers home at a showing at the Port Angeles high school auditorium, sponsored by Reverend James T. Albertson of the Methodist church. Shown was the main feature which 40,000 people had seen during the six-month tour, plus new travel footage filmed while on tour.

The auditorium was filled to capacity. Droves of disappointed, unhappy people were turned away. They showed again the next night, and the next, until everyone had been accommodated. There was no charge, but many people donated money anyway. This was the Crisler's way of saying thank you to Peninsula people for all the help they had provided.

Notes and Sources, Beyond The Trails, Chapter Fourteen

1. Lois Crisler, Port Angeles Evening News, 2 Dec., 1948

2. Ibid.

3. Ibid.

4. Ibid.

5. Ibid.

6. Herb Crisler, "Western Wildlife Photographer," courtesy Ruby El Hult.

7. Ibid

8. Lois Crisler, <u>Port Angeles Evening News,</u> 8 Jan., 1949

9. Lois Crisler, <u>Port Angeles Evening News,</u> 10 Jan., 1949

10. Ibid.

11. Ibid.

12.   Lois Crisler, <u>Port Angeles Evening News,</u> 9 Feb., 1949
    The bird was a Magnificent Frigatebird, a tropical bird with a forked tail, that catches gulls and terns in flight, and is occasionally seen along the Florida Keys, the northern part of its range.

13. Lois Crisler, <u>Port Angeles Evening News,</u> 17 Feb., 1949

14. Ibid.

15

Olympic Trail Talks

By the spring of 1949, Herb Crisler began growing a full beard, insisting it helped camouflage his face while photographing wildlife. Already a widely-recognized figure around the Pacific Northwest, the beard, at a time when beards were not fashionable, certainly caused Herb to stand out in a crowd.

Twenty-six of Lois' travel articles had been published by the <u>Port Angeles Evening News</u>. The articles, although irregular, had been popular. Lois hadn't written a summer column.

Subscribers commented that they wished Lois would write a regular column, instead of only while on tour, so that they could keep track of the Crislers' activities while at Hume's Ranch and in the mountains.

Editor Charles N. Webster, successor to his father, E. B. Webster, was intensely interested in all affairs of the Peninsula, especially its development, outdoor activities, pioneers and history.

Webster asked Lois if she would consider writing a weekly column about their activities on a year-around basis.

After some deliberation and consulting with Herb, Lois agreed. The column would be called OLYMPIC TRAIL TALKS, even when the Crislers were away on tour.

Ruby El Hult, who first met the Crislers about this time, and has been keenly interested in everything regarding both the Peninsula and the Crislers since, describes Lois' decision:

> In agreeing to turn out the columns, Lois set herself a difficult task. Not only did she follow Herb over ridges, around peaks, into basins, and up talus slopes, but at the end of each strenuous week must have a column ready for the newspaper. On the lecture circuit, she must travel day after day, appear on the platform numerous times, yet get her writing stint done.
>
> It speaks for her stamina and devotion that during 1949, 1950 and the spring of 1951 she turned out one hundred OLYMPIC TRAIL TALKS.
>
> A writer of extraordinary lucidity, she captures not only the unique life she and Herb (or Cris, as she called him) led in the mountains and on their tours, but includes rich material about the mountains, the wildlife, the history of the area and the lives of the pioneers.[1]

A more fitting name for the column could scarcely have been chosen. Most of Lois' columns were simple descriptions of life on the trail.

The first TRAIL TALK was published 10 June, 1949. After readers realized there would be a weekly column by Lois Crisler, the volume of her fan mail increased dramatically. Readers penned frequent letters directly to the Crislers. Sometimes they requested additional information. Lois, however much she treasured her fans, had the annoying habit of leaving readers hanging by a thread.

Crislers' fans, and they were not confined to the Peninsula by any means, regarded happenings at Hume's Ranch as important. Many hiked in to visit. Everyone received the famous Crisler hospitality. A few found the escape from the modern world which they needed, and returned to the ranch many times.

Photographing wildlife, camping in the mountains and traveling around the country showing films was considered (by those who had never tried it) a glamorous lifestyle.

People did not realize the physical difficulties, stress, expense and dangers imposed by such a rigorous life of continuous travel, both on foot and on the highways.

Few were aware of the financial drain of being away and on the road for months at a time either. Fortunately, most visitors knew the Crislers were not well off and brought along extra food.

Few professional wildlife photographers earn a good living. Crisler was no exception. They work atrocious hours and frequently risk their lives with wildlife, accidents, and other hazards. Crisler's "pay" was not measured in dollars. His was a much loftier ambition: Alert people to the values of wilderness and wildlife, especially in Olympic National Park. As long as he could pay his bills and accomplish his goal he was relatively happy.

Although Lois was capable of writing on a level far above the majority of her Peninsula audience, mostly common folks, she chose to simplify. Scarcely a word was used which couldn't have been found in a primary school textbook.

When possible, she read first drafts of the column to Herb. His ability to cut straight through to the heart of the topic, especially if it was about animal behavior or the Olympic Mountains, often improved the column.

Lois' column livened up many a reader's day. Herb had been correct when he told Lois, "Marry me and you'll have something to write about." Lois never lacked for something to write about once she decided to follow Herb, and made up her mind to write.

Actually, Herb, although having had practically no formal education, had considerable talent as a writer and poet. His powers of observation were acute and his sense of humor delightful. He wrote several manuscripts, none of which ever saw print, mainly because he didn't really try to get them published. Later, he composed innumerable poems and wrote and sang his own songs. He even sang one of his songs to Walt Disney. Disney loved it.

After joining the national lecture circuit, lecturing before distinguished audiences, meeting important people like Walt Disney, staying at such famous hotels as the Statler in Detroit, the Crislers became even more famous. Heady stuff for

Herb Crisler with movie camera somewhere in the Bailey Range.

Peninsula residents, many who lived a very quiet, backwoodsy life.

Lois wrote about things which local people could relate to: finding the rare Fletts violets, the thrill of hearing an Olympic marmot, **Marmota olympus,** whistle, the seriousness of spilling the salt supply while in the wilds and how they bathed out of a bucket while camped in the snow on a high, timberline ridge at Kimta Basin.

Readers, mostly robust, avid outdoor types, relished such lore and hungered for more.

Lois doled out minuscule tidbits of information, painting a vivid but terse picture, then frequently left her reader's imagination free to wander. Sometimes she literally left them dangling, which provided several humorous incidents.

There isn't space here for her columns. But the reader deserves a taste. In order to do so, judicious editing was necessary.

The very first TALK starts out in Lois' breezy, homey, delightful style, like a letter from a favorite aunt:

> Home at last, after our season of lecturing! We did not really get home for keeps until after our final showing of the season, which was for the Mountaineers in Seattle.
>
> Before that we just had a rushed day or two at old Hume's Ranch up the Elwha now and then, between showings, trying to get the "ga'den" in and the cabin re-organized after a winter by itself.
>
> We re-decorated the cabin.[2]

We can almost hear an audible gasp from readers at this startling statement. Had Lois stopped there, with, "We re-decorated the cabin," dozens of people's imaginations would have been fired up by vivid thoughts. What could they have possibly done to Grant Hume's old cabin? The building was becoming a shrine, even then, and certainly is now that it's been designated a National Historic Place by the National Park Service.

Some readers might have fired off an indignant letter inquiring: How dare they defile a local shrine by re-decorating? Others might have called on the phone, or hiked in for a look see.

Yes, Hume's Ranch was connected by Forest Service telephone wires. Elkhorn and Low Divide Ranger Stations, Hurricane Hill and Dodger Point Fire Lookouts were attached to the wire. Because frequent limbs, snags and other debris fell across the wires, telephone service was rather spasmodic.

Phones were the old hand crank, battery-powered, wall-hung party line variety. Each party had his own ring, two shorts and a long, or a short, long and a short, etc. Eavesdropping was expected. Sometimes those doing the eavesdropping broke into the conversation, much as people might do on Citizen Band radio today. Everyone on the party line knew everyone else's business. It became known as the Olympic "grapevine". The phone was the only link with civilization for people stationed at, for example, isolated Dodger Point Lookout.

On this occasion, Lois anticipated readers's concerns about redecorating Humes log cabin. She explained:

> Whenever we put new oilcloth on the nine-foot table in front of the cabin window, that is "re-decorating."[3]

Reader's must have sighed with relief. Instead of modern plumbing, interior plywood walls, new clapboard wood siding or electric lights, only a simple oilcloth. They could accept that.

What kind of oilcloth would anyone put on a hand-made table in an old log cabin? Lois not only described the oilcloth, but who picked it out:

> Cris picked out this oilcloth. It's not smart. It's not modest. It's just frankly pretty. It is bright blue with corsages of tulips, roses, poppies and dahlias on curly white palettes all over it. At the time I wondered who had the nerve to design it. Cris felt pretty audacious himself.
>
> Cris got rolling from Whiskey Bend with his load ahead of me. When I trudged up to the cabin door in the twilight with my pack board, there it was, unrolled the length of the table. Cris was no-where to be seen. The row of skunks [tiny wooden ones purchased in the East] glittered back of the moss center-piece. I stood and looked.
>
> When Cris brought in fresh-cut asparagus for supper, I said humbly, `the oilcloth is beautiful.'

PINK POTTERY

> Our brown plates went with it. For breakfast I set out the pink plates, and the pink napkins. Cris chose those pink plates. He chose the pink napkins. There is only one thing a southerner likes better than pink and that is the pearly gates themselves. Pink pearl.
>
> I put on clear glasses of orange juice and red goblets of buttermilk. The whole thing was not good taste. It went clear through bad taste and out on the other side. It was gorgeous taste. There was something about that audacious oilcloth that fitted right in with the age of pioneer log cabins.[4]

Next Lois explains they took everything out of the cabin so it could be thoroughly washed down. While she was standing outside a group of people from Port Angeles, who had seen their pictures, dropped by. Lois was weary, but she proudly showed them the inside of the cabin, bare-bones empty, but clean.

Then on to other things:

Cris' first project was the "ga'den." Spading. Hauling in dozens of loads of forest loam to add to the hard clay soil. Planting cabbages, onions, spinach, carrots, turnips, cucumbers, squash, tomatoes, corn. Taking care of the strawberries and raspberries.

It was hard to get him to take time enough to come in to eat his meals. When Cris gets interested in one project he forgets about everything else.

Down in the river bottom the bear was lifting stones to look for ants, the elk were getting ready to leave for their annual spring migration. Cris's new camera sat idle on the table. But he said he would get to the picture taking later. Then everything else would get neglected.

Tuesday Irving Petite from Issaquah and Betty Cornelius from Seattle dropped in. Irving is a writer and rancher. No books published yet. But the publisher read the first 30 pages of his first book and sent him $400. When the book was finished they did not like it.

Shucks, they said, keep the four hundred bucks. Forget it. All we ask is to have the first look at your next manuscript. We think in a few years you will be the most exciting writer in the U.S.

Betty's great grandmother was the first white woman in Whatcom county to have a child there.

Next morning the kids, both former students of mine at the University of Washington, had to leave at 4 a.m. to catch the 8 o'clock ferry from Port Ludlow.

WISE MEN ARRIVE

The following morning E.A. Kitchin and A. L. [Tommy] Thompson of Port Angeles strolled down the trail from Whiskey Bend. Tommy carried his camera. Kitch carried 50 years experience with birds in his head, and a package of nails for Cris in his pocket.

Kitch was much interested in the little carved wooden skunks from Maine and asked how much each one cost.

'Two bits,' I said.

'Is that with or without the smell?'

At 25¢ I said it was without.

'Oh, of course,' Kitch replied. 'The smell would be one scent more.'

After lunch Tommy prowled off with his camera and Kitch looked over the five deer in the barn pasture while I tried to film something very elusive--not Kitch's hawk-like visage, but the look of experience, authority and keen life-long interest in the bird man's face.[5]

In her next column, 17 June, Lois describes how popular Hume's Ranch had become:

About 50 people dropped in over Memorial Day weekend. We expected from one to 13 at the most.

The previous Wednesday I took a pencil and tried to figure out the possible number of people, mattresses, bedding and places to lay it down, including air mattresses and the lawn swing.

`You just wastin' yo time,' Cris said. `Things will work out themselves.' I went ahead figuring.

Ernst Freitag, an engineer from the state highway department at Olympia, has first choice of the tent and he was coming.

We had asked Kassowitz, the nationally known Leica portrait photographer from Seattle and his wife. The bedroom was for them.

Jim Mann of the Ryther Home in Seattle, and his wife were bringing a boy who was much interested in the outdoors. The bothy--Cris's log lean-to on the bluff--was for them.

Cris had just finished fixing up the saddle room with a built-in lounge and my great-great-grandfather's cherry spool bed. Cris planned this room for Mrs. Albertson and her two girls while Reverend James Albertson camped with a group of young folk by Idaho creek.[6]

With so much company coming, they worried about food. They knew from experience that the combination of fresh air and hiking resulted in colossal appetites. They had been late returning home that spring and the garden was not producing yet.

A trip to town seemed inevitable. They dreaded it. A round trip required a minimum of five precious hours. Herb went up to the root-cellar and took stock.

The root-house shelves held home-canned raspberries, blackcaps, apple sauce, beans and tomatoes. From time to time they had carried in extra supplies, canned sliced bacon, canned butter, yeast, powdered eggs, powdered milk and cases of canned milk. Herb decided they could make it without any additional supplies.

Then something happened which made them feel more relaxed:

> Down out of the forest strode Ernst with a heavy pack. He was beaming. Without a word he laid out on the kitchen table grapefruit, oranges, fresh eggs, cheese, fresh ham.
>
> I was awestruck. `Ernst,' I said, `you were inspired.'
>
> I made bread and put it to rise on the cedar shake above the jumbo heater in the corner of the cabin. I made a half dozen beds around the cabin and filled the old home-made wheelbarrow with bedding for Cris to roll up to the bothy in the woods.
>
> Ernst chopped and brought in a wheelbarrow of wood and kept the water pails filled.

LIKE GRAND HOTEL

> From now on the tide of people flowed in and out and over little old Hume's Ranch.
>
> Next to arrive were Edna Fagerberg from Kirkland and her brother Morley Bouch from Diablo. Unexpectedly with them were her sister and brother-in-law, Ada and Ed Marot from Marblemount. Bang went another bed.
>
> Then we found they were going on to camp at the ocean the next day. So that situation wound up with two extra beds for someone else.
>
> The kaleidoscope shifted fast. I could barely get in the minimum of appropriate worrying before the pieces somehow fitted into shape again.
>
> I heard voices at the water log and ran out eagerly. The Kassowitzes, I thought. It was four strangers getting a drink.
>
> `You have the life,' said the younger woman dreamily. `Never see another human being. Never have a thing to worry about.'
>
> `M-hm,' I said.[7]

All that worry for nothing. Everyone brought food. A few hikers missed the turn-off trail and continued on towards Lillian River, but eventually turned back and found the ranch. Others didn't come at all.

The Crislers needed pictures of calf elk, which are not easy to obtain. The cows hide their calves until they are large enough to run and keep up with the herd in case of danger.

A trip to the Hoh River was decided. The first stop was at the famous old John Huelsdonk ranch, then run by Huelsdonk's daughter Elizabeth (Bettine) and son-in-law John Fletcher.

The first time Lois had visited the Huelsdonk's she had walked 18 miles by trail to reach the ranch. This time they drove right to the door. Lois could not help but make comparisons between this visit and the one long ago, when the ranch was truly in the wilderness:

> A power plant hummed in the yard furnishing lights for the house. Bettine has an electric mixer with a churn attachment. From the big white refrigerator she took out steaks--not "forest beef"--and ice cream.
>
> John has a tractor and a truck to bring in gas to feed the tractor, wood-saw and power plant.
>
> Cris thinks Pa Huelsdonk actually had more "soluble" time than John and Bettine have.
>
> Pa cleared land by hand, but if the hound got after a cougar Pa could leave the stump burning, get his gun and follow the hound.

John hires machinery to clear land. At $80 a day for the bulldozer and driver you don't go following the old hound dog for cougar.

Cris wonders what becomes of all the time they save with the time-saving gadgets.[8]

They looked for elk on the South Fork of the Hoh without success. Then they backpacked up the main Hoh River trail. A few scattered elk tracks and the tracks of two different black bear dimpled the soft soil along the trail:

Cris rested his pack on a mossy log. `In 1924,' he said, `coming up here at this time of year there wouldn't be a leaf left on the maples as high as the elk could reach. The elk did a lot for this country. The upper Hoh was like a park. The elk kept the brush eaten out, making open glades under the trees.'

Now there is no apparent difference between the fenced-in elk forage study plots and the open forest.[9]

They heard an elk bark the alarm. A cow ran across the trail with her tongue hanging out. Herb climbed up onto a little bench and found the calf. A black bear had hold of it. The bear moved off at the sound of the camera. But the calf was bitten through and wouldn't live. Both the cow elk and Lois were crying.[10]

The parade of visitors continued. Paul and Margaret Granger arrived. Paul spent most of two weeks working on the woodpile. He loved it. `You couldn't have entertained me better,' he said.

Tales flowed like aged wine. Grant Humes, Dr. Ludden, Pa Huelsdonk, Billy Everett, the Mowich Man--pioneers who had a spark of greatness because they loved the land, were all discussed.

Superintendent Preston Macy of Olympic National Park, Lieutenant McCubben of Ediz Hook Coast Guard Air Detachment Base and his wife arrived.

Lt. McCubben listened attentively while Herb described the immense task of backpacking supplies 30 or 40 miles up steep mountains to some of his camps.

Lt. McCubben said the Coast Guard was perfecting the technique of air-dropping supplies and life-saving equipment, both at sea and on land. Training was going on now. He'd look into the matter of making air drops for the Crislers as a practice mission. If they could drop supplies to the Crislers, they should be able to do the same for stranded or injured mountain climbers, he reasoned.

However, such a project would have to be kept quiet, he cautioned, unofficial.

Superintendent Macy placed both hands over his ears as if he hadn't heard a thing.

The Reverend James Albertson, his wife and daughters Ann and Mary, and Leith and Mary Johnson, former aircraft observers, [during World War II] came to visit.

Also during this particular June, a woman writer made her first appearance at Hume's Ranch. Lois included this bit in her column:

Ruby El Hult was here for a day or two, thanks to Walter Green of the Black Ball Ferry Line.

Ruby is the author of Steamboats in the Timber, to be published by Caxton Press. It is a history of the roaring mining days in Coeur d'Alene, Idaho.

Ruby is a redheaded elf with honest live blue eyes. She said she used to just cry every time she went by a university, she wanted so bad to attend. Thought all the knowledge in the world was locked up in those people and buildings.

Finally she got there herself. As Cris said, `Ruby is a puhsistent little cuss.'  Now she says there are a lot of dumb ones in the university too. `No great secrets locked up there.'

Ruby plans a book on the history of the Olympics. She went in to see big Bill Thorniley in Seattle about it. He is the man who is reorganizing the Olympic Peninsula Hotel and Resort Owners Association.

Finally Bill got suspicious and Ruby admitted she had never been to the Peninsula.

`That's a hell of a background for writing a book,' Thorniley roared.

So Ruby came to the Peninsula! `I'm going to write a real book about this country,' she says.[11]

As June ended, the tide of visitors slowed:

Among the last friends to drop in were Dr. and Mrs. T. Eric Reynolds of Piedmont, California, and Hugo Holm of Oakland.

Holm is with the Pacific Telephone and Telegraph Company. Dr. Reynolds is president of the Alameda County Medical Association and a nature lover too.

He gave the keynote address at the national convention of the Audubon Society at Asilomar last April. His wife is a noted bird photographer and lecturer.[12]

Carol Preston, Herb Crisler and Helen Rupp making cider at Hume's Ranch about 1945.

Last to come were Lieutenant Commander McCubbin, his wife and two children and Mrs. McCubbin's brother Bob Budd. He had been considering the air drops with his airmen and decided they required more details. He brought maps and wanted to know exact locations where supplies could be dropped onto snow fields, where the goods had a better chance of landing without damage, and of being found. It could be arranged, he assured them.

But not without cost! The Crislers might be expected to show their films of the drops and maybe a few movies of wildlife to military gatherings. Herb agreed this would be the deal of the century.

The garden was laid by. Snow had melted enough in the high country to permit travel:

'For the next three months,' Cris said, 'I wish I was two people. One to go into the mountains and take pictures. The other to stay at home and enjoy the luxury of the Ga'den.'[13]

In typical Crisler fashion, Herb decided to "break in" by heading for the farthest end of the "traverse", Far or Kimta camp, about 50 miles from Whiskey Bend.

His pack weighed 100 pounds. Lois' half that. The packs were that heavy because of a 60-pound handicap of cameras and film. In addition, they carried emergency rations and sleeping bags, since on the first trip of the season they never knew whether or not one of the caches had been destroyed by windfall, animal or avalanche.

Bob Budd accompanied them as far as Hayes River on the main Elwha Trail. They inspected their cache at Chicago camp and found it in perfect condition, although it hadn't been visited for two years.

They stayed the second night at Low Divide shelter, building a fire in the big sheet-iron stove Ingar Olsen had carried in when the Geological Survey camped there years before. Someone had recently left hotcake flour and bacon grease. Herb mixed up a big batch of hotcakes and they feasted.

The next day both suffered from sore muscles and feet. Herb led up the north end of the Skyline Trail. It was his plan to reach their Lake Beauty cache, but they encountered iron-hard snow covering the trail along the steep slopes of Mount Seattle. Herb had to kick steps. With soft-soled boots they made miserably slow progress. He wished he had an ice axe.

Darkness caught them on a miserable, steep pitch. Both were so tired and sore they could hardly walk. They bivouacked for the night in a tiny cleared space beneath an alpine fir where the snow had melted.

The next day they reached Lake Beauty only to discover it was still frozen over. The cache, although not visited for two years, was in perfect shape.

The next morning they returned to the top of the divide and headed for Kimta camp. Only occasionally could they find the trail, as snow still covered the north slopes. The distance to Far Camp was only about five miles, but what a rugged five miles! Even without snow, the poorly-maintained Skyline Trail was sometimes difficult to determine from game trails. There were many ups and downs and wicked ravines to cross. Some were filled with snow, which may be undermined by melt water, creating the hazard of falling through.

They became thoroughly discouraged. From two to five feet of snow covered the area. They had seen no animals except chipmunks. This was mid-July. Had they come "upstairs" too soon?

At Promise Creek Pass they struck the first animal sign, a bear slide in a snow field, three fresh deer tracks headed west and a bull elk going east:

Our hearts lifted and Cris put the heavy Cine-Special camera on the tripod to carry over his shoulder.

We followed the crest of the ridge, sometimes swinging east over sun-thawed snow where we could easily step, sometimes west where Cris kicked steps, balancing the tripod and camera on his shoulder and carrying his pack.

Below us the snowfields slanted steeply down to crags and drop-offs. We climbed down gray crags via tree branches and instepped along knife-edges of snow sprung from cliffs.

Up one peak, down the other side and up the next we went, glorying in it all. "I'm like an ole bull elk," Cris said. "I like to be up on the ridge where I can see both ways."

It was hot. Our only water was snow melted in the furnace of our mouths.

FLORA AND FAUNA

Once we saw a herd of elk below us walking single file across the unbroken snow just under a saddle.

It was a pitifully small herd--only nine cows. But they handled themselves in the elk tradition. The lead cow was well ahead, bold, cautious, responsible, picking the way. The others loitered nonchalantly in her steps.

I heard the long, long war cry of a Townsend's solitaire, and Cris with his keen eyes spotted the bird for me, trim and gray on a snag against the blue.

The avalanche lilies arched their necks, gleaming with youth, and curled their petals back as daintily as a ballerina's thumb and finger.

In the afternoon there was one peak we could not get down the other side of. We had to come back a distance and contour below it.

At the head of a hard, precipitous snow finger I stuck like a postage stamp and Cris had to creep back and relay my pack.

It is hard for us to get over terrain like this because of our foot-gear. If we wore mountain climber's boots with caulks and tricouni we could dig in. But we wear composition soles in order to move noiselessly over rocks.

We rested in the first place where we could perch after Cris relayed my pack, and saw a bull elk across the ravine from us.

He stepped carefully off the rocks onto the snow, walking towards us in full sunlight.

Cris loves to study nature and this drives me wild. `His velvet's all shed,' he commented interestingly, dabbing Skol on his red face.

`Are you a photographer or a naturalist?' I whispered hoarsely. `Give me that Skol.'

`You got enough Skol already,' Cris retorted calmly but he did get up and film the bull.

Cautiously it started down the steep shadowed side of the snow ridge towards us. The surface was hard, the bull skidded and the snow from his hoofs flew up into the sunlight.

Cris looked at me with an admiring smile. For the elk, `They're a wonderful animal,' he said. `Those bulls will go almost anywhere.'

Late in the afternoon we encountered two bulls together. First we heard them, then we saw their tracks running hard in the snow.

Next we came to their bedroom high on a thawed-out shoulder with a commanding view of the world. It was flat and convenient, with a mucky shady place at one side and nipped-off beargrass at the other.

Finally we saw its owners, a big bull and a small one. They had caught our scent and were still running, though by now well below us, flying across the snow shoulder.

They lunged over the far side recklessly and disappeared. Regretfully we rested a while in their pleasant bedroom.

FAR CACHE

When we reached Far Cache, at the crest of a saddle, after sundown, we were disconcerted.

The cache itself, lodged in the crotch of four young alpine firs, seemed to be in good condition, and was. But the stone fireplace and sleeping space were three feet deep under solid snow.

We were tired and had little time to make camp before dark.

Cris took a sharpened pole and jabbed out boulders of snow. I up-ended them to the edge and rolled them over. They dashed to pieces in the scrub 20 feet below.

He cleared the fireplace, scooped out slushy snow and on a bark island built a fire.

I had a fine waist-high table to work on but it fooled me. I forgot it was solid snow and the gelatine turned leathery at the bottom of the can before I squeezed in the lemon.

In profound stillness and blackness, by a tiny fire in the warm night, we dried our socks. We were dead weary but heart-pleased, and crawled into our bags on the ground.

In the snow of the saddle just below camp next morning we saw a record of tracks. The big and the small bull had tried to traverse the saddle and return towards their bedroom.

Near camp the tracks bunched undecidedly, then turned back. The bulls had not dared to pass us.

Cris chipped out the entire camp spot, exposing under the heavy snow the green spears of avalanche lilies already two or three inches tall.

159

These alpine flowers were on their marks, set and waiting, clasping the bud in two cupped leaves.

After this hot day the buds spired white an inch above the leaves.

That evening the two bulls tried again to get past us and back to their bedroom.[14]

The above provides a graphic example of how rough the country is. The Olympic Mountains are some of the most recently-formed in America. They haven't had time to weather, not even as much as the Cascades. Sometimes only a narrow, cleaver-like summit provides a way for either man or elk to travel.

The next morning was stormy, so they decided to stay in camp. Suddenly an Olympic marmot whistled far below the campsite. This was the first marmot they had heard whistle in two years. They went to look. The marmot was located in a green spur of growth in a wild, steep earth slide. Neither cat, coyote nor man could possibly approach without being either seen or heard.

Towards evening the marmot began whistling rhythmically, a sure indication that something was bothering it. They walked to the brow of the drop-off and peered down.

A huge cloud of dust swirled upward on the wind. The marmot sat upright on a rock whistling excitedly. Below it, and 300 feet below where the Crislers stood, the two bulls were struggling along the nearly perpendicular rock slide, searching for footholds, creating the dust cloud. Again the bulls were trying to get past the Crisler's campsite, bent on returning to their comfortable bedroom. The Crislers whispered, instead of talking out loud, hoping this time the bulls would get past.

After several days of sweating, the Crislers needed a bath. Herb heated a bucket of hot water:

Cris's bath: Standing on a carpet of soft gray old bark by glowing bark coals. The steam clouding off his wet body, green hemlocks and snow all around. Luxury!

We thought of the mirrored bathrooms in deluxe hotels where we stay before big showings back east.

Cris ordered hoe cake. It was to be cooked as Aunt Maggie cooks it down in south Georgia--in a skillet.

But if Aunt Maggie could see us now, I thought. The wet abysses of fog below, the far-off roar of some mountain torrent rushing under unbroken snow, the drip overhead on our tarp, the cleaned-off place on the snow where we scooped it to melt for water, the avalanche lilies coming up by the fireplace.

Thousands of snow fleas hopping like coal dust in our tracks on the snow and a pine siskin peacefully pecking them up in the fog.

The evening the storm cleared we were near the top of the cloud. It would open up and let in bright mountains and soft sky, then close up in fog again.

I heard the marmot piping and started to the drop-off to see what had upset him. I uttered an exclamation.

Along the brink, the trunks of the alpine firs swung in black curves against a gauzy blue. On second glance this blue was thronged with thousands of plumy tree-tips lighted by sun, far down in the abyss.

The next morning we started for home.[15]

They retraced their steps towards Lake Beauty. The trail was still mostly obliterated by snow. They found a place where one of the bulls running from them that first afternoon had slipped and fallen. The steep earth was molded where his side hit. A jag of rock had ripped out clumps of hair. This concerned them greatly, it is not a trivial thing to run a wild animal.

Presently, Cris, up ahead, digging steps with his tripod, looked back and motioned to me with a smile.

On a flat shoulder of snow was a whole circus of bear tracks. A mother and cubs had played and nursed and slid here.

The mother had climbed back for a second slide but the cub had hoofed it cautiously down her track.

We saw three bears this morning. One was a huge fellow, half brown, awkwardly sliding down a steep green slope between two snow fields.

He stared at us intently, then sidled towards us, just a little higher than we were. He was eaten up with curiosity but Cris didn't want him above us, so he whistled.

The bear studied awhile then turned away.

One little fellow ahead came down a crag perpendicularly like a black caterpillar and started around a steep snow cirque towards us.

He paused and swung his little snout out over the world below him. How cute, I thought. He swung it around above him.

Then I caught on. The wind was full at our backs as we faced the bear. In a minute, without ever spotting us, he turned and gingerly backtracked to the crag.[16]

They met campers at Low Divide. It was cold and raining again. They welcomed the fire already built inside the shelter.

At Chicago Camp, still in rain, they built a fire and ate cans of home-canned chili, corn and pears and drank a quart of hot chocolate before turning in. The next morning they cached the cameras and headed down the trail for home.

After a day at home, where, among other things, they read the list of visitors who had come, and signed the guest book during their absence, they headed for Whiskey Bend and town.

A note on their car read: Dear Sir: Unwittingly you have become a Good Samaritan by very generously loaning us the use of your spare tire. Thank you very much. A Port Angeles address was given.

The next trip was by way of Queets Basin, then west towards Cream Lake, to open caches in the Bailey Range. After coming down off Mount Pulitzer they made an amazing discovery on Mount Ferry:

It was a botanist's paradise among the crags above the snow. Cris had just found and filmed one of the famous endemics of the Olympic Mountains. Endemics are plants that develop in a certain region and are found nowhere else. The Olympics are so isolated that they have 20 species of endemics. (Britain, for instance, has only one)

Within a few yards of the summit of Mount Ferry, Cris paused, astonished. On the hard, hot slope just below the summit rocks stood four clumps of one of the scarcest plants in the world.

It was the rare Olympic endemic Senecio Websteri[17] discovered on Mt. Angeles by the late E.B. Webster and named for him. Till this minute only about 100 of these plants were known to exist. These grew in only two places--Mt. Angeles and Marmot Pass, near Mt. Seattle.

These four clumps of several plants each beside our feet had only 25 blossoms and seed heads among them. They grew on the northeast slope of the mountain like those on Mt. Angeles. But they looked more hard-bitten.

Senecio Websteri is an exotic-looking plant 6 to 10 inches high. It has big glossy leaves and pale cream-colored blossoms. It looks like a Marlene Dietrich of dandelions.

FOLLOWED ICE AGE

Senecio Websteri lives very quietly now, in some of the grandest and loneliest scenery in the world. But it has a dramatic past.

When the last ice age crowded down over the Strait of Juan de Fuca, choked Puget Sound and reached its fangs up the north Olympic canyons, most of the local plants moved south.

In California they sat out the ice age in comparative luxury. When it was all over they moved north again.

But Senecio Websteri toughed it out right here in the Olympics. Pursued by ice, it crawled up to the highest slopes in the lee of the dark summit crags and hung on by its teeth.

161

During each short, thin alpine summer, <u>Senecio Websteri</u> looked out over the sea of ice, bloomed, then dug in for the winter again.

It looked as if the dogged little plant with the vein of iron in its nature might lose its bet with fate. The ice lost instead.

<u>Senecio Websteri</u> blooms now in the thin hot air far above the forests instead of the ice. But after the long struggle it has lost its pep. It has no ambition now to spread. Perhaps it needs the old whip of glacial cold.[18]

They were relieved to find the first few caches visited along the Bailey Range had come through the winter in good condition. It had been a season of extraordinarily deep snow. The Cream Lake cache had them worried:

As we came around Mt. Ferry and looked down into Cream Lake Basin we saw that a tremendous avalanche had occurred down right where Cris' shelter had stood.

'Our cache is gone,' Cris said. Below was a brown island of desolation. The lake water backed up onto the meadow, apparently dammed by debris.

Down the mountainside we could see a path of broken trees, meadows piled with dead trees, and great piles of avalanched snow.

In an hour we were on the floor of the basin. We approached a wall of snow, broken trees and logs hiding the spot where our shelter had stood. In the green meadow just in front of this wall of wreckage gazed a big black bear with its back towards us. In spite of Cris' anxiety to see what remained on the other side of that wall, he dutifully set up his camera to film the bear.

It was backlighted and against a dark background. So I offered to walk towards the bear to help the picture.

When I was 15 feet from the bear, who assumed he was alone in the world, Cris called:

`Address the bear. Say something to him,' he said.

The bear looked around astounded. Confronting me, he stood there hating to run and also dying of curiosity. Finally he walloped over to a little alpine fir and stood behind it.

This fig leaf made him feel better but it impaired his view. He stuck his head out from one side and then the other, peeking at us.

`He may stand up,' I called to Cris. The next second up he reared, a fine black monster towering over the tree. I glanced around to see if Cris was filming this.

Cris was stalking towards me, his tripod over his shoulder. He was too rattled by my failure to address the bear and by the nearness of his unseen cache to bother with bears.

FINDS CACHE SAFE

Cris climbed the avalanche wall and looked ahead. Then he looked back at me. His face was one smile of pure delight.

`Our sheltah's there, Lois,' he called softly.

What saved it was apparently about 12 feet of snow already on the ground where the avalanche struck. Young trees were bent over 12 feet above ground. One standing tree had its branches stripped from 12 feet high to 24 feet. So the avalanche had been about 12 feet deep.

Debris had been left on the roof of the shelter but no logs or trees. The sturdy, well-braced cross log had sagged under the weight of snow. No other harm had been done. The little gray shelter sat snug between two mighty paws of the avalanche.

It seems to have been about 50 years since the last big avalanche at this spot.[19]

The trees framing the famous view of Hoh Glacier across the lake are tipped at a crazy angle now. Probably the prettiest lake now in the Cream lake basin is not mangled Cream lake itself, but Billy Everett's lake in the upper basin.[20]

Outdoor photography, especially motion-picture photography, can be a frustrating endeavor, especially in the wet climate of the Olympic Peninsula. The peaks and high ridges of the Olympic Mountains catch moist, marine weather coming in off the Pacific Ocean. Vapory clouds cling to the peaks green-clad bosoms, obliterating, for weeks on end, what during clear weather is grand alpine scenery.

Lower elevations, especially on the rain-shadow or east side of the mountains, might at the same time be enjoying sunny, dry weather.

The Hoh and Quinault Valleys are the wettest places in the Continental United States. A new record was set at the Hoh in 1997. Officially measured at 190.42 inches, it could have been 200, according to Park Ranger Bill Rohde, but a road wash-out in mid December forced the Hoh Visitor Center to close temporarily. An inch a day is sometimes recorded in any one of the wettest months, and in March, 1997, 29.42 inches of rain fell. Even June can get about 10 inches. July, August and September are the driest months, but even then storms can suddenly sweep in off the nearby Pacific Ocean and dump inches of rain.

Lois explains the frustrations of bad weather in one of her Trail Talks:

Our caches were all open, inspected and replenished. Cris was all set for photography.

I returned to the ranch for a few days and left him in the high country to start his real photographic season.

The season is only about 45 days long, from the first of August to the middle of September. This period is when Cris does his year's work. All the rest of the year is either preparation for those 45 days or the aftermath of them.

After all the work of preparation is done, you would think there was nothing to the filming. That would just mean sauntering around with a camera.

Then it rained. Clouds wrapped the mountain meadows and hid the peaks. For four days Cris traveled alone up in the fog and snow and rain beyond the trails. He did not even have his camera out once.

Then he ran out the back way, down from Ludden's peak to the ranch to greet Hugh Brooks.

Hugh is a retired New York banker who takes an annual trip in the Olympics with Cris.[21]

Herb arrived at the ranch to a festive occasion. August 8th was Lois' birthday. His annual present to her was the first ears of corn from the garden. Present was Dr. William Graf, head of zoology at San Jose State College in California. Dr. Graf wrote his doctoral thesis on the Roosevelt elk and came to the Olympics to gather information on the Olympic variety.

In 1949, Olympic elk were considered a separate variety. They have now been lumped into the same classification as all Roosevelt elk **Cervus elaphus roosevelti**. Old-timers on the Olympic Peninsula still call them "Olympic" elk, although they are indistinguishable from other Roosevelt elk.

A dozen friends had gathered to help Lois celebrate her birthday. They came bearing gifts, sweet cream, a knitted rug, transparent apples and other items. Some helped hoe the garden. That evening A.L. "Tommy" Thompson, Port Angeles photographer, arrived at the ranch to make the next mountain trip with the Crislers.

How they entered the Bailey Range Lois doesn't say, but probably from Olympic Hot Springs, up the Boulder Creek trail to Castle in the Cat, then over the Catwalk.

The very first night rain began to pour down again. Tarps were stretched over sleeping bags, gear and cooking fire. Lois describes what followed:

Seven cameras, three photographers, wonderful scenery and a week of fog and rain!

It was beautiful but about as photogenic as a pan of milk. We five were alone in a world few humans ever see. It was a world that was wild, strange and grand.

The mists drove through the mountain passes. Their directions were confused. Mists climbed the mountainsides below us. They drove east, they drove west.

To the photographers this was very tantalizing. They would think the mountains were about to appear. But just as one curtain of fog lifted, another veil slipped in. It was an alpine strip-tease.

There was one magnificent evening when the mists opened and we saw the high snow fields on Mt. Olympus under the shadow of the cloud. The clouds below cut Mt. Olympus and us adrift in the sky.

Thompson got out his still color camera and tried for a slide. `It's a mood you seldom get,' he said. `Most mountain pictures are sunny. This will either be special or worthless.'

Brooks got discouraged and went back "downstairs" to civilization.[22]

Surrounded by wind, rain and snow flurries, the group spent their time trying to arrange the tarps so they could keep dry and dragging in more wet wood for the smoky fire.

Since elk, deer and bear photography was out of the question, they studied and photographed a mother field mouse and her brood of five. The little mouse was using all of her resources to defend herself and her family from the invasion of people. Every time she went out for more food, her brood would soon come tumbling out of the nest, anxious to see the bright new world outside the ball of grass which was their home.

They would be scattered when she returned. Could she count? You bet. Not until the last of the litter had been found and returned home did she plug the entrance with a ball of grass.

One afternoon, as they struggled along the alpine slopes, Thompson pointed ahead. Through the mists they saw a herd of 40 elk, "fat, velvety-looking and clean", a thrilling spectacle against a backdrop of fog and wet sub-alpine firs.

The weather didn't stop them from enjoying nature:

Another thing we enjoyed in the storm was the water-drenched flowers. In the Olympics you have to repeal the law that flower gardens should lie flat and in beds. These may be nearly perpendicular.

One wet green meadow tilted on edge and was the floweriest thing I ever saw. Pink mountain asters, orange tiger lilies, red and yellow columbine, big plumes of pine lilies, little plumes of creamy buckwheat, blue lupine, gold arnica, orchid elephant trunks--all were draped in a festoon of color.[23]

Avalanche lilies hung their bonnets straight down in the rain like white bells.

Cris made a new "locality record" on the famous Olympic endemic, Flett's violet.

One of the meanest places to travel in the rain is along the Catwalk.

The Catwalk is a jagged undulating rock cleaver between Mt. Carrie and Cat Mountain.

Rain shot up from the Hoh Valley three or four thousand feet below.

`I'm not partic'lar cold,' Cris shouted above the storm. `I'm not partic'lar tired. I'm not partic'lar hungry. But boy am I wet!'

Thompson shouted back, `I've been rained on many a time from above. But this is the first time I've been rained on from below!'

In a pass south of Mt. Ferry stands a lone tree that is known as The Tree. Its branches are all brushed to the east by the prevailing westerly gales.

Cris and Thompson wanted to get some pictures of The Tree. After Tommy took several shots both in color and black and white, Cris wanted a little movie of me standing in front of The Tree swinging my rain cape over my shoulders.

On the first take I swung so hard against the wind that I swung myself off balance and wrapped the cape around my neck.

Cris smiled. `You work too hard, Lois,' he called. `Just pitch it to the wind.'[24]

The Olympic Mountains tempt, flirt with and sometimes crush intruders. Photographers especially seem to become targets.

However, the mystical Olympian storm gods do not <u>always</u> carry a grudge against invaders, or Herb would never have been able to expose approximately 100,000 feet of film over a period of many years, some of which would eventually be incorporated into the future Walt Disney Production release, <u>The Olympic Elk.</u>

Notes and Sources, Chapter Fifteen.
1. Ruby El Hult, <u>Herb Crisler In The Olympic Mountain Wilds,</u> (Swallowtail Press, Puyallup, WA, 1992)

2. Lois Crisler, "Olympic Trail Talk--1," <u>Port Angeles Evening News</u> 10 Jun., 1949

3. Ibid.

4. Ibid.

5. Ibid.
   E.A. Kitchin's book is, <u>Birds of the Olympic Peninsula</u>.

6. Lois Crisler, Olympic Trail Talk--2. 15 July, 1949

7. Ibid.

8. Ibid.

9. Lois Crisler, "Olympic Trail Talk- 3" 24 June 1949

10. Ibid.

11. Lois Crisler, "Olympic Trail Talk--4," 1 July, 1949
    Ruby El Hult's book is <u>UNTAMED OLYMPICS</u>, Binford & Mort, Portland, OR. First edition (1954) Third edition, CP Publications, Inc., Port Angeles (1989)

12. Ibid.

13. Lois Crisler, "Olympic Trail Talk--6," 15 July, 1949

14. Lois Crisler, "Olympic Trail Talk--9," 5 Aug., 1949

15. Ibid.

16. Lois Crisler, "Olympic Trail Talk--10," 8 Aug., 1949

17. Lois refers to the Olympic Mountain Groundsel <u>Senecio neowebsteri,</u> of the sunflower family. Also known as Webster's Ragwort and Webster's Groundsel.

18. Lois Crisler, "Olympic Trail Talk--11," 12 Aug., 1949

19. Sometime after 1951 another avalanche completely destroyed this shelter, leaving no trace.

20. Lois Crisler, "Olympic Trail Talk--11," 12 Aug. 1949

21. Lois Crisler, "Olympic Trail Talk--13" 19 Aug., 1949

22. Ibid.

23. The "pine lilies" Lois referred to are probably Columbia Lily, <u>Lilium columbianum</u>, a lovely, large plant with a showy flower with curved, orange, maroon-spotted sepals and petals.
    Her "orchid elephant trunks" are Elephant Heads <u>Pedicularis groenlandica</u>, of the figwort family, which thrive in wet alpine meadows in many Olympic Mountain locations.

24. Lois Crisler, "Olympic Trail Talk--13," 19 Aug., 1949

16
Olympic Mountain History
Photographing Elk.

Summertime in the high elevations of the Olympic Mountains comes reluctantly, sometimes hardly at all. Deep snow often covers alpine regions until late July--even into late August during seasons of heavier than normal snowfall. Snow can occur at higher elevations any month of the year during cold, stormy spells.

When it comes to describing a wildlife viewing situation, or the Olympic back-country, without becoming a bore about it, Lois Crisler had talent. Her weekly column, OLYMPIC TRAIL TALKS, was increasingly popular.

Many of the ideas for Lois' columns were conceived while resting her pack on a rock or log to take the weight off, shoulders numb from tormenting pack straps, legs muscles complaining and sweat beading her brow. Few writers, especially those published in a newspaper, are inspired by such circumstances.

Or while waiting on a mountain "cleaver", the Crisler term for one of the many upthrust slabs of jagged rock so common in these newest of mountains, for a herd of elk to leave their beds on a snowfield so the photographers could shoot some footage.

Lois rarely missed getting these columns to Port Angeles to meet weekly deadlines! How she did so remains a mystery, but probably added a lot of trail miles to her season's accumulation. She may have submitted more than one at a time.

She frequently left Herb alone and returned to the ranch by herself--no small achievement. Any one of the three access routes to the Bailey Range, Elwha Snowfinger, Ludden Peak or Catwalk, present numerous obstacles which can cause a crippling, or even killing accident.

In this particular column Lois first indulges in reminiscence about mountaineers who had trod the Olympic Mountains long before Herb rambled there:

> When you are in the interior of the Olympic wilderness, it looks virgin and untouched. You might be the first person ever there. But it has a lot of history.

> On our recent trip, from the Elwha Basin to Queets Basin, we recalled a few of the things that have happened along this route.

> The Elwha basin, the Elwha Snowfinger, Dodwell-Rixon Pass,Queets Basin and Humes Glacier on the east side of Mt. Olympus--all have their stories.

> From my own point of view, the dazzling historical facet of Elwha Basin is that there I met a blue-eyed stranger, a ranger name of Herb Crisler.

> The Queets Basin is glorified by the further fact that there Herb made our first date. Characteristically it was to go game-stalking. But all that is a gleaming tale that has no end.

> SAD TALE OF TEXAN

> For instance, into Port Angeles in the early 20's came a Texan. He wore a sombrero and a goatee and said he had come to spend the winter trapping in the Elwha Basin.

> Dr. Ludden, who lived in the wilderness himself (half a mile from Hume's Ranch), tried to point out a few of the facts of life in the Olympics to the romantic trapper.

He ended up by canning bear meat sausage for him. The Texan had trapped a bear.

With a horse loaded with supplies and traps, the Texan moved into the Elwha Basin in the fall. He intended to build a shelter and a stable, harvest grass in the basin for the horse and trap fur-bearers. The Olympics did not play that way. The snow came early and it didn't go away. The larger animals did go away.

The only shelter the Texan got done was a lean-to against a rock a few feet off the trail.

Finally he brought the starving horse into this shelter with him. It died. He couldn't get it out.

In the spring he came out to Dr. Ludden's and on to Port Angeles, bitter, as romantics usually wind up by being.

RIXON SURVEY

Here in the Elwha Basin, Theodore Rixon of Port Angeles camped in 1899, along with helper Jack McGlone. They were engaged in the first survey of the Olympic mountains.

One September afternoon after the day's work was over, Rixon says that McGlone took off to climb Mt. Olympus.

He got back to camp about 2 o'clock in the morning. On the east peak he had left the first human record made on any of the three highest peaks of Olympus. It was a scrap of an August copy of a Shelton newspaper.

EARLY EXPLORERS

The way from the Elwha Basin to the Queets Basin is up the Elwha snowfinger. This is a narrow draw filled with varying amounts of snow according to the season.

The top of the Snowfinger is a pass between the Elwha and Queets watersheds. It is named in honor of Rixon and Dodwell, commissioned by the U.S. government to survey the Olympics. At the pass you suddenly emerge into a glorious outlook.

Opposite you is the black wall of the Olympic range. Below you the Queets Basin falls away to the Queets River Valley winding toward the Pacific.

But the great fact is that across from you rises Mt. Olympus itself, a tremendous, complex, rugged massif of snow and ice and black rock peaks.

Down it slants the Humes Glacier, to end in two pug noses of seamed, greenish-gray ice, like a gigantic mastodon's paws.

On August 15, 1900, H.B. (Bert) Herrick of Port Angeles broke out onto the crest of the Dodwell-Rixon pass. On a knoll in the pass he found a record of adventure in a 1-lb. Royal baking powder can.

`A.M. Godfrey, D.W. Starrett, W. Daggett, on our way to the Pacific from Port Townsend by Dungeness, over Dosewallups and Elwha Valleys--Aug. 25, 1894.'

Those words are blunt. But there is a great joy of adventure about them. The planet doesn't hold much excitement any more, of that particular rare quality.

Seven years later a party of 64 moved into the Elwha basin. It was the well-organized group of the Seattle Mountaineers.

Their packers were Will and Grant Humes. The Anderson boys had applied for the job and lost. They played a trick on the Humes brothers.

For the main climb of Mt. Olympus the Mountaineers wanted to camp in Queets Basin. The Humes boys told them there was no trail and horses could not get up there.

Meanwhile, the Anderson boys back-packed horseshoes and manure up to Queets Basin and trampled the place up with horseshoes on sticks.

When the Mountaineers sweated in with their backpacks some days later, they looked things over and asked Grant and Will Humes a few biting questions.

They liked the Humes brothers though. And in those days it was possible to give them the most romantic of accolades. They named Humes Glacier on Mt. Olympus for their packers.

EARLY ASCENTS

The Mountaineers made first ascents right and left. They climbed peaks named in 1890 by the Press Party but never climbed--unless Jack McGlone had sneaked up them without any newspaper.

They climbed Meany, named for Prof. Meany, then city editor on the <u>Seattle Press</u>. Barnes, named for the historian of the party. Christie, named for its leader. Mt. Seattle, etc.

The women of the party were regarded through the dim spectacles of the 19th century.

These females were instructed to wear "durable waists and short skirts--not much below the knees" and "bloomers" or better yet "knickerbockers."

They were told to bring heavy veils. Not for harem concealment but to protect their complexion on climbs.

When any of the women did climb, the other women regarded them as heroines. As they returned to camp, the others met them, carried in their packs and brought them tea and hot water for baths.

Discipline on climbs was military. "Companies," "double quick," "orders obeyed promptly."

CAN'T WALK ON MIST

On August 10, [1907] 37 of the Mountaineers attempted Olympus. Among them was a gentle little botanist, Winona Bailey.

When I first went out with the Mountaineers decades later Miss Bailey was always along on the trips. I asked old-timers about the hump at the back of her neck. "She tried to walk on a cloud," they told me dryly.

It was stormy on August 10, 1907, when the 37 started up Olympus. They tried it anyway. There is a wild delight in attempting a mountain in a storm. Besides, some of them had to start home the next day.

By the time they got up the Humes Glacier to Blizzard pass, 700 feet above the Hoh glacier, a 30-mile gale with snow and mist thundered through the pass.

Asahel Curtis, old-time northwest photographer, wrote, `The party appeared suspended in the heavens on the edge of some great cloud, with a white desolate world forming out of the chaos.'

They turned back. And Winona Bailey walked off the snow onto some mist of the same color. She fell 100 feet. Her back broke. But she wedged into snow and was not killed.

In the storm they got her down to their temporary camp in Queets Basin. A bit of canvas stretched to a rock made a wet shelter. There, in "Hospital Camp," she stayed, later was moved down to the Elwha Basin, still 60 miles from civilization.

The leader of the Mountaineers was pint-sized, blue-eyed L.A. Nelson, a fine mountaineer.

On August 13, three days after the accident, L.A. led the first ascent of West peak, the highest point of Mt. Olympus. There were ten men (six of them professors) in the party and one woman. In honor of the lone woman, Anna Hubert, they named Hubert Glacier.

Nelson recorded the outstanding impression of the first human beings ever to reach the true summit of Mt. Olympus. `One of the grandest views to be had in the American mountains--over unscathed forests and a wilderness of peaks.'

GEORGE WELCH FALLS

Another accident on the Humes Glacier was that of George Welch of Port Townsend.

Because the overhanging snout of the glacier could not be ascended the glacier was reached from the rock wall to the north. The ice had shrunk away from the rock and Welch slipped down between the rock and ice, scouring the vertebrae of his spine against the rock.

His two companions made a rope from strips of blankets and managed to get him out. One stayed with him while the other went for help.

Young Dr. Will Taylor of Port Angeles went up, treated him, and prepared him for the long trek out.[1]

During the summer of 1949 a first occurred in the Olympic Mountains. Supplies were air-dropped to the Crislers by the Coast Guard. The Coast Guard Air Detachment on Ediz Hook had recently acquired a helicopter. Both the chopper and fixed-wing aircraft were used in the air-drops. Pilots needed practice of this technique since it was something new for them.

The air-drops were not officially sanctioned, received no publicity and were not mentioned in Lois' columns. Herb agreed to photograph each drop, then show the film to the Coast Guard for evaluation of techniques used. Few people ever knew about the drops.

Plans had been carefully formulated. The drops were spaced out over the season. Herb needed to decide what he wanted to be dropped when and where, then pack and crate the goods with plywood.

The drop locations had to be carefully coordinated so Herb and Lois could be on scene before the flights. They cut and built crosses with evergreen boughs on snow fields as targets, because from the air one snow bank looks much like another.

Before the plane arrived over the drop area, Herb placed the motion-picture camera on its tripod in readiness.

When the aircraft approached the location, Herb flashed a signal with a mirror. The Crislers also wore bright clothing for this occasion. A smoke flare provided the pilot with wind direction. When the plane came in for the actual drop, Herb or Lois would begin filming.

Boxes dropped free-fall usually buried in the snow. Boxes with parachutes drifted on the wind and sometimes missed the snowbank. The plan included photographing the recovered boxes so the airmen could evaluate the damage.

Altogether, four drops were made. First was near Lake Beauty. Second was in Kimta Basin. Third was on Dodwell-Rixon Pass and fourth, the snowy slopes of Mount Ferry. All were chosen because adjacent snow fields were available and caches were in the vicinity.

Film and supplies were the main items in the drops. The air crews, however, couldn't resist adding special treats, such as buttermilk and fresh fruit and vegetables, much to the Crisler's delight.

The Dodwell-Rixon Pass drop went badly. Parachutes failed to open because of wind gusts. The boxes, one containing precious film, threw up a large plume of snow as it crashed and broke apart, spilling film and food.

At the Mount Ferry drop, made from a helicopter, four boxes were dropped safely. One contained a replacement for the damaged film.

August in the high country often brings a period of rain and fog, locally known as the "August bad spell." September usually provides delightful Indian summer weather. Although there are no guarantees about this marine climate any season of the year.

September is also the height of the elk's rutting period, which lasts about a month, and the best time to photograph elk. The bulls are gathering their harems and are more active than at other times. Preoccupied with mating, the elk sometimes allow the photographer to get much closer and stay in camera range longer.

Elk have complex social customs. Their behavior pattern changes according to the time of year. During the summer the bulls are usually off by themselves in bachelor clubs. The cows take care of the calves. They cannot go as high or into as difficult country as the bulls while the calves are young. The cows do get the calves up to the lower mountain meadows surprisingly early.

By late July the herds are at their largest. Various groups of cows which have separated while giving birth in June have come together again.

Now comes the easiest time of year for elk. Food is plentiful. Their most dangerous enemy, man, is far below. By moving a short distance, to take advantage of the almost constant alpine winds, they avoid the bugs and mosquitos which plague animals during the summer. By pristine mountain lakes, on snowfields and in lush, green meadows ablaze with wildflowers, the cows romp and frolic in wild abandon with their calves.

Never, however, do they forget that the cougar may be close by, and several cows will likely be on guard duty while the rest frolic.

By the middle of August the bulls begin the age-old competition for dominance which ensures the survival of the fittest. They spar, playfully at first, among themselves, until they establish dominant males. The early sparring matches are never very serious.

As the rutting season approaches, the bulls are attracted more and more to the cows, until mating becomes their driving obsession. Nature has caused this period to happen when it does simply because calves, in order to survive, must be born at a very exact time in the late spring. Born too early they might not survive because of a lack of food for the mother and because of bad weather. Born too late and they do not mature enough to survive the rigors of the coming winter.

At first the cows tend to ignore the bulls advances. They reluctantly accept the dominance of a herd bull. The herd bull, usually the strongest bull with the largest sets of antlers, attempts to accumulate as many cows as possible. Once he has them in his harem, he strives mightily to keep them for himself.

This reluctance on the part of the cows to remain in a bull's harem sometimes drives the bulls to distraction. Bulls must wait patiently for the cows to come into estrus. The period of time during which the cow will be receptive may be only a few hours.

The bull senses the approaching period by an odor discharged by the cow. He frequently takes a whiff of her posterior. As the time approaches, the bull becomes very attentive, staying close, not wishing to miss this opportunity to breed. He may also urinate, then wallow in the urine, which contains scents irresistable, as well as sexuallly exciting to the cows.

As the time draws near, the bull will lay his head and neck across the cow's rump or back, and sometimes he vigorously licks the hair along the cow's spine against the grain, obviously a form of foreplay intended to stimulate the sexual urge.

Herd of elk in the Bailey Range.

A large, experienced, mature bull is quite an adept lover.

The cows may have other ideas about which bull they wish for a boyfriend, although most are naturally attracted to the biggest bulls with the largest antlers, survival of the fittest.

The saddest of this gathering of harems are the immature bulls. Many are "momma's" boys, and wish to remain with their mothers. Some outriders have fairly respectable racks of antlers too.

Any herd bull refuses to tolerate the young bulls, and forces them out. Since elk are usually sociable animals, this causes the youngsters to feel lonely and rejected. They sometimes go off to the sidelines and actually pout, standing with lowered head, looking back frequently as if being abandoned by their family is the saddest thing which ever happened. Perhaps it is.

Herb's packboard somewhere in the Bailey Range. Mt. Olympus in distance.

A young yearling bull will breed if allowed to do so. The cows definitely prefer older, more experienced lovers. There's an excellent chance that the dominant herd bull is not a member of the herd, but has migrated in from elsewhere. Consequently, the larger bulls produce the majority of the calves, which is good animal husbandry, nature's answer to the weakening effects of in-breeding by close relatives.

On this particular trip the Crislers had been hampered by low clouds and fog during the days. Yet, the nights had mysteriously been clear. Finally, waiting paid off. At one of Herb's favorite locations, a spike camp at what is now known as Crisler Lake, on the north side of Steven Peak, they found and "worked" a large herd of elk:

When we broke out into the area above timberline, it looked as if the cameras were going to be useless today again. A fog finger had unrolled overhead.

But this day turned out to be a glorious one.

As we rested on top of a ridge, Cris suddenly purred, `I know where the elk are.'

I hunted stubbornly until I saw them too--half a dozen dots below summit crags far ahead.

Cris outlined our course and we set out. Finally we reached the cleaver facing our elk. We did not burst out on top. We reared our head cautiously through the scrub on top, dug in our toes and set up tripods.

We faced a grand sight. We were near the head of a U-shaped basin, floored with snow. Opposite us rose a steep, bare, green mountainside. From the summit crags almost perpendicular fingers of talus ran down into the green. Animal feeding trails crisscrossed it.

ELK COME INTO VIEW

And there were our elk--72 of them.

171

It was so steep they looked as if pinned to the mountainside. Some elk lay cradled on a bit of feed trail. Others stood motionless. Some grazed. A calf lay on a protruding rock. Only in one place were a few elk able to lie near each other.

Half a dozen cows incredibly stuck to the faint fingers of green just under the crags.

`We'll wait and see what they do,' Cris said. `They may go down to that snow after a while.'[2]

For an hour they waited, battling insects and praying something photogenic would happen. As the sun swung around to the south and began to beat onto the slope where the elk were, the heat began to bother them. Roosevelt elk do not like heat.

Finally a lone bull got to his feet and started cautiously down the mountainside towards the snow. A beautiful, raw wildlife drama unfolded, a scene witnessed by only a few people in the alpine section of the Olympics. Even Herb, the veteran elk watcher, became excited while observing this herd of elk at play.

The following was one of the "gold nuggets" which the Crislers often referred to, after perhaps weeks of prospecting, and not seeing any elk behavior worth photographing. Later, tens of thousands of movie watchers would thrill to the scene Lois describes:

About 100 feet above the snow the bull intersected a good elk trail that angled down to the snow. He struck out briskly but half way down decided to shortcut down a talus slide directly to the snow.

The idea spread to the herd about as fast as Woodrow Wilson's idea of world government spread to the U.S. But after a while they got it.

One calf squawked. Another thought of the same thing and mewed. The herd got into motion. Many calves cried.

`Lookit'm line out, Lois!' Cris exclaimed.

The ones higher up were still scattered. But ten were coming down. They lined out, passing a low crag. They hit the good elk trail and doubled pace. Above, others were lining out, elk fashion.

ELK ON `SKIS'

A calf flew down at a run between two files of cows. The calves remembered how nice the snowfields are.

The whole mountainside was in motion; 72 elk looping and zigzagging in single file downward.

Where the bull had short-cut down, one by one the elk left the trail and came straight down the talus slide. Their front feet dropped down and braced. Their hind feet humped and slid to the front.

Then one by one the elk hit the snow. Cris was almost crying with excitement. `I can't take them all. You better get up and help. Lookut'm. Ogee! Oh lookut'm!'

When each elk hit the snow she let go all caution. Down she came lickety split at a dead run. The calves flew like little brown streaks.

Then came the "buckers." They ran down the snow, bowed up their backs and bucked. The snow flew.

They whirled and headed uphill. One would run down, half turn and stop like a skier doing the Christie, waiting for her pal right after her.

`That bull's going to buck,' Cris said. The bull braced himself and stepped down sedately.

A troop of half a dozen calves already down on the level snow got together and ran back like mad to the oncoming elk.

Cris glanced at me with a smile. `They certainly do enjoy getting on a little place where they can kick up thuh heels,' he said.

The elk walked to the far edge of the snow. One or two went onto the rocks, then turned and moved back onto the snow. The whole group seethed, drifted, like a flock of birds about to light.

A brown body kneed down onto the snow, pressed it comfortably. The neck leaned up, holding the brown head so easily, as if feeling, "How good."

TOGETHER AGAIN

The herd settled. Now it didn't look as if there were 72 elk. It looked more like there was 30, they lay so close together. In their center rose the antlers of the herd bull.

`Oh, I missed that,' Herb moaned.

`What was it?' I was reloading. I had never shot up 50 feet so fast in my life.

`A cow struck at a bull!' Cris said. `She ran him! Happened so quick. She got up and struck her hoof at that young bull.'

The young bull stood now away from the group 20 feet or so. His head pointed sulkily away from them. After a couple of minutes brooding, he stalked off and lay down on the steep snow 100 yards from the herd.

The whole movement of the herd down to the snow had taken a half hour. By 12 o'clock they lay on the snow like table statuettes flat on the bottom. Each statuette had the long cream-colored curve of the body and the little chocolate brown head and neck rising at one end. Here and there one lay prone--abandoned, head, neck and all, to the coolness of the snow, the hotness of the sun.

DISAPPEARING ACT

We each found an easy chair--a rock ledge in the foot-deep juniper--and settled down to wait. We figured nothing would happen for about two hours.

By my rock grew big bells of blue gentian. Two red-tailed hawks found us and slid around flat-winged to look us over. Some small bird popped over the crest six feet away with a surprised flurp of its wings.

The sun was hot. We ate lunch quietly, then Cris crawled under the "petticoat" of an alpine fir to reload his magazine. I dozed.

Ten minutes later Cris wakened me. 'They're gone!' he said. 'You're a nice animal watcher.'

I raised my head and looked. The snow was bare. The elk had simply vanished.

Apparently the wind had shifted for just a whiff and they had caught our scent.[3]

Lois writes with an intoxication about her life in the alpine country. The challenge, the feeling of discovery and achievement, offset the miles of painful backpacking, the periods of rain, wind and storm. After "losing" the herd of elk, she describes a mountain meadow with lyric-like prose:

MOUNTAIN MEADOW

We moved down the cleaver to rest in a mountain meadow. What is a mountain meadow?

Heap together red-blue lupine and blue-red Indian paintbrush.

Sprinkle pink asters among them.

Float white plumes over them.

Shoot a little pure gold arnica among them.

Stick them in bright green grass.

Toss in a few gray rocks with mustard-color and soot-black lichen stains.

Mantle them all with clovery sweet air and hoist them a mile into the sky.

Fix a backdrop of snow peaks and a glacier or two.

There you have a mountain meadow.

Make this one the choicest kind of mountain meadow--the kind a connoisseur of human pleasures would choose.

That is, let it have the aroma of remoteness.

A mountain meadow you can Jeep or Cadillac to is the market variety. You want the rich, perishable flavor of the non-commercial kind.

To get that you have to change yourself. Hike for three or four days. Get over some difficult terrain. Then when you roll out onto your mountain meadow you savor the feeling of deep-breathing strength and relaxation, the delicious feeling of achievement.

That's what brings out the full flavor of the meadow. That's meadow plus you. A mountain meadow you drive to is like a home run without a ball game.[4]

The wildlife photographer who becomes a victim of his own emotions invariably misses action he regrets later. There's nothing quite as exasperating as waiting for hours, even days, to obtain a picture, then being either distracted, or so caught up in the unfolding drama, that the camera sits forgotten, unused. It happens frequently, even to 30-year veterans in the business like Herb. Remember he missed the shot of the Florida frigatebird catching a gull in midair! Lois tell of another time:

Take for instance the day Cris studied nature and called the shots.

We were contouring from Eleven Bull to Cream Lake, along the Bailey range. From its crest ridges roll down like paws bracing the range. Between the paws lies steep grassy basins.

Sure enough, below us at the edge of the timber were three elk, a bull and two cows.

Above us in the fog, we could hear a whole herd. Near us stood a lone outrider bull, half hidden by a clump of alpine firs.

The four visible elk were absorbed in a little domestic drama.

The two cows did not really have their hearts in the act. They lay beside the trees a little apart from each other.

It was the two bulls who took their roles earnestly. Both were outriders. Both were potential cow stealers and home wreckers.

The only difference between them was that the one below had already succeeded in cutting out two cows from under the herd bull's nose, from the main herd up in the fog. The other one was ambitious to steal cows. At the moment he was moving down toward the three by the woods, bugling his ambitions at every pause.

The bull below stood defiant and anxious in front of his reluctant two-cow harem. Antlers reared high, he bugled up at his rival. Then he glanced anxiously over his shoulder at his harem.

We were standing motionless beside a tree. Cris called the shot. `He's going over and get that cow up.'

The bull went over. Six feet from the cow he ducked his antlers at her. Hastily she scrambled to her feet and stood still.

Take 2. `He's going to run her back into the brush.'

The bull walked above the cow and herded her into the brush, out of sight.

He emerged and rolled center front again. Standing proudly in front of the green forest, he reared his antlered head and bugled up the mountainside. The bull beside us responded.

Take 3. `He's going over and get that other cow up. He wants to run them farther from the outrider.' The bull got the second cow up and ran her into the brush. Then he came back and stood ready again.

Suddenly I came to. `You didn't get a picture, Cris,' I hissed. `Here you stand, calling the shots, with your camera over your shoulder.'

Cris had been enjoying nature. Now he looked sheepish. All the rest of the way to Cream Lake I nursed my resignation. After we had made camp I decided to show Cris up.

On our way over we had heard elk bugling from the lower meadows and Cris said he would go down and photograph them the next day.

I took my little magazine camera and sneaked away from camp unobserved.

No sooner had I entered the first of the lower meadows than I heard a sound in the brush at the far side.

Moving back into the brush for cover would make too much noise. The only "cover" available was to use a trick.

I dropped to my knees, crouched and focused for 50 feet. The next second into the little green meadow strolled a cow elk who had wandered from the herd to graze.

When the movie camera started to buzz she looked up and bent her ears forward. Her dark brown animal face and eyes were a study in attention, suspicion and determination. She walked towards me!

`Oh boy,' I thought, `I won't tell Cris. Just wait till he views my film.'

I had to wind up. The movement, I feared, would scare the cow away. Instead she was more puzzled and curious than ever. She walked closer! Exultantly I changed focus to 25 feet.

She would eat a bite, study me, then step a little nearer. My heart purred with delight.

The cow could not decide exactly what I was. But she made up her mind that whatever it was, it was for no good. She gave the short contemptuous bark that is the elk's warning word, turned and stalked out of sight.

With revenge sweet in my mind, I started for camp. Then I glanced at the indicator on my camera. For 30 feet I had been out of film. I had not one inch of the cow.[5]

The Crislers' lectures and films were alerting people to the beauties of trekking in the wild Olympics. They began seeing people in places where they had never seen anyone before, unless it was Dr. Keith Thompson and his party, or Dick Owens or Jack Broadbent the Elwha ranger who sometimes patrolled the Bailey Range area.

The Crislers started a 20-day cross-country trip at Olympic Hot Springs, intending to come out at Three Prune shelter and the Quinault. As usual, they were loaded down with supplies for various camps. On the Boulder Creek trail, the morning they started, three young men steamed past them loaded with 60-pound packs and climbing gear. It was only a one-night trip, to Cream Lake and out by Whiskey Bend, the exuberant youths said!

An hour later they hear the boy's voices above them in the brush. They had lost the government trail in a rock slide! A half hour later the young men were lost again, not so exuberant by this time. Herb thought they would perhaps spend the night somewhere around Oyster Lake, then sneak back home.

Besides elk, bear were their favorite subject to film. On a steep mountainside overlooking the Queets River Herb was photographing wind-torn wisps of fog in the valley below when Lois whispered:

`There's a bear 10 feet from you.' Cris silently turned his head. Then his lens. A sober, earthy little face bristling with black fur had come up over the edge to see what on earth was going on.

I looked away, to give Cris the most of a chance. Animals feel easier if your eyes aren't on them.

A thumping and crashing of rocks. I looked around. Cris was grinning. `Just got focused and he left.' While we were still talking there was the little head again, sharp-eared, rearing up from behind a bush farther away. Dying to figure us out.

On a rocky knoll near Dodwell-Rixon Pass, a bear was picking huckleberries. Mt. Olympus rose in the background. Ice was in the wind and the bear was working briskly. The fur blew forward over his shoulders. At the first whisk of the camera he dodged around the rock.

Cris tiptoed after him and met the bear tiptoeing back. The bear stood up on hind legs then walloped off, uttering "foomph" at every jump.

SECRET ELK ROUTE

Bears are not clowns. No wild animals are. But a human being often doesn't take them seriously. But there is something splendid and gallant about the Olympic elk that makes you respect them even when you smile at them.

When you see the places where those elk go, and the trails they make, you can't help marveling.

There's a wild, high ridge of rock and snow where the Olympic range meets the Bailey range. Annually, along it we see the tracks of a lone bull.

Why he comes up there, how he gets up there, I do not know. This year the tracks were there as usual. And the day we returned he had just been through. We were astonished to see that he had gone through an even more difficult spot than before. Apparently following our track, he figured there must be a way through.

'A man fell there and had to be packed out,' Cris told me. But the bull's bones were not around. He made it.

We walked on quietly, wondering at the great lone animal. 'He must be proud of himself,' Cris said, 'comin' up here all by himself, knowing all these secret little routes.'

PATIENT FILMING

Cris has keen, trained vision. He can spot a patch of fur a mile away, pick a way to the animal along dense-forested, trackless mountain side, come up on it beside the wind and in the best possible place to photograph it.

He led us to herd after herd of elk, in country the average person would have said was bare of animals.

But Cris's idea of real skill is to film the animals and leave them undisturbed, without their ever detecting his presence.

When we got on a herd we would often stay with it for hours. The sun beat on us, mosquitos buzzed around our faces, flies bit us, we skipped lunch, went thirsty, "froze" if a head turned our way, doubled down and crawled if we had to move or change film.

I was the baby that put one herd to flight, and maybe a good thing at that. We had wonderful fun staying with this herd for hours. Cris was pleased. 'We done purty good,' he breathed in my ear. 'Didn't scare 'em.'

IN A TOUGH SPOT

We were on our way from cache to cache, no bags with us, by a route we had never gone before. It was nearly sundown. We shoved on fast but we missed it. That night we siwashed under the stars.

For a while it looked as if we were in one of the toughest spots we'd ever been in. We were wet with sweat, even my leather belt was soaked. Our bodies grieved for water. Coming down through the unknown timber we watched the light of the sky dim. Cache, bags, grub, fire and water were far below. It was too dry and dangerous where we were to make a fire.

We got down into jungely forest and avalanched trees. In the twilight I saw Cris' figure ahead of me walking a log. He wavered. 'Cris, be careful!' He lunged down. Unhurt! His toe had stubbed an unseen snag on the log.

In pitch darkness we still felt our way downward. About 10 p.m. Cris paused. He had intersected our usual trail and his foot had felt it. He struck a match. It really was the trail.

Foot by foot he felt along it to a creek. On the wet gravel he made a fire. Out into the glimmering forest he prowled, came back with wood for the night, and a 12-foot slab that made a cradle for each of us by the fire.

A strange night. The little fire, the stars among the tree tops. The great stillness and wonder of deep forest. For food the few scraps left from lunch.

SURPRISE

Three times on this trip Cris got so close to a lone bull that it was thrilling. The first time I pulled a boner. Stepping as quietly as a cougar, Cris had led down into a "bulls' basin." We both spied it at the same moment--the palms of antlers rising from a pocket ahead. We stopped. The palms wagged rhythmically. There lay the bull chewing his cud. We pulled back and looked at each other with pleased despair.

`If the camera starts, he'll go,' I breathed.  `Scare all the bulls in the basin.'

Some people sneak up on animals. We sneaked away.

I almost wrecked the next bull too. It was the next day and hot. Cris kept going down, down, until, sweaty and discouraged, I thought I could never climb back up.

Finally I blew up. `You don't find animals down in the timber on a day like this. They're up by the snowfields or lakes,' I whispered crossly. Explaining the facts of elk life to Herb Crisler!

Cris gave me an anxious look, trying to figure out how badly off I was. Then he changed course and started contouring.

In five minutes we came on a bull sound asleep not 50 feet away. After a beautiful session with him, Cris turned to me gently. `Elk,' he said, `you never know where they'll be.'

People's favorite reaction to bulls in mating season is fear. `The bull charged me!' Well, the third bull "charged" Cris.

At first he accepted us. He rose, looked us over, threatened a few cedar limbs to show who he was, then figured if we wanted to use the mountainside that was ok by him.

He actually lay down again. But Cris badgered him, stepping closer and burring the camera.

Up rose the bull and stalked majestically towards Cris. He bowed the curve of his antlers to the ground and hooked it. He strode closer, stripping bushes with a lift of his crown.

From where I watched it looked as if the bull rolled to within 15 feet of Cris. Cris said it was 20 or 25.

My own blood pressure was up with excitement and delight. But there was one small significant detail I noted. Every once in a while out licked the bull's pink tongue. This was Cris' protection. The bull had not got the scent and was trying to figure Cris out. He was defiant and curious.

When Cris ran out of film and turned his back on the bull and climbed to where I stood, he did not bother to reload. There was nothing more this bull could show him.

`Goodby, old man,' he called gratefully. Then that bull (a) went over and posed in front of a waterfall! (b) Went up on a snowfield and lifted a 30-foot tree on his antlers two times. Then shoved it down the snowfield![6]

One great embarrassment for any wildlife photographer is to be caught with an empty camera while something really exciting is going on within camera range. Or, which sometimes happens to me, to run out of film, period!

The climax of elk photography is an elk fight. Not that elk fights are so difficult to see, especially in such places as Yellowstone and other U.S. and Canadian national parks. In the Olympics most of the fights take place far beyond highways, which means carrying camping supplies and camera equipment on your back to some remote place.

What's difficult is to find an elk fight that you can actually photograph. It may be too dark, or two brushy, pouring rain or snowing, or may happen while you're changing film.

Lois writes about the frustrations of trying to film an elk fight, and that was with motion-picture film. Still photography is much more difficult. Combinations of fast action, poor light conditions and obstructions such as brush may prevent any pictures at all.

Lois explains the dilemma:

NEAR-MIRACLE PICTURES

When you stop to think of it, it is a wonder one gets any animal pictures at all. You travel over vast stretches of mountains. You come to the right place at the right time. (Things happen quickly when they do happen.) The light is right, the wind is right, the animals are out in the open. They do not see you. It is almost a miracle.

Then one time the near-miracle happened. Everything was right and we still lost the fight.

We were at Far Camp when Cris had a hunch to come clear across the mountains to the north side.

We traveled hard for 2 1/2 days, made camp and the same afternoon were out hunting with our cameras.

By some hunch Cris led directly to a mountain pass. As we approached we saw elk tracks. On the far side the stage was set. A steep mountainside above timberline, tawny in afternoon sunlight. Center-stage was a herd of elk.

`There's going to be a fight, Lois,' Cris said.

Tension is in the very air. The herd of cows stand tersely. Not a head lowers to eat.

Over on the "stage" abruptly the herd started hurrying uphill. They were trying to get out of the way. A nearby cow is sometimes gored accidentally during a fight between two bulls.

The cows failed to make it. They stopped laboring upward. Instead they crowded outward away from the herd bull, leaving him in an open circle.

Into the circle rolled the challenger. Cris focused his camera and filmed the two bulls clashing in the middle. Then he turned to me and gestured frantically.

`Get back, Lois. Get a picture of me getting a picture of the fight.'

Before I could obey I screamed. What happened over there was the most spectacular and appalling thing I ever saw in the mountains. It was over in a minute. While Cris was giving me directions he missed filming it.

The challenger was uphill from the big herd bull. He caught the herd bull off balance, struck him head on. The herd bull cartwheeled down the mountainside, end over end.

`He's killed him,' I cried.

The big bull slewed to a stop on his belly 100 yards below his herd. He got his feet under him.

Slowly he plodded down the mountainside to a snowfield that lay in a draw. He ate snow, rested, ate snow again.

Above, the outriders were bugling, parceling out his herd. With difficulty the wounded bull turned his head and looked upward.

THE VANQUISHED

Then occurred the most gallant thing I have ever seen an animal do. Slowly, with infinite difficulty, the bull forced himself up the mountain to his herd.

The outriders still knew him. They drew off.

But he could not stay. He had to have water. For the last time he left the herd.

Beyond the snow was a pool. We found him there alone beside it the next day.

The herd had moved far on down the valley, broken into three or four groups by younger bulls, none of whom could hold the entire herd.

The valley was walled by steep mountainsides and a precipitous drop-off at the lower end.

Three days later the herds left. The bull could not make the climb. He stayed alone, for his last fight--with winter.[7]

During the nine years Lois had been following Herb through the Olympics, they had seen only two elk fights. Before that Herb had seen only one. They often found evidence; clotted blood on trampled ground, bulls with one antler broken off, a bull with both antlers broken to stubs. Once, down in the timber, they found a dead bull with both antlers broken out of his skull.

In one remote basin they watched and photographed the same herd for four days. This is possible during the rut because once a herd bull has gathered a large harem and "staked" his territory, usually an area with open basins, he is very reluctant to leave. He knows that his chances of keeping his harem together, if the herd is on the move, are slim indeed.

Each morning the photographers climbed to a ridge above the herd and down wind from them. Often they were so close to elk they dared not move. Herb's new Eastman Kodak Cine Special camera was almost silent. Lois' little German Arriflex sounded like an airplane taking off, so she dared not photograph unless the elk were making noise. Lois describes the high drama which occurred the day they finally photographed the grand elk fight:

Our situation was uncomfortable, but grand. The hot sun beat on us. We lay low. For water we filled a plastic bag with snow and let it melt on the hot rocks.

Cris and I, silent on our ridge, might have been on another planet watching beings of another world. Around us rose crags black in the morning shadow, white peaks and the receding folds of distant mountains.

Below us rolled a velvety alpine basin dotted with clumps of alpine fir or hemlock on the tip of each rise.

Immediately below was a snow patch and beyond it two shallow lakelets. And on this theater, utterly unconscious of our presence, the elk were busy with their life.

They had a regular routine. Between 8 and 9 a.m., they moved in from the morning browsing to some cool place to spend the day. On two mornings they came onto the snow patch. For two hours after that the bulls were restless, bugling and whistling.

The next two hours, during the heat of the day, most of the outriders lay by the skirts of the alpine firs or in some other brushy, shady place. You could have passed nearby and thought not a living thing existed in the basin.

Almost on the dot of 3:30 the cows got up and either grazed or sought water.

Then all the outriders moved in amongst the herd. While the herd bull was running one out, two others would move in.

The whole herd was in commotion. Calves got separated from their mothers. Practically every outrider at one time or another had four or five cows rounded up. One rattled outrider even rounded up a calf.

The calves cried. The bulls bellowed. The herd bull told the cows what he would do to them if they didn't stay together. The air rang with whistles, bellows, barks, squeals, groans, bugles.

Once three outriders in a row started for the herd. Out towards them rolled the herd bull and they rolled back into the woods in unison. Suddenly one of them felt brave. He turned and headed back towards the H.B. on the run. H.B. stood and watched him. As suddenly as he had started, the outrider turned and sped back to the woods.

H.B. lay down for a moment behind a ledge of rock. One of the outriders looked up, saw he wasn't with the herd. He hopped up and headed for the herd on a trot. He just got to nose one cow when out bristled H.B. The little outrider trotted off just as fast as he had trotted up.

The outriders had troubles amongst themselves too. One had him a little bedroom in the shade of a tree clump. As bulls do, he had prepared his couch by hooking the ground with his antler tips, then pawing it.

Along came another outrider and intruded. They had a little fight and the owner knocked the intruder down the hill.

Two outriders sparred, to pass the time of day. The idle, languid clacking of their antlers was syncopated--cuh-lack, cuh-lack. Like the sound effects for a broadsword duel in the movies.

One little outrider had hemmed off two cows. All day long he petted and watched over them. If any other outrider so much as looked in their direction he ran him off. He thought he had himself a little harem.

About 3 o'clock, the H.B., restless and spoiling for trouble, suddenly came over and took the two cows away, back to the herd.

The little outrider just stood there looking after them for half an hour very dejected, his head hanging as low as his shoulders. Then he lay down and went to sleep.

The bulls had each other's measure. And the H.B. could bluff too. He would run at the outriders, get them started away, then throw on the brakes and stop with his hindquarters sliding under him.

COWS POINT OF VIEW

All this time the cows lay demurely on the snow, except that one or two would scramble to their feet and jump out of the H.B.'s way if he rolled past them towards some of the outriders.

`Oh, how sweet! He's protecting them.' I heard a lady coo once, years ago. It surely didn't look that way to the cows.

Once the wind varied and they caught a whiff of us. All were on their feet in an instant. They wanted to run but the H.B. wouldn't let them.

One cow did get off the snow. But she wouldn't leave without her girlfriends. H.B. glanced at her, but he was busy holding the herd on the snow. After a while they lay down. Then he went out and drove her back to the herd.

The bull cannot make the cows do what he wants. But he can keep them from doing what they want. For a while. In the long run they generally circumvent him and do go where they please, though maybe by a devious route.

CRIS GETS HIS ELK FIGHT

For some time we had noted one big outrider. He had come into the basin from elsewhere. He went up to a lakelet, drank a little, rested in the shade.

Suddenly Cris rose and manned his camera. I took one look and came to my knees focusing.

This big outrider was now approaching the herd. Very leisurely. But steadily. One of the local outriders challenged him. The big bull gave ground. He was not spending his strength on outriders.

The herd bull came off the snow to meet him. Deliberately, without haste, the big outrider came up. He halted. The two big bulls eyed each other.

Then began the preliminary footwork. They stalked parallel with each other, the outrider a little ahead.

Suddenly they whirled. They met head on. Their powerful haunches spread and squatted with the drive of their antlers.

Heads locked, there was no clacking of antlers, only grunting and the clashing of driving hoofs as the bulls circled and pushed and shoved.

Finally the herd bull gave a big toss. He threw the outrider off--pitched him aside. The outrider ran.

The herd bull still had his harem and Crisler had his fight.[8]

Now that the Crislers had new, exciting elk movies, including the long wished for elk fight, they looked forward to getting back to the ranch and editing film, in preparation for the winter lecture circuit.

Notes and Sources, Chapter Sixteen

1. Lois Crisler, "Olympic Trail Talk--14," 26 Aug., 1949
    According to Ruby El Hult, George was accompanied by three others; Bill Smith, Johnny Siebenbaum and George Clark Jr., called "Happy."
    Bill and Johnny stayed with Welch while Happy, the youngest, went for help. After examining the injured man, Dr. Taylor decided he did not have broken bones. Welch was brought out on a horse.

2. Lois Crisler, "Olympic Trail Talk--15," 2 Sept., 1949

3. Ibid.

4. Ibid.

5. Lois Crisler, "Olympic Trail Talk--18," 23 Sept., 1949

6. Ibid.

7. Lois Crisler, "Olympic Trail Talk--17, " 16 Sept. 1949

8. Lois Crisler, "Olympic Trail Talk--19," 30 Sept. 1949

17

Hume's Ranch Gets Modern
Movie, Beyond the Trails, Completed.
Mountain Mice Show for Hollywood Czar.

It was inky-dark in the old-growth forest, and nearly mid-night along the Elwha Trail, as Herb and Lois Crisler approached Hume's Ranch. They were weary beyond measure and glad to be home. Their legs and feet were swollen after walking 25 miles since dawn.

The beam of a flashlight dashed around the white-washed yard gate, flicked up at the weathered white elk antlers nailed over the top, then on into the yard.

It was mid-October, a magical time of year in the Elwha River Valley. Jack Frost had paid his first annual visit. Bigleaf maple leaves around the fringes of the meadow had turned calico; the leaves of vine maple, which grew along the river, bright crimson.

The night air carried the aroma of sun-cured meadow grass, rich, green garden plants, ripe corn and the tangy-sweet smell of apples.

Herb's flashlight beam swept the tall grass beneath the apple trees until he found what he had been dreaming of--ice cold Gravenstein apples, beaded with dew, lying in the grass. He filled both hands and sank his teeth into one before going into the cabin.

Lantern light flooded the inside of the log cabin. Lois sank down, totally exhausted. Herb stoked the old range with dry cedar. The fire popped and snapped, throwing sparks through cracks in the stove. They munched juicy apples.

After the teakettle began steaming, Herb took the lantern and disappeared into the garden. He returned with a bucket full of roasting ears and a can of butter from the root cellar. They feasted on steaming, yellow corn on the cob slathered in butter. Herb filled the galvanized wash tub, removed the lids from the stove and set the tub directly over the fire to heat so they could bathe their filthy, sweaty bodies.

It was after two o'clock when they tumbled into bed. Not in bags on the hard ground. On an innerspring mattress on their old cherry wood four-poster. They tossed and turned, too tired to sleep, unaccustomed to the softness of their own bed. For three months they had wandered the high, alpine country, experiencing beauty few people even dream exist.

Although weary of the rough life, there was a reluctance to abandon it for the season. Returning to their high caches and camps, where life, although hard, was still joyously free of the tediousness which they faced during the hectic winter, was impossible. Winter had closed the high country.

A few weeks later Lois was in the cabin reading when a strange purring noise drowned out the murmur of the river. The sound came from a shed out back. Suddenly the inside of the cabin was illuminated with a strange, bright light.

If Grant Humes spirit still wandered the Elwha Valley that October, it would have stopped dead in its tracks to see bright electric lights coming from Hume's Ranch. Herb had bought a small electric generating plant.

Ernst Freitag, a long-time friend and structural steel bridge draftsman with the state highway department in Olympic, and Herb came bouncing through the door, glad smiles on their faces. Everything glittered and shone.

Cobwebs never before visible in the corner over the wood range danced and shimmered. Lois laughed, grabbed a broom and knocked them down.

After half a century of coal oil lamps and Coleman gas lanterns Hume's Ranch had "gone modern."

Ernst had come up to help with the wiring. But it wasn't for lights they decided to install a light plant. They could now, for the first time, edit the summer's take of film without leaving home. Herb chinked up cracks in the old saddle shed until it was light-tight. Until then, they had kept their editing equipment and projector at the Methodist Church in Port Angeles.

They returned from the high country each fall with thousands of pieces of a giant jigsaw puzzle. And no picture on the cover to help them fit the pieces together. However, Herb had many years of experience, and considerable talent, at editing and composing a nature story with film.

Viewing and editing film at home was a luxury. More work could be accomplished. They decided they should view their film library, left-over footage from previous movies. After sorting through scores of reels, Herb decided reviewing them all would consume several days. They didn't have time.

The fall canning had to be done. Applesauce needed to be made. The wood pile had shrunk to alarming proportions. The garden needed attention. Berries, what few the birds hadn't stolen, needed to be picked. Lois skimped on the wood supply whenever possible so Herb could spend more time editing the new take of film.

The first major showing was in Seattle on November 17. Before then, the movie had to be completed. They needed to run through it at least three or four times so Lois could write the lecture and match words with scenes.

Herb helped with the script by suggesting changes. The introduction always fell to him. He was not only a more astute observer of wildlife than Lois, he had a flare for humor.

Film editing had, of necessity, always been a hurry-up job. There never seemed to be enough time between the end of filming and leaving on tour. Fortunately, Herb's memory of film already in the library was extraordinary.

Lois describes the process of editing:

One viewing does not familiarize me with thousands of feet of film. But Cris remembers it pretty well.

When the actual editing begins, I am Cris' man Friday. 'I want a valley scene,' Cris says.

I hunt through my scene lists for four or five valley scenes while he goes on cutting and viewing. I lay the 100-foot rolls out for him to project and choose from.

The scene not only has to have the right meaning. It also has to tie in with the preceding and following scenes. Altitude, time of year, time of day, coloring and amount of trees or snow in it, etc., must harmonize.

It must seem so natural and inevitable that when people look at the finished picture it never occurs to them that Cris did not just step up to some high point one afternoon and film the whole thing.

Actually, one short sequence may be made up of a dozen different bits of film, from 8 to 48 inches long, taken on different trips.

Sometimes we have six or seven scenes haunting our minds for days. They almost fit together. Cris tries them this way and that--splicing, cutting, putting them in the main film, running it off. Nope, that's not quite it.

It's tormenting. They are wonderful shots. They just have to be used. They obviously belong together. A logical sequence of elk activities perhaps, with superb close-ups.

Then suddenly, the evening of the third day, the insight comes. One scene from the library of Cris' old footage is the key. Put that in and three others that we hadn't thought of and the whole sequence fits together.

It looks so simple and natural that some lady will come up after our showing and say brightly, **'I'll bet you spent 15 minutes filming that. I'd like to go out some afternoon and film something like that myself.'**

STORY MUST TIE IN

      Most difficult of all is to get the story line. With an ordinary picture you prepare the script beforehand then film it. If something doesn't work right, you film it over. If you find later you need a little link or transition shot, you can film it. With wild animals it's different. You jolly well film what the spirit moves them to do. Right now or else. And if you had failed to film the build-up that's just too bad.[1]

The generator hummed. Lois prepared meals of roasting ears, carrots, cabbage and other vegetables fresh from the garden. They washed it down with drafts of cold apple cider.

As the film began to take form, Herb became totally absorbed in telling the story, his thoughts consumed by what to put in next. A good finished product depended upon keeping the thread of story running smoothly. Little bits of film, scenes which he may have shot years previously, he remembered, and Lois found. They were examined, then either discarded, or incorporated. A cow elk standing on her hind legs pawing at the sky, a chipmunk carrying a tiny, pink, hairless baby in its mouth. Storm clouds racing over the summit of Mount Ferry. Indian thistles nodding their delicate purple heads in the wind on the High Divide. Snow melt pouring off a granite ledge with wildflowers blooming on either side.

Lois was elected to make a trip to town for more gasoline. She hated to leave. The trip used up a precious day. Herb kept editing.

In the golden light of late afternoon Lois returned. She mopped her sweaty brow with a towel and drank from the water log, before entering the projection room.

Herb was bent over the splicing machine. He turned, a distant look in his eyes, smiled and nodded:

      `I had the brakes tightened,' I said.

      `I think I've fixed that little out-of-focus place in the projector,' Cris replied.

      `The Green boy had to go to the plant for white gas and I paced around lashing my tail for fear you'd run out of gas before I got home,' I answered.

      `The civet cat came in the door and hid under the bunk and I couldn't get him out.'

      `You didn't tell me you had enough gas for two hours yet,' I said. (I did. You didn't, etc.)

      `So I didn't put in the packing house,' Cris replied, his words tumbling out, giving a slight chiropractic yank to the English language en route. `I used an apple on the tree instead. And that's a lot pleasinger than showin' a lot of machinery.'[2]

The season's itinerary arrived from their agent in Chicago. One item, from the Chicago Geographic Society at Orchestra Hall, caught Lois' eye. She read it to Herb, who was sharpening a butcher knife:

      `It says here one of the requirements for this engagement is that the male speaker wear a dinner jacket.'

      `I won't do it,' Herb replied softly, then went on about his business.

      From Stockman Miller's supply house in Colorado Herb had just got a new tan suede shirt which he intended to wear on the platform the following winter.[3]

At breakfast the next morning, Lois discreetly laid a picture from <u>The Port Angeles Evening News</u> of two dinner jackets by his plate.

Herb looked them over. "The ad says they are lightweight wool, with or without cummerbund, whatever that is. I like wool." He gave Lois a shy, dewy glance, all eyelashes. "Wonder how I'd look in a dinner jacket?" he said.

He immediately forgot about the matter.

Before the Seattle engagement Lois needed to buy a formal. A task she evidently looked forward to with as much displeasure as facing an enraged bull elk in full rut or crossing the Catwalk during a fall snowstorm.

The tour included some very impressive engagements, including the Academy of Science and Art at Carnegie Hall in Pittsburgh and the Geographic Society at Witherspoon Hall in Philadelphia--places which had already informed them that they would be expected to be dressed in formal attire. Lois again reminded Herb that he was expected to wear formal clothing.

This information went in one of Herb's ears, zipped out the other and disappeared into the forest, without him even raising an eyebrow.

They drove to Seattle and stopped at Carol Preston's. Her friend and trail mate listened sympathetically while Lois spilled her tale of woe. Lois was badly in need of a new wardrobe.

Carol loaned Lois an outfit to wear shopping, provided her with references on where to shop, then coached her on what to say and how to act when the time came to confront the haughty sales staff. Then, most importantly, how to exit the store without buying anything with as much face-saving as possible.

At I. Magnin's & Company, a fashionable ladies' wear shop at Sixth and Pine, Lois was shown several scrumptious gowns adorning a tall, dark-complected graceful young model. Lois observed each gown in turn, thinking when left alone between showings, that perhaps she was out of her world:

> Lois Crisler, just changed at Whiskey Bend from zelan trail pants, boots and old wool shirt. Chief wardrobe from Chick's Marina and the army surplus store.

> Dizzily, I got off my line [Carol's advice] about my husband needing to approve such an expensive outfit and extracted myself from I. Magnin's."[4]

In the second store the saleslady took a long, appraising look at the outfit Lois was wearing, pursed her lips thoughtfully and said, "I believe I will show you the Adrians."

Out came African Sunset, an absolutely raw affront to Lois' taste.

Next came The Tiger Dress, a heavy silk that Lois later said, "Looked like a tiger's fur, drowned under moonlight."

Lois discreetly inquired about the price. The saleswoman's reply, $800, gave Lois what she described as, "an instant sickish feeling in her pocketbook." Again she took Carol's advice and told the saleslady that before spending such a sum, she would have to parade it by her stingy husband.

Later Lois described the Adrians to Herb. "Would a dress like that do anything for a person, even with all that price?" she asked.

"I don't know," Herb replied, "but I can say without pause that it would do something to an audience."

"It would do something to the Crislers too," added Lois.[5]

Lois devoted an entire TRAIL TALK to the shopping trip, titled, "Perils of Olympics Nothing Like Shopping for New Evening Dress."

This was the fall when Lois repeatedly placed her foot in her mouth, via her column. The shopping column caught the attention of many clothes-conscious female readers, and is still remembered by some today. However, Lois made several statements of poor taste. She named the store, and wrote unkindly about several of the store's employees. Of course the store read the column, was furious and wrote Lois a scathing retort. The Crislers were famous. The column was undoubtedly sent intentionally to the store by someone from the Peninsula.

Secondly, Lois left her readers dangling with suspense when she neglected to say whether or not she actually bought a dress. An oversight which caused her additional embarrassment later.

While in Seattle Lois called Ruby El Hult and invited her to pay a fall visit. Ruby was still writing, The Untamed Olympics and welcomed the idea of another visit to Hume's Ranch. At the time Ruby was assistant editor to the state nursing association's magazine, the Journal, published in Seattle. She arranged to take a week off the third week in October.

Ruby had visited Hume's Ranch that spring. She and Herb had hit it off from the first. He dubbed Ruby the little "red-haired elf."

Ruby had kept abreast of the Crisler's summer activities by reading Lois' column, about the elk fight, etc. She was anxious to hear more.

The Crislers were cordial hosts, but so busy editing they couldn't devote much time to their guest. They suggested she go for a drive around the Peninsula in their truck.

During the summer Ruby had obtained a driver's license. This would provide her the opportunity to research her book.

Ruby's adventure, and her driving career, ended suddenly only a few miles down the road. While trying to turn around Ruby backed the truck into the ditch where the Elwha road joined Highway 101.

Mortified, she telephoned Hume's Ranch. To add to Ruby's embarrassment, Lois had to hike all the way down and drive the truck out of the ditch. There was little damage, except to Ruby's pride. Ruby hasn't driven since.

That fall Lois found a letter and a curious box in the mail. She mentioned the incident in her column:

Ruby El Hult sitting in the swing at Hume's Ranch, 1949.

> A printed, unsigned note said, 5,000 readers want to know, Are You Or Are You Not Lecturing in a new Dress?
>
> This, by the way, would seem to be an understatement. For weeks perfect strangers--at Whiskey Bend, down in Portland, by letter from the East--have inquired, `Did you get a new dress?'
>
> To the 5,020 then, the answer is, Yep. I got one.
>
> The one I bought is uncrushable black velvet. Below the shoulders it is just night flowing down. Above the shoulders it zoops around in scallops edged with gold and pearls.
>
> What was in the box? A friend from California had impulsively sent me the apple of her eye, a beloved and ravishing dinner gown of hers, in black silk and gold, good for any occasion from dinner at the White House on down. [People from all over the country subscribed to the Port Angeles paper just to follow the Crislers].
>
> I have never felt so complete in my life. When you live in a log cabin in the mountains three miles from the road, there's nothing you need worse than a velvet evening gown and a silk one. Unless it's a man's dinner jacket--with cummerbund. [6]

One dark, stormy night about midnight, Herb blew three blasts on the whistle they used as a signal for Lois to come to the studio. The movie was finally done. They sat and watched most of it unfold on a tiny screen.

They estimated nine hundred man-hours, and tens of thousands of feet of film, had gone into the film's production.

They could not take time to relax, even after weeks of constant pressure. After one day of catching up on other chores, they carried film cans and projector out to Whiskey Bend.

In the recreation room at the Methodist Church they set up equipment for the first practice run. Thankfully, they were alone. They needed this solitary showing badly. Lois still hadn't seen the entire film. In a few days she would be expected to narrate it.

Lois started the music. <u>Beyond the Trails</u> began to unroll. A young man and a girl with a kerchief on her head slipped in. They had heard the commotion and wondered what was going on.

Our first audience, they thought. What if they walk out?

After the movie ended, the couple gave the Crislers a grave look, then left without saying as much as a word! Herb and Lois looked at one another, shrugged, then laughed nervously.

They took the show to a small club on Mercer Island which had been clamoring to see some of their films. The chairman introduced them: "Mr. Crisler is intelligent. Mrs. Crisler seems to be intelligent. They should be committed for their work." The new film was off to a terrific start!

Twice more they made practice appearances to small, local audiences. Then it was time for the first major showing.

The World Cavalcade Series itinerary that winter was an ambitious one. On the West Coast, Seattle, Portland, Salem and Fresno had engagements to fill. East of the Mississippi, Evanston and Chicago, Illinois; Dayton, Ohio; Sioux City and Des Moines, Iowa; Flint, Michigan; Pittsburgh and Philadelphia, Pennsylvania; New York City; Columbus, Ohio; Waterbury, Connecticut; and Washington D.C. Those were only the big shows. There were many fill-in shows at smaller places, churches and clubs, to keep them occupied.

Ruby El Hult and two friends attended the film's premier, at the Metropolitan Theater, Second and Seneca, Seattle. Ruby had been thrilled to watch while the movie was heavily advertised for several weeks. Tickets rapidly sold out.

Four decades later Ruby vividly remembered and described that exciting night:

We turned the corner and saw the theater marquee ablaze with lights that spelled out; HERB AND LOIS CRISLER--BEYOND THE TRAILS.

The entrance was jammed and a queue ran the length of the block. We joined the end of the line, and as we made our slow march up the block I kept my eyes on that wondrous sign. It seemed a huge shout into the colorful night, attesting to the success of Herb's long labors and artistry, and to the worth of Lois' devotion and inspiration. For in truth, Herb without Lois might well be the "farmer" agape with wonder, not the film producer whose triumph was written so brightly on the air.

The Met, as it was affectionately known to Seattleites, was of Moorish decor but had escaped the usual garish ostentation. In color it was rose and gray, highlighted with gold. Ceiling medallion designs, deep velvet hangings, great golden chandeliers--all were elegant and yet tastefully subdued.

On that cavernous stage, topped by a gilt proscenium arch, had appeared almost every major theatrical star, every concert artist of importance, and every topflight entertainer in the country. Anyone who followed in such hallowed footsteps had better be good, and I felt a nervous qualm for Herb.[7]

That evening, enroute to the theater, Herb and Lois turned to appraise one another:

I had on my new black velvet dress. Cris okayed me with his eyes. `You look like a little seal just outa watah,' he said. `Slick.'

When we turned the corner and saw the Metropolitan, we lost our breath for a minute. In neon signs over the marquee were our names, HERB AND LOIS CRISLER--BEYOND THE TRAILS. It was 45 minutes until show time, but a double line of people extended from the gallery door to the corner.

In a strange town I wouldn't have minded. But this scared me. Here at the Met I had always been on the receiving end. For a minute the conflict between the old glamour and current facts walloped my heart.

Then I burrowed down inside myself to where I could feel the old packboard straps bruising my shoulders. I relaxed and tromped in, all myself again.

We actually enjoyed our pictures that evening, we've seen the new ones so few times ourselves.

Afterward a friend had champagne for us. Cris tasted it. He looked like a man who has eaten a raw snail at a Chinese banquet and is trying to be polite about it.

`Don't you like it?' our host inquired incredulously.

Cris thankfully flung politeness to the winds and blurted out the truth. `You know that muddy pool in the pictures, where the cow elk's been trampling it up? Well, this tastes like that muddy watah if you'd throw a bushel of rotten apples in it and letm lay for a month.'[8]

At Portland, a number of friends who had watched the movie in Seattle drove down to see it again. People stood along the walls of the crowded theater. Wherever they showed in the Pacific Northwest a few people who had previously seen the film came to watch it a second time.

They needed all the encouragement they could get. The previous fall they had received a letter from the Walt Disney Studio. The studio was looking for material for Disney's True-Life Adventure Series. National Geographic had recommended them. Could they come to Hollywood and show some of their film?

Lois replied that they would be passing through southern California that winter, and would stop by.

The tour had hardly started until winter storms sought to stop their southern progress. Gales of wind and lashing rain sent their truck weaving from side to side as they motored down Highway 99 in southern Oregon.

After the Oakland appearance, they stayed the night with Dr. and Mrs. Eric Reynolds. Laurel Reynolds was a nationally-known Audubon lecturer and bird movie photographer.

In Hollywood, December 7, 1949, at the entrance to the Disney Studio, they looked at each other, took a deep breath and went in, wondering what the next few hours might bring.

They still owed for the truck and other things. Herb disliked being in debt. Expenses while on tour ate up the fees.

The "mountain mice" winced at the Disney receptionist's appearance. She wore a startling, henna-ed crimson wig, severe brown dress, yellow jockey vest and flowing polka dot tie.

Chewing gum furiously, she dialed a number. A man who's patronizing manner caused Lois to later refer to him in her column as "Bird Dog" appeared.

"I'll just look at a little bit of your footage," he said hurriedly.

Herb patiently explained that their stuff was in two 1,600 foot reels accompanied by lecture and music.

Their host recoiled, thought a moment, then relented and motioned them to one of several tiny viewing theaters called "sweat boxes."

Apparently no one else was to attend. Herb was about to object, when in walked the production manager, dapper, thin little Ben Sharpsteen, whom Lois would later refer to as the Thread. He was followed by a young red-headed fellow.

They went through the first reel, and half of the second, before the projector lost the sprocket holes on a splice. The lights came on:

> The Thread said coolly, `I don't think you need show any more. This is just wasting time.'
> `Well!'
> The Thread continued. `We have no authority to decide whether to buy this or not. I think Walt should see it. He's the one that will have to decide. So, we have to go through it all again anyway.'
> `Oh!'
> The Thread explained. `Movie photographers all over the U.S. think they have the best pictures in the world and they want us to look at it. Most of it is awful--just animal portraits. So we're kind of a screening committee to decide whether it's worth Walt's time.' [9]

Walt Disney was nowhere to be found. They were taken to lunch at the cafeteria by the red-haired young man. He was considerate and kind. Lois dubbed him Human-Red.

Talk got around to the True-Life Adventure Series. Herb mentioned that they had never seen Seal Island.[10] Their host graciously offered to show the film while they waited. In another sweatbox they stretched out on comfortable reclining chairs. The room's acoustics were "pin-fall" sharp.

Watching the Pribilof seal movie took the Crislers away from their immediate concerns. The photography was superb. The editing very professional. They drooled over the animation which accompanied the title.

Their host beamed. He was the film's director. Their estimation of Human-Red increased dramatically.

They were told that Walt would appear at 2:30. Human-Red, the Thread and Bird-Dog whiled away the time by reviewing some of Crisler's leftover footage.

At 2:25 someone said, `We'd better stop. Mount the other reels.' Walt, who Lois later referred to unkindly in her column as the "Presence," was due any minute. Then Walt Disney himself walked it. Disney and the Crislers had met briefly when they had been invited to visit the studio by some of Walt's associates.

Disney, Herb noticed, soon became quite animated, jabbing his finger at specific scenes and whispering excitedly to one of his associates sitting beside him.

After the film was finished the associate said softly to Herb, `Your photography is breathtaking!' This was the only comment anyone made about the film!

Disney told them that in the ravine below the new house he was building, a pair of coyotes had their den. It excited and pleased him to have wildlife living nearby.

Sharpsteen spoke affectionately about 360 acres of wild redwood forests he owned in northern California.

Then the meeting ended.

Lois' reaction to Disney's mention of wildlife near his home and Sharpsteen's chatter about wild redwood forests was stated in her column:

> We could see that to a lot of people in the United States the wildness that we take for granted up
>
> in the Olympics was becoming one of the choicest things they could contact.[11]

As the Crislers tumbled bewildered out of the sprawling studio into the balmy Hollywood air that evening after the Disney meeting, it occurred to them that it was their eighth anniversary. It seemed something unusual always happened on that day, starting with the bombing of Pearl Harbor.

Lois devoted an entire column, "Crislers Tangle With Hollywood But Walt (Himself) Disney Sees Films," published in the Evening News barely a week later, on December 16, 1949.

The column made no mention about sale of the film, or even whether or not Disney liked it. The column's contents, however, were fraught with bad taste.

Lois certainly never expected anyone at the studio to read it, but they did. The column may have been sent to Disney by someone who didn't like the Crislers. Most creative people, especially if they are productive, have jealous critics.

Lois' derogatory remarks and the use of nicknames, such as Bird Dog, instead of real names, created hostility towards Lois Crisler at the studio. This hostility didn't do their reputation any good, but most eventually forgot about it, except the man Lois dubbed "Bird Dog". He never forgave Lois. There's no indication that Lois ever made a formal apology either.

After Lois' column failed to mention whether or not they had sold the film to Disney or not, many readers, some who were also close friends, were, again, left dangling.

Lois could be naive. She sometimes wrote sans sensitivity; as if she assumed no one mentioned would read her column. Several of her closest friends complained that Lois frequently simply "blanked them out."

After the "Meets Disney" column, readers waited patiently for some indication of what had happened. Column after column appeared, in fact, during the following year, but not one mention about Disney appeared in her column! This bewildered many readers who had been closely following the Crislers' career for a long time and wanted to know what was going on.

Probably no other period of the Crisler's rather public lives are surrounded by more secrecy, misquotes and untruths than the original Disney meetings.

What transpired, as accurately as can be reconstructed by the available facts, gleaned from a variety of sources, are as follows:

Disney, an astute businessman, was tremendously interested, after viewing the film. He also wisely declined to comment, until he had time to think about the film's possibilities.

After promising to meet with the Crislers the following day, Walt returned home.

According to Walt's associates, in a statement published in the Port Angeles Evening News almost a year later, the film had excited Disney so much he was unable to sleep that night. He tossed and turned, got up, paced and returned to bed. Creative thoughts about what the studio could do with such material kept him pacing the floor.

The following day Disney, some of his advisors and legal staff met with the Crislers. Although Disney was interested in buying the film, there were legal glitches involved.

Herb explained that they were under contract to The World Adventure Series for the winter of 1949-50. A few bookings had already been made for 1950-51. He had to meet those obligations, but was willing to sell the film under those conditions.

A compromise was arranged. Disney agreed to buy the film, provide a copy for Herb to use, and keep the original in the safe until the Crislers completed their contract. The Crislers were to inform their agent that no additional engagements would be allowed.

Then came the big surprise! Disney offered to place the Crislers under contract on special assignment! They would continue to photograph in the Olympics, especially elk behavior and calf elk. Whatever film they shot would become Disney property. Photographing for Disney was a gigantic decision which they hadn't expected.

The terms of the contract are vague, but according to an article by Jim Casey in the Everett Herald-Western Sun, September 24, 1977, Disney agreed to pay them $10,000 for exclusive rights to the film used in the movie, Beyond the Trails.

Regarding the photography assignment, the studio would furnish film, travel and living expenses and a fee of $13,000 a year. Exactly when the assignment began isn't clear. We assume it started the following spring.

Disney's contracts with employees, as well as independent photographers, included a gag provision prohibiting public disclosure about projects under development.

How Lois' derogatory column, published only about one week after the Disney meetings, escaped the gag clause isn't known.

A year went by before the word Disney appeared in Olympic Trail Talks. She mentioned that they had stopped at the studio while on their way home the following winter. Even then she only mentioned they watched a preview, "of Cris' picture, so far called The Olympic Elk."

The Crislers must have had plenty to contemplate as they headed east on Route 66 on their way to their first mid-west engagement at Evanston, Illinois on January 3, 1950.

After many miles of icy highway driving throughout the mid-west, they were back in Chicago. The Chicago appearance, at Orchestra Hall, sponsored by the Geographic Society, was the first engagement where formal dress was an absolute must.

Lois had given up on Herb wearing a dinner jacket. She decided to let events take their course:

A crucial skirmish was due first; Herb vs. the Dinner Jacket.

Cris' wardrobe has not hitherto included a dinner jacket. When I first met him, he had on stagged-off khaki trousers and a red bandanna tied around his head.

He did wear a suit of clothes at our wedding, and once thereafter.

But a dinner jacket was mandatory for Orchestra Hall, according to his contract.

Cris was walking softly but didn't consider himself licked--yet. He was prepared for either defeat or victory. But most of his preparations were for the latter.

Then we went to see the secretary for the Orchestra Hall showing. She was the epitome of Chicago. Fascinating, but ravaged prettiness. Nervous and driving.

The Olympic squirrel conferred softly with the red-haired Chicago Jaguar. Finally she half growled, half purred, "You have to give and take. All right. We'll forget about the dinner jacket."[12]

Herb triumphantly marched out onto the stages of the top lecture circuits in the country, including the Geographic Society, Witherspoon Hall, in fashion-conscious New York City, wearing his tan doeskin. No one said a word. But Lois, decked out in her evening gown, thought plenty!

The zenith of any illustrated lecturer's career was considered to be the National Geographic Society, Constitution Hall, Washington, D.C. The Society screened prospective entertainers very, very carefully. Crisler's film had passed this scrutiny the previous year.

Preparations for this big event, the evening of March 17, 1950, were a model of efficiency. Every detail was thrashed out in advance. The Crislers were "stroked and petted" throughout the day in an effort to relax them. Even the exact shade of color for Lois' corsage was wrangled over by the staff at a florist shop.

Constitution Hall was filled to capacity, with 3,500 city-bound souls, many who obviously, from the enthusiastic response to the film, thirsted for nature and the outdoors.

The screen was 20 feet wide. In order to project the length of the auditorium, the projector's powerful beam was cooled with water so it would not damage film.

Lois had trouble with the audience. They insisted on applauding the good shots. There were many, many good shots. Her voice frequently became lost in the medley.

After the performance a long line of well-wishers gathered to wring the Crisler's hands. For weeks afterwards Lois could hardly grasp anything.

With the last appearance behind them, the Crislers left the cold midwest and drove south, headed for a visit to Herb's family.

After the visit they headed west along the snow-free winter route, now Interstate 10, which crosses the United States near the Mexican border.

They put on their program at San Jose and Berkeley. The Berkeley showing was sponsored by the Sierra Club and Wilderness Society.

The Crislers were now back in an area where they felt more at home than in the east. Each engagement brought people they knew backstage. Some had driven great distances to see Beyond the Trails.

But they were not free to drive straight home to Hume's Ranch yet. They did not forget their friends. For months their movie had been headline news in Pacific Northwest publications and in the news nationally. So many people wanted to see it, they despaired how to get the task done. Finally, after showing at almost every town in western Washington, they arrived home. At Port Angeles high school gymnasium they had to show several evenings to accommodate the crowds. They also showed the movie to the Wilderness Society which met that fall in Port Angeles.

They had driven 15,000 miles and been gone more than four months!

Upon returning to Port Angeles, amongst a huge accumulation of mail, they discovered a letter from their agent, George F. Pierrot. In part, the letter stated:

> You'll be happy to know that your OUTDOOR ADVENTURES IN THE PACIFIC NORTHWEST ranked sky-high in our annual popularity contest. That's an accolade indeed, from a big audience that sees more illustrated programs each year than any other.
>
> The reason isn't hard to guess. Your photography is remarkably spirited and artistic. The color is uniformly brilliant. Not only do you show us America's remote Last Wilderness--high country that is breathtakingly beautiful--but you have an uncanny talent for picking human interest shots, shots that have life, and humor, and are well remembered. A nice combination of action, atmosphere, and appealing narration.
>
> Unobtrusively, too, you strike some telling blows for conservation. Our people seem to like the way you told your story, so often from the standpoint of the big and little animals themselves.[13]

From Olaus J. Murie, director of the Wilderness Society, Moose, Wyoming, came another review:

> Your film, which you presented at the Annual Meeting of the Wilderness Society Council on the Olympic Peninsula, was an inspiration to us all. The photography was of course excellent, and you have a happy choice of subject matter. The artistry and warmth of feeling which permeates the whole film presented the wilderness quality of Olympic National Park in a manner that can hardly be excelled. You are doing a great service for the American people in showing this film and I only wish it were possible for all the millions of Americans to have he privilege of seeing and experiencing its inspiration.[14]

With the praise of experts ringing in their ears, and a steady paycheck coming in for a change, they looked forward to another summer with more than the usual enthusiasm.

Notes and Sources, Chapter Seventeen

1. Lois Crisler, "Olympic Trail Talk--22," 21 Oct., 1949

2. Ibid.

3. Lois Crisler, "Olympic Trail Talk-24," 4 Nov., 1949
   According to Ruby El Hult, who has the garment in question hanging in her closet, it is not a shirt, as Lois described it, and it isn't suede. It's a beautiful doeskin jacket.

4. Ibid.

5. Ibid.

6. Lois Crisler, "Olympic Trail Talk-24," 4 Nov., 1949

7. Ruby El Hult, <u>An Olympic Mountain Enchantment,</u> CP Publications, Port Angeles, WA. Pgs. 132-133. (1988)

8. Lois Crisler, "Olympic Trail Talk--27," 25 Nov., 1949

9. Ibid.

10. <u>Seal Island,</u> filmed by Al and Elma Milotte on Alaska's Pribilof Islands, was the first of Walt Disney Production's True-Life Adventure Series. Interestingly, before embarking on this nature film project, Disney's idea, his financial advisors reportedly attempted every way they knew to discourage the Series. They were positive no one would pay money to see films containing only wildlife. <u>Seal Island</u> won an Oscar! As did most of the rest of the series. And Disney's name became a household word. So much for financial advisors!

11. Lois Crisler, "Olympic Trail Talk--30," 18 Dec., 1949

12. Lois Crisler, "Olympic Trail Talk--37," 3 Feb., 1950

13. Compliments Ruby El Hult's Crisler scrapbook.

14. Ibid.

18

Cameras Alone Do Not Make a Wildlife Photographer.
Lois Crisler's Definition of Wilderness. End of an Era.

****

In the wilderness you are not a slave. But to experience its finest joy, you have to give up any wish to become its master. You behold and enjoy the life of the great living wilderness itself.[1]

****

Elbow room--usable elbow room--is going to become one of the scarcest, most priceless of our national resources--if only it isn't all recklessly squandered before we realize it's gone.

The adult personalities of today were shaped on the last of the wilderness. When wilderness goes, the psychology of a country changes from free to slavish.[2]

****

Springtime at Hume's Ranch was a captivating, yet busy time. The return of the sun, after months of dismal, gray light, a period during which the weak winter sun lacked enough height and energy to penetrate the murky depths of the Elwha Valley, was welcomed by all living things.

Everything in the rain forest, abandoned machinery, the privy door knob, the shakes on the cabin roof, the trunks, bark and branches of apple, maple, alder and fir, the ground itself, was covered either with a fine new sheen of green mosses, or older, hanging tapestries of Douglas' Neckera **Neckera douglasii,** or a half dozen kinds of lichen.

Month upon month of mist, rain, fog and lack of sunshine are what create the Olympic Rain Forest, one of the largest temperate rain forests in the world.

The sun, high enough in March to stab with renewed vigor down through the perpetual mists and fir boughs for a few mid-day hours, awakened long dormant seeds and caused buds to swell. Birds began their mating rituals and dormant animals emerged from hibernation.

New shoots of grass struggled through the dead, decaying brown mass of last year's crop. Crocus bobbed in the breeze by the water log and along the greenhouse foundation wall.

Down in the big meadow, once a source of hay for Grant Humes horse herd, or in the shade of the nearby forest, two bull elk, their knobby new antlers in velvet, whiled away the days waiting for instinct to tell them the high country was free of snow. Sometimes they were joined by several cows, heavy with unborn calves.

Eight to 12 deer drifted silent and ghost-like through the meadows and fringes of timber. They habitually circled Herb's fenced garden to see if by chance he'd forgotten to close the gate. The forbidden delicacies inside that wire enclosure had long been a temptation to deer and elk.

Before Herb fenced the yard and the precious fruit trees, the deer usually beat them to any drop-off pears, plums or apples. Herb purposely ran the fence alongside one apple tree, whose fruit wasn't much good, so half the apples would fall outside the fence. When apples were on the tree, he would go out before bed time and give the tree a good shake so the deer wouldn't be disappointed when they arrived.

Up along the trail to Whiskey Bend a ruffed grouse sat motionless, her nest hidden amongst budding wild currant bushes, amidst a wild jumble of gray, lifeless Douglas fir windfalls. Everything she owned and hoped for lay beneath her feathers. Her egg's only protection from a host of hungry predators, both feathered and four-footed, was her natural camouflage and ability to sit motionless, without even blinking an eye, whenever danger drew near.

Above the log cabin Herb had built a dam across the tiny forest brook which trickles past the ranch. The little pond behind the dam was their water supply, and a favorite foot-bath for the local cougar as he made his rounds. They often noticed the cat's wet paw marks where he'd dipped his pads into their drinking water.

They sometimes delighted in telling thirsty guests that the water they were drinking came from a pond where a cougar sometimes washed his feet. That statement always resulted in immediate, humorous and unusual reactions; especially from guests used to living in Los Angeles, where they had been drinking water contaminated far beyond anything a cougar might do.

The lecture circuit of 1949-50 had been a particularly strenuous one. The Crislers didn't drag themselves up the trail to Hume's Ranch to stay until late May, the twenty-fifth to be exact.

Lois Crisler standing by moss tapestries in the Hoh Rain Forest.

The first thing Herb did upon arriving, even before going into the cabin, was take a spade from the shed, walk out into the garden and start turning over sod.

Herb noticed that the woven wire fencing over the top of the berry patch had, again, been flattened by a heavier than normal winter snow. More extra work to do. The garden was in bad shape. Grass and weeds already ankle high. This was the latest he had ever planted the garden.

After a restful respite at Hume's Ranch (two whole days) Herb decided on Sunday, May 28 to drive out to the Hoh River after the calf elk pictures Disney needed.

At first they were unsuccessful; locating calf elk in the rain forest is nearly impossible. They kept reminding themselves they were on Disney's payroll. The solitude of the rain forest revived spirits that had sagged to alarming levels during the rigors of the tour.

The tranquility of green, moss and lichen-covered forest floor, knee-high ferns and undisturbed old-growth forest soothed highway-frazzled nerves. The silence calmed ears grown accustomed to the racket of automobiles and multitudes of yapping people. The air seemed cleaner (recent air tests have proved this to be true) and they inhaled deeply, as if to rid their lungs of the carbon monoxide accumulated during 15,000 miles of highway travel.

They camped at Happy Four, 5.1 miles from the trailhead, poked up the fire, ate and smiled smugly at each other. But baby elk they failed to find.

Eventually their luck changed:

At twilight one evening in camp, we heard one of the eeriest of the forest sounds, the warning bark of a cow elk, off in the deep forest.

It means that she had a calf and that the calf was in danger. A glance at the wind showed that it was not our "tails" that had disturbed her.

I wanted to struggle through the forest to try and help her. Cris looked somberly at the darkening great forest. `It's hard to help a wild thing, Lois,' he said.

FILMING BABY ELK

There was one morning in the forest when we seemed suddenly to snap out of our city tiredness. Our wilderness antennae that had been beaten down all winter in the big cities across the continent just all at once straightened themselves up.

It was a good, contented, alive feeling.

Cris whispered, `Sometime we'll step over a log and on the other side there will be a calf elk.'

The next day we hunted in a new part of the forest. It was the most beautiful and park-like I had ever seen.

Hardly a sun ray penetrated the canopy far overhead.

We passed silently from one green, moss-cush-ioned "room" of the forest to another.

Roosevelt elk in the Rain Forest

Suddenly a cow elk barked.

She was not down wind from us. That meant that she had not smelled us. She had seen us! That meant in turn that she had been keeping a lookout in our direction.

And that meant that her calf was near us. We separated, searching for it.

I was crossing the deep forest carpet towards a long, mossy log. All at once my sense of timing began.

Probably you can have that wonderful sense of timing with people. But then it's complex. This was absolutely pure. As deep and soft as the pressure of velvet. Pause. (I even backed up a step.) But then, Now, go ahead. Softly.

Beyond the log lay the baby elk.

It lay on moss in a triangle formed by the log and a mossy root. Only one small "door" led in to its bed.

Cris filmed the baby elk. This was what he wanted. This was what our whole trip was about. We smiled at each other, triumphant with delight. With awe too.

The silken calf lay there perfect and beautiful, watching us, but not moving.

Off in the forest its mother barked, circling us, out of sight.

As quickly as we could, we withdrew, without touching the little creature. We felt that we should hurry and leave it and the mother to themselves. There should be a sense of honor toward the wild things. When you have gained what you want you don't crowd.[3]

195

The somewhat strange (for that period) and unfamiliar theory that a section or portion of the planet should remain exactly as created was an alien one for most people of Crisler's generation. They tended to ask, "What in the world for?"

Herb & Lois Crisler on backpack trip up the Hoh River Trail in 1947.

The idea that public land should be set aside for wilderness, per se, and for recreation, instead of used for logging, mining, hunting, trapping and other commercial exploits was new and strange. Wilderness recreation had little actual value placed upon it during the first half of the twentieth century. Although the Sierra Club had been formed half a century previous, their efforts and support had not become effective nationwide as they have since.

Protection of vast pieces of wild land may, perhaps, seem costly, in terms of jobs and state and government economics, but at this writing, over 98 million Americans engage in fish and wildlife-related activities. Included are 76 million who participate in feeding, observing and photographing wildlife. Wildlife-related recreation pumped $59.5 billion into the U.S. economy in 1991, according to a 1991 U.S. Fish and Wildlife Service survey. These figures do not include backpacking, paddle sports and other outdoor activity.

How do we put a price on destroying the mosses, trees and lichens of the rain forest? Because they act as a giant air purifier, a sponge the size of some states, to retain rainwater and generate oxygen.

Wildlife films, especially in vivid color, were something new to theater goers during this period. Viewing such films brought about a new awareness and changed people's opinions regarding the non-consumptive value of wild animals. Not that I do not believe in consumptive use of certain species. Hunters are the best supporters of deer, elk and other game animals. They pour millions of dollars annually into that support, while the anti-hunting crowd contributes little in the way of habitat enhancement. Their money goes mostly into more media hype to support their cause. I believe in wise use, and conservation of wild animals. Preservation should only be applied to wild animal environment, and, of course, to truly endangered species, of which there are many, many species.

Watching elk, bear, birds or a chipmunk in a color movie brought on a new awareness of these animals, and the importance of protecting their habitat. Perspectives changed. Attitudes flip-flopped: From "couldn't care less" to "genuine concern." Animals became movie stars. Like most stars, the animals had fans. People clapped and cheered and laughed at the antics of animals and birds they may never have heard of before. Once people became aware of these animals, it was only a short step to thinking about, and supporting protection of the animal's **environment** (a scarcely-used word during the 1940's and 1950's). It, or at least a portion of it, needed to be protected.

Wildlife photography was in its infancy during the post-war period. Portable motion-picture cameras, with lens long enough for wildlife, had been available for some time. Still photography was crippled because of a lack of decent 35mm cameras, long lens and suitable film. The first color transparency film was Kodachrome(R), ASA-12, which later was "souped" up to an astonishing speed of ASA-25, while today's wildlife photographers enjoy ASA-50 and 100. Color print film was also new, and not very good, compared to today.

The first 35mm camera I owned was an Argus C-3, which I bought in 1957. It had only one 50mm lens. I used Kodachrome ASA 25. Herb never owned a long lens for a still camera. By 1954 he was using an Eastman Kodak

16mm Cine Special with a 400mm lens, the camera the people of the Olympic Peninsula presented him with out of gratitude for his work.

We could have counted the number of photographers who were photographing wildlife with motion-picture cameras during this period on our fingers and toes. The number of truly serious professionals on our fingers.

The Olympic Peninsula was fortunate to have two of the best; Crisler and Lloyd Beebe. Both, in their unique way, contributed greatly to the profession. Both were avid hunters during their youth. There were two major differences between them; Crisler was a widely-recognized photographer, having worked at the trade since 1920. He believed in strictly, un-manipulated, natural footage of wild animals.

Beebe, a logger and renowned bounty hunter of cougar and wildcats, was inexperienced as a photographer during his youth. He loved, and had a rare rapport with wild animals, kept captives and became an outstanding, world-recognized, award-winning pioneer in the use, and photography of captive animals for motion-pictures.

During the late nineteen forties, Lloyd and his wife Catherine bought an 85-acre farm in the Dungeness River Valley near Sequim, began milking cows and expanding the number of captive wild animals on the farm. Beebe saw his first motion-picture camera in 1945. Like Crisler, Beebe decided photography was an excellent excuse to spend more time in the wilds. Eventually he bought a camera and began filming wildlife, including captive wild animals kept, and trained, on the Beebe farm.

This coincided with the time Walt Disney Studios began producing the <u>True Life Adventure Series,</u> pictures of animals which Disney's advisors staunchly claimed would never, never sell! Lloyd wrote Disney that he had some wildlife footage of cougars, etc., and was invited to the Studio. This was the beginning of a long association with Disney, both as a supplier of wild animals, as a wild animal trainer and photographer. Beebe trained cougar, wolves, black and grizzly bears, bobcats, even the wily and little understood wolverines, for use in Disney movies. During his long career, Lloyd traveled to the Antarctic, Arctic, South America, Alberta and Arizona for work on Disney productions. He also canoed down the Back and Thelon Rivers in the Northwest Territories in 1954 searching for musk oxen. This expedition included the first white men to see that still remote wilderness country during the previous century.

The Beebes (Catherine Beebe, and their two children, have been an important part of the enterprise) supplied expertise, filming, wild animals, animal trainers and worked on about fifty Disney films. They also provided animals and trainers for 60, one-hour Grizzly Adams Television shows. Presently, the Beebes are working on a self-produced movie featuring wolves, about the period when wolves were common in what is now Olympic National Park.

At present, professional outdoor photographers are having a hot debate about "truth" and "deception" that has become rampant in wildlife and nature photography. Two issues are involved. Manipulation of existing images and the use of captive wild animals. While composites (merging two transparencies) have been used for a long time, the availability of digital manipulation with high-tech computers has heaped fuel on the deception fires. Some of the world's foremost wildlife and nature photographers are involved, and have been accused of, using manipulated images. The main issue is **disclosure**, or "truth in advertising" so to speak; whether viewers should be informed the images are altered, or, if captive animals were used. Still photography, not motion-pictures is the medium under fire. Use of captive animals and deception have been widely accepted (perhaps expected) by viewers in the production of most motion-pictures. Walt Disney Studio, and Lloyd and Catherine Beebe were pioneers in the use of manipulated, captive, "wild" animals. Movie fans have, we suppose, benefitted by deceptive practices, since photographing animals in the wild isn't likely to produce the spectacular drama movie fans have been conditioned to expect. On the other hand, altered, deceptive animal behavior, as seen by the movie audience, may provide false conceptions of what actually happens in the wild. This is no attempt to evaluate the pros and cons of this issue.

Crisler was a staunch believer in presenting reality and truth in his photography. He refused to disturb any wild animal to produce footage. Although the Crislers did keep wild wolf pups while working for Disney in the Arctic while documenting the Porcupine caribou herd, footage used in <u>The White Wilderness,</u> and he produced footage of the pups, they were not overly manipulated.

Previous to going to Alaska, Herb spent a year, under contract for Disney, documenting Bighorn sheep in the Tarryall Mountains of Colorado. During the fall he almost froze while filming the rams peculiar behavior during the rut. The rams charge into each other from a distance, resulting in a tremendous crash as their heads collide. Then they stand motionless (perhaps regaining their senses) for a long, long period of time, before backing off, then repeating the charge. Crisler filmed the scenes exactly as they happened. The Bighorn scenes were used in The Vanishing Prairie.

After returning from the Arctic, the Crislers went to see the movie, released while they were in Alaska, at a theater in Colorado Springs. When the Bighorn fight appeared on the screen, instead of the long pause after crashing into each other, and then backing off a distance, the Disney editors had manipulated the scene to suit themselves. The rams now stood close to each other and repeatedly butted heads rapid fire. Disgusted, the Crislers got up and left the theater without watching the rest of the film. They wrote a letter of protest to the Studio. The Studio replied that viewers didn't want to sit in a movie while sheep stood motionless, waiting to resume the attack! Viewers wanted action.

Lloyd and Catherine Beebe's farm became known as Walt Disney's Wild Animal Ranch. After a 28-year relationship with Disney Studios, they became independent and changed the name to Olympic Game Farm.

Other motion-picture photographers of the period were, Ben East, Al and Elma Milotte, who I once met in Alaska, and who filmed one of the very first True Life Adventure Series films for Disney, "Seal Island", (which won an Oscar) filmed on the stormy, remote Pribilof Islands of Alaska. Leonard Lee Rue III, Carl Ackley, from the Museum of Natural History, Arthur Allen of Cornell University, Martin and Osa Johnston, who startled the world with their African lion pictures during the 1930s and Hugh Wilmar, killed in a train wreck near Machu Picchu, Peru while working for Disney, were well known during this period.

Not until the heavy 35mm motion-picture "newsreel" cameras were replaced by the lighter, 16mm, and good 35mm still cameras, with interchangeable lenses became available, did wildlife photography become more practical. Eastman Kodak's Kodachrome(R) film, popular with wildlife photographers over the decades for still photography, was the first color film designed to be used in motion-picture photography. Crisler, remember, was chosen to test this film for Eastman Kodak. The transparency film was used in the old "newsreel" cameras that weighed about 90 pounds, the kind we old-timers used to watch in the newsreels shown before every movie, if you're old enough to remember. Today, with modern video equipment available, and an expanded public appetite for nature films, there are thousands of photographers in the business documenting nature and wildlife world-wide.

Even after the lighter, more modern photography and backpacking equipment became available (plastics replaced many wood, leather and canvas items used in camping) backpacking is a laborious activity.

Lois sometimes left Herb filming while she came "downstairs" to Humes Ranch to deliver her column, water the garden and pick up food supplies.

Following are Lois's remarkable thoughts about the benefits of scrambling through un-tracked, steep, brushy mountains under a sweaty backpack. Remarkable, because at the time she wrote the following, Lois was 53, an age when few women backpack, especially alone. Much of Lois's backpacking was through the rugged wilderness, without trails, where one slip could mean big trouble.

Lois Crisler's definition of backpacking:

I've had a lot of kinds of fun in my life. But the most fun I've ever had has been backpacking in the Olympics.

This season Cris and I start our ninth consecutive season of filming in the Olympic high country beyond the trails.

`I hope you love it, Lois,' a Quaker friend in Los Angeles wrote doubtfully the other day.

THE CHALLENGE

I wonder if I can tell her why I do.

It is a record of strengths and of delights. In the wilderness you experience kinds of delights you did not know about beforehand. There is nothing in civilization to acquaint you with them.

To me they came one by one as a total surprise. They were my own discoveries. No one had ever told me about them. Now I know that every wilderness goer knows them.[4]

One personal discovery (perhaps not her first, as Lois had climbed Mount Rainier, and other peaks previously) was backpacking over Dodwell-Rixon pass with the Seattle Mountaineers and unexpectedly finding Queets Basin still deep in snow. Each person fended for themselves. Since it was raining, prospects for a miserable, wet night were excellent. Lois found a little dry, bare cubbyhole beneath the limbs of an alpine fir which was clear of snow, spread her bag on some boughs, climbed in and spent a comfortable night. She woke up refreshed and delighted with herself.

Another was while on a backpack trip to Mount Tom, a peak just southwest of Mount Olympus, elevation 7,046 feet, with Bettine, the daughter of John "Pa" and Dora Huelsdonk, John Fletcher, Bettine's husband, and a hired hand, a trip already mentioned.

They walked from the Huelsdonk homestead. Lois was soft and completely pooped when her three tough, work-hardened companions finally decided to call it a day somewhere on the South Fork and stopped to camp. Lois sank down, wondering if she had enough strength to eat and crawl into her bag, attended to by the others.

But Bettine left to gather wood. Lois felt guilty so she forced herself to get up and help, discovering that she had an extra, unknown reserve of stamina, enough to do just a little more, if she had to. Lois described that feeling:

That wasn't "fun." That was something more gratifying. It was new experience that makes you more of a person than you ever were before. You like that.

There is another delight to wilderness travel that is so common and necessary to me that it seems incredible that other people neither know it or desire it.

It is the glorious superb feeling of health and strength you get from being outdoors 24 hours a day, breathing outdoor air, working hard, getting hard, seeing hard things to do and being more than able to do them.

Nothing tops that.

Perhaps the most valuable thing a real genuine wilderness does for a human being is to be dangerous.

Not much dangerous. Just a little bit dangerous.

Everybody needs a trace of exploit in his life. I don't know why one needs it. That's just a fact of nature. Like needing a trace of copper in one's diet.

The absence of exploits in people's lives may cause their personalities to fade and turn gray.

Most older people cease to try for adventurous exploits.[5]

Was this the literature instructor, the bookworm, the intellectual writing this? The lady who didn't know how to cook or keep house when she finally married Herbert Crisler?

While the Crislers were making up their packs, ready to leave for the high country, a Coast Guard helicopter passed over Humes Ranch. The "whirlybird" circled, like an orange dragon fly, then came in low over the meadow and dropped a package suspended below a tiny parachute. It landed right beside the back porch. A note inside said:

Confucius say:
When you want rice china
And the store ain't nigh
Drop your work, Mme. Crisler,
And look to the sky.

The package contained two fragile blue and gold Chinese rice cups from Josephine Gould, wife of Lieutenant Commander Bob Gould, stationed at Coast Guard Air Station/Group Port Angeles, located on Ediz Hook.

On that positive note they shouldered heavy packs and proceeded "upstairs." The precious rice cups remained safely behind in the cabin. They were headed for tin cup country.

At her apartment in West Seattle, Ruby El Hult was hard at work on her book, The Untamed Olympics. She was writing about Makah and Nittinat Indians and a prospective wedding scene at Neah Bay when suddenly the phone rang:

`Ruby?' queried a male voice. `You've still got the same number? The same name? It's been so long I wondered. This is Cris--or Herb--I answer to anything.'

`Herb,' I cried. `Where are you? Aren't you in the mountains? I thought you were in the mountains!'

`We hiked out yesterday. I'm in Port Angeles. Came down to mail some film. Lois and I thought maybe you could come up. I know it's short notice, but then our time at the ranch will be short too. Four days, and I don't know when we'll be down again. I'd like it a lot if you could come.'

Three hours later I stood at a ferry boat railing enroute to the Peninsula and Port Angeles.....[6]

It was Lois, not Herb, who appeared in Port Angeles to pick up their guest. Ruby was disappointed. Lois was very kind and considerate, as usual.

Ruby found Herb busy hoeing in the garden. After the initial greetings, Ruby got right to the most important question on her mind:

`Lois never said in her column, and I still don't know. Was Disney interested in your film or wasn't he?'

`Yes, very interested.'

`What I mean--interested in **buying** it.'

`We sold it.'

I let out a crow of triumph. `Oh! That's wonderful. I'm so happy for you.'

He looked up doubtfully. `I'm not sure I'm happy. I wonder if it was the best thing to do, to sell it.'

`Not the best thing to do? Why would you feel like that?'

`Well, it ends my long project.'

It was a road he never thought of as ending at all. Still...such a spectacular ending! `Surely you'll be rich and famous,' I said.

`Rich and famous! Where'd you get any such stuff?'

I stopped, rather nonplussed, then said rather lamely, `I thought it was the whole idea. That if Disney wanted the film he'd pay a fortune for it.'

`Well, a fortune isn't what we got. After we paid off our debts we have little left.'

`But I counted on it making you rich and independent,' I cried. `All right, if you got so little, then why did you sell it?'

`Because, I owed for the truck and other debts as well. I don't think it right for people to have to wait for money that belongs to them. This way I'm paid up, free and clear, ready to start over.'

Swallowing my disappointment, I asked, `What of the lecture tours?'

`Finished--except for a few engagements next winter.' They were dates their agent had accepted before the sale; the studio would provide a copy of the film for fulfilling those final obligations.

`After that, what?'

Herb's somewhat doubtful look brightened. `It'll cheer you to know the Crislers are now gainfully employed. We're on the Disney payroll! For this summer and next.'

`Oh, that's great!' I beamed.

Herb explained that when Disney Studio people were re-editing the film, they would give it a different emphasis, concentrating more closely on the elk herds. For that they would need more elk footage, especially more footage of calf elk. So, for the next two summers he would focus all his attention on the herds.

`Which explains,' I said in sudden enlightenment, `why you rushed off to the Hoh for calf elk pictures after those two ridiculous days at home. Maybe there is method in your madness after all. Though your public--meaning me--sometimes wonders!'[7]

Herb asked Ruby to come into the film studio and close her eyes. He placed a stationery box in her hands:

`Remember that day on Hurricane Ridge when you asked how I changed from being a hunter! And remember last fall on the way to Olympia I promised I'd tell you what happened! Well, there it is. It's all in the script. How I got converted.'

His eager eyes and earnest expression told me he had long awaited this moment--yes ever since the conversation in the truck that day en route to Olympia. During the winter I had probed, doubted and agonized over our relationship. Not Herb. He had traveled thousands of difficult miles, put on many showings, returned home only to rush into the mountains. All he remembered was that he had made me a promise. He had held to that thought, biding his time. Home at last, even for these few days, and with all this work nagging at him, an opportunity had presented itself.

Hugging the box tightly to me, I said, `I might prove a severe critic, you know.'

He shrugged. `Good or bad, there it is. At least you'll get the answer to your question. What turned me against hunting.'

Outside, he left me to go back to the garden. I walked into the cabin with the manuscript box, saying to Lois, who was still at the table, `Can you imagine it! Herb gave me his book to read. Oh, I'm excited.'

I set the box down on the bed and as I turned, saw Lois regarding me intently, almost as if for the first time.

`You can be flattered,' she said dryly. `He's shown the book to no one. That is, except to the publisher he sent it to. After that he just tossed it in a drawer.'

`Oh, I am flattered,' I said. `But I didn't know he'd sent it to a publisher. What happened!'

`The publisher liked it. Would have published it with a few revisions. But Cris would never make the changes.'

`Why not?'

`You'll have to ask him.'

I thought maybe I already knew the answer. After all, he'd proved his point. Even he could write a book. Why should he bother after that?[8]

Ruby went outside and sat in the swing. The manuscript kept her busy the remainder of the day. It was Herb's story about his 1930 survival trip across the Olympics. She read it through. Herb could really write, although, of course the manuscript needed work.

Ruby returned to Seattle confused. Her relationship with Herb grew closer each time they were together. She tried to visualize a place for her in his life. Although Herb and Lois didn't appear to have a warm, affectionate relationship, Ruby realized that a strong bond of partnership existed between them.

Para-dropping supplies into the Crisler's camps saved them a lot of work and time, but had one disadvantage. They no longer had an excuse to return as often to Hume's Ranch for fresh vegetables and supplies. Lois still had to file her weekly column though.

During the summer and fall of 1950 they had two more para-drops, one in Cat Creek drainage and one in Queets Basin.

Now that they were under contract for Disney Studios, what film they exposed belonged to Disney. They would have an unlimited amount of footage to expose, for the first time, and would not be faced with the annual editing job during the fall.

Dapper little Ben Sharpsteen became their liaison man with the studio. Lois no longer referred to him as the "Thread."

Herb worked very hard at filming elk calves. They dreaded the coming of the "August bad spell", a period of several weeks when fog, rain and cold usually envelop the Olympic high country. Herb's birthday was July 23. Lois was always at a loss to find anything to give him for his birthday.

On July 22, along the Bailey Range, they had left one of their caches early one morning, intending to return. They carried only cameras and camera knapsacks. They had bad luck finding elk in the area. Shortly after leaving camp Lois had an idea. Always it was Herb's hunches they followed. This time she suddenly said:

`Let's go to your next cache.'

Cris looked at me thoughtfully.`Okay,' he said.

We beat it back to camp, made up our travel packs on our packboards and set off for the next cache in Cris' string of wilderness caches, which are about a day's travel apart across the interior.

It was near sundown when we arrived. I started supper. Cris disappeared. He came back with very bright eyes. `Come with me,' he said.

He led to a vantage point. `Look over there,' he said. There spread out on the mountainside grazed a herd of more than 100 elk.

`That,' I said to Cris, `is my birthday present to you.'

From there Herb took over. For ten days we followed that herd--a feat that took both muscle and woodsmanship.[9]

Now that they were concentrating on calf behavior shots, they began to observe traits which had not registered before. Such as watching a mischievous calf attempt to nurse the wrong cow and the cow knocking the calf flat.

They also watched and filmed a three-ringed elk "circus," several herds of elk playing with wild abandon in a snow-covered alpine basin, which Lois described as one of the, "most thrilling, wild and singular events Cris and I have ever witnessed in the wilderness." [10]

They found another large herd and followed it for 15 days! They observed "teenage gangs," spike, or yearling bull elk devotedly following an older bull, a four-legged role model, imitating everything the older animal did.

They watched the formation of a "bachelor's club." They observed mature cow elk "baby sitting" lively calves while the calves mothers wandered off to feed.

They photographed a black bear attempting to retake what he had thought of as "his" private meadow from a group of elk which had moved in. The bear made gallant, unsuccessful rushes at the elk. The elk ignored him. Finally the bear lumbered unhappily off.

Once a herd moved in so close, on the opposite side of a cleaver of rock they were hiding behind, they could hear them cropping grass, a sound "like a thousand Chinese eating with chopsticks."

Lois left Herb alone in the high country several times, hiking out alone, checked the mail, dropped off her column at the newspaper, watered the garden, then returned with a heavy pack of fresh supplies. Remarkable feats of courage and endurance for a woman of her age. She makes light of these single excursions in her columns, never mentioning the weariness, the soaking, cold wind and rain storms endured, the tired feet, unwashed body. During the August "bad spell," they took a break and returned to Hume's Ranch for Lois's birthday. Birds had taken over the berry patch since that the wire enclosure over the top had collapsed during the previous winter's heavy snowfall. The cherry tree had also been raided.

A stream of visitors came to help Lois celebrate her birthday. Among them were the James Albertsons. Jim and Herb took off right away on a trip to the high country with a load of supplies. Lois, Gladys Albertson and her girls, and several other visitors, hiked to Lillian Shelter and held a hotcake flipping contest.

Two carloads from California and Seattle arrived. For once these guests had brought everything they needed, from chicken to sleeping bags to toilet paper. Lois was "flabbergasted."

Then the bad spell of weather broke. The top of Mount Fitzhenry (6050 feet elevation), the Crislers' barometer, visible from out in the big meadow, became visible again.

They loaded their packboards and disappeared up the trail. This time they went via Boulder Creek, Castle-In-The-Cat, then the Catwalk. Herb considered good time across the Catwalk as 20 minutes, with a full pack, of course. Forty minutes was Lois' top speed.

From the pond end, Boston Charlie's camp, to Eleven Bull Basin cache, Herb could go in an hour. Lois took two. One of their male friends required five hours! The Crislers were careful of who accompanied them on their trips. Few could keep up.

Along the steep flanks of the Bailey Range Lois had a close call. They frightened a black bear above them, on a very steep mountainside. The bear, in its haste to depart, dislodged a large rock. The rock began hurtling straight down towards Lois. She ran, with a heavy pack! The rock disappeared down the mountain towards the Hoh River.

From Eleven Bull to Cream Lake they took two and a half hours. They only lunched at Cream Lake. Too many bugs. They pushed on to High Camp. No bugs could survive the constant winds there.

They followed along the high ridge leading towards Mount Childs, passed through the "Defile of the Prophets" and spent the next night in Queets Basin. From Queets Basin they crossed over Dodwell-Rixon pass and down the Elwha Snowfinger to Chicago camp to pick up supplies which had been cached there by a horse packer.

They continued on up the Elwha to Low Divide, turned up the steep Skyline Trail to Lake Beauty, spent one day resting during a storm, then continued along the Skyline Trail to Promise Creek pass, Kimta Peak, and Far Camp.

They watched four elk calves trying to nurse one cow on the edge of a herd. The cow turned her head and sniffed the nearest calf on one side, then the other side. She stalked disdainfully out of this calf-pile, leaving one calf licking his red tongue.

They hiked with only day packs on down as far as Three Prune shelter. Finding little elk sign, they retraced their steps, ending up 10 days later at Olympic Hot Springs and the car.

While this is a total distance, round trip, of only about 120 miles, enough energy was expended on the ups and downs to carry a pack three hundred miles or more on the level.

Billy Everett died. His passing caused a great deal of sadness amongst old-time Peninsula dwellers. Billy, like "Pa" Huelsdonk, had been respected and liked.

Lois devoted a column to him, A TRIBUTE TO BILLY EVERETT, GRAND OLD MAN OF THE OLYMPIC WILDERNESS, recalling some of many experiences she and Herb had shared with Billy, both at his farm and while on the trail.

Fall appeared from out of the monotonous clouds and perpetual mists. It came overnight, with a quick, determined vengeance, as if Jack Frost had only allowed summer to creep in by accident for a few weeks.

One day the landscape was emerald green. That night the sky turned clear. Stars glittered above the jagged peaks like jack-o-lanterns. At dawn the alpine meadows were coated with silver-white, hard frost.

After a hot sun seared the land that day, the succulent green vegetation transformed into wilted corpses, unfit for animal consumption. By the following day the stricken plants had flattened into useless heaps of decay.

Except for the patches of hearty, blue-leaf huckleberry, **Vaccinium deliciosum**, with leaves that had magically transformed into a pallet of wine-red, flaming orange. The dark blue berries hung thick and sweet on the bushes.

Now that the tender plants and grasses, which had lured elk up to this mountain wonderland in the first place, were unfit to eat, they began migrating down into the timber, where sheltering evergreens had kept Jack Frost at bay.

Herb and Lois hurried to close each camp before leaving for the season. To do so, they needed sunshine and wind to dry the canvas tarps. The caches were covered with tarps, then either buried in rock slides or covered with slabs of heavy, dead bark to keep the fierce winds and wildlife from disturbing their precious possessions.

Once the caches were closed they too, like the elk and deer, descended to lower elevations, where Indian summer might last for weeks.

In mid-October, 1950, Ruby El Hult returned, by invitation, to Hume's Ranch for a week. The mutual attraction which both Ruby and Herb felt for each other had been progressing ever since they first met, but had not erupted into anything but friendly admiration. Nor did Ruby intend it to. Although she had secretly contemplated the possibilities of a future with Herb, she had no intentions of letting those feelings out...

One day during Ruby's vacation, Lois decided to make a trip to town. Herb retired to his studio to edit film. Ruby took a seat in the swing overlooking the river and began working on her book.

Suddenly, the light plant stopped. Herb appeared and sat beside her. "Hard to work with a red-haired girl around," he quipped. They talked. Herb held her hand, the most intimate action between them yet, except for an innocent good night kiss Herb had planted on her one night. Then Herb reached over and kissed Ruby. She protested. His beard was scratchy. He grabbed her and rubbed his beard on her face playfully.

Suddenly they heard the door slam. Lois had returned and walked within 10 feet of the swing. She may have stood out in the woods watching them for some time! She disappeared into the cabin without saying a word.

Herb went inside and questioned Lois. Asking why she had returned so quickly. She claimed she could not get the truck started.

This little-third-person-out episode caused everyone present embarrassment. Although Lois didn't mention the affair to Ruby and kept up her usual hospitality towards their guest, the air was charged with the expectation of disaster.

Herb stalked off to "fix" the car only to return, angrily claiming nothing was wrong with it. Lois, suspicious, had tricked them.

Ruby feigned an excuse to leave: She had to return to Seattle earlier than expected to meet someone.

Lois said she would go to town the next day. Ruby could ride with her.

No one slept that night.

Before she left the following morning, Herb got Ruby into the garden with the excuse that she was to pick out what she wished in the way of vegetables to take home. This provided them with a brief chance to talk privately.

Herb did most of the talking. He said he had lain awake all night thinking about leaving with Ruby in the morning. Towards dawn he abandoned such a plan. He would be walking away from the marriage with only the clothes on his back. Not even his cameras could accompany him.

He had already suffered from a similar experience during the Depression. Besides, he claimed that he felt obligated to many people who had helped him, such as the citizens of Port Angeles who had taken up a collection to help pay for the expensive motion-picture camera and projector. He also had obligations to Disney. The fact that he was fifty-seven probably influenced his decision not to abandon what little he owned, although that certainly wasn't much.

However, considering Herb contemplated such a radical change was an indication that something was lacking in their marriage. He didn't say what it was.

Although the thought of eloping with Herb was enticing, Ruby agreed that they couldn't be that ruthless. Ruby decided the solution was to leave Hume's Ranch and drop all contact with the Crislers, which she did. She lost track of the Crisler's whereabouts for 16 years. For all she knew Herb could have been dead.

After the interlude with the "red-haired elf" Herb threw himself into the badly neglected work around Hume's Ranch. It was a difficult time. Now that they were no longer making their own movie, he felt at loose ends, although they were under contract with Disney for another year. What then?

One day a strange racket approached the old log cabin. Herb arrived down the trail driving a half-brother for lonesome Step'n Fetchit. The new machine was a yellow Agri-cat(T), with tracks 36 inches wide, narrow enough to move along the trail.

Herb had seen the little cat and fell in love with it, borrowing $1,000 from Ernst to buy the machine. He was so proud of the charming little cat he asked Verne Samuelson to accompany him to the Black Ball dock to receive it.

Several months after acquiring the cat, the Crislers carried their "work" clothes (Lois' formal gowns and Herb's doeskin coat) out to the green Ford truck. It was time for them to meet their obligations on the last winter tour. All engagements were in the mid-west or east. The first engagement was 14 January in Denver.

They left a week before Christmas, drove over Stevens Pass to Wenatchee, where the Albertsons had been transferred, and spent the holiday with them.

Then began the long drive south. Since this would be their last tour, they decided to cram as many tourist sites into their itinerary as possible. They visited the big Palomar Observatory, went to Mexico, Carlsbad Caverns, Henry Ford's Museum in Detroit and a few other places they had long wished to see.

In Charlotte, North Carolina, they visited Herb's brothers Lester and Albert. They learned, not from Al, who was too modest to say so, that he was one of the flying instructors at the naval training station, rated second from the top amongst 500 instructors.[11]

They also visited Herb's mother Adora, and his sister Vara and her family in Savannah. An article in the Savannah Morning News, on Saturday, March 17, 1951, called Herb a "nationally-known figure in the world of wildlife photography, now under contract to Walt Disney Studios, a lecturer for National Geographic Society, an explorer of the great Northwest country, and by far the most fascinating interview of the year."[12]

Finally, more than half way home, they drove into Los Angeles and a scheduled meeting with Walt Disney:

At the Disney Studio we saw the first previews of Cris's picture. So far, it's called The Olympic Elk.

His picture will appear in about six months. It is one in a new series that Disney is putting out--the True-Life Adventure Series.

These are not cartoons. They are nature pictures, showing wildlife with no human beings in the picture.

The first picture in the series was "Seal Island," filmed in the Pribilofs. It won an Oscar.

The second was "Beaver Valley." Last Sunday in Hollywood, "Beaver Valley" too received an Oscar.

As far we know, the third in the series will be "Nature's Half Acre," and Cris's picture will be fourth.

The music for "The Olympic Elk" will be written by the same composer who wrote the music for "Beaver Valley."[13]

On the way up the coast the Crislers arrived in Berkeley in time for the annual Wilderness Conference of the Sierra Club and attended its two-day session. They heard Starker Leopold, son of famous wildlife expert Aldo Leopold, and others speak on wilderness.

The superintendent of Sequoia and King's Canyon National Parks told how 24 packers with 1,600 head of horses were destroying alpine meadows in his parks.

"Accessibility is the Achilles heel of wilderness. There is more danger from over-use and wilderness bad manners than from other things more talked about," he said. [14]

They listened in awe while Carl Russell, superintendent of Yosemite National Park warned: "The time is coming when people will have to make reservations to go into a wilderness, just as they have to go into a hotel. Why? Simply to preserve the very thing they're going for--wilderness and the authenticity of the wilderness."[15]

With these and other warnings ringing in their ears, Herb and Lois started north, thankful that Olympic National Park did not have the problems that California had, not yet anyway. They became more resolved to fight for preservation of what wilderness was left.

The Crislers had no sooner reached home than the usual swarm of admiring visitors appeared. In fact, they took one home from Port Angeles with them, a likable young man they'd met in Ohio who had just arrived in Port Angeles via bus. They'd promised he could visit.

They'd not been home long before Carol Preston[16] and Ernst Freitag showed up. They took one look at the sad state of the wood pile, donned gloves and went to work.

Herb brought out one of their old motion-pictures, The Living Wilderness, and polished it up for showing to several Washington state sponsors who were anxious to see some of his films.

The Reverend James Albertson wanted them to bring their picture to Wenatchee and show to his new church congregation.

They'd no sooner returned than Mrs. Edward Petite and her son Irving from Seattle arrived, bringing Amos Burg, world traveler and lecturer. Mr. Burg had canoed the length of the Columbia River before it was blocked by dams.

They went to Seattle to put on a show. Amos Burg introduced them to Mr. Robert Hitchman, a businessman by day and Washington state historian by night. Mr. Hitchman told them how, in 1937, he had tracked down James Christie, the leader of the famous Press Expedition, which had crossed the Peninsula during the winter of 1889-90.

Christie had been born in Scotland, December 14, 1854. Hitchman located Christie living in a log cabin in the forest in western Canada. Hitchman showed them a photograph he had made of Christie, which thrilled them immensely.

Back in Port Angeles Lois picked up the mail. The first thing she opened was a letter with the Walt Disney Studio logo on the envelope. She scanned it quickly and looked questioningly at Herb.

Herb asked her to read it out loud. The studio had all the elk pictures they needed. Sharpsteen wanted the Crislers to move to the Tarryall Mountain of Colorado right away to spend the summer photographing bighorn sheep.

The news was not unexpected. During their stop at the studio Ben Sharpsteen and Herb had discussed alternate plans for the summer. They had asked Herb if there was any place he would like to go. Herb remembered that at one of their showings in Denver a local game biologist had mentioned that he should come and photograph bighorn sheep in the nearby Tarryall Mountains. Herb suggested this to Sharpsteen. Sharpsteen thought that a wonderful idea, as they could use sheep pictures for a movie they were planning, to be called "The Vanishing Prairie."

Herb and Lois were strangely silent as they drove up the Elwha, hiked the trail to Hume's Ranch, and began to pack.

Finally, everything they thought they needed, camping equipment, camera gear and clothing, had been transported, packboard load at a time, out to the truck. They returned for one last load, to close the cabin and gather up a few personal items. While Herb secured everything, storing perishables inside five-gallon cans, hanging a few possessions from rafters in the shed that might tempt varmints, he could hear the old Underwood typewriter going, "clackey-clack" as Lois sat at the table and pecked out her column. No one needed to know they were headed for Colorado. In fact, the studio had forbidden them to announce the summer's work. They would drop the copy off at the newspaper office on their way through town.

When Herb came into the cabin he noticed Lois brush away a tear as she silently placed her beat-up typewriter into it's worn case and lashed it to her packboard.

She glanced up. "Well, you told me if I married you and moved into this cabin I'd finally have something to write about," she said, a forced smile on her lips. "This column is number one hundred! Not counting the travel articles."

Herb nodded, then began to gather up last minute items. Pack. Unpack. It seemed they were forever on the go. It was a glad, but hard life. Now they were going far away from what they were accustomed to. What would it mean? Where would future trails lead?

They picked up their packs. Herb gently closed the door. They had never locked it. No one had ever bothered or taken anything. With a last look around the clearing, they opened the gate and started out along the trail. Every bush, windfall, stone and stump were familiar.

A slender, pale-gray, long-tailed Townsend's solitaire flitted from limb to limb, following them up the trail. The bird sang: a haunting, melodious, ringing "c-r-eek, cr-eek, eeeeek."

Near Krause Bottom cutoff, where one of the Press Expedition's old trail blazes was still visible on an old-growth fir, a doe deer and her twin fawns stood below the trail. The doe stopped browsing tender shoots of wild currant and watched nervously. The fawns took advantage of their mother standing motionless and began nursing, one on each side, butting their heads savagely against the doe's flanks, in an attempt to obtain more milk.

Herb stopped to watch, a smile on his face. Where was his camera? Packed away deep in the truck."Only when you don't have a camera," Herb muttered, "do animals pose like that!"

Although they expected to return in the fall, and had left Hume's Ranch many, many times previously, both had a premonition that what lay ahead might open a new era in their lives. For the first summer in over a decade they would not be returning to their old haunts in the Bailey Range.

Herb suddenly remembered something Billy Everett said one night years earlier, as they huddled around a cheerful fire in Cream Lake Basin. Removing his pipe, Billy said softly, "In here," with a great swinging sweep of his pipe that took in the surrounding mountains, "in this beautiful place, where few men have ever trod, where the elk and bear and cougar roam, that's where I feel closest to God."

Herb had been startled. He'd never heard Billy mention God before. "Of course," Herb had said. "Of course." He didn't mention to Billy that he felt exactly the same way.

They stopped at the newspaper office. Herb sat in the truck while Lois went in and handed the copy to the lady behind the desk. She glanced at it, saw the title, and read it aloud, "Number 100. Trail Talk Columns Signing Off As Crislers Prepare to Go Upstairs." She looked up at Lois with a perplexed stare. "Kind of early to be going into the mountains, isn't it Lois? Lots of snow up there yet."

Lois agreed. It was too early. Lois turned and left, thinking, well, it's true, we are going upstairs. She got into the truck and slammed the door. Herb started the motor and drove east, along First Street. The article was published 25 May, 1951. It would be the last article Lois would write for the paper.

Epilogue

Lois wasn't lying. The Crislers truly were going "upstairs". They would spend the summer in a tent at 11,000 feet elevation, twice the height they were accustomed to working. The place where Herb chose to photograph bighorn sheep was McCurdy Park, Pike National Forest, in what is now the Lost Creek Scenic Area.

The Crislers fell in love with Colorado's high, dry climate and the Rocky Mountains. They located an unfinished miner's cabin on an abandoned mining claim, filed for possession, and named it Crag Cabin. Herb put his carpenter's skills to work finishing the cabin. They decided to stay in Colorado, as Disney wanted them to film the sheep rut, which occurs in late fall. They made a quick trip to Humes Ranch and carried away their belongings, including the Agri-cat, to Colorado.

Although many more years of hiking, backpacking and wilderness photography lay ahead, including two seasons on Alaska's North Slope documenting the Porcupine herd of caribou, and almost a decade of living with and breeding wild Alaska tundra wolves at Crag Cabin, they never returned to Hume's Ranch to live.

AUTHOR'S NOTES: Several books have been published that describe the Crislers' adventures in Colorado and Alaska.

Lois Crisler's first book, Arctic Wild, describes two years in the Arctic while filming the Porcupine caribou herd on the North Slope for Walt Disney Productions.

While in the Arctic, they obtained a litter of five tundra wolf pups from the Eskimos. They wanted the wolves so they could photograph them. Instead of the Crislers' adopting the wolves, the wolves adopted the Crislers as their parents. No one lived within a hundred miles from their camp on the tundra. It was a lonely life, photographing, hiking, watching for wildlife. The Crislers, and their wolves, quickly became a close-knit family, roving across the tundra carefree and wild.

Herb taught them to howl, although they did so naturally as they grew older and heard other nearby wolves howl. Every morning upon awakening the wolf pups would pile onto the Crislers bed and enjoy a roughhouse romp and a "good, long period of howling," while Lois buried her head under the covers and held her fingers in her ears.

Before they realized what was happening, the relationship between human and wolf had become far too close. They joined many others who, over the years, have adopted young wild animals and become so fond of them they refused to let them go.

When it came time to leave, they had three choices, turn the wolves loose to starve (they had never learned to hunt), kill them, or take them to Colorado.

After days of agonizing they finally admitted they really had no choice. They simply couldn't part with the boisterous, lovable wolf pups. To kill them was not an option. If they turned them loose, the animals would quickly starve, or become easy prey for Eskimo guns or traps. They applied for, and received, permission to take the wolves to Colorado. Had they known the trouble, and expense, those wolves would cause them over the next decade, their decision might have been different.

Lois' next, and last book, <u>Captive Wild</u>, (both books by Harper & Brothers) is a detailed description of nearly a decade of raising and breeding wolves at Crag Cabin in Colorado. It was not an uneventful experience, especially when storms tore down fences and wolves escaped. Local ranchers went hunting for the animals, thinking they would kill their livestock.

As previously mentioned, Herb and Ruby had been respectably attracted to each other while the Crislers were still living at Humes Ranch, until Lois caught them smooching in the swing one day. After that, they lost contact with each other.

Ruby is the author of three books about Herb Crisler's experiences. They are listed in the Appendix.

The wolves kept the Crislers broke. To keep money coming in, Herb began mining. Herb was away from Crag Cabin during the week working in his mine. He returned home one Friday night to discover that Lois had killed the remaining wolves, taken her belongings and departed for Seattle. Herb had been fond of the wolves, probably more than Lois. It took him a long time to recover the loss of both wife and wolves.

Despite all they had been through together, the Crislers divorced. According to Ruby El Hult, because the book, **Captive Wild** was published after the Crislers divorced, much of the original mention of Herb was removed from the manuscript.

Some think the wolves were responsible. The animals certainly kept the Crislers broke, and tied down, during this decade.

Herb remained in Colorado for several years and remarried. He returned to the Olympic Peninsula in 1966, when he was 73, and made a solo trip, starting at the South Fork, Quinault. Near Lake Beauty he fell and seriously injured himself. Rather than retreat, he spent several days recuperating, then continued across the Crisler Traverse. Long overdue at Olympic Hot Springs, a search began. Searchers had difficulty locating Crisler. He arrived at the Hot Springs 16 days overdue! He had been in the mountains 30 days. The Associated Press ran the story which was widely published.

Ruby had married and was living in California. She read the newspaper account about Crisler being lost in the Olympics, the first she'd heard about him for 16 years! She wrote to him in Colorado, and their friendship resumed. Herb's third wife died.

Again, in 1973, at age 80, Crisler decided to make a last traverse of his beloved Olympic Mountains. He and Don McQuade hired a cinematographer, still photographer and several assistants and packers, and a group of about 15 headed for the Bailey Range. The packers were sent back after one day and 10 carried on for a successful trip to the Quinault. McQuade's movie showed twice in Seattle but was not successful.

After discovering that I intended to write the Crisler story, Ruby graciously shared her extensive notes, a copy of Herb's unpublished manuscript, "Western Wildlife Photographer" and her scrapbook, containing newspaper clippings and material about Crisler gathered over several decades. Without the above sources, and Ruby's patient monitoring of the manuscript, this book would never have been completed. Ruby had intended to write the Crisler biography, but age and time caught up with her. For her patience and help, I shall always be grateful.

I'm also grateful to Hazle M. Chapman for allowing me the use of her black and white photos and for several interviews. Hazle lives in a retirement home at Lacey, Washington.

Herb and Ruby did have a chance to enjoy each other's company again for a few years after Ruby's husband died. They lived in Puyallup, Washington. Herb died 15 December, 1985 of natural causes. He was 92.

Lois Crisler died June 3, 1971 in Seattle, at age 74.

The "Spirit of the Olympics" finally came home to rest. Herb's ashes were carried up the Elwha River Trail by his adopted son, Robert Bruce Crisler, and buried somewhere around Hume's Ranch, now on the National List of Historic Places. He can sleep in peace. Thanks to his earlier efforts to inform people nationwide about the values of establishing

Olympic National Park, no chainsaw or bulldozer will ever disturb the beautiful Elwha Valley, with its stands of old-growth forest. No new trails will be built in Olympic National Park.

Cream Lake Basin, majestic Mount Olympus and its glaciers, the Bailey Range, Queets Basin, the land "beyond the trails" that many of the pioneers, such as Boston Charlie, Billy Everett and a few others loved, and fought for, will forever remain wild and pristine---a reminder of what wilderness is really like---unless some future generation fails to support the national park concept.

Carol Preston Stands before Olympus Ranger Station on the Hoh River, 1947.

Sources and Notes, Chapter Eighteen

1. Lois Crisler, "Olympic Trail Talk--58," 7 July, 1950

2. Lois Crisler, commenting after a man in Iowa complained to her: "There is no elbow room around Iowa City. If you want to hike, you are soon trespassing on someone's private property."

3. Ibid.

4. Lois Crisler, "Olympic Trail Talk--58," 7 July, 1950

5. Ibid.

6. Ruby El Hult, <u>An Olympic Mountain Enchantment,</u> CP Publications, Inc., Port Angeles, WA Pgs. 150-151 (1988)

7. Ibid. Pgs. 162-164.

8. Ibid. Pgs. 165-166.

9. Lois Crisler, "Olympic Trail Talk--62," 4 Aug., 1950

10. Lois Crisler, "Olympic Trail Talk--63," 18 Aug., 1950

11. Albert Crisler died in 1992 while this manuscript was being written.

12. Compliments Ruby El Hult's Crisler scrapbook.

13. Lois Crisler, "Olympic Trail Talk--94," 6 April, 1951

14. Lois Crisler, "Olympic Trail Talk--95," 13 April, 1951

15. Ibid.

16. Caroline Preston studied psychology at the University of Washington, then switched to psychiatry and graduated. She joined the staff of the Department of Psychiatry and Behavioral Sciences as an Associate Professor 9-5-1949. She retired as an Associate Professor Emeritus 7-7-84 and died 5-7-87. (University of Washington Faculty Records Office)

Index

Index

Index

Index

Index

Bibliography

Island Of Rivers. An anthology, edited by Nancy Beres, Mitzi Chandler & Rusell Dalton.
    Seattle, WA: Pacific Northwest National Parks & Forests Association, 1988.

Jimmy Come Lately. An anthology, edited by Jervis Russell.
    Port Orchard, WA: Clallam County Historical Society, 1971.

Forest Conditions in the Olympic Reserve, WA. Washington D.C.: Geological Survey, 1902.

Hult, Ruby El. *Untamed Olympics*. Portland, OR: Binford & Mort, 1954.
    Reprinted, Third Edition, Port Angeles, WA: WACP Publications, 1989.

Hult, Ruby El. *Herb Crisler Films the Rocky Mountain Bighorn Sheep*.
    Puyallup, WA: Swallowtail Press, 1980 & 1986.

Hult, Ruby El. *Herb Crisler in the Olympic Mountain Wilds*. Puyallup, WA: Swallowtail Press, 1977 & 1992.

Hult, Ruby El. *An Olympic Mountain Enchantment*. Port Angeles, WA: CP Publications, 1989.

Kitchin, E.A. *Birds of the Olympic Peninsula*. Port Angeles, WA: Olympic Stationers, 1949.

Olympic Mountain Rescue. *Climber's Guide to the Olympic Mountains*.
    Seattle, WA: The Mountaineers, 3rd. Ed., 1988.

Lucia, Ellis. *The Big Woods: Logging and Lumbering--From Bull Teame to Helicopters in the Pacific Northwest*.
    New York, 1975.

Martin, Paul J. *Port Angeles, Washington, A History*.   Port Angeles, WA: Peninsula Publishing, Inc., 1983.

Parratt, Smitty. *Gods & Goblins, A Field Guide to Place Names of Olympic National Park*.
    Port Angeles, WA: CP Publications, 1984.

Smith, LeRoy.   *Pioneers of the Olympic Peninsula*. Forks, WA: Olympic Graphic Arts, Inc., 1977.

Stewart, Charles. *Wildflowers of the Olympic Peninsula*. Port Angeles, WA: Education Enterprises, 1988.

Webster, E.B. *Fishing in the Olympics*. The Port Angeles Evening News, 1923.

Wood, Robert L. *Olympic Mountain Trail Guide*. Seattle, WA & Vancouver B.C.: The Mountaineers, 1984.

Beebe, Lloyd. *Wilderness Trails and a Dream*. Forks, WA: Olympic Graphic Arts, Inc., 1997.